Yamaha Kodiak and Grizzly Owners Workshop Manual

by Alan Ahlstrand
and John H Haynes
Member of the Guild of Motoring Writers

Models covered:
Kodiak 400, 1993 through 2005
Kodiak 450, 2003 through 2005
Grizzly 600, 1998 through 2001
Grizzly 660, 2002 through 2005

(2567 - 10U5)   ABCDE

Haynes Publishing
Sparkford Nr Yeovil
Somerset BA22 7JJ England

Haynes North America, Inc
859 Lawrence Drive
Newbury Park
California 91320 USA
www.haynes.com

Acknowledgments

Our thanks to Grand Prix Yamaha/Kawasaki/Suzuki of Santa Clara, California, for providing the facilities used for these photographs; to Mark Zueger, service manager, for arranging the facilities and fitting the mechanical work into his shop's busy schedule; and to Craig Wardner, service technician, for doing the mechanical work and providing valuable technical information.

© Haynes North America, Inc. 2005

With permission from J.H. Haynes & Co. Ltd.

A book in the Haynes Owners Workshop Manual Series

Printed in Malaysia

All rights reserved. No part of this book may be reproduced or transmitted in any form or by any means, electronic or mechanical, including photocopying, recording or by any information storage or retrieval system, without permission in writing from the copyright holder.

ISBN-10: 1-56392-567-2
ISBN-13: 978-1-56392-567-2

Library of Congress Control Number 2005927256

British Library Cataloguing in Publication Data
A catalogue record for this book is available from the British Library

We take great pride in the accuracy of information given in this manual, but vehicle manufacturers make alterations and design changes during the production run of a particular vehicle of which they do not inform us. No liability can be accepted by the authors or publishers for loss, damage or injury caused by any errors in, or omissions from, the information given.

Contents

Introductory pages
About this manual	0-5
Introduction to the Kodiak and Grizzly	0-5
Identification numbers	0-6
Buying parts	0-6
General specifications	0-7
Maintenance techniques, tools and working facilities	0-8
Safety first!	0-14
ATV chemicals and lubricants	0-15
Troubleshooting	0-16

Chapter 1
Tune-up and routine maintenance   1-1

Chapter 2
Engine, clutch and transmission   2-1

Chapter 3
Cooling system   3-1

Chapter 4
Fuel and exhaust systems   4-1

Chapter 5
Ignition system   5-1

Chapter 6
Steering, suspension and final drive   6-1

Chapter 7
Brakes, wheels and tires   7-1

Chapter 8
Frame and bodywork   8-1

Chapter 9
Electrical system   9-1

Chapter 10
Wiring diagrams   10-1

Conversion factors/Fractions/Trail rules/Service record

Index   IND-1

Yamaha - 2005 Grizzly 660 model

About this manual

Its purpose

The purpose of this manual is to help you get the best value from your vehicle. It can do so in several ways. It can help you decide what work must be done, even if you choose to have it done by a dealer service department or a repair shop; it provides information and procedures for routine maintenance and servicing; and it offers diagnostic and repair procedures to follow when trouble occurs.

We hope you use the manual to tackle the work yourself. For many simpler jobs, doing it yourself may be quicker than arranging an appointment to get the vehicle into a shop and making the trips to leave it and pick it up. More importantly, a lot of money can be saved by avoiding the expense the shop must pass on to you to cover its labor and overhead costs. An added benefit is the sense of satisfaction and accomplishment that you feel after doing the job yourself.

Using the manual

The manual is divided into Chapters. Each Chapter is divided into numbered Sections, which are headed in bold type between horizontal lines. Each Section consists of consecutively numbered paragraphs.

At the beginning of each numbered Section you will be referred to any illustrations which apply to the procedures in that Section. The reference numbers used in illustration captions pinpoint the pertinent Section and the Step within that Section. That is, illustration 3.2 means the illustration refers to Section 3 and Step (or paragraph) 2 within that Section.

Procedures, once described in the text, are not normally repeated. When it's necessary to refer to another Chapter, the reference will be given as Chapter and Section number. Cross references given without use of the word "Chapter" apply to Sections and/or paragraphs in the same Chapter. For example, "see Section 8" means in the same Chapter.

References to the left or right side of the vehicle assume you are sitting on the seat, facing forward.

All-terrain vehicle manufacturers continually make changes to specifications and recommendations, and these, when notified, are incorporated into our manuals at the earliest opportunity.

Even though we have prepared this manual with extreme care, neither the publisher nor the author can accept responsibility for any errors in, or omissions from, the information given.

NOTE

A **Note** provides information necessary to properly complete a procedure or information which will make the procedure easier to understand.

CAUTION

A **Caution** provides a special procedure or special steps which must be taken while completing the procedure where the Caution is found. Not heeding a Caution can result in damage to the assembly being worked on.

WARNING

A **Warning** provides a special procedure or special steps which must be taken while completing the procedure where the Warning is found. Not heeding a Warning can result in personal injury.

Introduction to the Yamaha Kodiak and Grizzly

The Yamaha YFM400/450 Kodiak and YFM600/660 Grizzly are highly successful and popular all-terrain vehicles.

The engine on 1993 through 1999 Kodiak 400 models and 1998 through 2001 Grizzly 600 models is air cooled, with an auxiliary oil cooler. The engine on all other models is liquid cooled. All engines have a single cylinder and overhead camshaft.

1993 through 1999 400 models use a five-speed transmission with high and low ranges. All other models use a constantly variable belt drive transmission, coupled with a range box that lets the rider select high, low (some models) or reverse.

Fuel is delivered to the cylinder by a single Mikuni carburetor.

The front suspension consists of upper and lower control arms on all models except the 1998 through 2001 Grizzly 600. These models use front struts. The rear suspension consists of a swingarm and single shock absorber-coil spring unit on all except the 2005 Kodiak 450 and 2002 and later Grizzly 660. These models use an independent rear suspension.

1993 through 1998 400 models use hydraulic drum brakes at the front wheels. All other models use front disc brakes. Rear drum or rear disc brakes are used, depending on model.

Shaft final drive is used at the rear of all models covered in this manual. At the front of 4WD models, a front driveshaft, which is operated by the engine's middle gear shaft, transmits power to the front differential, driveaxles and wheel hubs.

Identification numbers

The frame serial number is stamped into the left side of the frame. The engine number is stamped into the right side of the crankcase. Both of these numbers should be recorded and kept in a safe place so they can be furnished to law enforcement officials in the event of a theft.

The frame serial number, engine serial number and carburetor identification number should also be kept in a handy place (such as with your driver's license) so they are always available when purchasing or ordering parts for your machine.

The models covered by this manual are as follows:
Kodiak 400, 1993 through 2005
Kodiak 450, 2003 through 2005
Grizzly 600, 1998 through 2001
Grizzly 660, 2002 through 2005

The frame serial number is located on the left side of the frame

The engine serial number is located on the right side of the crankcase

Buying parts

Once you have found all the identification numbers, record them for reference when buying parts. Since the manufacturers change specifications, parts and vendors (companies that manufacture various components on the machine), providing the ID numbers is the only way to be reasonably sure that you are buying the correct parts.

Whenever possible, take the worn part to the dealer so direct comparison with the new component can be made. Along the trail from the manufacturer to the parts shelf, there are numerous places that the part can end up with the wrong number or be listed incorrectly.

The two places to purchase new parts for your vehicle - the accessory store and the franchised dealer - differ in the type of parts they carry. While dealers can obtain virtually every part for your vehicle, the accessory dealer is usually limited to normal high wear items such as shock absorbers, tune-up parts, various engine gaskets, cables, chains, brake parts, etc. Rarely will an accessory outlet have major suspension components, cylinders, transmission gears, or cases.

Used parts can be obtained for roughly half the price of new ones, but you can't always be sure of what you're getting. Once again, take your worn part to the wrecking yard (breaker) for direct comparison.

Whether buying new, used or rebuilt parts, the best course is to deal directly with someone who specializes in parts for your particular make.

General specifications

Kodiak 400

  1993 through 1995
    Wheelbase .... 1210 mm (47.6 inches)
    Overall length .... 1925 mm (75.8 inches)
    Overall height .... 1130 mm (44.5 inches)
    Seat height .... 830 mm (32.7 inches)
    Ground clearance .... 180 mm (7.09 inches)
  1996 through 1998
    Wheelbase .... 1210 mm (47.6 inches)
    Overall length .... 1956 mm (77.0 inches)
    Overall height .... 1144 mm (45.0 inches)
    Seat height
      US .... 830 mm (32.7 inches)
      Except US .... 835 mm (32.9 inches)
  1999
    Wheelbase .... 1236 mm (48.7 inches)
    Overall length .... 1945 mm (76.6 inches)
    Overall height .... 1165 mm (45.9 inches)
    Seat height .... 835 mm (32.9 inches)
    Ground clearance .... 245 mm (9.65 inches)
    Weight (with oil and full fuel tank)
      Except Oceania .... 269 kg (593 lbs)
      Oceania .... 275 kg (606 lbs)
  2000 through 2002
    Wheelbase .... 1225 mm (48.23 inches)
    Overall length .... 1965 mm (77.36 inches)
    Overall height .... 1120 mm (44.09 inches)
    Seat height .... 820 mm (32.28 inches)
    Ground clearance .... 245 mm (9.65 inches)
    Weight (with oil and full fuel tank) .... 262 kg (578 lbs)
  2003 through 2004
    Wheelbase .... 1233 mm (48.5 inches)
    Overall length .... 1984 mm (78.1 inches)
    Overall height .... 1120 mm (44.1 inches)
    Seat height .... 827 mm (32.6 inches)
    Ground clearance .... 245 mm (9.7 inches)
    Weight (with oil and full fuel tank)
      2WD .... 250 kg (551 lbs)
      4WD .... 265 kg (584 lbs)
  2005
    Wheelbase .... 1233 mm (48.5 inches)
    Overall length .... 1993 mm (78.5 inches)
    Overall height .... 1120 mm (44.1 inches)
    Seat height .... 830 mm (32.7 inches)
    Ground clearance .... 245 mm (9.7 inches)
    Weight (with oil and full fuel tank)
      US and Canada .... 279 kg (615 lbs)
      All others .... 283 kg (624 lbs)

Kodiak 450

  Wheelbase .... 1233 mm (48.5 inches)
  Overall length
    2003, 2004 .... 1984 mm (78.1 inches)
    2005 .... 1993 mm (78.5 inches)
  Overall height .... 1120 mm (44.1 inches)
  Seat height
    2003, 2004 .... 827 mm (32.6 inches)
    2005 .... 830 mm (32.7 inches)
  Ground clearance .... 245 mm (9.7 inches)
  Weight (with oil and full fuel tank)
    2003, 2004 .... 267 kg (589 lbs)
    2005
      All except Europe .... 285 kg (628 lbs)
      Europe .... 289 kg (637 lbs)

Grizzly 600

  Wheelbase .... 1254 mm (49.3 inches)
  Overall length
    1998 .... 2079 mm (81.9 inches)
    1999 through 2001 .... 2068 mm (81.4 inches)
  Overall height .... 1215 mm (47.8 inches)
  Seat height .... 865 mm (34.1 inches)
  Ground clearance .... 178 mm (7.0 inches)
  Weight (with oil and full fuel tank)
    1998 .... 307 kg (675 lbs)
    1999 through 2001
      US and Canada .... 289 kg (637 lbs)
      Except US and Canada .... 290 kg (639 lbs)

Grizzly 660

  Wheelbase .... 1275 mm (50.2 inches)
  Overall length .... 2085 mm (82.1 inches)
  Overall height .... 1210 mm (47.6 inches)
  Seat height .... 880 mm (34.6 inches)
  Ground clearance .... 275 mm (10.83 inches)
  Weight (with oil and full fuel tank) .... 290 kg (639 lbs)

Maintenance techniques, tools and working facilities

Basic maintenance techniques

There are a number of techniques involved in maintenance and repair that will be referred to throughout this manual. Application of these techniques will enable the amateur mechanic to be more efficient, better organized and capable of performing the various tasks properly, which will ensure that the repair job is thorough and complete.

Fastening systems

Fasteners, basically, are nuts, bolts and screws used to hold two or more parts together. There are a few things to keep in mind when working with fasteners. Almost all of them use a locking device of some type (either a lock washer, locknut, locking tab or thread adhesive). All threaded fasteners should be clean, straight, have undamaged threads and undamaged corners on the hex head where the wrench fits. Develop the habit of replacing all damaged nuts and bolts with new ones.

Rusted nuts and bolts should be treated with a penetrating oil to ease removal and prevent breakage. Some mechanics use turpentine in a spout type oil can, which works quite well. After applying the rust penetrant, let it "work" for a few minutes before trying to loosen the nut or bolt. Badly rusted fasteners may have to be chiseled off or removed with a special nut breaker, available at tool stores.

If a bolt or stud breaks off in an assembly, it can be drilled out and removed with a special tool called an E-Z out (or screw extractor). Most dealer service departments and vehicle repair shops can perform this task, as well as others (such as the repair of threaded holes that have been stripped out).

Flat washers and lock washers, when removed from an assembly, should always be replaced exactly as removed. Replace any damaged washers with new ones. Always use a flat washer between a lock washer and any soft metal surface (such as aluminum), thin sheet metal or plastic. Special locknuts can only be used once or twice before they lose their locking ability and must be replaced.

Tightening sequences and procedures

When threaded fasteners are tightened, they are often tightened to a specific torque value (torque is basically a twisting force). Over-tightening the fastener can weaken it and cause it to break, while under-tightening can cause it to eventually come loose. Each bolt, depending on the material it's made of, the diameter of its shank and the material it is threaded into, has a specific torque value, which is noted in the Specifications. Be sure to follow the torque recommendations closely.

Fasteners laid out in a pattern (i.e. cylinder head bolts, engine case bolts, etc.) must be loosened or tightened in a sequence to avoid warping the component. Initially, the bolts/nuts should go on finger tight only. Next, they should be tightened one full turn each, in a criss-cross or diagonal pattern. After each one has been tightened one full turn, return to the first one tightened and tighten them all one half turn, following the same pattern. Finally, tighten each of them one quarter turn at a time until each fastener has been tightened to the proper torque. To loosen and remove the fasteners the procedure would be reversed.

Disassembly sequence

Component disassembly should be done with care and purpose to help ensure that the parts go back together properly during reassembly. Always keep track of the sequence in which parts are removed. Take note of special characteristics or marks on parts that can be installed more than one way (such as a grooved thrust washer on a shaft). It's a good idea to lay the disassembled parts out on a clean surface in the order that they were removed. It may also be helpful to make sketches or take instant photos of components before removal.

When removing fasteners from a component, keep track of their locations. Sometimes threading a bolt back in a part, or putting the washers and nut back on a stud, can prevent mixups later. If nuts and bolts can't be returned to their original locations, they should be kept in a compartmented box or a series of small boxes. A cupcake or muffin tin is ideal for this purpose, since each cavity can hold the bolts and nuts from a particular area (i.e. engine case bolts, valve cover bolts, engine mount bolts, etc.). A pan of this type is especially helpful when working on assemblies with very small parts (such as the carburetors and the valve train). The cavities can be marked with paint or tape to identify the contents.

Whenever wiring looms, harnesses or connectors are separated, it's a good idea to identify the two halves with numbered pieces of masking tape so they can be easily reconnected.

Gasket sealing surfaces

Throughout any vehicle, gaskets are used to seal the mating surfaces between components and keep lubricants, fluids, vacuum or pressure contained in an assembly.

Many times these gaskets are coated with a liquid or paste type gasket sealing compound before assembly. Age, heat and pressure can sometimes cause the two parts to stick together so tightly that they are very difficult to separate. In most cases, the part can be loosened by striking it with a soft-faced hammer near the mating surfaces. A regular hammer can be used if a block of wood is placed between the hammer and the part. Do not hammer on cast parts or parts that could be easily damaged. With any particularly stubborn part, always recheck to make sure that every fastener has been removed.

Avoid using a screwdriver or bar to pry apart components, as they can easily mar the gasket sealing surfaces of the parts (which must remain smooth). If prying is absolutely necessary, use a piece of wood, but keep in mind that extra clean-up will be necessary if the wood splinters.

After the parts are separated, the old gasket must be carefully scraped off and the gasket surfaces cleaned. Stubborn gasket material can be soaked with a gasket remover (available in aerosol cans) to soften it so it can be easily scraped off. A scraper can be fashioned from a piece of copper tubing by flattening and sharpening one end. Copper is recommended because it is usually softer than the surfaces to be scraped, which reduces the chance of gouging the part. Some gaskets can be removed with a wire brush, but regardless of the method used, the mating surfaces must be left clean and smooth. If for some reason the gasket surface is gouged, then a gasket sealer thick enough to fill scratches will have to be used during reassembly of the components. For most applications, a non-drying (or semi-drying) gasket sealer is best.

Hose removal tips

Hose removal precautions closely parallel gasket removal precautions. Avoid scratching or gouging the surface that the hose mates against or the connection may leak. Because of various chemical reactions, the rubber in hoses can bond itself to the metal spigot that the hose fits over. To remove a hose, first loosen the hose clamps that secure it to the spigot. Then, with slip joint pliers, grab the hose at the clamp and rotate it around the spigot. Work it back and forth until it is completely free, then pull it off (silicone or other lubricants will ease removal if they can be applied between the hose and the outside of the spigot). Apply the same lubricant to the inside of the hose and the outside of the spigot to simplify installation.

If a hose clamp is broken or damaged, do not reuse it. Also, do not reuse hoses that are cracked, split or torn.

Maintenance techniques, tools and working facilities

Spark plug gap adjusting tool

Feeler gauge set

Control cable pressure luber

Hand impact screwdriver and bits

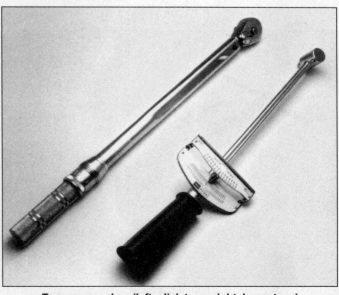
Torque wrenches (left, click type; right, beam type)

Tools

A selection of good tools is a basic requirement for anyone who plans to maintain and repair a vehicle. For the owner who has few tools, if any, the initial investment might seem high, but when compared to the spiraling costs of routine maintenance and repair, it is a wise one.

To help the owner decide which tools are needed to perform the tasks detailed in this manual, the following tool lists are offered: Maintenance and minor repair, Repair and overhaul and Special. The newcomer to practical mechanics should start off with the Maintenance and minor repair tool kit, which is adequate for the simpler jobs. Then, as confidence and experience grow, the owner can tackle more difficult tasks, buying additional tools as they are needed. Eventually the basic kit will be built into the Repair and overhaul tool set. Over a period of time, the experienced do-it-yourselfer will assemble a tool set complete enough for most repair and overhaul procedures and will add tools from the Special category when it is felt that the expense is justified by the frequency of use.

Maintenance and minor repair tool kit

The tools in this list should be considered the minimum required for performance of routine maintenance, servicing and minor repair work. We recommend the purchase of combination wrenches (box end

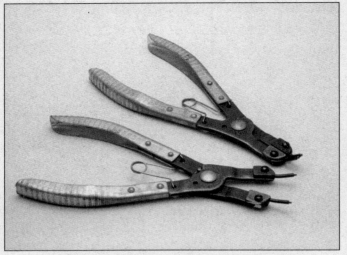
Snap-ring pliers (top - external; bottom - internal)

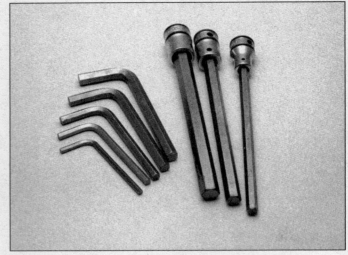
Allen wrenches (left), and Allen head sockets (right)

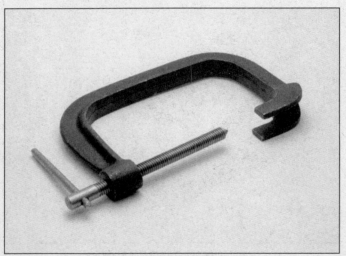
Valve spring compressor

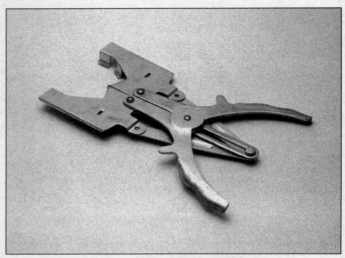
Piston ring removal/installation tool

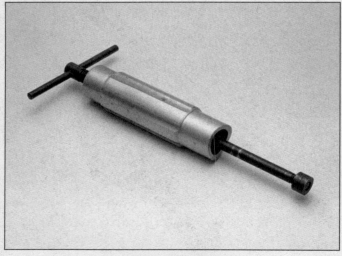
Piston pin puller

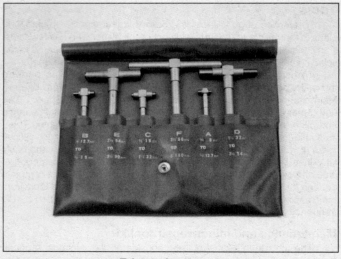
Telescoping gauges

Maintenance techniques, tools and working facilities

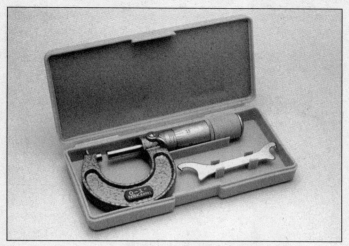
0-to-1 inch micrometer

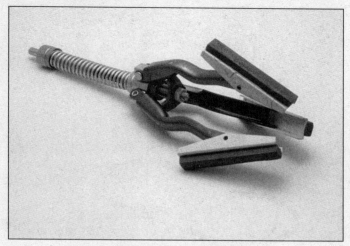
Cylinder surfacing hone

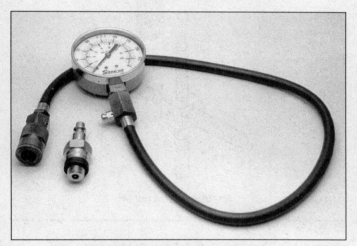
Cylinder compression gauge

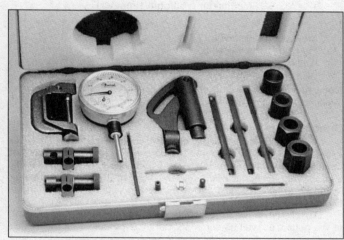
Dial indicator set

and open end combined in one wrench); while more expensive than open-ended ones, they offer the advantages of both types of wrench.

Combination wrench set (6 mm to 22 mm)
Adjustable wrench - 8 in
Spark plug socket (with rubber insert)
Spark plug gap adjusting tool
Feeler gauge set
Standard screwdriver (5/16 in x 6 in)
Phillips screwdriver (No. 2 x 6 in)
Allen (hex) wrench set (4 mm to 12 mm)
Combination (slip-joint) pliers - 6 in
Hacksaw and assortment of blades
Tire pressure gauge
Control cable pressure luber
Grease gun
Oil can
Fine emery cloth
Wire brush
Hand impact screwdriver and bits
Funnel (medium size)
Safety goggles
Drain pan
Work light with extension cord

Repair and overhaul tool set

These tools are essential for anyone who plans to perform major repairs and are intended to supplement those in the Maintenance and minor repair tool kit. Included is a comprehensive set of sockets which, though expensive, are invaluable because of their versatility (especially when various extensions and drives are available). We recommend the 3/8 inch drive over the 1/2 inch drive for general vehicle maintenance and repair (ideally, the mechanic would have a 3/8 inch drive set and a 1/2 inch drive set).

Alternator rotor puller tool
Socket set(s)
Reversible ratchet
Extension - 6 in
Universal joint
Torque wrench (same size drive as sockets)
Ball peen hammer - 8 oz
Soft-faced hammer (plastic/rubber)
Standard screwdriver (1/4 in x 6 in)
Standard screwdriver (stubby - 5/16 in)
Phillips screwdriver (No. 3 x 8 in)
Phillips screwdriver (stubby - No. 2)
Pliers - locking
Pliers - lineman's
Pliers - needle nose
Pliers - snap-ring (internal and external)
Cold chisel - 1/2 in
Scriber
Scraper (made from flattened copper tubing)
Center punch
Pin punches (1/16, 1/8, 3/16 in)

0-12   Maintenance techniques, tools and working facilities

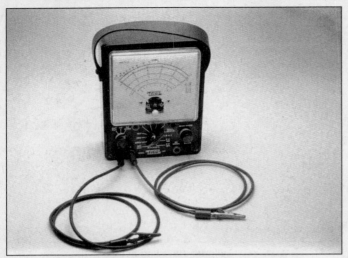

Multimeter (volt/ohm/ammeter)

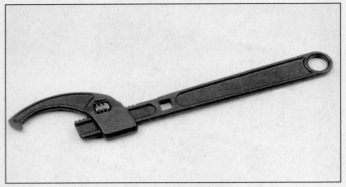

Adjustable spanner

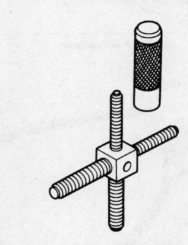

Alternator rotor puller

Steel rule/straightedge - 12 in
Pin-type spanner wrench
A selection of files
Wire brush (large)

Note: *Another tool which is often useful is an electric drill with a chuck capacity of 3/8 inch (and a set of good quality drill bits).*

Special tools

The tools in this list include those which are not used regularly, are expensive to buy, or which need to be used in accordance with their manufacturer's instructions. Unless these tools will be used frequently, it is not very economical to purchase many of them. A consideration would be to split the cost and use between yourself and a friend or friends (i.e. members of a vehicle club).

This list primarily contains tools and instruments widely available to the public, as well as some special tools produced by the vehicle manufacturer for distribution to dealer service departments. As a result, references to the manufacturer's special tools are occasionally included in the text of this manual. Generally, an alternative method of doing the job without the special tool is offered. However, sometimes there is no alternative to their use. Where this is the case, and the tool can't be purchased or borrowed, the work should be turned over to the dealer service department or a vehicle repair shop.

Valve spring compressor
Piston ring removal and installation tool
Piston pin puller
Telescoping gauges
Micrometer(s) and/or dial/Vernier calipers
Cylinder surfacing hone
Cylinder compression gauge
Dial indicator set
Multimeter
Adjustable spanner
Manometer or vacuum gauge set
Small air compressor with blow gun and tire chuck

Buying tools

For the do-it-yourselfer who is just starting to get involved in vehicle maintenance and repair, there are a number of options available when purchasing tools. If maintenance and minor repair is the extent of the work to be done, the purchase of individual tools is satisfactory. If, on the other hand, extensive work is planned, it would be a good idea to purchase a modest tool set from one of the large retail chain stores. A set can usually be bought at a substantial savings over the individual tool prices (and they often come with a tool box). As additional tools are needed, add-on sets, individual tools and a larger tool box can be purchased to expand the tool selection. Building a tool set gradually allows the cost of the tools to be spread over a longer period of time and gives the mechanic the freedom to choose only those tools that will actually be used.

Tool stores and vehicle dealers will often be the only source of some of the special tools that are needed, but regardless of where tools are bought, try to avoid cheap ones (especially when buying screwdrivers and sockets) because they won't last very long. There are plenty of tools around at reasonable prices, but always aim to purchase items which meet the relevant national safety standards. The expense involved in replacing cheap tools will eventually be greater than the initial cost of quality tools.

It is obviously not possible to cover the subject of tools fully here. For those who wish to learn more about tools and their use, there is a book entitled *Vehicle Workshop Practice Manual* (Book no. 1454) available from the publishers of this manual. It also provides an introduction to basic workshop practice which will be of interest to a home mechanic working on any type of vehicle.

Care and maintenance of tools

Good tools are expensive, so it makes sense to treat them with respect. Keep them clean and in usable condition and store them properly when not in use. Always wipe off any dirt, grease or metal chips before putting them away. Never leave tools lying around in the work area.

Some tools, such as screwdrivers, pliers, wrenches and sockets, can be hung on a panel mounted on the garage or workshop wall, while others should be kept in a tool box or tray. Measuring instruments, gauges, meters, etc. must be carefully stored where they can't be damaged by weather or impact from other tools.

When tools are used with care and stored properly, they will last a very long time. Even with the best of care, tools will wear out if used frequently. When a tool is damaged or worn out, replace it; subsequent jobs will be safer and more enjoyable if you do.

Working facilities

Not to be overlooked when discussing tools is the workshop. If anything more than routine maintenance is to be carried out, some sort of suitable work area is essential.

It is understood, and appreciated, that many home mechanics do not have a good workshop or garage available and end up removing an engine or doing major repairs outside (it is recommended, however, that the overhaul or repair be completed under the cover of a roof).

A clean, flat workbench or table of comfortable working height is an absolute necessity. The workbench should be equipped with a vise that has a jaw opening of at least four inches.

As mentioned previously, some clean, dry storage space is also required for tools, as well as the lubricants, fluids, cleaning solvents, etc. which soon become necessary.

Sometimes waste oil and fluids, drained from the engine or cooling system during normal maintenance or repairs, present a disposal problem. To avoid pouring them on the ground or into a sewage system, simply pour the used fluids into large containers, seal them with caps and take them to an authorized disposal site or service station. Plastic jugs are ideal for this purpose.

Always keep a supply of old newspapers and clean rags available. Old towels are excellent for mopping up spills. Many mechanics use rolls of paper towels for most work because they are readily available and disposable. To help keep the area under the vehicle clean, a large cardboard box can be cut open and flattened to protect the garage or shop floor.

Whenever working over a finished surface (such as the fuel tank) cover it with an old blanket or bedspread to protect the finish.

Safety first!

Professional mechanics are trained in safe working procedures. However enthusiastic you may be about getting on with the job at hand, take the time to ensure that your safety is not put at risk. A moment's lack of attention can result in an accident, as can failure to observe simple precautions.

There will always be new ways of having accidents, and the following is not a comprehensive list of all dangers; it is intended rather to make you aware of the risks and to encourage a safe approach to all work you carry out on your bike.

Essential DOs and DON'Ts

DON'T start the engine without first ascertaining that the transmission is in neutral.
DON'T attempt to drain oil until you are sure it has cooled sufficiently to avoid scalding you.
DON'T grasp any part of the engine or exhaust system without first ascertaining that it is cool enough not to burn you.
DON'T allow brake fluid to contact the machine's paint work or plastic components.
DON'T siphon toxic liquids such as fuel, hydraulic fluid or antifreeze by mouth, or allow them to remain on your skin.
DON'T inhale dust - it may be injurious to health (see *Asbestos* heading).
DON'T allow any spilled oil or grease to remain on the floor - wipe it up right away, before someone slips on it.
DON'T use ill fitting wrenches or other tools which may slip and cause injury.
DON'T attempt to lift a heavy component which may be beyond your capability - get assistance.
DON'T rush to finish a job or take unverified short cuts.
DON'T allow children or animals in or around an unattended vehicle.
DON'T inflate a tire to a pressure above the recommended maximum. Apart from over stressing the carcase and wheel rim, in extreme cases the tire may blow off forcibly. ATV tires, which are designed to operate at very low air pressures, may rupture if overinflated.
DO ensure that the machine is supported securely at all times. This is especially important when the machine is blocked up to aid wheel or suspension removal.
DO take care when attempting to loosen a stubborn nut or bolt. It is generally better to pull on a wrench, rather than push, so that if you slip, you fall away from the machine rather than onto it.
DO wear eye protection when using power tools such as drill, sander, bench grinder etc.
DO use a barrier cream on your hands prior to undertaking dirty jobs - it will protect your skin from infection as well as making the dirt easier to remove afterwards; but make sure your hands aren't left slippery. Note that long-term contact with used engine oil can be a health hazard.
DO keep loose clothing (cuffs, ties etc. and long hair) well out of the way of moving mechanical parts.
DO remove rings, wristwatch etc., before working on the vehicle - especially the electrical system.
DO keep your work area tidy - it is only too easy to fall over articles left lying around.
DO exercise caution when compressing springs for removal or installation. Ensure that the tension is applied and released in a controlled manner, using suitable tools which preclude the possibility of the spring escaping violently.
DO ensure that any lifting tackle used has a safe working load rating adequate for the job.
DO get someone to check periodically that all is well, when working alone on the vehicle.
DO carry out work in a logical sequence and check that everything is correctly assembled and tightened afterwards.
DO remember that your vehicle's safety affects that of yourself and others. If in doubt on any point, get professional advice.
IF, in spite of following these precautions, you are unfortunate enough to injure yourself, seek medical attention as soon as possible.

Asbestos

Certain friction, insulating, sealing and other products - such as brake pads, clutch linings, gaskets, etc. - may contain asbestos. *Extreme care must be taken to avoid inhalation of dust from such products since it is hazardous to health*. If in doubt, assume that they *do* contain asbestos.

Fire

Remember at all times that gasoline (petrol) is highly flammable. Never smoke or have any kind of naked flame around, when working on the vehicle. But the risk does not end there - a spark caused by an electrical short-circuit, by two metal surfaces contacting each other, by careless use of tools, or even by static electricity built up in your body under certain conditions, can ignite gasoline (petrol) vapor, which in a confined space is highly explosive. Never use gasoline (petrol) as a cleaning solvent. Use an approved safety solvent.

Always disconnect the battery ground (earth) terminal before working on any part of the fuel or electrical system, and never risk spilling fuel on to a hot engine or exhaust.

It is recommended that a fire extinguisher of a type suitable for fuel and electrical fires is kept handy in the garage or workplace at all times. Never try to extinguish a fuel or electrical fire with water.

Fumes

Certain fumes are highly toxic and can quickly cause unconsciousness and even death if inhaled to any extent. Gasoline (petrol) vapor comes into this category, as do the vapors from certain solvents such as trichloroethylene. Any draining or pouring of such volatile fluids should be done in a well ventilated area.

When using cleaning fluids and solvents, read the instructions carefully. Never use materials from unmarked containers - they may give off poisonous vapors.

Never run the engine of a motor vehicle in an enclosed space such as a garage. Exhaust fumes contain carbon monoxide which is extremely poisonous; if you need to run the engine, always do so in the open air or at least have the rear of the vehicle outside the workplace.

The battery

Never cause a spark, or allow a bare light bulb near the vehicle's battery. It will normally be giving off a certain amount of hydrogen gas, which is highly explosive.

Always disconnect the battery ground (earth) terminal before working on the fuel or electrical systems (except where noted).

Do not charge the battery at an excessive rate or the battery may burst.

Take care when cleaning or carrying the battery. The acid electrolyte, even when diluted, is very corrosive and should not be allowed to contact the eyes or skin. Always wear rubber gloves and goggles or a face shield. If you ever need to prepare electrolyte yourself, always add the acid slowly to the water; never add the water to the acid.

Electricity

When using an electric power tool, inspection light etc., always ensure that the appliance is correctly connected to its plug and that, where necessary, it is properly grounded (earthed). Do not use such appliances in damp conditions and, again, beware of creating a spark or applying excessive heat in the vicinity of fuel or fuel vapor. Also ensure that the appliances meet national safety standards.

A severe electric shock can result from touching certain parts of the electrical system, such as the spark plug wires (HT leads), when the engine is running or being cranked, particularly if components are damp or the insulation is defective. Where an electronic ignition system is used, the secondary (HT) voltage is much higher and could prove fatal.

ATV chemicals and lubricants

A number of chemicals and lubricants are available for use in vehicle maintenance and repair. They include a wide variety of products ranging from cleaning solvents and degreasers to lubricants and protective sprays for rubber, plastic and vinyl.

Contact point/spark plug cleaner is a solvent used to clean oily film and dirt from points, grime from electrical connectors and oil deposits from spark plugs. It is oil free and leaves no residue. It can also be used to remove gum and varnish from carburetor jets and other orifices.

Carburetor cleaner is similar to contact point/spark plug cleaner but it usually has a stronger solvent and may leave a slight oily residue. It is not recommended for cleaning electrical components or connections.

Brake system cleaner is used to remove grease or brake fluid from brake system components (where clean surfaces are absolutely necessary and petroleum-based solvents cannot be used); it also leaves no residue.

Silicone-based lubricants are used to protect rubber parts such as hoses and grommets, and are used as lubricants for hinges and locks.

Multi-purpose grease is an all purpose lubricant used wherever grease is more practical than a liquid lubricant such as oil. Some multi-purpose grease is colored white and specially formulated to be more resistant to water than ordinary grease.

Gear oil (sometimes called gear lube) is a specially designed oil used in transmissions and final drive units, as well as other areas where high friction, high temperature lubrication is required. It is available in a number of viscosities (weights) for various applications.

Motor oil, of course, is the lubricant specially formulated for use in the engine. It normally contains a wide variety of additives to prevent corrosion and reduce foaming and wear. Motor oil comes in various weights (viscosity ratings) of from 5 to 80. The recommended weight of the oil depends on the seasonal temperature and the demands on the engine. Light oil is used in cold climates and under light load conditions; heavy oil is used in hot climates and where high loads are encountered. Multi-viscosity oils are designed to have characteristics of both light and heavy oils and are available in a number of weights from 5W-20 to 20W-50. On these machines, the same oil supply is shared by the engine and transmission.

Gas (petrol) additives perform several functions, depending on their chemical makeup. They usually contain solvents that help dissolve gum and varnish that build up on carburetor and intake parts. They also serve to break down carbon deposits that form on the inside surfaces of the combustion chambers. Some additives contain upper cylinder lubricants for valves and piston rings.

Brake fluid is a specially formulated hydraulic fluid that can withstand the heat and pressure encountered in brake systems. Care must be taken that this fluid does not come in contact with painted surfaces or plastics. An opened container should always be resealed to prevent contamination by water or dirt.

Chain lubricants are formulated especially for use on the final drive chains of vehicles so equipped (all models covered in this manual are equipped with shaft drive). A good chain lube should adhere well and have good penetrating qualities to be effective as a lubricant inside the chain and on the side plates, pins and rollers. Most chain lubes are either the foaming type or quick drying type and are usually marketed as sprays.

Degreasers are heavy duty solvents used to remove grease and grime that may accumulate on engine and frame components. They can be sprayed or brushed on and, depending on the type, are rinsed with either water or solvent.

Solvents are used alone or in combination with degreasers to clean parts and assemblies during repair and overhaul. The home mechanic should use only solvents that are non-flammable and that do not produce irritating fumes.

Gasket sealing compounds may be used in conjunction with gaskets, to improve their sealing capabilities, or alone, to seal metal-to-metal joints. Many gasket sealers can withstand extreme heat, some are impervious to gasoline and lubricants, while others are capable of filling and sealing large cavities. Depending on the intended use, gasket sealers either dry hard or stay relatively soft and pliable. They are usually applied by hand, with a brush, or are sprayed on the gasket sealing surfaces.

Thread cement is an adhesive locking compound that prevents threaded fasteners from loosening because of vibration. It is available in a variety of types for different applications.

Moisture dispersants are usually sprays that can be used to dry out electrical components such as the fuse block and wiring connectors. Some types can also be used as treatment for rubber and as a lubricant for hinges, cables and locks.

Waxes and polishes are used to help protect painted and plated surfaces from the weather. Different types of paint may require the use of different types of wax polish. Some polishes utilize a chemical or abrasive cleaner to help remove the top layer of oxidized (dull) paint on older vehicles. In recent years, many non-wax polishes (that contain a wide variety of chemicals such as polymers and silicones) have been introduced. These non-wax polishes are usually easier to apply and last longer than conventional waxes and polishes.

Troubleshooting

Contents

Symptom	Section
Engine doesn't start or is difficult to start	
Starter motor doesn't rotate	1
Starter motor rotates but engine does not turn over	2
Starter works but engine won't turn over (seized)	3
No fuel flow	4
Engine flooded	5
No spark or weak spark	6
Compression low	7
Stalls after starting	8
Rough idle	9
Poor running at low speed	
Spark weak	10
Fuel/air mixture incorrect	11
Compression low	12
Poor acceleration	13
Poor running or no power at high speed	
Firing incorrect	14
Fuel/air mixture incorrect	15
Compression low	16
Knocking or pinging	17
Miscellaneous causes	18
Overheating	
Engine overheats	19
Firing incorrect	20
Fuel/air mixture incorrect	21
Compression too high	22
Engine load excessive	23
Lubrication inadequate	24
Miscellaneous causes	25
Clutch problems	
Clutch slipping	26
Clutch not disengaging completely	27
Gear shifting problems	
Doesn't go into gear, or lever doesn't return	28
Jumps out of gear	29
Overshifts	30
Abnormal engine noise	
Knocking or pinging	31
Piston slap or rattling	32
Valve noise	33
Other noise	34

Symptom	Section
Abnormal driveline noise	
Clutch noise	35
Transmission noise	36
Transfer case noise	37
Final drive noise	38
Abnormal frame and suspension noise	
Suspension noise	39
Driveaxle noise (4WD models)	40
Brake noise	41
Oil level indicator light comes on	
Engine lubrication system	42
Electrical system	43
Excessive exhaust smoke	
White smoke	44
Black smoke	45
Brown smoke	46
Poor handling or stability	
Handlebar hard to turn	47
Handlebar shakes or vibrates excessively	48
Handlebar pulls to one side	49
Poor shock absorbing qualities	50
Braking problems	
Front brakes are spongy, don't hold	51
Brake lever pulsates	52
Brakes drag	53
Electrical problems	
Battery dead or weak	54
Battery overcharged	55
Automatic transmission problems	
Drivebelt slipping	56
Drivebelt upside down in pulleys	57
Burn marks or thin spots on drivebelt	58
Harsh engagement	59
Grabby or erratic engagement	60
Noisy operation	61
Melted or broken belt cover	62
Engine rpm too low when vehicle is driven	63
Engine rpm too high when vehicle is driven	64
Engine rpm erratic when vehicle is driven	65

Troubleshooting 0-17

Engine doesn't start or is difficult to start

1 Starter motor does not rotate

1 Engine kill switch Off.
2 Fuse blown. Check fuse (Chapter 9).
3 Battery voltage low. Check and recharge battery (Chapter 9).
4 Starter motor defective. Make sure the wiring to the starter is secure. Test starter relay (Chapter 9). If the relay is good, then the fault is in the wiring or motor.
5 Starter relay faulty. Check it according to the procedure in Chapter 9.
6 Starter switch not contacting. The contacts could be wet, corroded or dirty. Disassemble and clean the switch (Chapter 9).
7 Wiring open or shorted. Check all wiring connections and harnesses to make sure that they are dry, tight and not corroded. Also check for broken or frayed wires that can cause a short to ground (see *Wiring Diagrams*, Chapter 10).
8 Ignition (main) switch defective. Check the switch according to the procedure in Chapter 9. Replace the switch with a new one if it is defective.
9 Engine kill switch defective. Check for wet, dirty or corroded contacts. Clean or replace the switch as necessary (Chapter 9).
10 Starting circuit cut-off relay, neutral relay, neutral switch, reverse switch or front brake switch defective. Check the switches according to the procedure in Chapter 9. Replace the switch with a new one if it is defective.

2 Starter motor rotates but engine does not turn over

1 Starter motor clutch defective. Inspect and repair or replace (Chapter 9).
2 Damaged starter idle or wheel gears. Inspect and replace the damaged parts (Chapter 9).

3 Starter works but engine won't turn over (seized)

Seized engine caused by one or more internally damaged components. Failure due to wear, abuse or lack of lubrication. Damage can include seized valves, valve lifters, camshaft, piston, crankshaft, connecting rod bearings, or transmission gears or bearings. Refer to Chapter 2 for engine disassembly.

4 No fuel flow

1 No fuel in tank.
2 Tank cap air vent obstructed. Usually caused by dirt or water. Remove it and clean the cap vent hole.
3 Clogged strainer in fuel tap. Remove and clean the strainer (Chapter 1).
4 Fuel line clogged. Pull the fuel line loose and carefully blow through it.
5 Inlet needle valve clogged. A very bad batch of fuel with an unusual additive may have been used, or some other foreign material has entered the tank. Many times after a machine has been stored for many months without running, the fuel turns to a varnish-like liquid and forms deposits on the inlet needle valve and jets. The carburetor should be removed and overhauled if draining the float chamber doesn't solve the problem.

5 Engine flooded

1 Float level too high. Check as described in Chapter 4 and replace the float if necessary.
2 Inlet needle valve worn or stuck open. A piece of dirt, rust or other debris can cause the inlet needle to seat improperly, causing excess fuel to be admitted to the float bowl. In this case, the float chamber should be cleaned and the needle and seat inspected. If the needle and seat are worn, then the leaking will persist and the parts should be replaced with new ones (Chapter 4).
3 Starting technique incorrect. Under normal circumstances (i.e., if all the carburetor functions are sound) the machine should start with little or no throttle. When the engine is cold, the choke should be operated and the engine started without opening the throttle. When the engine is at operating temperature, only a very slight amount of throttle should be necessary. If the engine is flooded, turn the fuel tap off and hold the throttle open while cranking the engine. This will allow additional air to reach the cylinder. Remember to turn the fuel tap back on after the engine starts.

6 No spark or weak spark

1 Ignition switch Off.
2 Engine kill switch turned to the Off position.
3 Battery voltage low. Check and recharge battery as necessary (Chapter 9).
4 Spark plug dirty, defective or worn out. Locate reason for fouled plug using spark plug condition chart and follow the plug maintenance procedures in Chapter 1.
5 Spark plug cap or secondary (HT) wiring faulty. Check condition. Replace either or both components if cracks or deterioration are evident (Chapter 5).
6 Spark plug cap not making good contact. Make sure that the plug cap fits snugly over the plug end.
7 CDI magneto defective. Check the unit, referring to Chapter 5 for details.
8 CDI unit defective. Check the unit, referring to Chapter 5 for details.
9 Ignition coil defective. Check the coil, referring to Chapter 5.
10 Ignition or kill switch shorted. This is usually caused by water, corrosion, damage or excessive wear. The kill switch can be disassembled and cleaned with electrical contact cleaner. If cleaning does not help, replace the switches (Chapter 9).
11 Wiring shorted or broken between:
   a) *Ignition switch and engine kill switch (or blown fuse)*
   b) *CDI unit and engine kill switch*
   c) *CDI and ignition coil*
   d) *Ignition coil and plug*
   e) *CDI unit and CDI magneto*

Make sure that all wiring connections are clean, dry and tight. Look for chafed and broken wires (Chapters 4 and 8).

7 Compression low

1 Spark plug loose. Remove the plug and inspect the threads. Reinstall and tighten to the specified torque (Chapter 1).
2 Cylinder head not sufficiently tightened down. If the cylinder head is suspected of being loose, then there's a chance that the gasket or head is damaged if the problem has persisted for any length of time. The head nuts and bolts should be tightened to the proper torque in the correct sequence (Chapter 2).
3 Improper valve clearance. This means that the valve is not closing completely and compression pressure is leaking past the valve. Check and adjust the valve clearances (Chapter 1).

4 Cylinder and/or piston worn. Excessive wear will cause compression pressure to leak past the rings. This is usually accompanied by worn rings as well. A top end overhaul is necessary (Chapter 2).
5 Piston rings worn, weak, broken, or sticking. Broken or sticking piston rings usually indicate a lubrication or carburetion problem that causes excess carbon deposits or seizures to form on the pistons and rings. Top end overhaul is necessary (Chapter 2).
6 Piston ring-to-groove clearance excessive. This is caused by excessive wear of the piston ring lands. Piston replacement is necessary (Chapter 2).
7 Cylinder head gasket damaged. If the head is allowed to become loose, or if excessive carbon build-up on a piston crown and combustion chamber causes extremely high compression, the head gasket may leak. Retorquing the head is not always sufficient to restore the seal, so gasket replacement is necessary (Chapter 2).
8 Cylinder head warped. This is caused by overheating or improperly tightened head nuts and bolts. Machine shop resurfacing or head replacement is necessary (Chapter 2).
9 Valve spring broken or weak. Caused by component failure or wear; the spring(s) must be replaced (Chapter 2).
10 Valve not seating properly. This is caused by a bent valve (from over-revving or improper valve adjustment), burned valve or seat (improper carburetion) or an accumulation of carbon deposits on the seat (from carburetion or lubrication problems). The valves must be cleaned and/or replaced and the seats serviced if possible (Chapter 2).

8 Stalls after starting

1 Improper choke action. Make sure the choke knob or lever is getting a full stroke and staying in the out position.
2 Ignition malfunction. See Chapter 5.
3 Carburetor malfunction. See Chapter 4.
4 Fuel contaminated. The fuel can be contaminated with either dirt or water, or can change chemically if the machine is allowed to sit for several months or more. Drain the tank and float bowl and refill with fresh fuel (Chapter 5).
5 Intake air leak. Check for loose carburetor-to-intake joint connections or loose carburetor top (Chapter 4).
6 Engine idle speed incorrect. Turn throttle stop screw until the engine idles at the specified rpm (Chapter 1).

9 Rough idle

1 Ignition malfunction. See Chapter 5.
2 Idle speed incorrect. See Chapter 1.
3 Carburetor malfunction. See Chapter 4.
4 Idle fuel/air mixture incorrect. See Chapter 4.
5 Fuel contaminated. The fuel can be contaminated with either dirt or water, or can change chemically if the machine is allowed to sit for several months or more. Drain the tank and float bowl (Chapter 4).
6 Intake air leak. Check for loose carburetor-to-intake joint connections, loose or missing vacuum gauge access port cap or hose, or loose carburetor top (Chapter 4).
7 Air cleaner clogged. Service or replace air cleaner element (Chapter 1).

Poor running at low speed

10 Spark weak

1 Battery voltage low. Check and recharge battery (Chapter 9).
2 Spark plug fouled, defective or worn out. Refer to Chapter 1 for spark plug maintenance.
3 Spark plug cap or secondary (HT) wiring defective. Refer to Chapters 1 and 5 for details on the ignition system.
4 Spark plug cap not making contact.
5 Incorrect spark plug. Wrong type, heat range or cap configuration. Check and install correct plug listed in Chapter 1. A cold plug or one with a recessed firing electrode will not operate at low speeds without fouling.
6 CDI unit defective. See Chapter 5.
7 CDI magneto defective. See Chapter 5.
8 Ignition coil defective. See Chapter 5.

11 Fuel/air mixture incorrect

1 Pilot screw out of adjustment (Chapter 4).
2 Pilot jet or air passage clogged. Remove and overhaul the carburetor (Chapter 3).
3 Air bleed holes clogged. Remove carburetor and blow out all passages (Chapter 3).
4 Air cleaner clogged, poorly sealed or missing.
5 Air cleaner-to-carburetor boot poorly sealed. Look for cracks, holes or loose clamps and replace or repair defective parts.
6 Float level too high or too low. Check and replace the float if necessary (Chapter 4).
7 Fuel tank air vent obstructed. Make sure that the air vent passage in the filler cap is open.
8 Carburetor intake joint loose. Check for cracks, breaks, tears or loose clamps or bolts. Repair or replace the rubber boot and its O-ring.

12 Compression low

1 Spark plug loose. Remove the plug and inspect the threads. Reinstall and tighten to the specified torque (Chapter 1).
2 Cylinder head not sufficiently tightened down. If the cylinder head is suspected of being loose, then there's a chance that the gasket and head are damaged if the problem has persisted for any length of time. The head nuts and bolts should be tightened to the proper torque in the correct sequence (Chapter 2).
3 Improper valve clearance. This means that the valve is not closing completely and compression pressure is leaking past the valve. Check and adjust the valve clearances (Chapter 1).
4 Cylinder and/or piston worn. Excessive wear will cause compression pressure to leak past the rings. This is usually accompanied by worn rings as well. A top end overhaul is necessary (Chapter 2).
5 Piston rings worn, weak, broken, or sticking. Broken or sticking piston rings usually indicate a lubrication or carburetion problem that causes excess carbon deposits or seizures to form on the pistons and rings. Top end overhaul is necessary (Chapter 2).
6 Piston ring-to-groove clearance excessive. This is caused by excessive wear of the piston ring lands. Piston replacement is necessary (Chapter 2).
7 Cylinder head gasket damaged. If the head is allowed to become loose, or if excessive carbon build-up on the piston crown and combustion chamber causes extremely high compression, the head gasket may leak. Retorquing the head is not always sufficient to restore the seal, so gasket replacement is necessary (Chapter 2).
8 Cylinder head warped. This is caused by overheating or improperly tightened head nuts and bolts. Machine shop resurfacing or head replacement is necessary (Chapter 2).
9 Valve spring broken or weak. Caused by component failure or wear; the spring(s) must be replaced (Chapter 2).
10 Valve not seating properly. This is caused by a bent valve (from over-revving or improper valve adjustment), burned valve or seat (improper carburetion) or an accumulation of carbon deposits on the seat (from carburetion, lubrication problems). The valves must be cleaned and/or replaced and the seats serviced if possible (Chapter 2).

Troubleshooting 0-19

13 Poor acceleration

1 Carburetor leaking or dirty. Overhaul the carburetor (Chapter 4).
2 Timing not advancing. The CDI magneto or the CDI unit may be defective. If so, they must be replaced with new ones, as they can't be repaired.
3 Engine oil viscosity too high. Using a heavier oil than that recommended in Chapter 1 can damage the oil pump or lubrication system and cause drag on the engine.
4 Brakes dragging. Usually caused by debris which has entered the brake piston sealing boots, corroded wheel cylinders or calipers, sticking brake cam (drum brakes), or from a warped drum, warped disc or bent axle. Repair as necessary (Chapter 7).

Poor running or no power at high speed

14 Firing incorrect

1 Air cleaner restricted. Clean or replace element (Chapter 1).
2 Spark plug fouled, defective or worn out. See Chapter 1 for spark plug maintenance.
3 Spark plug cap or secondary (HT) wiring defective. See Chapters 1 and 5 for details of the ignition system.
4 Spark plug cap not in good contact. See Chapter 5.
5 Incorrect spark plug. Wrong type, heat range or cap configuration. Check and install correct plugs listed in Chapter 1. A cold plug or one with a recessed firing electrode will not operate at low speeds without fouling.
6 CDI unit or CDI magneto defective. See Chapter 5.
7 Ignition coil defective. See Chapter 5.

15 Fuel/air mixture incorrect

1 Pilot screw out of adjustment. See Chapter 4 for adjustment procedures.
2 Main jet clogged. Dirt, water or other contaminants can clog the main jets. Clean the fuel tap strainer and in-tank strainer, the float bowl area, and the jets and carburetor orifices (Chapter 4).
3 Main jet wrong size. The standard jetting is for sea level atmospheric pressure and oxygen content. See Chapter 4 for high altitude adjustments.
4 Throttle shaft-to-carburetor body clearance excessive. Refer to Chapter 4 for inspection and part replacement procedures.
5 Air bleed holes clogged. Remove and overhaul carburetor (Chapter 4).
6 Air cleaner clogged, poorly sealed, or missing.
7 Air cleaner-to-carburetor boot poorly sealed. Look for cracks, holes or loose clamps, and replace or repair defective parts.
8 Float level too high or too low. Check float level and replace the float if necessary (Chapter 4).
9 Fuel tank air vent obstructed. Make sure the air vent passage in the filler cap is open.
10 Carburetor intake joint loose. Check for cracks, breaks, tears or loose clamps or bolts. Repair or replace the rubber boots (Chapter 4).
11 Fuel tap clogged. Remove the tap and clean it (Chapter 1).
12 Fuel line clogged. Pull the fuel line loose and carefully blow through it.

16 Compression low

1 Spark plug loose. Remove the plug and inspect the threads. Reinstall and tighten to the specified torque (Chapter 1).
2 Cylinder head not sufficiently tightened down. If the cylinder head is suspected of being loose, then there's a chance that the gasket and head are damaged if the problem has persisted for any length of time. The head nuts and bolts should be tightened to the proper torque in the correct sequence (Chapter 2).
3 Improper valve clearance. This means that the valve is not closing completely and compression pressure is leaking past the valve. Check and adjust the valve clearances (Chapter 1).
4 Cylinder and/or piston worn. Excessive wear will cause compression pressure to leak past the rings. This is usually accompanied by worn rings as well. A top end overhaul is necessary (Chapter 2).
5 Piston rings worn, weak, broken, or sticking. Broken or sticking piston rings usually indicate a lubrication or carburetion problem that causes excess carbon deposits or seizures to form on the pistons and rings. Top end overhaul is necessary (Chapter 2).
6 Piston ring-to-groove clearance excessive. This is caused by excessive wear of the piston ring lands. Piston replacement is necessary (Chapter 2).
7 Cylinder head gasket damaged. If a head is allowed to become loose, or if excessive carbon build-up on the piston crown and combustion chamber causes extremely high compression, the head gasket may leak. Retorquing the head is not always sufficient to restore the seal, so gasket replacement is necessary (Chapter 2).
8 Cylinder head warped. This is caused by overheating or improperly tightened head nuts and bolts. Machine shop resurfacing or head replacement is necessary (Chapter 2).
9 Valve spring broken or weak. Caused by component failure or wear; the spring(s) must be replaced (Chapter 2).
10 Valve not seating properly. This is caused by a bent valve (from over-revving or improper valve adjustment), burned valve or seat (improper carburetion) or an accumulation of carbon deposits on the seat (from carburetion or lubrication problems). The valves must be cleaned and/or replaced and the seats serviced if possible (Chapter 2).

17 Knocking or pinging

1 Carbon build-up in combustion chamber. Use of a fuel additive that will dissolve the adhesive bonding the carbon particles to the crown and chamber is the easiest way to remove the build-up. Otherwise, the cylinder head will have to be removed and decarbonized (Chapter 2).
2 Incorrect or poor quality fuel. Old or improper grades of fuel can cause detonation. This causes the piston to rattle, thus the knocking or pinging sound. Drain old fuel and always use the recommended fuel grade.
3 Spark plug heat range incorrect. Uncontrolled detonation indicates the plug heat range is too hot. The plug in effect becomes a glow plug, raising cylinder temperatures. Install the proper heat range plug (Chapter 1).
4 Improper air/fuel mixture. This will cause the cylinder to run hot, which leads to detonation. Clogged jets or an air leak can cause this imbalance. See Chapter 4.

18 Miscellaneous causes

1 Throttle valve doesn't open fully. Adjust the cable slack (Chapter 1).
2 Clutch slipping (1993 through 1999 models). May be caused by improper adjustment or loose or worn clutch components. Refer to Chapter 1 for adjustment or Chapter 2 for clutch overhaul procedures.
3 Timing not advancing.
4 Engine oil viscosity too high. Using a heavier oil than the one recommended in Chapter 1 can damage the oil pump or lubrication system and cause drag on the engine.
5 Brakes dragging. Usually caused by debris which has entered the brake piston sealing boot, or from a warped drum, warped disc or bent axle. Repair as necessary.

Troubleshooting

Overheating

19 Engine overheats

1 Engine oil or coolant level low. Check and add oil or coolant (Chapter 1).
2 Wrong type of oil. If you're not sure what type of oil is in the engine, drain it and fill with the correct type (Chapter 1).
3 Air leak at carburetor intake joint. Check and tighten or replace as necessary (Chapter 4).
4 Fuel level low. Check and adjust if necessary (Chapter 4).
5 Worn oil pump or clogged oil passages. Replace pump or clean passages as necessary.
6 Clogged external oil line. Remove and check for foreign material (see Chapter 2).
7 Carbon build-up in combustion chambers. Use of a fuel additive that will dissolve the adhesive bonding the carbon particles to the piston crown and chambers is the easiest way to remove the build-up. Otherwise, the cylinder head will have to be removed and decarbonized (Chapter 2).
8 Operation in high ambient temperatures.
9 Cooling fan not working (see Chapter 3).
10 Radiator clogged (liquid-cooled models) (see Chapter 3).
11 Thermostat stuck shut (liquid-cooled models) (see Chapter 3).

20 Firing incorrect

1 Spark plug fouled, defective or worn out. See Chapter 1 for spark plug maintenance.
2 Incorrect spark plug (see Chapter 1).
3 Faulty ignition coil(s) (Chapter 5).

21 Fuel/air mixture incorrect

1 Pilot screw out of adjustment (Chapter 4).
2 Main jet clogged. Dirt, water and other contaminants can clog the main jet. Clean the fuel tap strainer, the float bowl area and the jets and carburetor orifices (Chapter 4).
3 Main jet wrong size. The standard jetting is for sea level atmospheric pressure and oxygen content.
4 Air cleaner poorly sealed or missing.
5 Air cleaner-to-carburetor boot poorly sealed. Look for cracks, holes or loose clamps and replace or repair.
6 Fuel level too low. Check fuel level and float level and adjust or replace the float if necessary (Chapter 4).
7 Fuel tank air vent obstructed. Make sure that the air vent passage in the filler cap is open.
8 Carburetor intake manifold loose. Check for cracks or loose clamps or bolts. Check the carburetor-to-manifold gasket and the manifold-to-cylinder head O-ring Chapter 4).

22 Compression too high

1 Carbon build-up in combustion chamber. Use of a fuel additive that will dissolve the adhesive bonding the carbon particles to the piston crown and chamber is the easiest way to remove the build-up. Otherwise, the cylinder head will have to be removed and decarbonized (Chapter 2).
2 Improperly machined head surface or installation of incorrect gasket during engine assembly.

23 Engine load excessive

1 Clutch slipping (1993 through 1999). Can be caused by damaged, loose or worn clutch components. Refer to Chapter 2 for overhaul procedures.
2 Engine oil level too high. The addition of too much oil will cause pressurization of the crankcase and inefficient engine operation. Check Specifications and drain to proper level (Chapter 1).
3 Engine oil viscosity too high. Using a heavier oil than the one recommended in Chapter 1 can damage the oil pump or lubrication system as well as cause drag on the engine.
4 Brakes dragging. Usually caused by debris which has entered the brake piston sealing boots, corroded wheel cylinders or calipers, sticking brake cam (drum) or from a warped drum, warped disc or bent axle. Repair as necessary (Chapter 7).

24 Lubrication inadequate

1 Engine oil level too low. Friction caused by intermittent lack of lubrication or from oil that is overworked can cause overheating. The oil provides a definite cooling function in the engine. Check the oil level (Chapter 1).
2 Poor quality engine oil or incorrect viscosity or type. Oil is rated not only according to viscosity but also according to type. Some oils are not rated high enough for use in this engine. Check the Specifications section and change to the correct oil (Chapter 1).
3 Camshaft or journals worn. Excessive wear causing drop in oil pressure. Replace cam or cylinder head. Abnormal wear could be caused by oil starvation at high rpm from low oil level or improper viscosity or type of oil (Chapter 1).
4 Crankshaft and/or bearings worn. Same problems as paragraph 3. Check and replace crankshaft assembly if necessary (Chapter 2).

25 Miscellaneous causes

Modification to exhaust system. Most aftermarket exhaust systems cause the engine to run leaner, which makes it run hotter. When installing an aftermarket exhaust system, always rejet the carburetor.

Clutch problems (1993 through 1999 models)

26 Clutch slipping

1 Secondary clutch friction plates worn or warped. Overhaul the secondary clutch assembly (Chapter 2).
2 Secondary clutch metal plates worn or warped (Chapter 2).
3 Secondary clutch spring(s) broken or weak. Old or heat-damaged spring(s) (from slipping clutch) should be replaced with new ones (Chapter 2).
4 Secondary clutch release mechanism defective. Replace any defective parts (Chapter 2).
5 Secondary clutch boss or housing unevenly worn. This causes improper engagement of the plates. Replace the damaged or worn parts (Chapter 2).
6 Primary (centrifugal) clutch weight linings or drum worn (Chapter 2).

27 Clutch not disengaging completely

1 Secondary clutch improperly adjusted (see Chapter 1).
2 Secondary clutch plates warped or damaged. This will cause clutch drag, which in turn will cause the machine to creep. Overhaul the clutch assembly (Chapter 2).
3 Sagged or broken secondary clutch spring(s). Check and replace the spring(s) (Chapter 2).

Troubleshooting　　0-21

4 Engine oil deteriorated. Old, thin, worn out oil will not provide proper lubrication for the discs, causing the secondary clutch to drag. Replace the oil and filter (Chapter 1).
5 Engine oil viscosity too high. Using a thicker oil than recommended in Chapter 1 can cause the secondary clutch plates to stick together, putting a drag on the engine. Change to the correct viscosity oil (Chapter 1).
6 Secondary clutch housing seized on shaft. Lack of lubrication, severe wear or damage can cause the housing to seize on the shaft. Overhaul of the clutch, and perhaps transmission, may be necessary to repair the damage (Chapter 2).
7 Secondary clutch release mechanism defective. Worn or damaged release mechanism parts can stick and fail to apply force to the pressure plate. Overhaul the release mechanism (Chapter 2).
8 Loose secondary clutch center nut. Causes housing and center misalignment putting a drag on the engine. Engagement adjustment continually varies. Overhaul the clutch assembly (Chapter 2).
9 Weak or broken primary clutch springs (Chapter 2).

Gear shifting problems

28 Doesn't go into gear or lever doesn't return

1 Clutch not disengaging (1993 through 1999). See Section 27.
2 Shift fork(s) bent or seized. May be caused by lack of lubrication. Overhaul the transmission (Chapter 2).
3 Gear(s) stuck on shaft. Most often caused by a lack of lubrication or excessive wear in transmission bearings and bushings. Overhaul the transmission (Chapter 2).
4 Shift drum binding. Caused by lubrication failure or excessive wear. Replace the drum and bearing (Chapter 2).
5 Shift lever return spring weak or broken (Chapter 2).
6 Shift lever broken. Splines stripped out of lever or shaft, caused by allowing the lever to get loose. Replace necessary parts (Chapter 2).
7 Shift mechanism pawl broken or worn. Full engagement and rotary movement of shift drum results. Replace shaft assembly (Chapter 2).
8 Pawl spring broken. Allows pawl to float, causing sporadic shift operation. Replace spring (Chapter 2).

29 Jumps out of gear

1 Shift fork(s) worn. Overhaul the transmission (Chapter 2).
2 Gear groove(s) worn. Overhaul the transmission (Chapter 2).
3 Gear dogs or dog slots worn or damaged. The gears should be inspected and replaced. No attempt should be made to service the worn parts.

30 Overshifts

1 Pawl spring weak or broken (Chapter 2).
2 Shift cam stopper lever not functioning (Chapter 2).

Abnormal engine noise

31 Knocking or pinging

1 Carbon build-up in combustion chamber. Use of a fuel additive that will dissolve the adhesive bonding the carbon particles to the piston crown and chamber is the easiest way to remove the build-up. Otherwise, the cylinder head will have to be removed and decarbonized (Chapter 2).
2 Incorrect or poor quality fuel. Old or improper fuel can cause detonation. This causes the pistons to rattle, thus the knocking or pinging sound. Drain the old fuel (Chapter 4) and always use the recommended grade fuel (Chapter 1).
3 Spark plug heat range incorrect. Uncontrolled detonation indicates that the plug heat range is too hot. The plug in effect becomes a glow plug, raising cylinder temperatures. Install the proper heat range plug (Chapter 1).
4 Improper air/fuel mixture. This will cause the cylinder to run hot and lead to detonation. Clogged jets or an air leak can cause this imbalance. See Chapter 4.

32 Piston slap or rattling

1 Cylinder-to-piston clearance excessive. Caused by improper assembly. Inspect and overhaul top end parts (Chapter 2).
2 Connecting rod bent. Caused by over-revving, trying to start a badly flooded engine or from ingesting a foreign object into the combustion chamber. Replace the damaged parts (Chapter 2).
3 Piston pin or piston pin bore worn or seized from wear or lack of lubrication. Replace damaged parts (Chapter 2).
4 Piston ring(s) worn, broken or sticking. Overhaul the top end (Chapter 2).
5 Piston seizure damage. Usually from lack of lubrication or overheating. Replace the pistons and bore the cylinder, as necessary (Chapter 2).
6 Connecting rod upper or lower end clearance excessive. Caused by excessive wear or lack of lubrication. Replace worn parts.

33 Valve noise

1 Incorrect valve clearances. Adjust the clearances by referring to Chapter 1.
2 Valve spring broken or weak. Check and replace weak valve springs (Chapter 2).
3 Camshaft or cylinder head worn or damaged. Lack of lubrication at high rpm is usually the cause of damage. Insufficient oil or failure to change the oil at the recommended intervals are the chief causes.

34 Other noise

1 Cylinder head gasket leaking.
2 Exhaust pipe leaking at cylinder head connection. Caused by improper fit of pipe, damaged gasket or loose exhaust flange. All exhaust fasteners should be tightened evenly and carefully. Failure to do this will lead to a leak.
3 Crankshaft runout excessive. Caused by a bent crankshaft (from over-revving) or damage from an upper cylinder component failure.
4 Engine mounting bolts or nuts loose. Tighten all engine mounting bolts and nuts to the specified torque (Chapter 2).
5 Crankshaft bearings worn (Chapter 2).
6 Camshaft chain tensioner defective. Replace according to the procedure in Chapter 2.
7 Camshaft chain, sprockets or guides worn (Chapter 2).

Abnormal driveline noise

35 Clutch noise (1993 through 1999 models)

1 Secondary clutch housing/friction plate clearance excessive (Chapter 2).

2   Loose or damaged secondary clutch pressure plate and/or bolts (Chapter 2).
3   Broken primary clutch springs (Chapter 2).

36 Transmission noise

1   Bearings worn. Also includes the possibility that the shafts are worn. Overhaul the transmission (Chapter 2).
2   Gears worn or chipped (Chapter 2).
3   Metal chips jammed in gear teeth. Probably pieces from a broken gear or shift mechanism that were picked up by the gears. This will cause early bearing failure (Chapter 2).
4   Engine oil level too low. Causes a howl from transmission. Also affects engine power and clutch operation (Chapter 1).

37 Transfer case noise (1993 through 1998 models)

1   Bearings worn. Also includes the possibility that the shafts are worn. Have the transfer case overhauled (Chapter 6).
2   Gears worn or chipped (Chapter 6).
3   Metal chips jammed in gear teeth. This will cause early bearing failure (Chapter 6).
4   Engine oil level too low. Causes a howl from transmission. Also affects engine power and clutch operation (Chapter 1).

38 Final drive noise

1   Final drive oil level low (Chapter 1).
2   Final drive gear lash out of adjustment. Checking and adjustment require special tools and skills and should be done by a Yamaha dealer.
3   Final drive gears damaged or worn. Overhaul requires special tools and skills and should be done by a Yamaha dealer.

Abnormal chassis noise

39 Suspension noise

1   Spring weak or broken. Makes a clicking or scraping sound.
2   Steering shaft bearings worn or damaged. Clicks when braking. Check and replace as necessary (Chapter 6).
3   Shock absorber fluid level incorrect. Indicates a leak caused by defective seal. Shock will be covered with oil. Replace shock (Chapter 6).
4   Defective shock absorber with internal damage. This is in the body of the shock and can't be remedied. The shock must be replaced with a new one (Chapter 6).
5   Bent or damaged shock body. Replace the shock with a new one (Chapter 6).

40 Driveaxle noise (4WD models)

1   Worn or damaged outer joint. Makes clicking noise in turns. Check for cut or damaged seals and repair as necessary (see Chapter 6).
2   Worn or damaged inner joint. Makes knock or clunk when accelerating after coasting. Check for cut or damaged seals and repair as necessary (see Chapter 6).

41 Brake noise

1   Brake linings worn or contaminated. Can cause scraping or squealing. Replace the shoes or pads (Chapter 7).
2   Brake linings warped or worn unevenly. Can cause chattering. Replace the linings (Chapter 7).
3   Brake drum out of round or disc warped. Can cause chattering. Replace brake drum or disc (Chapter 7).
7   Loose or worn knuckle or rear axle bearings. Check and replace as needed (Chapter 6).

Oil temperature indicator light comes on

42 Engine lubrication system

1   High oil temperature due to operation in high ambient temperatures. Shut the engine off and let it cool.
2   Engine oil level low. Inspect for leak or other problem causing low oil level and add recommended oil (Chapters 1 and 2).

43 Electrical system

1   Oil temperature sensor defective. Check the sensor according to the procedure in Chapter 9. Replace it if it's defective.
2   Oil temperature indicator light circuit defective. Check for pinched, shorted, disconnected or damaged wiring (Chapter 9).
3   Oil temperature thermistor defective. Check according to the procedure in Chapter 9. Replace it if it's defective.

Excessive exhaust smoke

44 White smoke

1   Piston oil ring worn. The ring may be broken or damaged, causing oil from the crankcase to be pulled past the piston into the combustion chamber. Replace the rings with new ones (Chapter 2).
2   Cylinders worn, cracked, or scored. Caused by overheating or oil starvation. If worn or scored, the cylinders will have to be rebored and new pistons installed. If cracked, the cylinder block will have to be replaced (see Chapter 2).
3   Valve oil seal damaged or worn. Replace oil seals with new ones (Chapter 2).
4   Valve guide worn. Perform a complete valve job (Chapter 2).
5   Engine oil level too high, which causes the oil to be forced past the rings. Drain oil to the proper level (Chapter 1).
6   Head gasket broken between oil return and cylinder. Causes oil to be pulled into the combustion chamber. Replace the head gasket and check the head for warpage (Chapter 2).
7   Abnormal crankcase pressurization, which forces oil past the rings. Clogged breather or hoses usually the cause (Chapter 2).

45 Black smoke

1   Air cleaner clogged. Clean or replace the element (Chapter 1).
2   Main jet too large or loose. Compare the jet size to the Specifications (Chapter 4).
3   Choke stuck, causing fuel to be pulled through choke circuit (Chapter 4).

Troubleshooting 0-23

4   Fuel level too high. Check the fuel level and float level and adjust if necessary (Chapter 4).
5   Inlet needle held off needle seat. Clean the float chamber and fuel line and replace the needle and seat if necessary (Chapter 4).

46 Brown smoke

1   Main jet too small or clogged. Lean condition caused by wrong size main jet or by a restricted orifice. Clean float chamber and jets and compare jet size to Specifications (Chapter 4).
2   Fuel flow insufficient. Fuel inlet needle valve stuck closed due to chemical reaction with old fuel. Float level incorrect; check and replace float if necessary. Restricted fuel line. Clean line and float chamber.
3   Carburetor intake tube loose (Chapter 4).
4   Air cleaner poorly sealed or not installed (Chapter 1).

Poor handling or stability

47 Handlebar hard to turn

1   Steering shaft nut too tight (Chapter 6).
2   Lower bearing or upper bushing damaged. Roughness can be felt as the bars are turned from side-to-side. Replace bearing and bushing (Chapter 6).
3   Steering shaft bearing lubrication inadequate. Causes are grease getting hard from age or being washed out by high pressure car washes. Remove steering shaft and replace bearing (Chapter 6).
4   Steering shaft bent. Caused by a collision, hitting a pothole or by rolling the machine. Replace damaged part. Don't try to straighten the steering shaft (Chapter 6).
5   Front tire air pressure too low (Chapter 1).

48 Handlebar shakes or vibrates excessively

1   Tires worn or out of balance (Chapter 1 or 7).
2   Swingarm bearings worn. Replace worn bearings by referring to Chapter 6.
3   Wheel rim(s) warped or damaged. Inspect wheels (Chapter 7).
4   Wheel bearings worn. Worn front or rear wheel bearings can cause poor tracking. Worn front bearings will cause wobble (Chapter 7).
5   Wheel hubs installed incorrectly (Chapter 6 or Chapter 7).
6   Handlebar clamp bolts or bracket nuts loose (Chapter 6).
7   Steering shaft nut or bolts loose. Tighten them to the specified torque (Chapter 6).
8   Motor mount bolts loose. Will cause excessive vibration with increased engine rpm (Chapter 2).

49 Handlebar pulls to one side

1   Uneven tire pressures (Chapter 1).
2   Frame bent. Definitely suspect this if the machine has been rolled. May or may not be accompanied by cracking near the bend. Replace the frame (Chapter 6).
3   Wheel out of alignment. Caused by incorrect toe-in adjustment (Chapter 1) or bent tie-rod (Chapter 6).
4   Swingarm bent or twisted. Caused by age (metal fatigue) or impact damage. Replace the swingarm (Chapter 6).
5   Steering shaft bent. Caused by impact damage or by rolling the vehicle. Replace the steering stem (Chapter 6).

50 Poor shock absorbing qualities

1   Too hard:
   a) *Shock internal damage.*
   b) *Tire pressure too high (Chapters 1 and 7).*
2   Too soft:
   a) *Shock oil insufficient and/or leaking (Chapter 6).*
   d) *Fork springs weak or broken (Chapter 6).*

Braking problems

51 Front brakes are spongy, don't hold

1   Air in brake line. Caused by inattention to master cylinder fluid level or by leakage. Locate problem and bleed brakes (Chapter 7).
2   Linings worn (Chapters 1 and 7).
3   Brake fluid leak. See paragraph 1.
4   Contaminated linings. Caused by contamination with oil, grease, brake fluid, etc. Clean or replace linings. Clean drum or disc thoroughly with brake cleaner (Chapter 7).
5   Brake fluid deteriorated. Fluid is old or contaminated. Drain system, replenish with new fluid and bleed the system (Chapter 7).
6   Master cylinder internal parts worn or damaged causing fluid to bypass (Chapter 7).
7   Master cylinder bore scratched by foreign material or broken spring. Repair or replace master cylinder (Chapter 7).
8   Drum or disc warped. Replace drum or disc (Chapter 7).

52 Brake lever or pedal pulsates

1   Axle bent. Replace axle (Chapter 6).
2   Wheel warped or otherwise damaged (Chapter 7).
3   Hub or axle bearings damaged or worn (Chapter 7).
4   Brake drum or disc out of round (front) or disc warped (rear). Replace brake drum or disc (Chapter 7).

53 Brakes drag

1   Master cylinder piston seized. Caused by wear or damage to piston or cylinder bore (Chapter 7).
2   Lever balky or stuck. Check pivot and lubricate (Chapter 7).
3   Wheel cylinder piston seized in bore. Caused by wear or ingestion of dirt past deteriorated seal (Chapter 7).
4   Brake shoes or pads damaged. Lining material separated from shoes or pads. Usually caused by faulty manufacturing process or from contact with chemicals. Replace shoes or pads (Chapter 7).
5   Shoes or pads improperly installed (Chapter 7).
6   Rear brake pedal or lever free play insufficient (Chapter 1).
7   Front brake springs weak (drum brakes). Replace brake springs (Chapter 6).

Electrical problems

54 Battery dead or weak

1   Battery faulty. Caused by sulfated plates which are shorted through sedimentation or low electrolyte level. Also, broken battery terminal making only occasional contact (Chapter 9).

2 Battery cables making poor contact (Chapter 9).
3 Load excessive. Caused by addition of high wattage lights or other electrical accessories.
4 Ignition switch defective. Switch either grounds/earths internally or fails to shut off system. Replace the switch (Chapter 9).
5 Regulator/rectifier defective (Chapter 9).
6 Stator coil open or shorted (Chapter 9).
7 Wiring faulty. Wiring grounded or connections loose in ignition, charging or lighting circuits (Chapter 9).

55 Battery overcharged

1 Regulator/rectifier defective. Overcharging is noticed when battery gets excessively warm or boils over (Chapter 9).
2 Battery defective. Replace battery with a new one (Chapter 9).
3 Battery amperage too low, wrong type or size. Install manufacturer's specified amp-hour battery to handle charging load (Chapter 9).

Automatic transmission problems

56 Drivebelt slipping

1 Too much belt deflection. Adjust the belt (see Chapter 1).
2 Worn belt. Replace the belt (see Chapter 2).
3 Oil or grease on belt. Clean the belt and check for leaking seals (see Chapter 2).
4 Water (not engine coolant) on belt. Check belt cover for proper sealing.

57 Drivebelt upside down in pulleys

1 Wrong drivebelt for that model ATV. Check part number on belt and replace with the correct belt if necessary.
2 Pulleys out of alignment. Check the alignment and correct if necessary.
3 Loose or broken engine mount. Check and tighten or replace as necessary (see Chapter 2).

58 Burn marks or thin spots on drivebelt

1 Excessive load on vehicle (weight on racks, heavy trailer, oversized accessory). Remove excessive weight.
2 Brakes dragging. Repair as necessary (see Chapter 7).
3 Applying throttle and continuously raising engine speed when the vehicle is not moving.

59 Harsh engagement

1 Worn drivebelt. Replace the belt (see Chapter 2).
2 Worn or damaged centrifugal clutch (see Chapter 2).

60 Grabby or erratic engagement

1 Thin spots or overall wear on drivebelt. Inspect the belt and replace if necessary (see Chapter 2). If there are thin spots, check possible causes described in Section 58 above.
2 Centrifugal clutch worn or contaminated (see Chapter 2).

61 Noisy operation

1 Loose belt. Inspect the belt tension.
2 Worn belt or separated belt plies. Inspect the belt (Chapter 1) and replaced it if necessary (Chapter 2).
3 Thin spots on drivebelt. Inspect the belt and replace if necessary (see Chapter 2). If there are thin spots, check possible causes described in Section 58 above.

62 Melted or broken belt cover

1 Air intake or outlet clogged. Check the inlet and outlet for obstructions and clean as necessary.
2 Belt slipping due to contamination and rubbing on cover. Clean away contamination. Check the cover for proper sealing against outside water. Check the engine for sources of oil or grease leaks.
3 Rotating mechanical components hitting cover. Check for damage and repair as necessary.

63 Engine rpm too low when vehicle is driven

1 Engine out of tune. Tune up engine (see Chapter 1).
2 Belt slipping. Inspect belt and replace as necessary. Clean any excess grease from pulleys.
3 Driven pulley spring broken or installed incorrectly. Inspect the spring and have it replaced if necessary (see Chapter 2).

64 Engine rpm too high when vehicle is driven

1 Incorrect shift weights for that model ATV. Verify part number and install correct shift weights if necessary.
2 Binding drive clutch. Have the clutch inspected a dealer service department or other qualified shop.
3 Binding driven clutch. Have the clutch inspected a dealer service department or other qualified shop.

65 Engine rpm erratic when vehicle is driven

1 Thin or burned spots on the drivebelt. Inspect the belt and replace if necessary (see Chapter 2). If there are thin spots, check possible causes described in Section 58 above.
2 Binding drive clutch. Have the clutch inspected a dealer service department or other qualified shop.
3 Binding driven clutch. Have the clutch inspected a dealer service department or other qualified shop.

Chapter 1
Tune-up and routine maintenance

Contents

	Section		Section
Air cleaner - filter element and drain tube cleaning	14	Fuel system - check and filter cleaning	15
Battery electrolyte level/specific gravity - check	4	Idle speed - check and adjustment	19
Brake lever and pedal freeplay - check and adjustment	6	Introduction to tune-up and routine maintenance	2
Brake system - general check	5	Lubrication - general	12
Choke - operation check	11	Routine maintenance intervals	1
Clutch - check and freeplay adjustment	9	Shift linkage - check and adjustment	8
Coolant - draining, flushing and refilling	24	Spark plug - replacement	17
Drivebelt - inspection	23	Steering system - inspection and toe-in adjustment	22
Engine/transfer case oil/filter and differential oil - change	13	Suspension - check	21
Exhaust system - inspection	16	Throttle freeplay and speed limiter - check and adjustment	10
Fasteners - check	20	Tires/wheels - general check	7
Fluid levels - check	3	Valve clearances - check and adjustment	18

Specifications

Engine

Spark plug

Type
- 1993 through 1995 Kodiak
  - US .... NGK D8EA or Nippondenso X24ES-U
  - Except US .... NGK DR8EA
- 1996 through 2002 Kodiak .... NGK D8EA or Nippondenso X24ES-U
- 2003 and later Kodiak .... NGK DR8EA
- Grizzly 600
  - US .... NGK DP8EA-9
  - Canada and Europe .... NGK DPR8EA-9
- Grizzly 660 .... NGK DPR8EA-9

Gap
- Kodiak .... 0.6 to 0.7 mm (0.024 to 0.028 inch)
- Grizzly .... 0.8 to 0.9 mm (0.031 to 0.035 inch)

Idle speed

- 1993 through 1998 Kodiak .... 1350 to 1450 rpm
- 1999 and later Kodiak .... 1450 to 1550 rpm
- Grizzly 600 .... 1350 to 1450 rpm
- Grizzly 660 .... 1450 to 1550 rpm

Chapter 1 Tune-up and routine maintenance

Valve clearance (COLD engine)
Kodiak
    Intake .... 0.06 to 0.10 mm (0.002 to 0.004 inch)
    Exhaust .... 0.16 to 0.20 mm (0.006 to 0.008 inch)
Grizzly 600
    Intake .... 0.05 to 0.10 mm (0.002 to 0.004 inch)
    Exhaust .... 0.12 to 0.17 mm (0.005 to 0.007 inch)
Grizzly 660
    Intake .... 0.10 to 0.15 mm (0.004 to 0.006 inch)
    Exhaust .... 0.15 to 0.20 mm (0.006 to 0.08 inch)

Chassis
Brakes
Front brake shoe lining thickness (drum brakes)
    New .... 4 mm (0.16 inch)
    Limit .... 1 mm (0.04 inch)
Rear brake shoe lining thickness (drum brake)
    New .... 4 mm (0.16 inch)
    Limit
        1993 through 1998 Kodiak, Grizzly 600 .... 1 mm (0.04 inch)
        1999, 2003 and 2004 Kodiak 400 .... 2 mm (0.08 inch)
Front pad lining thickness (disc brakes)
    Kodiak
        New .... 4.5 mm (0.18 inch)
        Limit .... 1.0 mm (0.04 inch)
    Grizzly
        New .... 4.2 mm (0.17 inch)
        Limit .... 1.0 mm (0.04 inch)
Rear pad lining thickness (disc brake)
    2000 through 2002 Kodiak
        New .... 5.6 mm (0.22 inch)
        Limit .... 1.0 mm (0.04 inch)
    2003 and later Kodiak 450, 2005 Kodiak 400
        New .... 5.0 mm (0.20 inch)
        Limit .... 1.0 mm (0.04 inch)
    Grizzly 660
        New .... 7.0 mm (0.28 inch)
        Limit .... 1.0 mm (0.04 inch)
Front brake lever freeplay
    1993 through 1998 Kodiak
        Before adjuster touches master cylinder piston .... 3 to 5 mm (0.1 to 0.2 inch)
        Before brake starts to work .... 25 to 30 mm (1.0 to 1.2 inch)
    1999 Kodiak .... 2 to 5 mm (0.08 to 0.20 inch)
    2000 and later Kodiak .... Zero
    Grizzly 600 .... 2 to 5 mm (0.08 to 0.20 inch)
    Grizzly 660 .... Not specified
Rear brake pedal freeplay
    All except Grizzly 660 .... 20 to 30 mm (0.8 to 1.2 inch)
    Grizzly 660 .... Not specified
Rear brake pedal height
    1993 through 1999 Kodiak .... 5 mm (0.2 inch)
    2000 through 2002 Kodiak .... 53 to 60 mm (2.09 to 2.36 inches)
    2003 and 2004 Kodiak .... Not specified
    2005 Kodiak .... 67 to 77 mm (2.64 to 3.03 inches)
    Grizzly 600 .... 20 to 30 mm (0.8 to 1.2 inch)
    Grizzly 660 .... 45 mm (1.77 inch)
Rear brake lever freeplay
    1993 through 1998 Kodiak .... 4 to 8 mm (0.16 to 0.31 inch)
    1999 Kodiak .... 5 to 8 mm (0.20 to 0.31 inch)
    2000 through 2002 Kodiak .... 0.5 to 2.0 mm (0.02 to 0.08 inch)
    2003 and 2004 Kodiak .... 3 to 5 mm (0.12 to 0.20 inch)
    2005 Kodiak .... 0.5 to 2.0 mm (0.02 to 0.08 inch)
    Grizzly 600 .... 5 to 7 mm (0.20 to 0.28 inch)
    Grizzly 660 .... 0.5 to 2.0 mm (0.02 to 0.08 inch)
Rear brake pin and slot gap .... Zero to 1 mm (0 to 0.04 inch)
Throttle lever freeplay .... 3 to 5 mm (0.1 to 0.2 inch)

Chapter 1 Tune-up and routine maintenance

1-3

Choke freeplay
   1999 through 2001 Kodiak .... Not specified
   2003 and later Kodiak, Grizzly 660 .... 15 mm (0.59 inch)
   Grizzly 600 .... Not specified
Speed limiter screw standard length .... 12 mm (0.47 inch)
Minimum tire tread depth .... 3 mm (0.12 inch)
Tire pressures (cold)
   1993 through 1998 Kodiak
     Front
       Minimum .... 17 kPa (2.5 psi)
       Standard .... 20 kPa (2.9 psi)
       Maximum .... 23 kPa (3.3 psi)
     Rear
       Minimum .... 22 kPa (3.2 psi)
       Standard .... 25 kPa (3.6 psi)
       Maximum .... 28 kPa (4 psi)
   1999 and later Kodiak
     Front and rear
       Minimum .... 22 kPa (3.2 psi)
       Standard .... 25 kPa (3.6 psi)
       Maximum .... 28 kPa (4 psi)
   Grizzly 600
     Front
       Minimum .... 27 kPa (3.8 psi)
       Standard .... 30 kPa (4.3 psi)
       Maximum .... 33 kPa (4.7 psi)
     Rear
       Minimum .... 24.5 kPa (3.5 psi)
       Standard .... 27.5 kPa (4.0 psi)
       Maximum .... 30.5 kPa (4.3 psi)
   Grizzly 660
     Front
       Minimum .... 32 kPa (4.6 psi)
       Standard .... 35 kPa (5.0 psi)
       Maximum .... 38 kPa (5.5 psi)
     Rear
       Minimum .... 27 kPa (3.9 psi)
       Standard .... 30 kPa (4.3 psi)
       Maximum .... 33 kPa (4.8 psi)
Front wheel toe-in
   1993 through 1999 Kodiak, 2003 and later Kodiak .... Zero to 10 mm (zero to 0.39 inch)
   2000 through 2002 Kodiak .... 10 mm out to 10 mm in (0.40 inch out to 0.40 inch in)
   Grizzly 600 .... 5 mm out to 5 mm in (0.20 inch out to 0.20 inch in)
   Grizzly 660 .... Zero to 10 mm (zero to 0.39 inch)

Torque specifications

Engine oil drain plug (with filter screen) .... 32 Nm (23 ft-lbs)
Engine oil drain plug (without filter screen)
   All except Grizzly 660 .... 23 Nm (17 ft-lbs)
   Grizzly 660 .... 30 Nm (22 ft-lbs)
Transfer case drain plug (1993 through 1998 Kodiak only) .... 20 Nm (14 ft-lbs)
Oil filter cover bolts (cartridge type filter) .... 10 Nm (86 inch-lbs)
Oil filter (spin-on type) .... 17 Nm (144 inch-lbs)
Oil gallery plug .... 7 Nm (62 inch-lbs)
Clutch adjusting screw locknut
   1993 through 1998 Kodiak .... 15 Nm (132 inch-lbs)
   1999 Kodiak .... 20 Nm (14 ft-lbs)
   2000 and later Kodiak, all Grizzly .... Not applicable
Valve adjuster cover bolts .... 10 Nm (86 inch-lbs)
Valve adjuster covers (Grizzly exhaust valves)
   Grizzly 600 .... Not specified
   Grizzly 660 .... 12 Nm (104 inch-lbs)
Valve adjusting screw locknuts
   Kodiak .... 20 Nm (14 ft-lbs)
   Grizzly .... 14 Nm 120 inch-lbs)
Spark plug .... 18 Nm (156 inch-lbs)

1-4   Chapter 1   Tune-up and routine maintenance

Torque specifications (continued)

Front differential filler plug
  1993 through 1998 Kodiak .... 23 Nm (17 ft-lbs)
  1999 Kodiak .... 12 Nm (104 inch-lbs)
  2000 and later Kodiak, all Grizzly .... 23 Nm (16 ft-lbs)
Front differential drain plug(s)
  1993 through 1998 Kodiak
    Rearward plug (2-plug type) .... 16 Nm (132 inch-lbs)
    Forward plug (2-plug type) .... 23 Nm (17 ft-lbs)
  1999 Kodiak .... 12 Nm (104 inch-lbs)
  2000 and later Kodiak .... 10 Nm (86 inch-lbs)
  Grizzly 600 .... 19 Nm (156 inch-lbs)
  Grizzly 660 .... 10 Nm 986 inch-lbs)
Rear final drive unit filler plug
  1993 through 1998 Kodiak .... 20 Nm (14 ft-lbs)
  1999 Kodiak .... 25 Nm (18 ft-lbs)
  2000 and later Kodiak, all Grizzly .... 23 Nm (16 ft-lbs)
Rear final drive unit drain plug
  1993 through 1998 Kodiak .... 23 Nm (17 ft-lbs)
  1999 Kodiak .... 25 Nm (18 ft-lbs)
  2000 and later Kodiak, all Grizzly .... 23 Nm (16 ft-lbs)
Rear final drive unit check bolt (Grizzly 660) .... 10 Nm (86 inch-lbs)
Tie-rod locknuts
  1993 through 1999 Kodiak .... 30 Nm (22 ft-lbs)
  2000 through 2002 Kodiak .... 15 Nm (132 inch-lbs)
  2003 and later Kodiak .... 40 Nm (29 ft-lbs)
  Grizzly 600 .... 25 Nm (18 ft-lbs)
  Grizzly 660 .... 15 Nm (132 inch-lbs)

Electrical

Battery
Specific gravity (fillable type) .... 1.280 at 20-degrees C/68-degrees F

Recommended lubricants and fluids

Engine/transmission oil
  Type .... API service SE, SF, SG or higher*
  Viscosity
    Above 5-degrees C (40-degrees F) 20W-40
    Above 10-degrees C (-10-degrees F) 10W-30
    Zero-degrees C (32-degrees F or below) 5W-30
Capacity
  1993 through 1998 Kodiak
    Without filter change .... 2.7 liters (2.5 qt)
    With filter change .... 2.8 liters (3.0 qt)
  1999 Kodiak
    Without filter change .... 2.9 liters (3.1 qt)
    With filter change .... 3.0 liters (3.2 qt)
  2000 and later Kodiak
    Without filter change .... 2.3 liters (2.4 qt)
    With filter change .... 2.4 liters (2.5 qt)
  Grizzly
    Without filter change .... 1.9 liters (2.0 qt)
    With filter change .... 2.0 liters (2.1 qt)
Air filter oil .... Foam air filter oil or 10W-30 engine oil
Coolant
  Type .... 50/50 mixture of ethylene glycol-based antifreeze and water
  Capacity
    2000 through 2002 Kodiak
      Radiator .... 0.55 liters (0.58 quarts)
      Reservoir .... 0.25 liters (0.26 qt)
    2003 and 2004 Kodiak
      Radiator .... 0.70 liters (0.74 qt)
      Reservoir .... 0.39 liters (0.41 qt)
    2005 Kodiak (total, including hoses) .... 1.32 liters (1.4 qt)
    Grizzly 660 (total, including hoses) .... 1.9 liters (1.9 qt)

Chapter 1 Tune-up and routine maintenance 1-5

Differential and final drive oil
  Type
    All Kodiak except 1999, all Grizzly .... API GL-4 gear oil
    1999 Kodiak
      Rear.. API GL-4 gear oil
      Front... API GL-5 gear oil for limited slip differentials
  Viscosity
    1993 through 1998 Kodiak .... SAE 80
    1999 Kodiak.. SAE 80 or 80W-90
    2000 and later Kodiak, all Grizzly .... SAE 80
  Capacity
    1993 through 1998 Kodiak
      Front differential .... 0.47 liters (0.5 qt)
      Rear final drive .... 0.19 liters (0.2 qt)
    1999 Kodiak
      Front differential .... 0.18 liters (0.19 qt)
      Rear final drive .... 0.19 liters (0.2 qt)
    2000 and 2001 Kodiak
      Front differential .... 0.35 liters (0.37 qt)
      Rear final drive .... 0.19 liters (0.2 qt)
    2003 and later Kodiak
      Front differential .... 0.35 liters (0.37 qt)
      Rear final drive (2003 and 2004)... 0.23 liters (0.24 qt)
      Rear final drive (2005)... 0.16 liters (0.17 qt)
    Grizzly 600
      Front differential .... 0.67 liters (0.71 qt)
      Rear final drive .... 0.19 liters (0.2 qt)
    Grizzly 660
      Front differential .... 0.28 liters (0.3 qt)
      Rear final drive .... 0.25 liters (0.26 qt)
Brake fluid .... DOT 4
Miscellaneous
  Wheel bearings .... Medium-weight, lithium-based multipurpose grease
  Swingarm pivots... Medium-weight, lithium-based multipurpose grease
  Brake pedal/shift pedal/throttle lever pivots .... Medium-weight, lithium-based multipurpose grease
  Knuckle pivots (independent rear suspension) .... Medium-weight, lithium-based multipurpose grease
  Driveshaft grease fittings .... Medium-weight, lithium-based multipurpose grease

*On 1993 through 1999 Kodiak models, use a motorcycle oil compatible with multi-plate wet clutches. Automotive oils may cause clutch slippage.

1 Yamaha Kodiak and Grizzly Routine maintenance intervals

Note: *The pre-ride inspection outlined in the owner's manual covers checks and maintenance that should be carried out on a daily basis. It's condensed and included here to remind you of its importance. Always perform the pre-ride inspection at every maintenance interval (in addition to the procedures listed). The intervals listed below are the shortest intervals recommended by the manufacturer for each particular operation during the model years covered in this manual. Your owners manual may have different intervals for your model.*

Daily or before riding

Check the engine oil level (including transfer case oil on 4WD models so equipped)
Check coolant level (liquid cooled models)
Check the fuel level and inspect for leaks
Check the operation of both brakes - check the fluid level of front drum and all disc brakes and look for leakage; check rear brake pedal and lever for correct freeplay
Check the tires for damage, the presence of foreign objects and correct air pressure
Check the rear final drive (and front differential on 4WD models) for visible oil leaks
Check the throttle for smooth operation and correct freeplay
Make sure the steering operates smoothly
Check for proper operation of the headlight, tail light, brake light (if equipped) and indicator lights
Make sure the engine kill switch works properly
Check the front driveaxle boots for damage or deterioration (4WD models)
Check the air cleaner drain tube and clean it if necessary
Check all fasteners, including wheel nuts and axle nuts, for tightness
Check the underbody for mud or debris that could start a fire or interfere with vehicle operation
Make sure any cargo is properly loaded and securely fastened

Every 20 to 40 operating hours

Clean the air filter element (1)
Clean the air cleaner housing drain tube (2)

Every 1500 miles (2400 km) or 150 operating hours

Perform all of the daily checks plus:
Check and adjust the valve clearances
Check the cleanliness of the fuel system and the condition of the fuel line
Clean the fuel tap strainer screen
Check/adjust the idle speed
Check/adjust the throttle lever freeplay
Check choke operation
Change the engine oil and oil filter; clean the oil strainer
Inspect the suspension
Clean and gap the spark plug
Check/adjust the drive select system freeplay
Check the skid plates for looseness or damage
Adjust the clutch
Check the exhaust system for leaks and check fastener tightness
Inspect the wheels and tires
Check the wheel bearings for looseness or damage
Inspect the steering system and steering shaft bearing
Lubricate the steering knuckle shafts and suspension arm pivots and steering shaft bearing (2WD models)
Lubricate the driveshaft universal joints (if equipped)
Lubricate the rear knuckle pivots (independent rear suspension)

Every 3000 miles (4800 km) or 300 operating hours

Check the brake shoes for wear (drum brakes)
Change the final drive oil and front differential oil
Check the driveaxle boots (if equipped)

Every two years

Overhaul the brake master and wheel cylinders or calipers
Change the coolant

Every four years

Replace the brake fluid hoses (2)

(1) More often in dusty or wet conditions.
(2) Or whenever cracks or damage are visible.

Chapter 1 Tune-up and routine maintenance

1-7

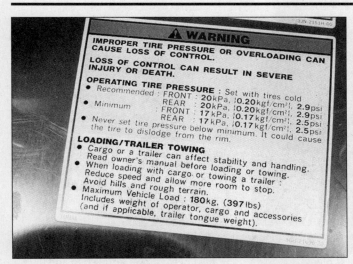

2.1a Decals on the vehicle include maintenance information such as tire pressure . . .

2.1b . . . and safety recommendations

2 Introduction to tune-up and routine maintenance

Refer to illustrations 2.1a and 2.1b

This Chapter covers in detail the checks and procedures necessary for the tune-up and routine maintenance of your vehicle. Section 1 includes the routine maintenance schedule, which is designed to keep the machine in proper running condition and prevent possible problems. The remaining Sections contain detailed procedures for carrying out the items listed on the maintenance schedule, as well as additional maintenance information designed to increase reliability. Maintenance information is also printed on decals, which are mounted in various locations on the vehicle **(see illustrations)**. Where information on the decals differs from that presented in this Chapter, use the decal information.

Since routine maintenance plays such an important role in the safe and efficient operation of your vehicle, it is presented here as a comprehensive checklist. For the rider who does all the vehicle's maintenance, these lists outline the procedures and checks that should be done on a routine basis.

Deciding where to start or plug into the routine maintenance schedule depends on several factors. If you have a vehicle whose warranty has recently expired, and if it has been maintained according to the warranty standards, you may want to pick-up routine maintenance as it coincides with the next mileage or calendar interval. If you have owned the machine for some time but have never performed any maintenance on it, then you may want to start at the nearest interval and include some additional procedures to ensure that nothing important is overlooked, If you have just had a major engine overhaul, then you may want to start the maintenance routine from the beginning. If you have a used machine and have no knowledge of its history or maintenance record, you may desire to combine all the checks into one large service initially and then settle into the maintenance schedule prescribed.

The Sections which actually outline the inspection and maintenance procedures are written as step-by-step comprehensive guides to the actual performance of the work. They explain in detail each of the routine inspections and maintenance procedures on the checklist. References to additional information in applicable Chapters are also included and should not be overlooked.

Before beginning any actual maintenance or repair, the machine should be cleaned thoroughly, especially around the oil filter housing, spark plug, cylinder head covers, side covers, carburetor, etc. Cleaning will help ensure that dirt does not contaminate the engine and will allow you to detect wear and damage that could otherwise easily go unnoticed.

3 Fluid levels - check

Engine/transfer case oil

Refer to illustrations 3.4a, 3.4b and 3.4c

1   The engine and transfer case on 1993 through 1998 Kodiak models share a common oil supply, which is checked through the crankcase filler plug/dipstick. No other models have a separate transfer case.
2   Support the vehicle in a level position, then start the engine and allow it to reach normal operating temperature. **Caution:** *Do not run the engine in an enclosed space such as a garage or shop.*
3   Stop the engine and allow the machine to sit undisturbed in a level position for about five minutes.
4   On all except Grizzly 600 models, with the engine off, unscrew the dipstick from the crankcase **(see illustrations)**. Pull it out, wipe it off with a clean rag, and reinsert it (let the dipstick rest on the threads; don't screw it back in). Pull the dipstick out and check the oil level on the dipstick scale. The oil level should be between the upper and lower level marks on the scale **(see illustration)**. On Grizzly 600 models, look at the sight glass on the side of the crankcase. The oil level should be between the upper and lower marks.

3.4a Unscrew the oil filler cap . . .

Chapter 1 Tune-up and routine maintenance

3.4b On belt-drive models, you'll need to remove this access plate . . .

3.4c . . . and pull out the dipstick; the engine oil level must be between the upper and lower marks

3.8a The brake fluid level must be above the Lower mark on the reservoir; remove the cover screws (arrows) to add fluid

5   If the level is below the Minimum mark, add oil through the dipstick hole. Add enough oil of the recommended grade and type to bring the level up to the Maximum mark. Do not overfill.

3.8b The rear brake fluid reservoir (left arrow) and radiator cap (right arrow) are at the front of the vehicle (Kodiak shown)

3.8c The rear brake fluid level can be seen through the reservoir; it must be between the marks

Brake fluid (hydraulic brakes)

Refer to illustrations 3.8a, 3.8b and 3.8c

6   In order to ensure the proper operation of hydraulic brakes, the fluid level in the master cylinder reservoir(s) must be properly maintained.

7   With the vehicle supported in a level position, turn the handlebars until the top of the front brake master cylinder is as level as possible. The rear reservoir is located toward the front of the vehicle on the right side. On Kodiak models, you'll need to remove the front upper trim panel (see Chapter 8).

8   The fluid level is visible through the master cylinder reservoir. Make sure that the fluid level is above the Lower mark on the reservoir **(see illustrations)**.

9   If the level is low, the fluid must be replenished. Before removing the master cylinder cap, place rags beneath the reservoir (to protect the paint from brake fluid spills) and remove all dust and dirt from the area around the cap.

10 To top up a front master cylinder, remove the cover screws, then lift off the cover, rubber diaphragm and float (if equipped). To top up a rear master cylinder, unscrew the cover. **Note:** *Don't operate the brake lever with the cover removed.*

11 Add new, clean brake fluid of the recommended type to bring the level above the Lower mark. Don't mix different brands of brake fluid in the reservoir, as they may not be compatible. Also, don't mix different specifications (DOT 3 or DOT 5 with DOT 4).

12 On front master cylinders, reinstall the float (if equipped), rubber diaphragm and cover. Tighten the cover screws securely, but don't overtighten and strip the threads. On rear master cylinders, screw the cover on tightly by hand.

13 Wipe any spilled fluid off the reservoir body.

14 If the brake fluid level was low, inspect the front or rear brake system for leaks.

Differential and final drive oil

Refer to illustrations 3.16a, 3.16b and 3.17

15 Park the vehicle on a level surface.

16 On all except Grizzly 660 rear final drive units, remove the filler cap **(see illustrations)**. Feel the oil level inside the differential or final drive unit; it should be up to the bottom of the filler threads. Add oil if necessary of the type recommended in this Chapter's Specifications.

17 On Grizzly 660 rear final drive units, remove the oil level check bolt **(see illustration)**. Oil should flow out of the hole. If it doesn't, unscrew the filler cap, then add oil through the filler cap hole until it runs out of the check bolt hole.

18 Reinstall the filler cap and tighten securely.

Chapter 1 Tune-up and routine maintenance

3.16a Unscrew the filler plug (arrow) to check the front differential oil level

3.16b On all except Grizzly models, unscrew the filer plug (arrow) to check the rear final drive oil level

3.17 On Grizzly 660 models, unscrew the check bolt (lower arrow) to check rear final drive oil level; unscrew the filler plug (upper arrow) to add oil

Coolant (liquid cooled models)

Refer to illustration 3.21

19   Remove the seat and the fuel tank left side panel (see Chapter 8).
20   Warm the engine to normal operating temperature.
21   Check the coolant level in the reservoir **(see illustration)**. If necessary, add ethylene glycol-based antifreeze to bring it between the marks. **Note:** *In an emergency, you can add distilled water, but the antifreeze concentration should be checked and corrected as soon as possible.*

4   Battery electrolyte level/specific gravity check

Refer to illustrations 4.3 and 4.7
Warning: *Be extremely careful when handling or working around the battery. The electrolyte is very caustic and an explosive gas (hydrogen) is given off when the battery is charging.*

1   This procedure applies to batteries on 1993 through 1998 Kodiak models, which have removable filler caps, which can be removed to add water to the battery. On all other models, which have a sealed maintenance-free battery, the electrolyte can't be topped up.
2   Remove the battery cover under the rear fender.
3   The electrolyte level is visible through the translucent battery case - it should be between the Upper and Lower level marks **(see illustration)**.
4   Disconnect the negative cable and remove the battery retainer bolt **(see illustration 4.3)**. Slide the retainer to the right, lift the battery cover and disconnect the positive cable. **Warning:** *Always disconnect the negative cable first and reconnect it last to avoid sparks which could cause a battery explosion.*
5   If the electrolyte is low, remove the cell caps and fill each cell to the upper level mark with distilled water. Do not use tap water (except in an emergency) and do not overfill. The cell holes are quite small, so it may help to use a plastic squeeze bottle with a small spout to add the water. If the level is within the marks on the case, additional water is not necessary.
6   Next, check the specific gravity of the electrolyte in each cell with a small hydrometer made especially for motorcycle and ATV batteries. These are available from most dealer parts departments or ATV accessory stores.
7   Remove the caps, draw some electrolyte from the first cell into the hydrometer **(see illustration)**, then note the specific gravity. Compare the reading to the value listed in this Chapter's Specifications. **Note:** *Add 0.004 points to the reading for every 10-degrees F above*

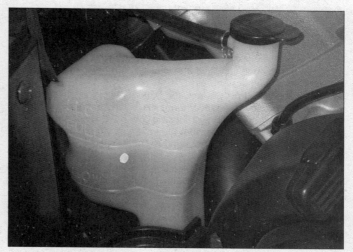

3.21 Coolant level must be between the upper and lower marks on the reservoir

4.3 Battery electrolyte should be between the horizontal lines on the battery; unbolt the negative cable and retainer (right arrows), then unbolt the positive cable (left arrow)

1-10　　Chapter 1　Tune-up and routine maintenance

4.7 Check the specific gravity with a hydrometer

5.7 Remove the adjusting hole plug (arrow) from the brake drum

68-degrees F (20-degrees C) - subtract 0.004 points from the reading for every 10-degrees below 68-degrees F (20-degrees C).

8 Return the electrolyte to the appropriate cell and repeat the check for the remaining cells. When the check is complete, rinse the hydrometer thoroughly with clean water.

9 If the specific gravity of the electrolyte in each cell is as specified the battery is in good condition and is apparently being charged by the machine's charging system.

10 If the specific gravity is low, the battery is not fully charged. This may be due to corroded battery terminals, a dirty battery case, a malfunctioning charging system, or loose or corroded wiring connections. On the other hand, it may be that the battery is worn out, especially if the machine is old, or that infrequent use of the machine prevents normal charging from taking place.

11 Be sure to correct any problems and charge the battery if necessary. Refer to Chapter 9 for additional battery maintenance and charging procedures.

12 Install the battery cell caps, tightening them securely. Reconnect the cables to the battery, attaching the positive cable first and the negative cable last. Make sure to install the insulating boots over the terminals.

13 Install all components removed for access and route the battery vent tube correctly. Be very careful not to pinch or otherwise restrict the tube, as the battery may build up enough internal pressure during normal charging system operation to explode.

14 If the vehicle will be stored for an extended time, fully charge the battery, then disconnect the negative cable before storage.

5 Brake system - general check

1 A routine general check of the brakes will ensure that any problems are discovered and remedied before the rider's safety is jeopardized.

2 Check the brake levers and pedal for loose connections, excessive play, bends, and other damage. Replace any damaged parts with new ones (see Chapter 8).

3 Make sure all brake fasteners are tight. Check the brake for wear as described below.

4 Make sure the fluid level in the front brake reservoir (and rear reservoir on rear disc brake models) is correct (see Section 3). Look for leaks at the hose connections and check for cracks in the hoses. If the lever or pedal is spongy, bleed the brakes as described in Chapter 6.

5 Make sure the brake light (if equipped) operates when the front brake lever is depressed. The front brake light switch is not adjustable. If it fails to operate properly, replace it with a new one (see Chapter 8). On rear disc brake models, the switch can be adjusted (see Chapter 9).

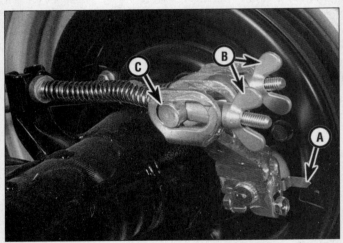

5.9 If the pointer aligns with the mark when the rear brake is applied, it's time to replace the brake shoes

A Pointer and mark
B Adjusting wing-nuts
C Gap between cable pin and slot (measured during adjustment)

6 Operate the rear brake lever and pedal. If operation is rough or sticky on a rear drum brake model, refer to Section 12 and lubricate the cables.

Front drum brakes
Refer to illustration 5.7

7 Remove the adjusting hole plug from the brake drum **(see illustration)**. Look through the hole to inspect the thickness of the lining material on the brake shoes (use a flashlight if necessary). If it's worn to near the limit listed in this Chapter's Specifications, refer to Chapter 7 and replace the brake shoes.

8 Look at the adjusting bolt on the rear brake (see Section 6). If the adjusting bolt is near the locknut with the rear brake properly adjusted, refer to Chapter 6 and replace the brake pads.

Rear drum brake
Refer to illustration 5.9

9 A rear drum brake is used on 1993 through 1999 Kodiak and all Grizzly 600 models. To check the linings for wear, have an assistant hold down the pedal while you look at the wear indicator on the brake drum **(see illustration)**. If the pointer is at the limit line (and the brakes are properly adjusted), replace the brake shoes (see Chapter 7).

Chapter 1 Tune-up and routine maintenance

5.11 If the wear hole next to the backing material (arrow) is exposed, replace the pads

Disc brakes

Refer to illustration 5.11

10 Raise the front of the vehicle and support it securely on jackstands. Remove the front wheels.

11 Look at the friction material on the brake pads. Some pads are equipped with wear indicator holes next to the metal backing material **(see illustration)**. Others have a groove along one edge of the friction material, while others have one or more slits in the friction material. If the friction material is worn to or almost to the wear indicator hole, groove or slits, replace the pads (see Chapter 7). Replace all four pads (front) or both pads (rear), even if only one is worn.

6   Brake lever and pedal freeplay - check and adjustment

Front brake lever (drum brakes only)

Refer to illustrations 6.1a, 6.1b and 6.3

1 Operate the front brake lever and note the amount of play from rest until just before the adjuster touches the master cylinder piston **(see illustration)**. Measure play at the outer end of the lever **(see illustration)**. If it's not within the range listed in this Chapter's Specifications, loosen the locknut, turn the adjusting screw to obtain the correct freeplay, then tighten the locknut.

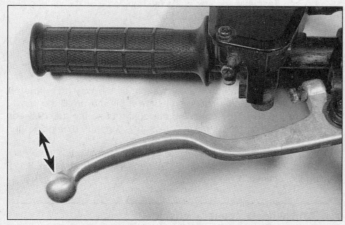

6.1b ... at this point, measure how far the outer tip of the brake lever has traveled

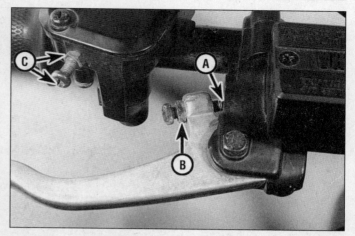

6.1a Squeeze the front brake lever until the adjusting screw just contacts the master cylinder piston ...

- A   Contact point of adjusting screw and master cylinder piston
- B   Adjusting screw locknut
- C   Speed limiter screw and locknut

2 Jack up the front end of the vehicle and support it securely. Spin the front wheels by hand (you'll probably need an assistant to do this) and pull the front brake lever. Note the amount of travel required to lock the wheels (measured at the tip of the lever). If it's not within the range listed in this Chapter's Specifications, adjust the front wheel cylinders.

3 To adjust the brakes, remove the adjusting hole plug **(see illustration 5.7)**. There's an adjuster wheel at each wheel cylinder, located at the sides of the brake panel **(see illustration)**.

4 Insert a screwdriver through the adjusting hole and turn the adjuster wheel out (away from the center of the wheel) until the tire can't be turned by hand, then back it off three notches. Spin the tire by hand to make sure the brake lining isn't dragging on the drum; if it is, back off the adjuster just enough so the dragging stops. Then align the hole with the second adjuster wheel and repeat the adjustment.

5 Push the adjusting hole cap securely into its hole with a screwdriver.

6 Repeat the adjustment on the other front wheel, then remove the jackstands and lower the vehicle.

6.3 There's an adjuster on each wheel cylinder; turn the adjusters out, in the direction of each wheel cylinder, to expand the shoes against the drum (drum removed for clarity)

A   Adjusters   B   Arrows

Chapter 1 Tune-up and routine maintenance

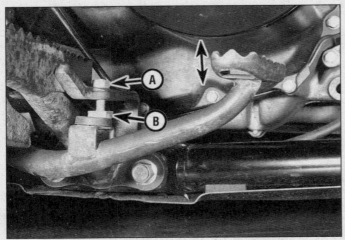

6.7 On rear drum brake models, measure freeplay at the pedal; loosen the locknut (A) and turn the adjuster (B) to adjust it

6.11 Loosen the lockwheel (right arrow) and turn the adjuster (left arrow) to adjust freeplay of the rear brake lever

6.16 Remove this cover for access to the rear brake pedal on rear disc brake models

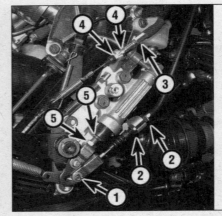

6.17 Rear brake pedal details - disc brake models (450 shown; 660 similar)

1. Cable pin and slot
2. Lever cable adjusting nuts
3. Lockout cable adjuster
4. Lockout cable mounting nuts
5. Master cylinder adjusting nuts

Rear drum brake

Refer to illustrations 6.7 and 6.11

7   Check pedal height (below or above the floorboard, depending on model (**see illustration**). If it's not within the range listed in this Chapter's Specifications, loosen the locknut, turn the adjuster to set the correct pedal height, then tighten the locknut.
8   Press the brake pedal two or three times.
9   Loosen the wingnut on the brake lever adjuster (farthest from the drum) all the way (**see illustration 5.9**).
10   Check freeplay at the brake pedal. If it's not within the range listed in this Chapter's Specifications, adjust it by turning the wingnut on the brake pedal adjuster (closest to the drum).
11   Loosen the brake lever adjuster at the handlebar all the way (**see illustration**). Then turn the wingnut on the brake cable to set the gap between the cable pin and the slot it rides in to the value listed in this Chapter's Specifications (**see illustration 5.9**).
12   Finally, use the brake lever adjuster at the handlebar to set lever freeplay (measured at the pivot gap) to the value listed in this Chapter's Specifications, then tighten the locknut.
13   After adjustment is complete, jack up both ends of the vehicle and support it securely on jackstands. Turn the rear wheels by hand and make sure the brakes don't drag. If they do, repeat the adjustment.

Rear disc brake

Refer to illustrations 6.16 and 6.17

14   Measure brake pedal height above the floorboard and compare it to the value listed in this Chapter's Specifications. Also check freeplay of the rear brake lever on the left handlebar (measured at the gap between lever and bracket). If either is incorrect, adjust as described below.
15   Loosen the cable adjuster at the left handlebar all the way (to give maximum cable slack) (**see illustration 6.11**).
16   Remove the rear master cylinder cover (**see illustration**).
17   If pedal height was incorrect, loosen the master cylinder locknut and turn the adjusting bolt to change it (**see illustration**). **Warning:** *Do not allow more than 6 mm (0.24 inch) of adjusting bolt threads to be exposed.* Once the adjustment is correct, tighten the locknut.
18   Loosen the locknut on the lever cable all the way (**see illustration 6.17**). Pull up on the cable, so its lower pin moves all the way to the right of the slot. Turn the cable adjusting nut so the gap between the adjusting nut and the bracket is less than 1 mm (0.039 inch), then tighten the locknut.
19   At the handlebar, turn the cable adjuster to obtain the lever freeplay listed in this Chapter's Specifications (**see illustration 6.11**). Tighten the locknut.

7   Tires/wheels - general check

Refer to illustration 7.4

1   Routine tire and wheel checks should be made with the realization

Chapter 1 Tune-up and routine maintenance

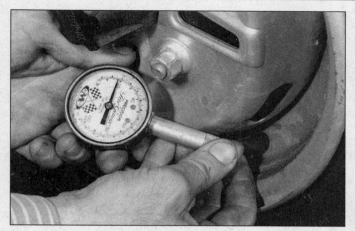

7.4 Check tire pressure with a gauge that will read accurately at the low pressures used in ATV tires

8.2a The spring (A) is attached to the top of the brake pedal . . .

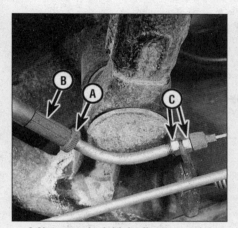

8.2b . . . make initial adjustments by loosening the lockwheel (A) and turning the adjuster (B); if further adjustment is necessary, loosen the cable locknuts (C) and reposition the cables

8.4a Remove the cotter pin and washer (arrow) and pull the clevis pin out of the cable and lever . . .

8.4b . . . if the holes in the pin and lever don't align perfectly, loosen the locknuts and reposition the cable until they do

that your safety depends to a great extent on their condition.
2   Check the tires carefully for cuts, tears, embedded nails or other sharp objects and excessive wear. Operation of the vehicle with excessively worn tires is extremely hazardous, as traction and handling are directly affected. Measure the tread depth at the center of the tire and replace worn tires with new ones when the tread depth is less than that listed in this Chapter's Specifications.
3   Repair or replace punctured tires as soon as damage is noted. Do not try to patch a torn tire, as wheel balance and tire reliability may be impaired.
4   Check the tire pressures when the tires are cold and keep them properly inflated (see illustration). Proper air pressure will increase tire life and provide maximum stability and ride comfort. Keep in mind that low tire pressures may cause the tire to slip on the rim or come off, while high tire pressures will cause abnormal tread wear and unsafe handling.
5   The steel wheels used on these machines are virtually maintenance free, but they should be kept clean and checked periodically for cracks, bending and rust. Never attempt to repair damaged wheels; they must be replaced with new ones.
6   Check the valve stem locknuts to make sure they're tight. Also, make sure the valve stem cap is in place and tight. If it is missing, install a new one made of metal or hard plastic.

8   Shift linkage - check and adjustment

Caution: *Be sure the machine is at a complete stop with the throttle closed before making adjustments or transmission damage could occur.*

1993 through 1999 Kodiak models
Refer to illustrations 8.2a, 8.2b, 8.4a and 8.4b
1   Press in the button on the side of the lever and move the lever to Low. Make sure the button returns to its out position.
2   Inspect the spring attached to the no. 2 cable **(see illustration)**. The spring should be pulled just tight enough to remove all slack, but not stretched. If not, loosen the locknut, turn the adjuster to achieve the correct amount of spring tension and tighten the locknut. If the adjuster doesn't provide the correct setting, loosen the locknuts on the cable bracket, reposition the cable as necessary and tighten the locknuts **(see illustrations)**.
3   Make sure the select lever can be shifted into Reverse only when the brake pedal is pressed, If Reverse can be selected when the pedal is not pressed (or when it's pressed only slightly and the rear brake is not actually operating), check the adjustment of the brake pedal and recheck the no. 2 cable adjustment.
4   Remove the cotter pin, washer and clevis pin from the end of no. 1 cable **(see illustration)**. The clevis pin holes in the cable and lever should align exactly. If they don't, loosen the locknuts on the cable

8.13 Loosen the locknuts (left and right arrows) and turn the rod with the flat (center arrow) to adjust the shifter

9.2 Loosen the locknut, then hold it with a wrench while you turn the adjusting screw

(see illustration), reposition the cable until the holes align exactly, then tighten the locknuts.
5 Slip the clevis pin through the holes. It should go easily. If it does, pull it back out, lubricate it lightly with silicone grease and reinstall it.
6 Secure the clevis pin with the washer and a new cotter pin.
7 Pull back the ends of the cable boot and lubricate the exposed areas of the cable with grease.

All other models

Refer to illustration 8.13

8 The linkage includes a safety lockout that prevents the transmission from being shifted into Reverse unless the rear brake is engaged. Since the rear brake pedal must be pressed before the transmission can be shifted into Reverse, adjust the rear brakes before adjusting the shift linkage (see Section 6).
9 Make sure the vehicle is stopped and the throttle lever is in the closed position. Place the select lever in Neutral.
10 Check the adjustment of the lockout cable (see illustration 6.21). There should be no slack in the return spring, and there should be no freeplay in the cable. If necessary, loosen the locknut and turn the adjuster to reposition the cable. **Note:** *If you can't achieve the correct adjustment with the adjuster, try repositioning the cable-to-bracket locknuts.*
11 Try to shift into Reverse while pressing the brake pedal. With the rear brake not engaged (pedal pressed less than 1 to 1-1/4 inch), it should not be possible to shift into Reverse. With the rear brake engaged (pedal pressed to 1-1/4 inch or more), it should be possible to shift into Reverse.

 a) *If the select lever and brake pedal work as described, go on to Step 12.*
 b) *If the select lever and brake pedal don't work as described, repeat the lockout cable adjustment.*

12 Once the brake pedal and select lever are working properly together, check to make sure the cable locknuts are tight.
13 Check the shifting action of the selector lever. If it's smooth and places the transmission in the correct range, no adjustment is needed. If not, place the lever in Neutral. Loosen the locknuts at the ends of the shift rod (see illustration) and rotate it to change its length. Once smooth shifting is obtained, tighten the locknuts.

9 Clutch - check and freeplay adjustment

Refer to illustration 9.2

1 The clutch release mechanism on 1993 through 1999 Kodiak models disengages the secondary clutch automatically when the shift lever is operated, so there is no clutch lever. If shifting gears becomes difficult, the clutch may be in need of adjustment.
2 Loosen the locknut on the right side of the engine. Carefully turn the adjusting screw counterclockwise until you feel resistance, then turn it back in 1/8 turn while holding the locknut with a wrench (see illustration). Hold the screw in this position and tighten the locknut to the torque listed in this Chapter's Specifications.

10 Throttle freeplay and speed limiter - check and adjustment

Throttle check

1 Make sure the throttle lever moves easily from fully closed to fully open with the front wheel turned at various angles. The grip should return automatically from fully open to fully closed when released. If the throttle sticks, check the throttle cable for cracks or kinks in the housings. Also, make sure the inner cable is clean and well-lubricated.
2 Check for a small amount of freeplay at the lever and compare the freeplay to the value listed in this Chapter's Specifications.

Throttle adjustment

Refer to illustrations 10.4 and 10.5

3 Before making adjustments, check and adjust idle speed (see Section 20).
4 Make the initial adjustment at the carburetor end of the cable (see illustration). Slide back the rubber boot, loosen the adjuster locknut and turn the adjuster. Once correct freeplay is obtained, tighten the locknut.
5 If correct freeplay can't be obtained at the carburetor end of the

10.4 Here's the 400/450 throttle cable adjuster (arrow) (600/660 similar); slide back the rubber boot to expose the locknut

Chapter 1 Tune-up and routine maintenance

1-15

10.5 Loosen the lockwheel (right arrow) and turn the adjuster (left arrow) to adjust throttle freeplay

11.1 Early models have a choke knob; later models have a choke lever on the left handlebar

A Choke knob   B Fuel line

cable, make the adjustment at the handlebar end. Pull back the boot from the adjuster **(see illustration)**. Loosen the lockwheel, turn the adjuster as needed to obtain correct freeplay, then tighten the lockwheel.

Speed limiter adjustment

6 The speed limiter can be used to restrict maximum throttle opening **(see illustration 6.1a)**. Turning the screw all the way in reduces the maximum throttle opening; turning it out to the maximum length listed in this Chapter's Specifications allows maximum throttle opening.

7 To make adjustments, loosen the locknut, turn the screw in or out as necessary and tighten the locknut. Screw length is measured from the underside of the screw head to the throttle housing. Never turn the screw out farther than the maximum specified length.

11 Choke - operation check

Refer to illustration 11.1

1 Operate the choke knob or lever while you feel for smooth operation **(see illustration)**.

2 If the knob doesn't move smoothly, refer to Chapter 4 and remove the choke mechanism for inspection.

12 Lubrication - general

Refer to illustrations 12.3, 12.7a and 12.7b

1 Since the controls, cables and various other components of a vehicle are exposed to the elements, they should be lubricated periodically to ensure safe and trouble-free operation.

2 The throttle and brake levers and brake pedal, should be lubricated frequently. In order for the lubricant to be applied where it will do the most good, the component should be disassembled. However, if chain and cable lubricant is being used, it can be applied to the pivot joint gaps and will usually work its way into the areas where friction occurs. If motor oil or light grease is being used, apply it sparingly as it may attract dirt (which could cause the controls to bind or wear at an accelerated rate). **Note:** *One of the best lubricants for the control lever pivots is a dry-film lubricant (available from many sources by different names).*

3 The throttle, brake and shift select cables should be removed and treated with a commercially available cable lubricant which is specially formulated for use on ATV control cables. Small adapters for pressure lubricating the cables with spray can lubricants are available and ensure that the cable is lubricated along its entire length **(see illustration)**. When attaching the cable to the lever, be sure to lubricate the barrel-shaped fitting at the end with multi-purpose grease.

4 To lubricate the cables, disconnect them at the lower end, then lubricate the cable with a pressure lube adapter **(see illustration 12.3)**. See Section 8 (drive select cables), Chapter 4 (throttle cable) or Chapter 7 (brake cables).

5 Refer to Chapter 6 for the following lubrication procedures:
 a) Swingarm bearing and dust seals
 b) Front driveaxle splines (4WD models)
 c) Rear driveshaft coupling spline
 d) Rear axle shaft splines

6 Refer to Chapter 7 for brake pedal removal procedures.

7 On models so equipped, apply multi-purpose grease to the

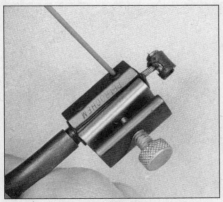

12.3 Lubricating a cable with a pressure lube adapter (make sure the tool seats around the inner cable)

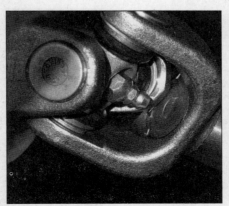

12.7a Driveshafts on some models have a grease fitting at each end

12.7b Rear knuckles on independent rear suspension vehicles have upper and lower grease fittings (arrows)

Chapter 1 Tune-up and routine maintenance

13.6a The transfer case drain plug (1993 through 1998 models only) is at the lower rear of the case (arrow)

13.6b 1999 and later Kodiak models have an oil strainer/drain plug and a rear drain plug (arrows)

13.6c Unscrew the oil drain plug and remove the O-ring, spring and strainer

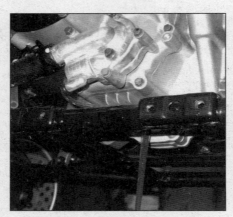

13.6d Grizzly models have a single oil drain plug in the bottom of the crankcase

13.9a Remove the filter cover bolts (arrows) and lift off the cover and its O-ring . . .

driveshaft universal joints and independent rear suspension knuckles through the grease fittings **(see illustrations)**.

13 Engine/transfer case oil/filter and differential oil - change

Engine/transfer case oil/filter

Refer to illustrations 13.6a, 13.6b, 13.6c and 13.6d

1 The transfer case on 1993 through 1998 models shares a common oil supply with the engine, but has a separate drain plug. 1999 and later Kodiak models and Grizzly 600 models have an oil drain plug at the rear of the crankcase, as well as an oil strainer screen/drain plug in the bottom center of the crankcase. Grizzly 660 models have a single oil drain plug in the bottom center of the crankcase.

2 Consistent routine oil and filter changes are the single most important maintenance procedure you can perform on a vehicle. The oil not only lubricates the internal parts of the engine, transmission, clutch and 4WD transfer case (if equipped), but it also acts as a coolant, a cleaner, a sealant, and a protectant. Because of these demands, the oil takes a terrific amount of abuse and should be replaced often with new oil of the recommended grade and type. Saving a little money on the difference in cost between a good oil and a cheap oil won't pay off if the engine is damaged.

3 Before changing the oil and filter, warm up the engine so the oil will drain easily. Be careful when draining the oil, as the exhaust pipe, the engine and the oil itself can cause severe burns.

4 Park the vehicle over a clean drain pan.

5 Remove the dipstick/oil filler cap to vent the crankcase and act as a reminder that there is no oil in the engine.

6 Next, remove the drain plug(s) from the engine (and transfer case if equipped) **(see illustrations)** and allow the oil to drain into the pan. On models with an oil screen plug, the O-ring, spring and strainer will probably fall out as the plug is removed, so be careful not to lose them.

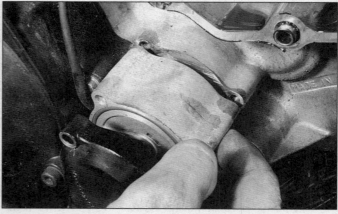

13.9b . . . early Kodiak models also have an inner cover with oil hose fittings . . .

Chapter 1 Tune-up and routine maintenance

13.9c ... the open end of the inner cover faces the engine ...

13.9d ... as does the open end of the filter element; be sure to install them facing the proper direction

13.10 If the snap-ring is loose, remove it and install a new one

Cartridge filter models

Refer to illustrations 13.9a, 13.9b, 13.9c, 13.9d, 13.10 and 13.11

7   If you're working on a Kodiak, unbolt the retainer that secures the two oil hoses running to the filter cover.

8   If you're working on a Kodiak, remove the shift pedal (see Chapter 2A).

9   Remove the oil filter cover bolts **(see illustration)**, then remove the outer cover. If you're working on a Kodiak, remove the inner cover with O-rings **(see illustrations)**. On Kodiak and Grizzly models, remove the filter element **(see illustration)**. If additional maintenance is planned for this time period, check or service another component while the oil is allowed to drain completely.

10   If you're working on a Kodiak, check the inside of the inner cover to make sure the snap-ring, washer, spring and plug are securely in position **(see illustration)**.

11   Wipe any remaining oil out of the filter housing area of the crankcase and make sure the oil passage is clear **(see illustration)**. Clean the oil strainer with solvent and let it dry completely.

12   Check the condition of the drain plug threads and the O-rings.

13   Install the filter element **(see illustrations 13.9c and 13.9d)**. **Caution:** *The filter must be installed facing the correct direction or oil starvation may cause severe engine damage.*

14   Install a new O-ring on the outer filter cover. If you're working on a Kodiak, also install a new O-ring on the inner filter cover **(see illustrations 13.9b and 13.9c)**. Install the cover(s). Apply gasket sealant to the threads of the outer cover bolts, install them and tighten them to the torque listed in this Chapter's Specifications.

13.11 Make sure the oil passage in the filter housing (arrow) is clear

Spin-on filter models

Refer to illustrations 13.15a and 13.15b

15   Place rags beneath the filter to catch dripping oil. Unscrew the filter from the engine **(see illustrations)**. Use a filter wrench or strap wrench if it's tight.

16   Lightly coat the gasket on a new filter with clean engine oil. Thread the filter on, then tighten it to the torque listed in this Chapter's Specifications, using a filter wrench.

13.15a Here's the spin-on oil filter used on later Kodiak models ...

13.15b ... and here's the filter on Grizzly 660 models

1-18   Chapter 1 Tune-up and routine maintenance

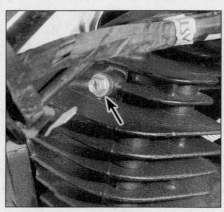

13.23a Loosen the oil gallery plug (arrow) slightly; oil should seep from the plug within one minute of idling the engine - this is a 1993-1998 Kodiak . . .

13.23b . . . this is a 1999 and later Kodiak . . .

13.23c . . . and this is a Grizzly 660 (600 similar)

13.26a The front differential drain plug(s) (arrows), two-plug model shown) are accessible from below

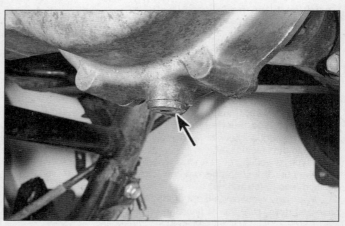

13.26b Unscrew the rear final drive drain plug (arrow) and let the oil drain into a pan

All models

Refer to illustrations 13.23a, 13.23b and 13.23c

17   Install the oil strainer, spring and engine drain plug (if equipped), using a new O-ring if the old one is worn or damaged. Tighten the plug to the torque listed in this Chapter's Specifications. Avoid overtightening, as damage to the engine case will result.

18   If you're working on a 1993 through 1998 model, install the transfer case drain plug with a new sealing washer and tighten it to the torque listed in this Chapter's Specifications.

19   If you're working on a 1999 or later Kodiak, install the rear crankcase drain plug, using a new sealing washer, and tighten it to the torque listed in this Chapter's Specifications.

20   Before refilling the engine, check the old oil carefully. If the oil was drained into a clean pan, small pieces of metal or other material can be easily detected. If the oil is very metallic colored then the engine is experiencing wear from break-in (new engine) or from insufficient lubrication. If there are flakes or chips of metal in the oil, then something is drastically wrong internally and the engine will have to be disassembled for inspection and repair.

21   On 1993 through 1998 Kodiak models, if there are pieces of fiber-like material in the oil, the secondary clutch is experiencing excessive wear and should be checked.

22   If the inspection of the oil turns up nothing unusual, refill the crankcase and transfer case (if equipped) to the proper level with the recommended oil and install the dipstick/filler cap. Start the engine and let it run for two or three minutes. Shut it off, wait a few minutes, then check the oil level. If necessary, add more oil to bring the level up to the upper level mark on the dipstick. Check around the drain plug(s) and filter cover for leaks.

23   Loosen the oil gallery plug on the cylinder head slightly **(see illustrations)**. Start the engine and let it idle. Oil should seep from the plug within one minute. If not, oil is not flowing properly. Shut the engine off and find out the problem before running it further.

24   The old oil drained from the engine cannot be reused in its present state and should be disposed of. Check with your local refuse disposal company, disposal facility or environmental agency to see whether they will accept the oil for recycling. Don't pour used oil into drains or onto the ground. After the oil has cooled, it can be drained into a suitable container (capped plastic jugs, topped bottles, milk cartons, etc.) for transport to one of these disposal sites.

Differential oil

Refer to illustrations 13.26a and 13.26b

25   Place a drain pan beneath the differential being drained.

26   Remove the oil filler plug, then the drain bolt and sealing washer **(see illustrations 3.16a, 3.16b and the accompanying illustrations)**. 1993 through 1998 Kodiak front differentials have two drain plugs; all other models have one. Let the oil drain for several minutes, until it stops dripping.

27   Clean the drain bolt and sealing washer. If the sealing washer is in

Chapter 1 Tune-up and routine maintenance   1-19

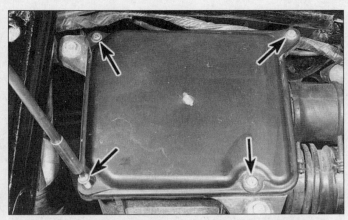

14.2 Remove the cover screws (arrows) or loosen the clips

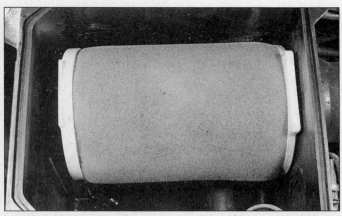

14.3 Detach the filter element from the housing and lift out the element and core

14.4a Turn the cover so the tab aligns with the slot and remove it; on assembly, make sure the tab aligns with the two arrows molded in the cover

14.4b Separate the foam element from the metal core

14.10 Open the clip and pull the drain tube (arrow) off its fitting; if it's full of clean oil, like this one, the element may have been oversaturated

good condition, it can be reused; otherwise, replace it.
28   Install the drain bolt and tighten it to the torque listed in this Chapter's Specifications.
29   Add oil of the type and amount listed in this Chapter's Specifications, then install the filler plug and tighten it to the torque listed in this Chapter's Specifications.
30   Refer to Step 24 to dispose of the drained oil.

14 Air cleaner - filter element and drain tube cleaning

Element cleaning

Refer to illustrations 14.2, 14.3, 14.4a and 14.4b
1   Remove the seat (see Chapter 8).
2   Remove the screws or pull back the clips that secure the filter cover and lift it off **(see illustration)**.
3   Detach the element from the case and lift it out **(see illustration)**.
4   Compress the tap, rotate it 1/4 turn to align the slot with the tab and take the cap off **(see illustration)**. Pull the foam element off the metal core **(see illustration)**.
5   Clean the element and core in a high flash point solvent, squeeze the solvent out of the foam and let the core and element dry completely.
6   Soak the foam element in the amount and type of foam filter oil listed in this Chapter's Specifications, then squeeze it firmly to remove

the excess oil. Don't wring it out or the foam may be damaged. The element should be wet through with oil, but no oil should drip from it.
7   Place the element on the core.
8   Install the cap and rotate it 1/4 turn to lock it in position **(see illustration 14.4a)**.
9   Install the element in the case so its squared-off ends align with the slots in the case.

Drain tube cleaning

Refer to illustration 14.10
10   Check the drain tube for accumulated water and oil **(see illustration)**. If oil or water has built up in the tube, squeeze its clamp, remove it from the air cleaner housing and clean it out. Install the drain tube on the housing and secure it with the clamp. **Note:** *A drain tube that's full indicates the need to clean the filter element and the inside of the case.*

15 Fuel system - check and filter cleaning

Refer to illustrations 15.5a, 15.5b, 15.9a and 15.9b
Warning: *Gasoline is extremely flammable, so take extra precautions when you work on any part of the fuel system. Don't smoke or allow open flames or bare light bulbs near the work area, and don't work in a garage where a gas-type appliance (such as a water heater or clothes dryer) is present. Since gasoline is carcinogenic, wear latex gloves*

1-20　Chapter 1　Tune-up and routine maintenance

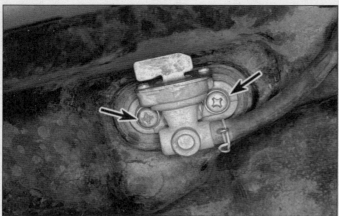

15.5a Remove the fuel tap screws (arrows) . . .

15.5b . . . and separate the tap and strainer from the tank

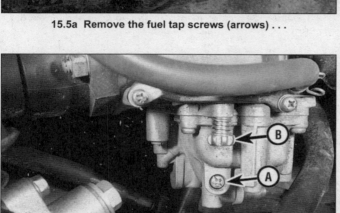

15.9a Here is the float chamber drain screw (A) and throttle stop screw (B) on early Kodiak models

15.9b Here is the float chamber drain screw (left) and throttle stop screw (right) on later Kodiak models (Grizzly similar)

when there's a possibility of being exposed to fuel, and, if you spill any fuel on your skin, rinse it off immediately with soap and water Mop up any spills immediately and do not store fuel-soaked rags where they could ignite. When you perform any kind of work on the fuel system, wear safety glasses and have a fire extinguisher suitable for a class B type fire (flammable liquids) on hand.

1   Check the carburetor, fuel tank, the fuel tap and the line for leaks and evidence of damage (see illustration 11.1).
2   If carburetor gaskets are leaking, the carburetor should be disassembled and rebuilt by referring to Chapter 4.
3   If the fuel tap is leaking, tightening the screws may help. If leakage persists, the tap should be disassembled and repaired or replaced with a new one.
4   If the fuel line is cracked or otherwise deteriorated, replace it with a new one.
5   Place the fuel tap lever in the Off position. Remove the fuel tap mounting screws and lower it out of the engine (see illustrations).
6   Clean the strainer with solvent and let it dry.
7   Installation is the reverse of the removal steps, with the following additions:
   a) Use a new gasket.
   b) Hand-tighten the screws firmly, but don't overtighten or the gasket will be squashed, resulting in fuel leaks.
8   After installation, run the engine and check for fuel leaks.
9   If the vehicle will be stored for a month or more, remove and drain the fuel tank. Also loosen the float chamber drain screw and drain the fuel from the carburetor (see illustrations).

16 Exhaust system - inspection

1   Periodically check the exhaust system for leaks and loose fasteners. If tightening the holder nuts at the cylinder head fails to stop any leaks, replace the gasket with a new one (a procedure which requires removal of the system).
2   The exhaust pipe flange nuts at the cylinder head are especially prone to loosening, which could cause damage to the head. Check them frequently and keep them tight.

17 Spark plug - replacement

Refer to illustrations 17.2a, 17.2b, 17.6a and 17.6b

1   This vehicle is equipped with a spark plug that has an 18 mm wrench hex.
2   Twist the spark plug cap to break it free from the plug, then pull it off. If available, use compressed air to blow any accumulated debris from around the spark plug. Remove the plug (see illustrations).
3   Inspect the electrodes for wear: Both the center and side electrodes should have square edges and the side electrode should be of uniform thickness. Look for excessive deposits and evidence of a cracked or chipped insulator around the center electrode. Compare your spark plug to the color spark plug reading chart on the inside of the back cover. Check the threads, the washer and the ceramic insulator body for cracks and other damage.

Chapter 1 Tune-up and routine maintenance

17.2a Unscrew the plug with a spark plug socket

17.2b The Grizzly 660 sparkplug is at the front of the engine, above the exhaust valve covers

17.6a Spark plug manufacturers recommend using a wire type gauge when checking the gap - if the wire doesn't slide between the electrodes with a slight drag, adjustment is required

17.6b To change the gap, bend the side electrode only, as indicated by the arrows, and be very careful not to crack or chip the ceramic insulator surrounding the center electrode

18.7a Remove the Allen bolts (arrows) and lift the cover off (this is an early exhaust cover) . . .

4   If the electrodes are not excessively worn, and if the deposits can be easily removed with a wire brush, the plug can be regapped and reused (if no cracks or chips are visible in the insulator). If in doubt concerning the condition of the plug, replace it with a new one, as the expense is minimal.
5   Cleaning the spark plug by sandblasting is permitted, provided you clean the plug with a high flash-point solvent afterwards.
6   Before installing a new plug, make sure it is the correct type and heat range. Check the gap between the electrodes, as it is not pre-set. For best results, use a wire-type gauge rather than a flat gauge to check the gap (see illustration). If the gap must be adjusted, bend the side electrode only and be very careful not to chip or crack the insulator nose (see illustration). Make sure the washer is in place before installing the plug.
7   Since the cylinder head is made of aluminum, which is soft and easily damaged, thread the plug into the head by hand. Slip a short length of hose over the end of the plug to use as a tool to thread it into place. The hose will grip the plug well enough to turn it, but will start to slip if the plug begins to cross-thread in the hole - this will prevent damaged threads and the accompanying repair costs.
8   Once the plug is finger tight, the job can be finished with a socket. If a torque wrench is available, tighten the spark plug to the torque listed in this Chapter's Specifications. If you do not have a torque wrench, tighten the plug finger tight (until the washer bottoms on the cylinder head) then use a spark plug socket to tighten it an additional 1/4 turn. Regardless of the method used, do not overtighten it.
9   Reconnect the spark plug cap.

18 Valve clearances - check and adjustment

Refer to illustrations 18.7a, 18.7b, 18.7c, 18.7d, 18.8, 18.9a, 18.9b, 18.11 and 18.12

1   The engine must be cool to the touch for this maintenance procedure, so if possible let the machine sit overnight before beginning.
2   Refer to Chapter 8 and remove the seat, front cargo rack and front fender.
3   If you're working on a Grizzly 600, remove the front air duct.
4   Disconnect the cable from the negative terminal of the battery (see Section 4, if necessary).
5   Refer to Chapter 4 and remove the fuel tank.
6   Refer to Section 17 and remove the spark plug. This will make it easier to turn the engine.
7   Remove the valve adjusting hole covers (there's one or two on each side of the cylinder head) (see illustrations).

Chapter 1 Tune-up and routine maintenance

18.7b ... replace the cover O-ring if its condition is in doubt; the ridge inside the cover goes upward

18.7c The Grizzly intake valve cover is secured by four bolts (660 shown)

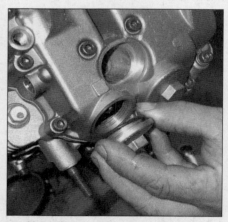

18.7d The Grizzly models have two exhaust valve covers with O-rings (660 shown)

18.8 Unscrew the timing hole plug - on early models (shown) the plug is in the top of the alternator cover; on later models, it's in the side

18.9a Align the notch on the alternator cover with the TDC line (the line next to the T mark on the rotor, right arrow) - the line by the F mark (left arrow) is used to check ignition timing (cover removed for clarity)

8   Remove the timing hole plug **(see illustration)**.
9   Position the piston at Top Dead Center (TDC) on the compression stroke. Do this by turning the crankshaft until the mark on the rotor is aligned with the timing notch on the crankcase **(see illustrations)**. You should be able to wiggle both rocker arms - if not (if the exhaust valve is open), the engine is positioned at TDC on the exhaust stroke; turn the crankshaft one complete revolution and realign the marks.
10 With the engine in this position, both of the valves can be checked.
11 To check, insert a feeler gauge of the thickness listed in this Chap-

18.9b On later models, the line is on the edge of the rotor; align it with the notch in the cover

18.11 Measure the clearance with a feeler gauge; to adjust it, loosen the locknut and turn the adjusting screw - the Yamaha special tool is convenient . . .

Chapter 1 Tune-up and routine maintenance

18.12 ... but you can use a box-end wrench on the locknut (left arrow) and an open-end wrench on the screw (right arrow)

ter's Specifications between the valve stem and rocker arm **(see illustration)**. Pull the feeler gauge out slowly - you should feel a slight drag. If there's no drag, the clearance is too loose. If there's a heavy drag, the clearance is too tight.

12 If the clearance is incorrect, loosen the adjuster locknut with a box-end wrench (ring spanner). Turn the adjusting screw with a wrench or special valve adjusting tool until the correct clearance is achieved, then tighten the locknut **(see illustration)**.

13 After adjusting, recheck the clearance with the feeler gauge to make sure it wasn't changed when the locknut was tightened.

14 Now measure the other valve(s), following the same procedure you used for the first valve. Make sure to use a feeler gauge of the specified thickness.

15 Once the clearance is within the Specifications, install the valve adjusting hole covers and timing hole plug. On covers with an internal ridge, the ridge faces upward. On Grizzly 600 models, the UP mark on the inside of the cover goes upright and the arrow mark points upward. Use new O-rings on the covers and plug if the old ones are hardened, deteriorated or damaged.

16 Install all components removed for access.

19 Idle speed - check and adjustment

1 Before adjusting the idle speed, make sure the valve clearances and spark plug gap are correct. Also, turn the handlebars back-and-forth and see if the idle speed changes as this is done. If it does, the throttle cable may not be adjusted correctly, or it may be worn out. Be sure to correct this problem before proceeding.

2 The engine should be at normal operating temperature, which is usually reached after 10 to 15 minutes of stop and go riding. Make sure the transmission is in Neutral.

3 Turn the throttle stop screw **(see illustration 15.9a or 15.9b)** until the idle speed listed in this Chapter's Specifications is obtained.

4 Snap the throttle open and shut a few times, then recheck the idle speed. If necessary, repeat the adjustment procedure.

5 If a smooth, steady idle can't be achieved, the fuel/air mixture may be incorrect. Refer to Chapter 4 for additional carburetor information.

20 Fasteners - check

1 Since vibration of the machine tends to loosen fasteners, all nuts, bolts, screws, etc. should be periodically checked for proper tightness. Also make sure all cotter pins or other safety fasteners are correctly installed.

2 Pay particular attention to the following:

Spark plug
Engine oil, transfer case (if equipped) and differential drain plugs
Oil filter or oil filter cover bolts
Gearshift lever
Brake pedal
Footpegs
Engine mount bolts
Shock absorber mount bolts
Front axle nuts
Rear axle nuts
Skid plate bolts

3 If a torque wrench is available, use it along with the torque specifications at the beginning of this, or other, Chapters.

21 Suspension - check

1 The suspension components must be maintained in top operating condition to ensure rider safety. Loose, worn or damaged suspension parts decrease the vehicle's stability and control.

2 Lock the front brake and push on the handlebars to compress the front shock absorbers several times. See if they move up-and-down smoothly without binding. If binding is felt, the shocks should be inspected as described in Chapter 6.

3 Check the tightness of all front suspension nuts and bolts to be sure none have become loose.

4 Inspect the rear shock absorber for fluid leakage and tightness of the mounting nuts and bolts. If leakage is found, the shock should be replaced.

5 Support the vehicle securely upright with its rear wheel off the ground. Grab the swingarm on each side, just ahead of the axle. Rock the swingarm from side to side - there should be no discernible movement at the rear. If there's a little movement or a slight clicking can be heard, make sure the swingarm pivot shaft is tight. If the pivot shaft is tight but movement is still noticeable, the swingarm will have to be removed and the bearings replaced as described in Chapter 6.

6 Inspect the tightness of the rear suspension nuts and bolts.

22 Steering system - inspection and toe-in adjustment

Inspection

1 This vehicle is equipped with a ball bearing at the lower end of the steering shaft and plastic bushings at the upper end. These can become dented, rough or loose during normal use of the machine. In extreme cases, worn or loose parts can cause steering wobble that is potentially dangerous.

2 To check block the rear wheels so the vehicle can't roll, jack up the front end and support it securely on jackstands.

3 Point the wheel straight ahead and slowly move the handlebar from side-to-side. Dents or roughness in the bearing or bushing will be felt and the bars will not move smoothly. **Note:** *Make sure any hesitation in movement is not being caused by the cables and wiring harnesses that run to the handlebar.*

4 If the handlebar doesn't move smoothly, or if it moves horizontally, refer to Chapter 6 to remove and inspect the steering shaft bushing and bearing.

5 Look at the tie-rod ends (inner and outer) while slowly turning the handlebar from side-to-side. If there's any vertical movement in the tie-rod ball-joints, refer to Chapter 6 and replace them.

Toe-in adjustment

Refer to illustrations 22.11a and 22.11b

6 Roll the vehicle forward onto a level surface and stop it with the front wheels pointing straight ahead.

7 Make a mark at the front and center of each tire, even with the centerline of the front hub.

Chapter 1 Tune-up and routine maintenance

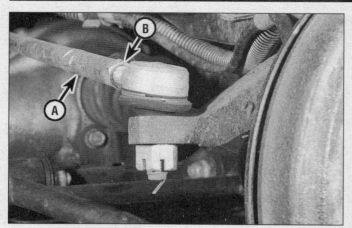

22.11a Hold and turn the tie-rod by placing an open-end wrench on the flats (A); loosen the locknuts (B) at the outer end . . .

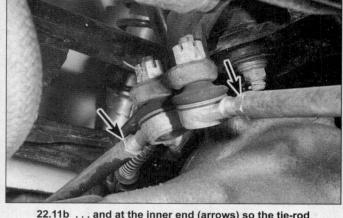

22.11b . . . and at the inner end (arrows) so the tie-rod can be turned

23.2 Pull out the drain plug at the bottom of the belt cover (arrow)

23.3 Open the clip and remove the catch tube for draining

8   Measure the distance between the marks with a toe-in gauge or steel tape measure.
9   Have an assistant push the vehicle backward while you watch the marks on the tires. Stop pushing when the tires have rotated exactly one-half turn, so the marks are at the backs of the tires.

10   Again, measure the distance between the marks. Subtract the front measurement from the rear measurement to get toe-in.
11   If toe-in is not as specified in this Chapter's Specifications, hold each tie-rod with a wrench on the flats and loosen the locknuts (see illustrations). Turn the tie-rods an equal amount to change toe-in. When toe-in is set correctly, tighten the locknuts to the torque listed in this Chapter's Specifications.

23 Drivebelt - inspection

Refer to illustrations 23.2, 23.3 and 23.5

1   A drivebelt connects the engine crankshaft to the transmission on all except 1993 through 1998 Kodiak models.
2   Remove the drain plug from the bottom of the drivebelt cover and let any water drain out (see illustration). Water will cause accelerated drivebelt wear, so it's important to inspect the belt if water is in the housing.
3   Remove the catch tube from the air duct(s) (see illustration). Let any water drain out. Again, it's important to inspect the belt if water is found.
4   Remove the belt cover (see Chapter 2B or 2C).
5   Check the belt for fraying, cracks, separation of the layers or missing pieces of material (see illustration). Measure the width of the belt and compare it to the value listed in this Chapter's Specifications. Replace it if any problems are found (see Chapter 2B).

23.5 Check the belt for wear and damage and measure its width

Chapter 1 Tune-up and routine maintenance

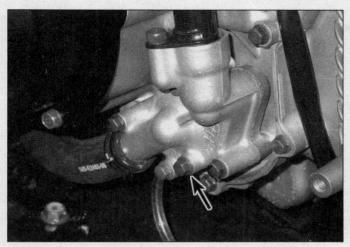

24.2a The drain bolt (arrow) has a copper washer (Kodiak shown; Grizzly similar)

24.2b The coolant will spurt out, so be ready to catch it

24 Coolant - draining, flushing and refilling

Warning: *Allow the engine to cool completely before performing this maintenance operation. Also, don't allow antifreeze to come into contact with your skin or painted surfaces of the vehicle. Rinse off spills immediately with plenty of water. Antifreeze is highly toxic if ingested. Never leave antifreeze lying around in an open container or in puddles on the floor; children and pets are attracted by its sweet smell and may drink it. Check with local authorities about disposing of used antifreeze. Many communities have collection centers which will see that antifreeze is disposed of safely. Antifreeze is also combustible, so don't store or use it near open flames.*

Draining

Refer to illustrations 24.2a and 24.2b

1 Loosen the pressure cap **(see illustration 3.8b)**. Place a large, clean drain pan under the water pump on the left side of the engine.
2 Remove the drain bolt from the water pump **(see illustration)** and allow the coolant to drain into the pan **(see illustration)**. **Note:** *The coolant will rush out with considerable force, so position the drain pan accordingly.* Remove the pressure cap completely to ensure that all of the coolant can drain.
3 If you're working on a Kodiak, remove the coolant drain plug from the front of the cylinder below the exhaust pipe (it can be identified by its copper washer).
4 Drain the coolant reservoir. Refer to Chapter 3 for the reservoir removal procedure. Wash the reservoir out with water.

Flushing

5 Flush the system with clean tap water by inserting a garden hose in the radiator filler neck. Allow the water to run through the system until it is clear when it exits the drain bolt hole. If the radiator is extremely corroded, remove it by referring to Chapter 3 and have it cleaned at a radiator shop.
6 Check the drain bolt washer(s). Replace them with new ones if necessary.
7 Clean the hole(s), then install the drain bolt(s) and tighten to the torque listed in this Chapter's Specifications.
8 Fill the cooling system with clean water mixed with a flushing compound. Make sure the flushing compound is compatible with aluminum components, and follow the manufacturer's instructions carefully.
9 Start the engine and allow it to reach normal operating temperature. Let it run for about ten minutes.
10 Stop the engine. Let the machine cool for a while, then cover the pressure cap with a heavy rag and turn it counterclockwise to the first stop, releasing any pressure that may be present in the system. Once the hissing stops, push down on the cap and remove it completely.
11 Drain the system once again.
12 Fill the system with clean water, then repeat Steps 8, 9 and 10.

Refilling

13 Fill the system with the proper coolant mixture (see this Chapter's Specifications). When the system is full (all the way up to the top of the radiator cap filler neck), install the cap and start the engine. Allow the engine to reach normal operating temperature, then shut it off.
14 Let the engine cool off for awhile, cover the radiator cap with a heavy rag and loosen it to the first stop to allow any pressure in the system to bleed off before the cap is removed completely. Recheck the coolant level in the radiator filler neck. If it's low, add more coolant until it reaches the top of the filler neck. Reinstall the cap.
15 Allow the engine to cool, then check the coolant level in the reservoir (see Section 3). If the coolant level is low, add the specified mixture until it reaches the FULL mark in the reservoir.
16 Check the system for leaks.
17 Do not dispose of the old coolant by pouring it down a drain. Instead, pour it into a heavy plastic container, cap it tightly and take it to an authorized disposal site or a service station.

Notes

2A-1

Chapter 2 Part A
Engine, clutch and transmission (1993 through 1999 400 models)

Contents

	Section		Section
Balancer gears - removal, inspection and installation	13	Major engine repair - general note	4
Cam chain tensioner - removal and installation	6	Oil pipe and pump - removal, inspection and installation	14
Crankcase - disassembly and reassembly	17	Operations possible with the engine in the frame	2
Cylinder - removal and installation	8	Operations requiring engine removal	3
Cylinder head, camshaft and rocker arms - removal, inspection and installation	7	Primary clutch - removal, inspection and installation	10
Engine - removal and installation	5	Recoil starter - removal, inspection and installation	15
External oil pipe and oil cooler - removal and installation	9	Reverse shift mechanism - removal, inspection and installation	12
External shift mechanism - removal, inspection and installation	16	Secondary clutch and release mechanism - removal, inspection and installation	11
General information	1	Transmission shafts, balancer shaft and shift cam - removal, inspection and installation	18

Specifications

General
Bore	83 mm (3.27 inches)
Stroke	71.5 m (2.81 inches)
Displacement	386 cc

Primary (centrifugal) clutch
Weight lining thickness
- Standard: 2 mm (0.08 inch)
- Limit: 1.5 mm (0.06 inch)

Clutch weight spring free length: 42.5 mm (1.67 inches)

Secondary clutch
Spring free length
- Standard: 44 mm (1.73 inches)
- Limit: Not specified

Metal plate thickness
- Nominal 2.0 mm plates: 1.5 to 1.7 mm (0.059 to 0.067 inch)
- Nominal 1.6 mm plates: 1.9 to 2.1 mm (0.075 to 0.083 inch)

Friction plate thickness
- Standard: 2.94 to 3.06 mm (0.116 to 0.120 inch)
- Limit: 2.8 mm (0.11 inch)

Friction and metal plate warpage limit: 0.2 mm (0.008 inch)

Transmission
Main axle and driveaxle runout limit: 0.08 mm (0.003 inch)

Chapter 2 Part A Engine, clutch and transmission (1993 through 1999 400 models)

Torque specifications

Cylinder head bolts	
M8 thread	20 Nm (14 ft-lbs)
M10 thread	40 Nm (29 ft-lbs)
Cylinder base Allen bolt	10 Nm (86 inch-lbs)
Cam sprocket cover Allen bolts	10 Nm (86 inch-lbs)
Oil check bolt	7 Nm (61 inch-lbs)
Camshaft bearing retainer bolts	8 Nm (70 inch-lbs)
Cam chain guide bolts	10 Nm (86 inch-lbs)
Camshaft sprocket bolt	60 Nm (43 ft-lbs)
Cam chain tensioner body bolts	10 Nm (86 inch-lbs)
Cam chain tensioner cap bolt	23 Nm (17 ft-lbs)
Crankcase bolts	10 Nm (86 inch-lbs)
Crankcase cover bolts	10 Nm (86 inch-lbs)
Main axle bearing retainer screws	7 Nm (61 inch-lbs)
Balancer shaft bearing retainer screws	7 Nm (61 inch-lbs)
Shift cam segment screw	12 Nm (104 inch-lbs)
Oil pump screws	7 Nm (61 inch-lbs)
Clutch boss nut	80 Nm (58 ft-lbs)
Clutch spring plate bolts	8 Nm (70 inch-lbs)
Primary clutch nut	140 Nm (100 ft-lbs)
Balancer shaft and driven gear nut	60 Nm (43 ft-lbs)
Middle driveaxle bearing retainer screws	25 Nm (18 ft-lbs)
Middle driveaxle pinion gear nut	120 Nm (85 ft-lbs)
Oil cooler bolts	7 Nm (61 inch-lbs)

1 General information

The engine/transmission unit is of the air-cooled, single-cylinder four-stroke design. The valves are operated by a chain and sprockets. The engine/transmission assembly is constructed from aluminum alloy. The crankcase is divided vertically.

The crankcase incorporates a wet sump, pressure-fed lubrication system which uses a gear-driven rotor-type oil pump, an oil filter and separate strainer screen and an oil temperature warning switch.

Power from the crankshaft is routed to the transmission via two clutches. The centrifugal clutch, which engages as engine speed is increased, connects the crankshaft to the change clutch, which is of the wet, multi-plate type. The change clutch transmits power to the transmission; it's engaged and disengaged automatically when the shift lever is moved from one gear position to another. The transmission has five forward gears and one reverse gear as well as high and low ranges.

2 Operations possible with the engine in the frame

The components and assemblies listed below can be removed without having to remove the engine from the frame. If, however, a number of areas require attention at the same time, removal of the engine is recommended.

Recoil starter
Starter motor
Starter reduction gears
Starter clutch
Alternator rotor and stator
Clutches (primary and secondary)
External shift mechanism
Cam chain tensioner
Camshaft
Rocker arms and shafts
Cylinder head
Rocker arms and pushrods
Cylinder and piston
Oil pump
Balancer gears

3 Operations requiring engine removal

It is necessary to remove the engine/transmission assembly from the frame and separate the crankcase halves to gain access to the following components:

Crankshaft and connecting rod
Transmission shafts
Shift drum and forks

4 Major engine repair - general note

1 It is not always easy to determine when or if an engine should be completely overhauled, as a number of factors must be considered.

2 High mileage is not necessarily an indication that an overhaul is needed, while low mileage, on the other hand, does not preclude the need for an overhaul. Frequency of servicing is probably the single most important consideration. An engine that has regular and frequent oil and filter changes, as well as other required maintenance, will most likely give many miles of reliable service. Conversely, a neglected engine, or one which has not been broken in properly, may require an overhaul very early in its life.

3 Exhaust smoke and excessive oil consumption are both indications that piston rings and/or valve guides are in need of attention. Make sure oil leaks are not responsible before deciding that the rings and guides are bad. Refer to Chapter 2D and perform a cylinder compression check to determine for certain the nature and extent of the work required.

4 If the engine is making obvious knocking or rumbling noises, the connecting rod and/or main bearings are probably at fault.

5 Loss of power, rough running, excessive valve train noise and high fuel consumption rates may also point to the need for an overhaul, especially if they are all present at the same time. If a complete tune-up does not remedy the situation, major mechanical work is the only solution.

6 An engine overhaul generally involves restoring the internal parts to the specifications of a new engine. During an overhaul the piston rings are replaced and the cylinder walls are bored and/or honed. If a rebore is done, then a new piston is also required. The crankshaft and connecting rod are permanently assembled, so if one of these compo-

Chapter 2 Part A Engine, clutch and transmission (1993 through 1999 400 models)

nents needs to be replaced both must be. Generally the valves are serviced as well, since they are usually in less than perfect condition at this point. While the engine is being overhauled, other components such as the carburetor and the starter motor can be rebuilt also. The end result should be a like-new engine that will give as many trouble-free miles as the original.

7 Before beginning the engine overhaul, read through all of the related procedures to familiarize yourself with the scope and requirements of the job. Overhauling an engine is not all that difficult, but it is time consuming. Plan on the vehicle being tied up for a minimum of two weeks. Check on the availability of parts and make sure that any necessary special tools, equipment and supplies are obtained in advance.

8 Most work can be done with typical shop hand tools, although a number of precision measuring tools are required for inspecting parts to determine if they must be replaced. Often a dealer service department or repair shop will handle the inspection of parts and offer advice concerning reconditioning and replacement. As a general rule, time is the primary cost of an overhaul so it doesn't pay to install worn or substandard parts.

9 As a final note, to ensure maximum life and minimum trouble from a rebuilt engine, everything must be assembled with care in a spotlessly clean environment.

5 Engine - removal and installation

Note: Engine removal and installation should be done with the aid of an assistant to avoid damage or injury that could occur if the engine is dropped. A hydraulic floor jack should be used to support and lower the engine if possible (they can be rented at low cost).

Removal

Refer to illustrations 5.9, 5.17a, 5.17b and 5.18

1 Drain the engine and transfer case oil and disconnect the spark plug wire (see Chapter 1).
2 Disconnect the ground cable from the engine and disconnect the battery cables.
3 Remove the seat, both footrests, the front and rear cargo racks, the front and rear fenders and the rear fender stay (see Chapter 8).
4 Remove the fuel tank, carburetor, air cleaner housing and exhaust system (see Chapter 4). The choke and throttle cables can be left connected. Plug the carburetor intake openings with rags.
5 Remove the shift linkage (see Section 16).
6 Remove the rear brake pedal rod and cable and the pedal (see Chapter 7).
7 Disconnect the speedometer/odometer cable (see Chapter 9).
8 Remove the starter motor (see Chapter 9).
9 Disconnect the crankcase breather hose **(see illustration)**.
10 Remove the clamp that secures the oil cooler hoses and remove the oil filter cover from the engine (see Chapter 1).
11 Label and disconnect the following wires (refer to Chapters 5 or 9 for component location if necessary):

Ignition pulse generator
Alternator
Oil temperature and gear position switches

12 Disconnect the reverse lock release cable (Section 12).
13 Remove the shift pedal (if equipped) (see Section 16).
14 Remove the rear final drive unit and swingarm (see Chapter 6). Make sure the rear of the vehicle is securely supported so it can't fall when the engine is removed.
15 Remove the front driveshaft protector, transfer case (1993 through 1998 models), middle driven gear assembly (1993 through 1998 models) and front driveshaft (see Chapter 6).
16 Support the engine securely from below. *Note: Use a jack (preferably a floor jack) that can be repositioned if necessary as the engine mounting bolts are removed.*
17 Remove the engine mounting bolts, nuts and brackets at the upper front, lower front, lower rear and upper rear **(see illustrations)**.
18 Have an assistant help you lift the engine and remove it to the left side of the vehicle **(see illustration)**.
19 Slowly lower the engine to a suitable work surface.

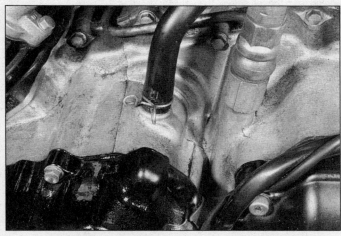

5.9 Disconnect the breather hose from the crankcase

5.17a With the engine securely supported, remove the upper front engine mounting bolt . . .

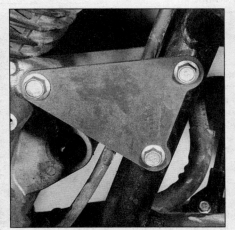

5.17b . . . and the lower front engine mounting brackets . . .

5.18 Have an assistant help you lift the engine out to the left

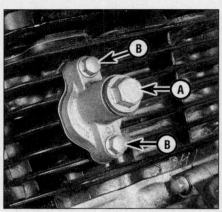

6.1 Loosen the tensioner cap bolt (A), then remove the tensioner bolts (B) and take the tensioner off

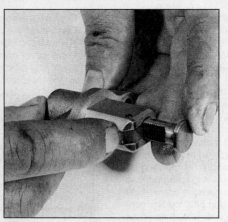

6.7a Lift the latch, press the piston into the tensioner and release the latch

6.7b The piston should be retracted like this when the tensioner is installed

Installation

20 Check the rubber engine supports for wear or damage and replace them if necessary before installing the engine.
21 Coat the driveshaft splines with moly-based grease. Install the engine from the left side of the vehicle.
22 Lift the engine to align the mounting bolt holes, then install the bolts from the right side of the vehicle.
23 Tighten the bolts in order to the torques listed in this Chapter's Specifications:

   a) *Engine stay to frame nuts (front)*
   b) *Engine stay to frame bolts (top)*
   c) *Upper mounting bolt nuts*
   d) *Front and rear mounting bolt nuts*

24 The remainder of installation is the reverse of the removal steps, with the following additions:

   a) *Use new gaskets at all exhaust pipe connections.*
   b) *Use new O-rings at the oil cooler hose connections.*
   c) *Adjust the throttle cable and select lever cable following the procedures in Chapter 1.*
   d) *Fill the engine and transfer case with oil and check the rear final drive oil level, also following the procedures in Chapter 1. Run the engine and check for leaks.*

6 Cam chain tensioner - removal and installation

Removal

Refer to illustration 6.1

Caution: *Once you start to remove the tensioner bolts you must remove the tensioner all the way and reset it before tightening the bolts. The tensioner extends and locks in place, so if you loosen the bolts partway and then tighten them, the tensioner or cam chain will be damaged.*

1 Loosen the tensioner cap bolt **(see illustration)**.
2 Remove the tensioner mounting bolts and detach it from the cylinder.
3 Remove the cap bolt and sealing washer from the tensioner body and wash them with solvent.

Installation

Refer to illustrations 6.7a and 6.7b

4 Clean all old gasket material from the tensioner body and engine.
5 Lubricate the friction surfaces of the components with moly based grease.
6 Install a new tensioner gasket on the cylinder.
7 Lift the latch, compress the tensioner piston all the way into the body and release the latch **(see illustrations)**.
8 Position the tensioner body on the cylinder and install the bolts, tightening them to the torque listed in this Chapter's Specifications.
9 Install the cap bolt with a new sealing washer and tighten it to the torque listed in this Chapter's Specifications.

7 Cylinder head, camshaft and rocker arms - removal, inspection and installation

Camshaft removal

Refer to illustrations 7.3, 7.4, 7.5, 7. 7a, 7.7b and 7.8

1 Remove the engine from the frame (see Section 5).
2 Remove the valve adjusting hole covers (see Chapter 1).
3 Remove the Allen bolts and take the cover off **(see illustration)**.
4 Refer to *Valve clearances - check and adjustment* in Chapter 1 and place the engine at top dead center on the compression stroke. The cam sprocket mark will align with the indicator cast into the cylinder head and the rocker arms will be loose when the cylinder is at TDC compression **(see illustration)**.

Models with recoil starter

5 Prevent the crankshaft from turning. To do this, remove the recoil starter as described in Section 15. Hold the recoil starter pulley (if

7.3 Remove the Allen bolts from the camshaft sprocket cover (arrows)

Chapter 2 Part A Engine, clutch and transmission (1993 through 1999 400 models)

7.4 With the engine at TDC compression, the sprocket line should be even with the cast indicator in the cylinder head (arrows)

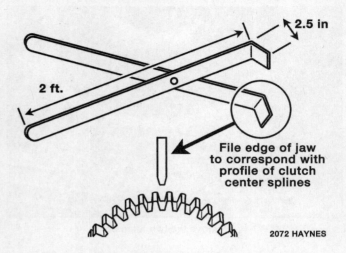

7.5 A clutch holding tool can be made from steel strap

7.7a The camshaft dowel aligns with the sprocket line and the cast indicator

7.7b Bend back the lockwasher tabs, remove the two bolts and take off the lockwasher and retainer

7.8 Thread a 10 mm bolt into the camshaft and pull on it to remove the camshaft and outer bearing

equipped) with a clutch holder tool. If the factory tool or an equivalent isn't available, you can make your own from some steel strap, bent at the ends and bolted together in the middle **(see Illustration)**.

Models without recoil starter
6   Remove the alternator outer cover (see Chapter 9) and place a wrench on the flats of the rotor (the rotor that fits into the outer cover, not the alternator rotor).

All models
7   Unbolt the cam sprocket and take it off the camshaft **(see illustration)**. Disengage the sprocket from the chain and support the chain with wire so it doesn't fall down off the crankshaft sprocket. Unbolt the camshaft retainer from the head **(see illustration)**.
8   Thread a 10 mm bolt into the end of the camshaft and use it as a handle to pull the camshaft out of the cylinder head **(see illustration)**. **Caution:** *The camshaft should come out easily. If it seems stuck, make sure it isn't caught on the rocker arms.*

Rocker arm removal
Refer to illustration 7.9
9   Thread a 6 mm bolt into the end of each rocker arm shaft **(see illustration)**. Support the rocker and use the bolt as a handle to pull out the shaft. **Note:** *If the shaft is stuck, it may be necessary to use a slide*

hammer. These can be rented from equipment rental yards (some auto parts stores also rent tools).

7.9 Thread a bolt into each rocker shaft and pull it out

7.10 Remove the two Allen bolts

7.11 Cylinder head bolt TIGHTENING sequence

Cylinder head removal

Refer to illustrations 7.10, 7.11 and 7.12

10   Remove the cylinder head Allen bolts **(see illustration)**.
11   Loosen the cylinder head bolts in several stages, in the reverse order of the tightening sequence **(see illustration)**.
12   Lift the cylinder head off the cylinder **(see illustration)**. If it's stuck, don't attempt to pry it off - tap around the sides with a plastic hammer to dislodge it. Be careful not to tap against the cooling fins - they're easily broken.
13   Locate the cover dowels **(see illustration 7.12)**. They may be in the cylinder or they may have come off with the head.

Cam chain and guide removal

Refer to illustrations 7.14a and 7.14b

14   Lift the front cam chain guide out of the cylinder **(see illustrations)**. The rear guide is bolted at the bottom, so the primary clutch will have to be removed for access if the guide or the cam chain need to be removed.
15   Stuff clean rags into the cam chain openings so dirt, small parts or tools can't fall into them.

Installation

16   Coat the rocker shafts and rocker arm bores with moly-based grease. Install the rocker shafts and rocker arms in the cylinder head. Be sure to install the intake and exhaust rocker arms and shafts in the correct sides of the head.
17   Install the inner camshaft bearing in the cylinder head and outer bearing on the camshaft (if they were removed). The sealed side of the outer bearing faces out (away from the cylinder head). Lubricate the camshaft bearings with engine oil.
18   Install the camshaft in the cylinder head with its lobes pointed down. The camshaft dowel should be up, so it aligns with the indica-

7.12 Lift the head off; the dowels and the O-ring that surrounds one of the dowels may come off with the head or stay in the cylinder (arrows)

7.14a Lift the front chain guide (arrow) . . .

7.14b . . . out of its cup (left arrow); to unbolt the rear chain guide (right arrows), you'll need to remove the primary clutch

Chapter 2 Part A Engine, clutch and transmission (1993 through 1999 400 models)

8.3 Remove the Allen bolt that attaches the cylinder to the crankcase (arrow)

8.4 Lift the cylinder off; the dowel inside the gasket loop has an O-ring (arrow) . . .

8.5 . . . there's also another dowel (left arrow); the dowels may stay in the crankcase or come off with the cylinder - the cylinder base O-ring (right arrow) should be replaced whenever the cylinder is removed

tor in the cylinder head, when the camshaft is installed (see illustration 7.4).
19   Install the bearing retainer and a new lockwasher (see illustration 7.7b). Tighten the bearing retainer bolts to the torque listed in this Chapter's Specifications.
20   Install the three dowel pins and the O-ring that surrounds one of the dowels, then place the new head gasket on the cylinder (see illustration 7.12). Never reuse the old gasket and don't use any type of gasket sealant.
21   Install the exhaust side cam chain damper, fitting the lower guide into its notch (see illustration 7.14b).
22   Carefully lower the cylinder head over the dowels and O-ring, guiding the cam chain through the slot in the cylinder head. It's helpful to have an assistant support the cam chain with a piece of wire so it doesn't fall and become kinked or detached from the crankshaft. When the head is resting on the cylinder, wire the cam chain to another component to keep tension on it.
23   Lubricate the threads of the cylinder head bolts with engine oil, then install them finger-tight. Tighten the four hex bolts in the correct sequence (see illustration 7.11), in several stages, to the torque listed in this Chapter's Specifications. After the hex bolts are tightened, tighten the two Allen bolts to the torque listed in this Chapter's Specifications.
24   Refer to the valve adjustment procedure in Chapter 1 and make sure the timing mark with the T next to it is aligned with the notch in the timing hole. If it's necessary to turn the crankshaft, hold the cam chain up so it doesn't fall off the crankshaft sprocket and become jammed.
25   Engage the camshaft sprocket with the timing chain so its dowel hole aligns with the dowel (see illustration 7.7a). Slip the sprocket onto the camshaft over the dowel, then install the sprocket bolt finger-tight. The line on the cam sprocket should be aligned with the cast indicator in the cylinder head (see illustration 7.4).
26   Twist the cam sprocket in both directions to remove the slack from the cam chain. Insert a screwdriver in the cam chain tensioner hole and push against the cam chain guide. With the guide pushed in, the cam sprocket line and cast indicator should line up (see illustration 7.4). If they don't, remove the cam sprocket from the chain, reposition it and try again. Don't continue with assembly until the marks are lined up correctly.
27   Tighten the cam sprocket bolt to the torque listed in this Chapter's Specifications.
28   Apply engine oil to a new O-ring for the cam sprocket cover. Install the O-ring and cover and tighten the Allen bolts to the torque listed in this Chapter's Specifications.
29   Install the cam chain tensioner (see Section 7).
30   Change the engine oil (see Chapter 1).
31   Adjust the valve clearances (see Chapter 1).
32   The remainder of installation is the reverse of removal.

8 Cylinder - removal and installation

Removal

Refer to illustrations 8.3, 8.4 and 8.5

1   Following the procedure given in Section 7, remove the cylinder head. Make sure the crankshaft is positioned at Top Dead Center (TDC).
2   Lift out the cam chain front guide (see illustration 7.14a).
3   Remove the Allen bolt the secures the base of the cylinder to the crankcase (see illustration).
4   Lift the cylinder straight up to remove it (see illustration). If it's stuck, tap around its perimeter with a soft-faced mallet (but don't tap on the cooling fins or they may break). Don't attempt to pry between the cylinder and crankcase as you'll ruin the mating surfaces.
5   Locate the dowel pins (they may have come off with the cylinder or still be in the crankcase (see illustration 8.4 and the accompanying illustration). Be careful not to let these drop into the engine. Stuff rags around the piston and remove the gasket and all traces of old gasket material from the surfaces of cylinder and crankcase.
6   Refer to Part D of this Chapter to inspect the cylinder.

Installation

Refer to illustration 8.10

7   Lubricate the cylinder bore with plenty of clean engine oil. Apply a thin film of moly-based grease to the piston skirt.

8.10 If you're experienced and very careful, the cylinder can be installed over the rings without a ring compressor, but a compressor is recommended

9.1 There's a sealing washer on each side of the banjo fitting (arrows)

9.3 Hold the fitting (A) with one wrench and undo the nut (B); remove the mounting nuts (C), then slide the cooler off the studs and lower it clear

8 Install the dowel pins, then lower a new cylinder base gasket over them **(see illustrations 8.4 and 8.5)**.
9 Attach a piston ring compressor to the piston and compress the piston rings. A large hose clamp can be used instead - just make sure it doesn't scratch the piston, and don't tighten it too much.
10 Install the cylinder and carefully lower it down until the piston crown fits into the cylinder liner **(see illustration)**. While doing this, pull the camshaft chain up, using a hooked tool or piece of stiff wire. Push down on the cylinder, making sure the piston doesn't get cocked sideways, until the bottom of the cylinder liner slides down past the piston rings. A wood or plastic hammer handle can be used to gently tap the cylinder down, but don't use too much force or the piston will be damaged.
11 Remove the ring compressor or hose clamp, being careful not to scratch the piston.
12 The remainder of installation is the reverse of the removal steps.

9 External oil pipe and oil cooler - removal and installation

Removal

External oil pipe

Refer to illustration 9.1

1 Remove the union bolt and sealing washers on the right side of the engine **(see illustration)**.
2 At the other end of the pipe, remove the oil temperature switch (see Chapter 9), union bolt and sealing washers. Detach the pipe from the engine and take it out.

Oil cooler

Refer to illustration 9.3

3 Hold the fitting at one of the oil cooler hoses with a wrench and loosen the nut with a second wrench **(see illustration)**. Unscrew the nut from the oil cooler.
4 Remove the oil cooler mounting nuts, lower the oil cooler so the top post clears its grommet and take the oil cooler out of the vehicle.
5 To remove the oil cooler hoses from the vehicle, remove the hose retainer. Detach the hoses from the oil filter outer housing on the left side of the engine in the same way they were disconnected from the oil cooler.

Installation

6 Installation is the reverse of the removal steps, with the following additions:

a) Replace the sealing washers whenever the union bolts or hose fittings are loosened.
b) Tighten the union bolts or hose fittings to the torques listed in this Chapter's Specifications.

10 Primary clutch - removal, inspection and installation

Removal

Refer to illustrations 10.5, 10.6a, 10.6b, 10.9a and 10.9b

1 Place the shift pedal in the Neutral position.
2 Drain the engine oil (see Chapter 1).
3 Remove the union bolt from the external oil pipe **(see illustration 9.1)**.
4 If necessary for access, remove the right footrest (see Chapter 8).
5 Unbolt the cover from the engine **(see illustration)**. Carefully pull the cover off so the clutch release mechanism isn't pulled from its hole in the crankcase. If the cover is stuck, tap it gently with a soft hammer to free it - don't pry it loose or the gasket surfaces will be damaged.
6 Locate the cover dowels **(see illustrations)**. Set them aside for safekeeping.
7 Bend back or grind away the staked portion of the locknut.
8 Wedge a rag between the gears of the primary clutch and the sec-

Chapter 2 Part A Engine, clutch and transmission (1993 through 1999 400 models)

10.5 Loosen the clutch cover bolts (arrows) in a criss-cross pattern

10.6a There's a cover dowel at the rear (arrow) . . .

10.6b . . . and one at the front (arrow)

10.9a Align one of the cutouts in the secondary clutch housing with the gear on the primary clutch housing, then pull it off the crankshaft

ondary clutch to prevent the primary clutch from turning, then unscrew the locknut.

9 Turn the secondary clutch so one of its cutouts aligns with the gear on the primary clutch housing **(see illustration)**, then pull the primary clutch off the crankshaft and remove the washer **(see illustration)**.

Inspection

Refer to illustrations 10.10, 10.11, 10.12 and 10.16

10 Take the weight assembly out of the drum and remove the plain washer **(see illustration)**.

10.9b Remove the plain washer

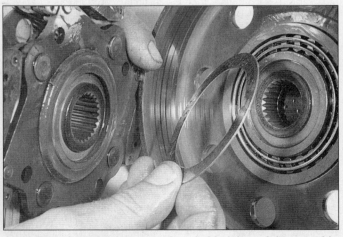

10.10 Remove the plain washer from behind the weight assembly

2A-10 Chapter 2 Part A Engine, clutch and transmission (1993 through 1999 400 models)

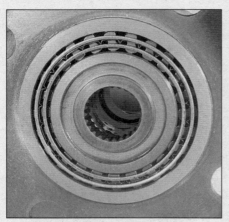

10.11 Check the one-way clutch for wear or damage

10.12 Measure the thickness of the friction material (arrow)

10.16 Remove the Torx screws and retainer to remove the bearing

10.20 Be sure the speedometer/odometer drive pin (upper arrow) engages the slot in the speedometer/odometer drive gear; make sure the shift guide is over the stopper bolt (lower arrow)

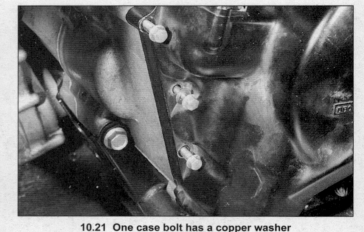

10.21 One case bolt has a copper washer

11 Check the one-way clutch rollers for signs of wear or scoring (see illustration). The rotors should be unmarked with no signs of wear such as pitting or flat spots. Replace the one-way clutch together with the drum if it's worn.
12 Measure the thickness of the lining material on the weights (see illustration). If it's thinner than the minimum listed in this Chapter's Specifications, replace the weights as a set.
13 Check the springs for breakage and the weights for wear or damage. Replace the weight assembly if problems are found.
14 Check the inside of the drum and replace it if it's worn or damaged.
15 Install the weight assembly in the drum.
16 Rotate the inner race of the ball bearing inside the crankcase cover with a finger. If the bearing is rough, loose or noisy, remove the Torx screws and retainer and install a new bearing (see illustration). Apply non-permanent thread locking agent to the threads of the Torx screws and tighten them securely.

Installation
Refer to illustrations 10.20 and 10.21

17 Slip the washer onto the crankshaft. Position one of the cutouts in the secondary clutch to make room, then install the primary clutch (see illustration 10.9a).
18 Install the locknut. Wedge a rag between the gears of the primary and secondary clutches to prevent the primary clutch from turning, then tighten the nut to the torque listed in this Chapter's Specifications.
19 Stake the lip of the locknut with a hammer and punch.
20 Make sure the dowels are in position and install a new gasket (see illustrations 10.6a and 10.6b). Position the cover on the crankcase. It the vehicle is equipped with a speedometer, make sure the pin in the speedometer gear drive aligns with the slot in the speedometer gear (see illustration). **Caution:** *Don't force the cover. If it won't go easily, the speedometer drive may not be properly aligned and it will be broken if force is used.*
21 Thread the cover bolts into their holes. One of the bolts has a copper washer (see illustration). Tighten the cover bolts in two or three stages, in a criss-cross pattern, to the torque listed in this Chapter's Specifications.
22 The remainder of installation is the reverse of the removal steps.
23 Refill the engine with oil (see Chapter 1).

11 Secondary clutch and release mechanism - removal, inspection and installation

Release mechanism
Removal
Refer to illustrations 11.2a through 11.2g

1 Remove the right crankcase cover (see Section 10).
2 Remove the release mechanism components from the crankcase (see illustrations).

Chapter 2 Part A Engine, clutch and transmission (1993 through 1999 400 models)

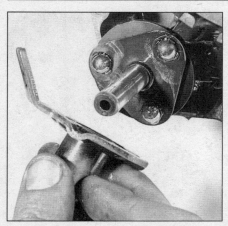
11.2a Pull off the no. 2 shift guide . . .

11.2b . . . the pawl holder . . .

11.2c . . . the no. 1 shift guide - make sure its dots (arrows) are lined up with each other on installation . . .

11.2d . . . a plain washer . . .

11.2e . . . the thrust bearing . . .

11.2f . . . a second plain washer . . .

Inspection

Refer to illustration 11.3

3 Check for visible wear or damage at the contact points of the lever and no. 1 shift guide and the friction points of the no. 1 shift guide, pawl holder and no. 2 shift guide. Check the spring for bending or distortion. Replace any parts that show problems. If the lever needs to be replaced, remove its cotter pin, washer and clevis pin and detach it from the cover **(see illustration)**. Replace the adjusting bolt O-ring in the crankcase cover whenever it's removed.

Installation

4 Installation is the reverse of the removal steps.
5 Refill the engine oil and adjust the clutch (see Chapter 1).

Secondary clutch

Removal

Refer to illustrations 11.7a through 11.7g

6 Remove the right crankcase cover and the primary clutch (see

11.2g . . . and the shaft

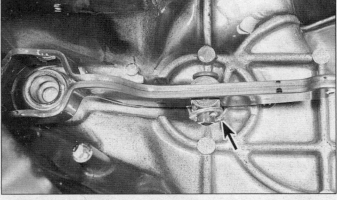
11.3 Remove the cotter pin (arrow), washer and pivot pin to remove the clutch release lever; use a new cotter pin on installation

2A-12 Chapter 2 Part A Engine, clutch and transmission (1993 through 1999 400 models)

11.7a Remove the pushrod and O-ring . . .

11.7b . . . undo the spring plate bolts evenly, in a criss-cross pattern . . .

11.7c . . . and remove the spring plate, bolts and springs

11.7d Bend back the lockwasher and undo the nut as described in the text

11.7e Pull off the clutch boss, plates, cushion springs and pressure plate as a pack

11.7f Remove the thrust washer (arrow) . . .

Section 10).

7 Refer to the accompanying illustrations to remove the clutch components (see illustrations). To prevent the clutch from turning while the nut is loosened, temporarily reinstall the primary clutch on the end of the crankshaft. Wedge a rag between the gears on the primary clutch and the secondary clutch drum, bend back the lockwasher and loosen the nut, then remove the rag and the primary clutch.

11.7g . . . then pull off the clutch housing and remove the collar

Inspection

Refer to illustrations 11.11, 11.12 and 11.13

8 Check the bolt posts and the friction surface on the pressure plate for damaged threads, scoring or wear. Replace the pressure plate if any defects are found.

9 Check the edges of the slots in the clutch housing for indentations made by the friction plate tabs. If the indentations are deep they can prevent clutch release, so the housing should be replaced with a new one. If the indentations can be removed easily with a file, the life of the housing can be prolonged to an extent. Also, check the driven gear teeth for cracks, chips and excessive wear and the springs on the back side for breakage. If the gear is worn or damaged or the springs are broken, the clutch housing must be replaced with a new one. Check the bearing surface in the center of the clutch housing for score marks, scratches and excessive wear.

10 Check the splines of the clutch boss for indentations made by the tabs on the metal plates. Check the clutch boss friction surface for wear or scoring. Replace the clutch boss if problems are found.

11 Measure the free length of the clutch springs (see illustration) and compare the results to this Chapter's Specifications. If the springs have sagged, or if cracks are noted, replace them with new ones as a set.

12 If the lining material of the friction plates smells burnt or if it is glazed, new parts are required. If the metal clutch plates are scored or discolored, they must be replaced with new ones. Measure the thickness of the friction plates (see illustration) and replace any friction plates that are worn with new parts.

Chapter 2 Part A Engine, clutch and transmission (1993 through 1999 400 models)   2A-13

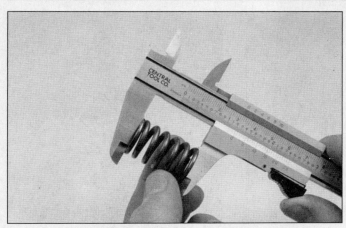

11.11 Measure the clutch spring free length

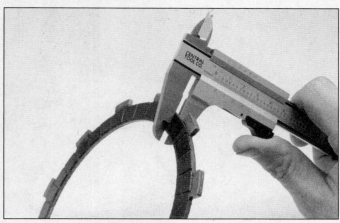

11.12 Measure the thickness of the friction plates

11.13 Check the metal plates for warpage

11.21 Align the arrows on clutch boss and pressure plate

13 Lay the metal plates, one at a time, on a perfectly flat surface (such as a piece of plate glass) and check for warpage by trying to slip a feeler gauge between the flat surface and the plate **(see illustration)**. The feeler gauge should be the same thickness as the maximum warp listed in this Chapter's Specifications. Do this at several places around the plate's circumference. If the feeler gauge can be slipped under the plate, it is warped and should be replaced with a new one.

14 Check the tabs on the friction plates for excessive wear and mushroomed edges. They can be cleaned up with a file if the deformation is not severe. Check the friction plates for warpage as described in Step 13.

15 Check the clutch collar for score marks, heat discoloration and evidence of excessive wear.

16 Check the clutch spring plate for wear and damage. Rotate the inner race of the bearing and check for roughness, looseness or excessive noise.

Installation

Refer to illustration 11.21

17 Lubricate the inner and outer surfaces of the clutch collar with moly-based grease and install it on the crankshaft.

18 Install the collar, clutch housing and thrust washer **(see illustrations 11.7g and 11.7f)**.

19 There are two different types of friction plate, one with a notch in one of its tabs and six without. The friction plate marked with a notch in one of its tabs goes on last (next to the clutch boss flange) **(see illustration 11.7e)**. There are two thicknesses of metal plate, two of them 2.0 mm thick and four of them 1.6 mm thick.

20 Coat the friction plates with engine oil, then install the friction plates, metal plates and cushion springs on the clutch boss. Be sure to install them in the correct order: friction plate, thin metal plate, friction plate, thin metal plate, friction plate, thick metal plate, friction plate, thick metal plate, friction plate, thin metal plate, friction plate, thin metal plate, then finally the friction plate with a notch in one of its tabs.

21 Install the pressure plate on the last friction plate, aligning the arrows on clutch boss and pressure plate **(see illustration)**.

22 Install a new lockwasher and the nut on the mainshaft. Hold the clutch as described in Step 8 and tighten the locknut to the torque listed in this Chapter's Specifications.

23 Bend one of the locknut tabs over to secure the nut.

24 Install the clutch springs and the spring plate. Tighten the bolts to the torque listed in this Chapter's Specifications in two or three stages, in a criss-cross pattern.

25 The remainder of installation is the reverse of the removal steps.

12 Reverse shift mechanism - removal, inspection and installation

Removal

Refer to illustrations 12.3 and 12.4

1 The reverse lock lever and shift cam detent ball are accessible from outside the engine. The crankcase must be disassembled for access to the reverse shift cam and forks.

2 To remove the reverse lockout lever, disconnect its cable (see Chapter 1).

2A-14 Chapter 2 Part A Engine, clutch and transmission (1993 through 1999 400 models)

12.3 Remove the bolt

12.4 Remove the bolt and sealing washer, then pull out the spring and remove the detent ball with a magnet

13.2 Balancer alignment marks

13.3 Bend back the lockwasher, wedge a rag between the gears to prevent rotation and unscrew the nut

13.4 Remove the balancer driven gear and the Woodruff key (arrow) . . .

13.5 . . . and slide off the collar

3 Remove the bolt, washer, spring, outer lever, inner lever and collar **(see illustration)**.
4 At the right rear corner of the engine, remove the bolt and sealing washer. Lift out the spring and detent ball with a magnet **(see illustration)**.

Installation

5 Installation is the reverse of the removal steps, with the following additions:

  a) Tighten the lever bolt securely, but don't overtighten it.
  b) Use a new sealing washer on the detent ball bolt if the old one is worn or damaged. Tighten the detent ball bolt to the torque listed in this Chapter's Specifications.

13 Balancer gears - removal, inspection and installation

Removal

Refer to illustrations 13.2, 13.3, 13.4, 13.5, 13.6a, 13.6b, 13.7a, 13.7b, 13.8, 13.9a, 13.9b and 13.9c

1 Remove the primary and secondary clutches (see Sections 10 and 11). Remove the oil pipe and pump for access to the balancer drive gear (see Section 14).
2 Turn the crankshaft so the match marks on the balancer boss and the balancer drive and driven gears align **(see illustration)**.
3 Bend back the tab on the balancer gear lockwasher **(see illustration)**. Wedge a rag between the teeth of the balancer drive and driven gears to prevent them from turning, undo the nut and remove the lockwasher.
4 Pull off the driven gear and remove the Woodruff key **(see illustration)**.
5 Slide the collar off the end of the balancer **(see illustration)**.
6 Remove the snap-ring **(see illustration)**. Remove the holding

13.6a Remove the drive gear snap-ring (if equipped) . . .

Chapter 2 Part A Engine, clutch and transmission (1993 through 1999 400 models)   2A-15

13.6b ... and the holding plate

13.7a Pull off the drive gear ...

13.7b ... the six springs and the three dowels; a dowel fits inside every other spring on assembly

13.8 Remove the buffer boss with a puller; replace the buffer boss and its Woodruff key with new ones whenever they're removed

13.9a Remove the plain washer and the oil pump drive gear ...

plate **(see illustration)**.

7   Grasp the drive gear and pull it off the buffer boss **(see illustration)**. The six springs and three pins will fall out as you do this, so be prepared to catch them **(see illustration)**.

8   Place a puller on the buffer boss and pull it free of the crankshaft

(see illustration). **Note:** *Yamaha recommends replacing the buffer boss and its Woodruff key with new ones whenever they are removed from the crankshaft.*

9   Once the buffer boss is loose, remove it, the plain washer, the collar, the oil pump drive gear and two Woodruff keys - one for the buffer boss and one for the oil pump drive gear **(see illustrations)**.

13.9b ... the buffer boss Woodruff key ...

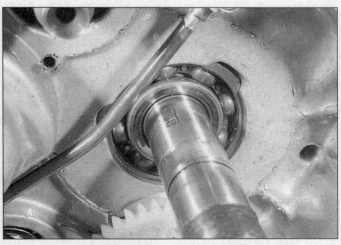

13.9c ... and the oil pump drive gear Woodruff key

2A-16 Chapter 2 Part A Engine, clutch and transmission (1993 through 1999 400 models)

13.14 Install the lockwasher so its tab fits into the shaft slot

14.2 Remove the union bolt and two sealing washers at each end of the pipe

Inspection
10 Check the gears for worn or damaged teeth and replace them as a set if problems are found.
11 Check the springs for distortion or fatigue and replace them as necessary.
12 Check the remaining components for wear and damage and replace any worn or damaged parts. Replace the lockwasher with a new one whenever it's removed.
13 Inspect the balancer and crankshaft ball bearings to the extent possible without disassembling the crankcase. If wear, looseness or roughness can be detected, the crankcase will have to be disassembled to replace the bearings.

Installation
Refer to illustration 13.14
14 Installation is the reverse of the removal steps, with the following additions:
   a) Use a new buffer boss and Woodruff key.
   b) Apply engine oil to the crankshaft after installing the oil pump drive gear Woodruff key, and again after installing the buffer boss Woodruff key.
   c) Install the buffer boss with the same tool used to install the crankshaft (see Part D of this Chapter). The basic tool is crankshaft installer set YM-90050; you'll also need pot extension YM-33280, adapter YM-33279 and buffer boss installer set 98890-04088. If you don't have the correct special tool, take the engine to a Yamaha dealer and have the buffer boss installed.
   d) Make sure the alignment marks on the buffer boss, drive gear and driven gear are lined up **(see illustration 13.2)**.
   e) Use a new lockwasher and make sure its tab fits in the slot in the balancer shaft **(see illustration)**. Tighten the nut to the torque listed in this Chapter's Specifications.

14 Oil pipe and pump - removal, inspection and installation

Note: *The oil pipe and pump can be removed with the engine in the frame.*

Oil pipe
Removal
Refer to illustration 14.2
1 Remove the primary and secondary clutches (see Sections 10 and 11).

14.8a Loosen the pump cover screw (A) if you plan to take the pump apart; remove the mounting screws (B) . . .

2 Remove the union bolt and hex bolts that secure the oil pipe and remove the pipe **(see illustration)**.

Inspection
3 Check the oil pipe for bending and for cracks, especially where the banjo fittings are brazed to the pipe. Replace it if problems are found.
4 Clean the inside of the pipe with solvent to remove any clogging.

Installation
5 Installation is the reverse of the removal steps, with the following additions:
   a) Use new sealing washers on each side of the banjo fitting at both ends of the pipe.
   b) Tighten the bolts to the torque listed in this Chapter's Specifications.

Oil pump
Removal, disassembly and assembly
Refer to illustrations 14.8a, 14.8b, 14.9 and 14.10
6 Remove the primary clutch (see Section 10).
7 Remove the balancer drive gear and oil pump drive gear (see Section 13).
8 Rotate the oil pump driven gear for access to the mounting screws **(see illustration)**. If you're planning to disassemble the pump, loosen the assembly screw now while the pump is secured to the engine.

Chapter 2 Part A Engine, clutch and transmission (1993 through 1999 400 models)   2A-17

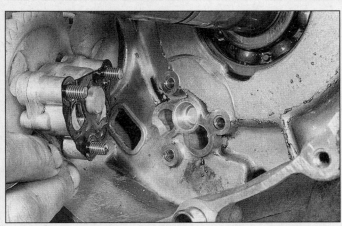

14.8b ... and take the pump and gasket off the engine

14.9 Remove the oil pump assembly screw

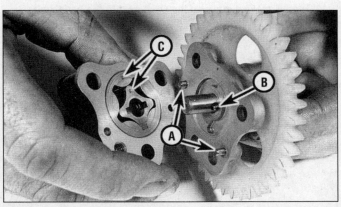

14.10 Take the cover and driven gear off the pump body and rotors; on reassembly, the dowels (A) must fit in the holes, the drive pin must fit in the slot (B) and the punch marks (C) must face the pump cover

Remove the mounting screws and take the pump and gasket off **(see illustration)**.

9   Remove the assembly screw **(see illustration)**.
10   Remove the driven gear, shaft and pump cover from the pump body **(see illustration)**.
11   Refer to Part D of this Chapter for oil pump inspection procedures.
12   Reassemble the pump by reversing the disassembly steps, with the following additions:
  a) Before installing the cover, pack the cavities between the rotors with petroleum jelly - this will ensure the pump develops suction quickly and begins oil circulation as soon as the engine is started.
  b) Make sure the cover dowels and drive pin are in position **(see illustration 14.10)**.
  c) Tighten the cover screw to the torque listed in this Chapter's Specifications.

Installation

13   Installation is the reverse of removal, with the following additions:
  a) Install a new gasket **(see illustration 14.8b)**.
  b) Tighten the oil pump mounting screws to the torque listed in this Chapter's Specifications.

15   Recoil starter - removal, inspection and installation

Removal

1   Unbolt the recoil starter case from the left side of the engine. Take the starter assembly off.
2   Pull the rope partway out and tie a knot in it so it won't be pulled into the case, then remove the cap and the starter handle.

Inspection

Warning: *Rewinding the coil spring is complicated and can be potentially dangerous. If you don't have experience with recoil starters, take the job to a Yamaha dealer or other qualified shop. If you do the job yourself, wear eye protection and heavy gloves in case the recoil spring flies out.*

3   Remove the nut, then the friction plate with its spring clip, the drive pawl, pawl spring, sheave drum and coil spring.
4   Check for obvious wear or damage, such as a broken rope. Replace worn or damaged parts.

Installation

5   Tie a knot in one end of the rope and pull it through the hole in the center of the sheave drum so the rope is in the sheave drum groove. Place the sheave drum on a work surface so the slit in its outer edge is up. Wind the rope 4-1/2 turns clockwise around the sheave drum, then lodge the rope in the slit in the edge of the sheave drum.
6   Install the pawl spring and pawl in the sheave drum.
7   Engage the hook on one end of the starter spring with the slit in the case (the slit closest to the outer edge of the case), then wind the spring clockwise, from the outside in, and engage the hook on its free end with the hook in the center of the case.
8   Install the spring clip and friction plate, engaging the ends of the spring clip with the starter pawl holes.
9   With the case down on a work surface, turn the sheave drum three turns clockwise to preload the starter spring. Pull the rope out through the starter case as you do this, then tie a temporary knot in the rope so it won't be pulled back into the case.
10   Slip the starter handle into the rope and tie a permanent knot in its end, then install the cap.
11   Untie the temporary knot in the rope and let it back into the case.
12   Install the recoil starter on the engine, engaging it with the rotor. Install the case bolts and tighten them to the torque listed in this Chapter's Specifications.

16   External shift mechanism - removal, inspection and installation

Shift pedal

Removal

Refer to illustration 16.1

1   Look for alignment marks on the end of the shift pedal and shift

2A-18 Chapter 2 Part A Engine, clutch and transmission (1993 through 1999 400 models)

16.1 If there aren't visible alignment marks on the shift shaft and pedal, make a mark on the shaft next to the pedal gap

16.7 Pull the shift shaft out of the crankcase and remove the thrust washer (arrow)

16.8 Remove the stopper lever and spring

16.11 Check the shift shaft components for wear or damage

shaft **(see illustration)**. If they aren't visible, make your own marks with a sharp punch.
2   Remove the shift pedal pinch bolt and slide the pedal off the shaft.

Inspection
3   Check the shift pedal for wear or damage such as bending. Check the splines on the shift pedal and shaft for stripping or step wear. Replace the pedal or shaft if these problems are found.
4   Check the shift shaft seal in the alternator cover for signs of leakage. If the seal has been leaking, remove the alternator cover (see Chapter 9). Pry the seal out of the cover, then tap in a new one with a seal driver or socket the same diameter as the seal.

Installation
5   Install the shift pedal. Line up its punch marks and tighten the pinch bolt to the torque listed in this Chapter's Specifications.

External shift linkage
Removal
Refer to illustrations 16.7 and 16.8
6   Remove the right crankcase cover (see Section 15).
7   Pull the shift shaft and its washer out of the crankcase **(see illustration)**.
8   Unbolt the stopper arm, then remove the arm and its spring **(see illustration)**.
9   Remove the Torx screw from the center of the shift drum segment.
10   Remove the shift drum segment and note the location of its dowel.

Inspection
Refer to illustrations 16.11 and 16.12
11   Check the shift shaft for bends and damage to the splines **(see illustration)**. If the shaft is bent, you can attempt to straighten it, but if the splines are damaged it will have to be replaced. Check the condition of the return spring, shift arm and the pawl spring. Replace the shift shaft if they're worn, cracked or distorted.
12   Make sure the return spring post isn't loose **(see illustration)**.

16.12 If the return spring post is loose, unscrew it, then reinstall it with thread locking agent and a new lockwasher

Chapter 2 Part A Engine, clutch and transmission (1993 through 1999 400 models) 2A-19

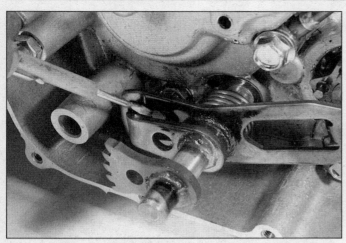

16.15a Pry apart the return spring and position it over the post

16.15b Make sure the ratchet pawls engage the shift drum pins

If it is, bend back its lockwasher and unscrew it. Apply a non-hardening locking compound to the threads, then reinstall the post with a new lockwasher and tighten it to the torque listed in this Chapter's Specifications.

Installation
Refer to illustrations 16.15a and 16.15b

13 Position the spring on the stopper arm, then install the stopper arm on the engine and tighten its bolt to the torque listed in this Chapter's Specifications.

14 Pull down the stopper arm and install the drum segment on the shift drum, making sure its dowel is located in the drum segment notch **(see illustration 16.8)**. Apply non-permanent thread locking agent to the threads of the shift cam segment Torx screw, then install it and tighten to the torque listed in this Chapter's Specifications. Make sure the stopper arm spring is correctly installed and that the roller end of the stopper arm engages a notch in the drum center.

15 Place the washer on the shift shaft and slide it into the engine **(see illustration 16.7)**. Slide the shaft all the way in, making sure the return spring fits over the post and the pawls engage the drum segment pins **(see illustrations)**.

16 The remainder of installation is the reverse of the removal steps.

17 Check the engine oil level and add some, if necessary (see Chapter 1).

17 Crankcase - disassembly and reassembly

1 To examine and repair or replace the crankshaft, connecting rod, bearings and transmission components, the crankcase must be split into two parts.

Disassembly
Refer to illustrations 17.11a, 17.11b, 17.11c, 17.12a, 17.12b, 17.12c, 17.12d and 17.13

2 Remove the engine from the vehicle (see Section 5).
3 Remove the carburetor (see Chapter 4).
4 Remove the alternator rotor and the starter motor (see Chapter 9).
5 Remove the primary and secondary clutches (see Sections 10 and 11).
6 Remove the external shift mechanism (see Section 16).
7 Remove the reverse shift cam detent ball and spring (see Section 12).
8 Remove the cam chain tensioner, cylinder head, cam chain, cylinder and piston (see Sections 6, 7, 8 and Part D of this Chapter).
9 Remove the oil pump (see Section 14).

10 Check carefully to make sure there aren't any remaining components that attach the halves of the crankcase together.
11 Loosen the crankcase bolts in two or three stages, in a criss-cross pattern **(see illustrations)**. Remove the bolts and label them; they are different lengths **(see illustration)**.

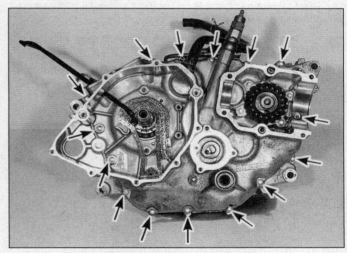

17.11a Crankcase bolts (arrows) . . .

17.11b . . . this bolt has a copper washer

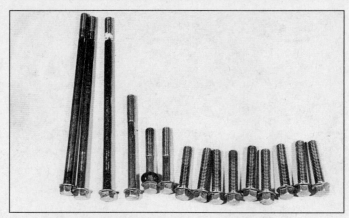

17.11c The bolts are different lengths; labeling them will speed reassembly

17.12a Using a soft face hammer, tap gently and evenly on the ends of the shafts as the case halves are separated

12 Tap gently on the ends of the transmission shafts, balancer shaft and crankshaft as the case halves are being separated **(see illustration)**. Carefully pry the crankcase apart at the pry points and lift the right half off the left half **(see illustrations)**. Don't pry against the mating surfaces or they'll develop leaks.

13 Locate the crankcase dowels **(see illustration)**. If they aren't secure in their holes, remove them and set them aside for safekeeping.

14 Refer to Section 17 and Part D of this Chapter for information on the internal components of the crankcase.

Reassembly

Refer to illustrations 17.17 and 17.18

15 Remove all traces of old gasket and sealant from the crankcase mating surfaces with a sharpening stone or similar tool. Be careful not to let any fall into the case as this is done and be careful not to damage the mating surfaces.

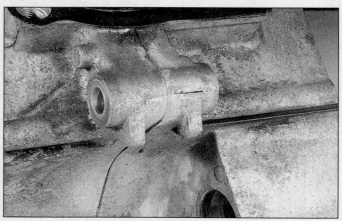

17.12b Pry only between the pry points . . .

17.12c . . . there's one at each end of the case

17.12d Lift the right case half off the left case half

17.13 Make sure the case dowels (arrows) are in place

Chapter 2 Part A Engine, clutch and transmission (1993 through 1999 400 models)   2A-21

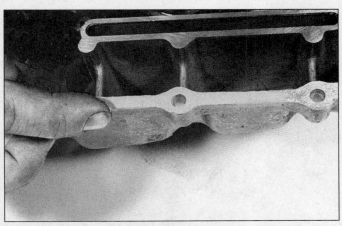

17.17 Coat both case halves with a thin film of sealant

17.18 Pour oil over the gears and shafts

18.3a Pull out the longer guide bar (arrow) . . .

18.3b . . . and remove its shift forks

16   Check to make sure the dowel pins are in place in their holes in the mating surface of the crankcase **(see illustration 17.13)**.
17   Coat both crankcase mating surfaces with Yamaha Quick Gasket (ACC-11001-05-01) or equivalent sealant **(see illustration)**.
18   Pour some engine oil over the transmission gears, balancer shaft and crankshaft bearing surfaces and the shift cams **(see illustration)**. Don't get any oil on the crankcase mating surfaces.
19   Carefully place the right crankcase half onto the left crankcase half.

While doing this, make sure the transmission shafts, shift drums, crankshaft and balancer fit into their ball bearings in the right crankcase half.
20   Install the crankcase half bolts in the correct holes and tighten them so they are just snug. Then tighten them in two or three stages, in a criss-cross pattern, to the torque listed in this Chapter's Specifications (don't forget to install the copper washer).
21   Turn the transmission shafts to make sure they turn freely. Also make sure the crankshaft and balancer shaft turn freely.
22   The remainder of installation is the reverse of removal.

18 Transmission shafts, balancer shaft and shift cam - removal, inspection and installation

Note: *When disassembling the transmission shafts, place the parts on a long rod or thread a wire through them to keep them in order and facing the proper direction.*

Removal
Refer to illustrations 18.3a, 18.3b, 18.3c, 18.4, 18.8, 18.10a, 18.10b, 18.10c, 18.11a, 18.11b and 18.12

1   Remove the engine, then separate the case halves (see Sections 5 and 17).
2   The transmission components and shift cams remain in the left case half when the case is separated.
3   Pull out the longer guide bar and the two no. 1 shift forks **(see illustrations)**. Lift the shift cam out of the case half, then remove the shorter guide bar and no. 2 shift fork **(see illustration)**.

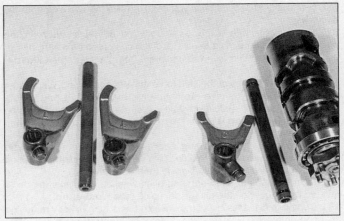

18.3c No. 1 shift cam, shift forks and shafts

2A-22 Chapter 2 Part A Engine, clutch and transmission (1993 through 1999 400 models)

18.4 Lift out the balancer shaft, then remove the plain washer (arrow), reverse wheel gear and reverse axle

18.8 Remove the driveaxle (left arrow) and main axle (right arrow) from the case

18.10a Note the positions of the shift forks and the numbers cast on them

18.10b Remove the snap-ring, plain washer and middle driven gear . . .

4   Lift the balancer shaft out of the crankcase (see illustration).
5   Remove the plain washer from the reverse wheel gear, then remove the gear from the reverse axle and lift the reverse axle out of the crankcase (see illustration 18.4 and the accompanying illustration).
6   From the driveaxle, remove the plain washer, high pinion gear, first wheel gear and second plain washer.
7   From the idle axle, remove the plain washer, high wheel gear with bearings and second plain washer. Remove the idle axle from the crankcase.
8   Remove the fifth wheel gear from the driveaxle, then lift the driveaxle and its remaining gears out of the case (see illustration).
9   Remove the main axle with its gears from the case (see illustration 18.8).
10 Note the positions of the shift forks that engage the no. 2 shift cam (see illustration). Remove the snap-ring, plain washer and middle driven gear from the middle driveaxle, then remove the middle driven gear holder (see illustrations). Remove the guide bar, shift forks and no. 2 shift cam.
11 Remove another snap-ring and plain washer from the middle driveaxle, then remove the middle drive gear (see illustration). Slide the dog clutch off the middle driveaxle (see illustration).
12 Remove another snap-ring and plain washer, then take the no. 2 reverse wheel gear off the middle driveaxle (see illustration).
13 Complete disassembly of the driveaxle and main axle by removing the snap-rings, plain washers and gears (see illustration 18.5).

18.10c . . . the middle driven gear holder . . .

18.11a ... the snap-ring (arrow), plain washer and middle drive gear ...

18.11b ... the dog clutch ...

18.12 ... and the snap-ring, plain washer and reverse wheel gear

18.23 Install the metal cup and spring on the guide bar

Inspection

14 Wash all of the components in clean solvent and dry them off. Rotate the middle driven shaft, feeling for tightness, rough spots, excessive looseness and listening for noises in the bearing or middle drive bevel gear. Replacement of the bevel gear or shaft will require setting up the gear backlash of the middle driven gear; take the case and middle driven gear assembly (which includes the transfer case on 4WD models) to a Yamaha dealer to have this procedure done.

15 Inspect the shift fork grooves in the gears, the middle driven gear holder and the dog clutch. If a groove is worn or scored, replace the affected part and inspect its corresponding shift fork.

16 Check the shift forks for distortion and wear, especially at the fork ears **(see illustration 18.3c)**. If they are discolored or severely worn they are probably bent. Inspect the guide pins for excessive wear and distortion and replace any defective parts with new ones.

17 Check the shift fork guide bars for evidence of wear, galling and other damage. Make sure the shift forks move smoothly on the guide bars. If the shafts are worn or bent, replace them with new ones.

18 Check the edges of the grooves in the shift cams for signs of excessive wear.

19 Hold the inner race of the shift cam bearing with fingers and spin the outer race. Replace the bearing if it's rough, loose or noisy. Replace the segment on the no. 1 shift cam if it's worn or damaged.

20 Check the gear teeth for cracking and other obvious damage.

Check the bushing surface in the inner diameter of the freewheeling gears for scoring or heat discoloration. Replace damaged parts.

21 Inspect the engagement dogs and dog holes on gears so equipped for excessive wear or rounding off. Replace the paired gears as a set if necessary.

22 Check the transmission shaft bearings in the crankcase for wear or heat discoloration and replace them if necessary (see Part D of this Chapter).

Installation

Refer to illustration 18.23

23 Installation is the basically the reverse of the removal procedure, but take note of the following points:

a) Use new snap-rings.
b) Align the flat on the end of the idle axle with the corresponding flat in the transmission case.
c) Don't forget the metal cup and spring on the guide bar for the no. 2 shift cam **(see illustration)**.
d) Lubricate the components with engine oil before assembling them.
e) After assembly, check the gears to make sure they're installed correctly. Move the shift cams through the gear positions and rotate the gears to make sure they mesh and shift correctly.

Notes

Chapter 2 Part B
Engine, clutch and transmission (2000 and later 400/450 models)

Contents

	Section
Balancer and crankshaft - removal and installation	14
Cam chain tensioner - removal and installation	5
Crankcase - disassembly and reassembly	12
Cylinder - removal and installation	9
Cylinder head, camshaft and rocker arms - removal, inspection and installation	6
Drivebelt and pulleys - general information, removal, inspection and installation	10
Engine - removal and installation	4
External oil pipe and oil pump gears - removal and installation	11
General information	1
Oil pump - removal and installation	13
Operations possible with the engine in the frame	2
Operations requiring engine removal	3
Recoil starter - removal, inspection and installation	8
Shift select mechanism - removal, inspection and installation	7
Transmission shafts, forks and shift cam - removal, inspection and installation	15

Specifications

General
Bore	84.5 mm (3.33 inches)
Stroke	
400 models	71.5 mm (2.81 inches)
450 models	75.0 mm (2.95 inches)
Displacement	
400 models	401 cc
450 models	421 cc

Centrifugal clutch
Lining thickness	
Standard	1.5 mm (0.08 inch)
Limit	1.0 mm (0.04 inch)
Drivebelt width	
Standard	30.7 mm (1.21 inches)
Limit	27.6 mm (1.09 inches)

Transmission
Main axle and driveaxle runout limit	0.06 mm (0.0024 inch)

Torque specifications
Cylinder head oil passage union bolt	7 Nm (61 inch-lbs)
Cylinder head bolts	
M6 thread	10 Nm (86 inch-lbs)
M10 thread	40 Nm (29 ft-lbs)
Cam sprocket cover Allen bolts	10 Nm (86 inch-lbs)
Oil check bolt	7 Nm (61 inch-lbs)
Camshaft bearing retainer bolts	8 Nm (70 inch-lbs)
Cam chain guide bolts	10 Nm (86 inch-lbs)
Camshaft sprocket bolt	60 Nm (43 ft-lbs)
Cam chain tensioner body bolts	11 Nm (96 inch-lbs)
Cam chain tensioner cap bolt	23 Nm (17 ft-lbs)

2B-2 Chapter 2 Part B Engine, clutch and transmission (2000 and later 400/450 models)

Torque specifications

Crankcase bolts	10 Nm (86 inch-lbs)
Shift lever cover bolts	10 Nm (86 inch-lbs)
Shift lever pivot bolt	14 Nm (120 inch-lbs)
Crankcase bearing retainer screws (left side)	10 Nm (86 inch-lbs)
Crankcase bearing retainer screw (right side)	11 Nm (96 inch-lbs)
Oil pump gear locknut	50 Nm (36 ft-lbs)
Oil pump mounting screws	8 Nm (70 inch-lbs)
Oil pump assembly screw	7 Nm (61 inch-lbs)
Centrifugal clutch nut	140 Nm (100 ft-lbs)
Centrifugal clutch housing bolts	10 Nm (86 inch-lbs)
Centrifugal clutch cover bolts	10 Nm (86 inch-lbs)
Drive and driven pulley nuts	100 Nm (72 ft-lbs)
Bearing housing bolts (inside pulley cover)	10 Nm (72 ft-lbs)
Middle driveaxle bearing retainer screws	25 Nm (18 ft-lbs)
Middle driveaxle bearing housing bolts	32 Nm (23 ft-lbs)
Middle driveaxle pinion gear nut	130 Nm (94 ft-lbs)

1 General information

The engine/transmission unit is of the liquid-cooled, single-cylinder four-stroke design. The valves are operated by a chain and sprockets. The engine/transmission assembly is constructed from aluminum alloy. The crankcase is divided vertically.

The crankcase incorporates a wet sump, pressure-fed lubrication system which uses a gear-driven rotor-type oil pump, oil filter and separate strainer screen.

Power from the crankshaft is routed to the internal transmission gears via a constantly variable transmission, consisting of a drivebelt and two variable-diameter pulleys. These change the effective gear ratio automatically, so no clutch or conventional transmission gears are needed. A one-way clutch in the front pulley allows the engine to provide compression braking when the throttle is released. The internal transmission gears provide forward and reverse ranges, as well as a low range on some models.

2 Operations possible with the engine in the frame

The components and assemblies listed below can be removed without having to remove the engine from the frame. If, however, a number of areas require attention at the same time, removal of the engine is recommended.

4.6 Here is the crankcase breather hose (center arrow) and camshaft cover bolts (outer arrows)

Recoil starter
Starter motor
Starter reduction gears
Starter clutch
Alternator rotor and stator
Drivebelt and pulleys
Shift select lever and linkage
Cam chain tensioner
Camshaft
Rocker arms and shafts
Cylinder head
Cylinder and piston

3 Operations requiring engine removal

It is necessary to remove the engine/transmission assembly from the frame and separate the crankcase halves to gain access to the following components:

Oil pump
Balancer
Crankshaft and connecting rod
Transmission shafts
Shift drum and forks

4 Engine - removal and installation

Note: *Engine removal and installation should be done with the aid of an assistant to avoid damage or injury that could occur if the engine is dropped. A hydraulic floor jack should be used to support and lower the engine if possible (they can be rented at low cost).*

Removal

Refer to illustrations 4.6, 4.7, 4.12a, 4.12b and 4.12c

1 Drain the engine oil and cooling system and disconnect the spark plug wire (see Chapter 1).
2 Remove the fuel tank, carburetor, air cleaner housing and exhaust system (see Chapter 4). Plug the carburetor intake openings with rags.
3 Remove the front and rear fenders and the footrests (see Chapter 8).
4 Disconnect the shift rod, then unbolt the select lever housing and take it off (see Section 7).
5 Remove the coolant reservoir and disconnect the inlet hose from the water pump (see Chapter 3).

Chapter 2 Part B Engine, clutch and transmission (2000 and later 400/450 models)   2B-3

4.7 Disconnect the engine ground cable (arrow)

4.12a Upper engine mount through-bolt (lower arrow) and mount-to-frame bolts (upper arrows)

6   Disconnect the breather hose from the cylinder head **(see illustration)**.
7   Disconnect the engine ground cable **(see illustration)**.
8   Label and disconnect the following wires (refer to Chapters 5 or 9 for component location if necessary):

Ignition pulse generator
Alternator
Gear position switches
Coolant temperature switch
Speed sensor

9   Remove the rear wheels (see Chapter 7).
10 Remove the swingarm or final drive unit (see Chapter 6).
11 Support the engine securely from below. **Note:** *Use a jack (preferably a floor jack) that can be repositioned if necessary as the engine mounting bolts are removed.*
12 Remove the engine mounting bolts, nuts and brackets at the rear, lower front and upper front **(see illustrations)**.
13 Have an assistant help you lift the engine. If you're working on a 4WD model, pull the engine rearward to disengage the front driveshaft from the engine.
14 Slowly lower the engine to a suitable work surface.

Installation

15 Check the rubber engine supports for wear or damage and replace them if necessary before installing the engine.
16 Coat the driveshaft splines with moly-based grease. Install the engine from the left side of the vehicle and move it forward to engage the driveshaft with the engine (refer to Chapter 6 if necessary).
17 Lift the engine to align the mounting bolt holes, then install the brackets and mounting bolts in the following order, but don't tighten them yet:

a) Upper front bracket to engine
b) Upper front bracket to frame
c) Lower front bracket to engine
d) Lower front bracket to frame
e) Upper rear mounting bolt
f) Lower rear mounting bolt

18 Tighten the mounts in the same order they were installed to the torques listed in this Chapter's Specifications.
19 The remainder of installation is the reverse of the removal steps, with the following additions:

a) *Use new gaskets at all exhaust pipe connections.*
b) *Adjust the shift linkage following the procedures in Chapter 1.*
c) *Fill the engine oil and coolant and check the differential oil level, also following the procedures in Chapter 1. Run the engine and check for leaks.*

5 Cam chain tensioner - removal and installation

This is the same as for 1993 through 1999 models. Refer to Part A for procedures and to this Chapter's Specifications for tightening torques.

4.12b Here's the lower left engine mount (there's another one on the opposite side of the engine) . . .

4.12c . . . and here are the rear upper and lower through-bolts (arrows)

2B-4 Chapter 2 Part B Engine, clutch and transmission (2000 and later 400/450 models)

6.4 The camshaft dowel aligns with the sprocket line and the cast indicator

6.6a Remove the camshaft sprocket bolt and oil thrower

6 Cylinder head, camshaft and rocker arms - removal, inspection and installation

Camshaft removal

Refer to illustrations 6.4, 6.6a, 6.6b and 6.7

1 Remove the fuel tank, front fenders and air cleaner housing (see Chapters 4 and 8).
2 Remove the valve adjusting hole covers (see Chapter 1).
3 Remove the Allen bolts and take the sprocket cover off (see illustration 4.6).
4 Refer to *Valve clearances - check and adjustment* in Chapter 1 and place the engine at top dead center on the compression stroke. The cam sprocket notch will align with the indicator cast into the cylinder head and the rocker arms will be loose when the cylinder is at TDC compression (see illustration).
5 Prevent the crankshaft from turning. To do this, remove the recoil starter as described in Section 8. Hold the recoil starter pulley (if equipped) with a clutch holder tool. If the factory tool or an equivalent isn't available, you can make your own from some steel strap, bent at the ends and bolted together in the middle (see illustration 7.5 in Chapter 2A).
6 Unbolt the plate and cam sprocket and take them off the camshaft (see illustration). Disengage the sprocket from the chain and support the chain with wire so it doesn't fall down off the crankshaft sprocket.

Unbolt the camshaft bearing retainer from the head (see illustration).
7 Thread a 10 mm bolt into the end of the camshaft and use it as a handle to pull the camshaft out of the cylinder head (see illustration 7.8 in Chapter 2A). **Caution:** *The camshaft should come out easily. If it seems stuck, make sure it isn't caught on the rocker arms.*

Rocker arm removal

Refer to illustration 6.8

8 Thread a 6 mm bolt into the end of each rocker arm shaft (see illustration 7.9 in Chapter 2A). Support the rocker and use the bolt as a handle to pull out the shaft. **Note:** *If the shaft is stuck, it may be necessary to use a slide hammer. These can be rented from equipment rental yards (some auto parts stores also rent tools).* Once the shaft has been removed, remove the rocker arm through the camshaft hole (see illustration).

Cylinder head removal

Refer to illustrations 6.11 and 6.12

9 Disconnect the spark plug wire if you haven't already done so (see Chapter 1).
10 Remove the two small cylinder head bolts (see illustration 7.10 in Chapter 2A).
11 Loosen the four main cylinder head bolts 1/4-turn each, in the reverse order of the tightening sequence (see illustration). Then loosen them the rest of the way and remove them.

6.6b Bend back the lockwasher tabs, remove the bolts (arrows) and take off the lockwasher, bearing retainer and rocker shaft retainers

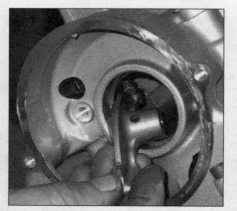

6.8 Once the camshaft and rocker shafts have been removed, the rocker arms can be withdrawn through the camshaft hole

6.11 Loosen and tighten the main head bolts (arrows) in a criss-cross pattern

Chapter 2 Part B Engine, clutch and transmission (2000 and later 400/450 models)   2B-5

6.12 Here are the cylinder head dowels; one has an O-ring (upper arrow)

6.21 The exhaust side chain guide fits in a pocket (left arrow); the intake side guide is bolted (right arrows)

7.1 Remove the bolt and washer and slip the shift lever off the shaft

12   Lift the cylinder head off the cylinder (**see illustration**). If it's stuck, don't attempt to pry it off - tap around the sides with a plastic hammer to dislodge it. Be careful not to tap against the cooling fins; they're easily broken.
13   Locate the cylinder head dowels (**see illustration 6.12**). They may be in the cylinder or they may have come off with the head.

Cam chain and guide removal
14   Lift the front cam chain guide out of the cylinder (**see illustration 6.12**). The rear guide is bolted at the bottom, so the recoil starter and alternator rotor will have to be removed for access if the guide or the cam chain need to be removed.
15   Stuff clean rags into the cam chain openings so dirt, small parts or tools can't fall into them.

Installation
Refer to illustration 6.21
16   Install a new O-ring on each rocker shaft. Coat the rocker shafts and rocker arm bores with moly-based grease. Thread a 6 mm bolt into the end of each rocker shaft to use as a handle. Insert each rocker arm into the valve adjusting hole, hold it in its installed position and install the rocker shaft in the rocker arm and cylinder head. Be sure to install the intake and exhaust rocker arms and shafts in the correct sides of the head.
17   Install the inner camshaft bearing in the cylinder head and outer bearing on the camshaft (if they were removed). The sealed side of the outer bearing faces out (away from the cylinder head). Lubricate the camshaft bearings with engine oil.
18   Install the camshaft in the cylinder head. The camshaft dowel should be up, so it aligns with the indicator in the cylinder head, when the camshaft is installed (**see illustration 6.4**).
19   Install the bearing retainer and a new lockwasher (**see illustration 6.6b**). Tighten the bearing retainer bolts to the torque listed in this Chapter's Specifications.
20   Install the dowel pins and the O-ring that surrounds one of the dowels, then place the new head gasket on the cylinder (**see illustration 6.12**). Never reuse the old gasket and don't use any type of gasket sealant.
21   Install the exhaust side cam chain damper, fitting the lower guide into its notch (**see illustration**).
22   Carefully lower the cylinder head over the dowels and O-ring, guiding the cam chain through the slot in the cylinder head. It's helpful to have an assistant support the cam chain with a piece of wire so it doesn't fall and become kinked or detached from the crankshaft. When the head is resting on the cylinder, wire the cam chain to another component to keep tension on it.
23   Lubricate the threads of the cylinder head bolts with engine oil, then install them finger-tight. Tighten the four main bolts in the correct sequence (**see illustration 6.11**), in several stages, to the torque listed in this Chapter's Specifications. After the main bolts are tightened, tighten the two small bolts to the torque listed in this Chapter's Specifications.
24   Refer to the valve adjustment procedure in Chapter 1 and make sure the timing mark with the T next to it is aligned with the notch in the timing hole. If it's necessary to turn the crankshaft, hold the cam chain up so it doesn't fall off the crankshaft sprocket and become jammed.
25   Engage the camshaft sprocket with the timing chain so its dowel hole aligns with the dowel (**see illustration 6.6**). Slip the sprocket onto the camshaft over the dowel, then install the sprocket bolt finger-tight. The line on the cam sprocket should be aligned with the cast indicator in the cylinder head (**see illustration 6.4**).
26   Twist the cam sprocket in both directions to remove the slack from the cam chain. Insert a screwdriver in the cam chain tensioner hole and push against the cam chain guide. With the guide pushed in, the cam sprocket line and cast indicator should line up (**see illustration 6.4**). If they don't, remove the cam sprocket from the chain, reposition it and try again. Don't continue with assembly until the marks are lined up correctly.
27   Tighten the cam sprocket bolt to the torque listed in this Chapter's Specifications.
28   Apply engine oil to a new O-ring for the cam sprocket cover. Install the O-ring and cover and tighten the Allen bolts to the torque listed in this Chapter's Specifications.
29   Install the cam chain tensioner (see Section 7).
30   Change the engine oil and fill the cooling system (see Chapter 1).
31   Adjust the valve clearances (see Chapter 1).
32   The remainder of installation is the reverse of removal.

7   Shift select mechanism - removal, inspection and installation

Shift lever and linkage
Removal
Refer to illustrations 7.1, 7.2a and 7.2b
1   Disconnect the lockout cable at the lower end (see Chapter 1). Detach the shift rod from the engine (**see illustration**).

2B-6   Chapter 2 Part B   Engine, clutch and transmission (2000 and later 400/450 models)

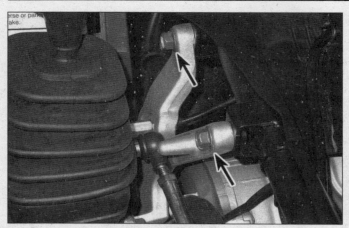

7.2a Remove the mounting bolts (arrows) . . .

7.2b . . . and take the shift lever off, together with the shift rod and lockout cable

7.8a Remove the cover and gasket, then pull out the no. 1 (upper) shift lever and its O-ring

2   Remove the mounting bolts and take the lever housing off, together with the shift rod and lockout cable **(see illustrations)**.

Inspection
3   Check the rubber boot for cracks or deterioration. If problems are found, undo its rubber retainer and pull it off. Install a new boot, using a new retainer.

4   Check the inside of the housing for worn or damaged parts. Replace the housing as an assembly if problems are found.

Installation
5   Installation is the reverse of the removal steps, with the following additions:
   a) Tighten the housing bolts to the torque listed in this Chapter's Specifications.
   b) Adjust the cable and rod (see Chapter 1).

External shifter
Removal
Refer to illustrations 7.8a, 7.8b and 7.9

6   Remove bodywork components as necessary for access.
7   Detach the shifter lever from the shaft, then unbolt the shifter cover and take it off the engine **(see illustrations 7.1 and 4.7)**.
8   On models with high and low ranges, remove the no. 1 shift lever and O-ring **(see illustration)**. On all models, unscrew the shifter bolt, then remove the plate washer, spring, second plate washer, lever, collar and second lever **(see illustration)**.
9   Turn the shifter back to the neutral position with an open-end wrench after unbolting the shift lever **(see illustration)**.

Inspection
Refer to illustrations 7.10a and 7.10b
10   Check all parts for wear and damage and replace them as needed.

7.8b Slowly and carefully unscrew the bolt and remove the no. 2 shift lever . . .

7.9 . . . after removing the shift lever, use an open-end wrench to return the shaft to the neutral position

7.10a Inspect the no. 2 shift lever components . . .

Chapter 2 Part B Engine, clutch and transmission (2000 and later 400/450 models)

7.10b ... but don't disassemble them unless there's a problem

7.11 Position the single upper mark between the two lower marks (arrows)

9.4 Lift the cylinder off and remove the base O-ring (arrow) ...

Don't disassemble the no. 2 shift lever unless necessary **(see illustrations)**.

Installation

Refer to illustration 7.11

11 Installation is the reverse of the removal steps. On models with a low range, align the dots on the two gears **(see illustration)**. Tighten the shifter bolt to the torque listed in this Chapter's Specifications.

8 Recoil starter - removal, inspection and installation

This is the same as for 1993 through 1999 models. See Part A of this Chapter.

9 Cylinder - removal and installation

Removal

Refer to illustrations 9.4 and 9.5

1 Drain the engine oil and coolant (see Chapter 1).
2 Following the procedure given in Section 7, remove the cylinder head. Make sure the crankshaft is positioned at Top Dead Center (TDC).
3 Lift out the cam chain front guide **(see illustration 6.21)**.
4 Lift the cylinder straight up to remove it **(see illustration)**. If it's stuck, tap around its perimeter with a soft-faced mallet (but don't tap on the cooling fins or they may break). Don't attempt to pry between the cylinder and crankcase as you'll ruin the mating surfaces.
5 Locate the dowel pins (they may have come off with the cylinder or still be in the crankcase **(see illustration)**. Be careful not to let these drop into the engine. Stuff rags around the piston and remove the gasket and all traces of old gasket material from the surfaces of cylinder and crankcase.
6 Refer to Part D of this Chapter to inspect the cylinder.

Installation

7 Lubricate the cylinder bore with plenty of clean engine oil. Apply a thin film of moly-based grease to the piston skirt.
8 Install the dowel pins, then lower a new cylinder base gasket over them **(see illustrations 9.4 and 9.5)**. Install the base O-ring.
9 Attach a piston ring compressor to the piston and compress the piston rings. A large hose clamp can be used instead - just make sure it doesn't scratch the piston, and don't tighten it too much.
10 Install the cylinder and carefully lower it down until the piston crown fits into the cylinder liner **(see illustration 8.10 in Chapter 2A)**. While

9.5 Locate the dowels and note that one of them (upper arrow) has an O-ring

doing this, pull the camshaft chain up, using a hooked tool or piece of stiff wire. Push down on the cylinder, making sure the piston doesn't get cocked sideways, until the bottom of the cylinder liner slides down past the piston rings. A wood or plastic hammer handle can be used to gently tap the cylinder down, but don't use too much force or the piston will be damaged.
11 Remove the ring compressor or hose clamp, being careful not to scratch the piston.
12 The remainder of installation is the reverse of the removal steps.

10 Drivebelt and pulleys - general information, removal, inspection and installation

General information

1 All of the vehicles covered in this Chapter use a belt-drive constantly variable transmission (CVT). This consists of a centrifugal clutch, one-way clutch, drive pulley, drivebelt and driven pulley, all mounted in a sealed housing on the right side of the machine. The CVT connects the engine to the transmission. The transmission on these models is a separate unit from the CVT. It allows the operator to select forward range (high or low on some models) or reverse range. Transmission service is covered in Section 14.
2 The CVT's drive and driven pulleys are variable in diameter. The drive pulley is mounted on the end of the engine crankshaft. The driven pulley is mounted on the transmission input shaft.

10.10a Unscrew the clamp to detach the front duct from the engine . . .

10.10b . . . the upper end of the front duct (arrow) is located beneath the front panel

10.10c Loosen the clamp (arrow) and detach the rear duct from the short duct connecting it to the engine . . .

3 At idle, the centrifugal clutch is disengaged, so no power is transmitted from the crankshaft to the drive pulley. As engine speed increases, the centrifugal clutch engages, and power is transmitted from the crankshaft, through the centrifugal clutch, to the drive pulley.

4 At low engine speeds, the drive pulley has a small diameter and the driven pulley has a large diameter. As engine speed increases, the drive pulley diameter gets larger and the driven pulley diameter gets smaller. This changes the effective gear ratio of the CVT.

5 The drive pulley changes its diameter in response to changes in engine speed. At idle and low engine speed, the tension of the drivebelt forces the pulley halves apart, so the pulley diameter is small. As engine speed increases, the drive pulley spins faster. The centrifugal force causes the four shift weights to move outward, sliding along the drive pulley cam and pushing the outer pulley half toward the inner pulley half, which is fixed in position. This makes the pulley groove narrower, so the drive belt rides higher in the pulley groove (closer to the outer edge of the pulley). This causes the driven pulley to be rotated more times for each rotation of the drive pulley (higher gearing).

6 Since the drive belt doesn't change length, the driven pulley must become smaller in diameter as the drive pulley becomes larger. To make this happen, the driven clutch pulley changes diameter in response to the load placed on it by the drive belt. At low engine speeds, the spring in the driven clutch pushes the pulley halves together, which causes the drive belt to ride higher in the groove (closer to the outer edge of the pulley). This is the equivalent of a low gear in a conventional transmission. As engine speed increases, more power is applied to the drive belt. The belt forces the driven pulley halves apart, causing the belt to ride lower in the pulley groove (closer to the center of the pulley). This is the equivalent of a higher gear in a conventional transmission.

7 Some drivebelt CVT systems disengage when the throttle is released, which disengages the wheels from the engine so there is no engine braking (going downhill, for example). On these models, however, engine braking is provided by a one-way clutch in the center of the centrifugal clutch. When the vehicle is moving forward under engine power, the one-way clutch is disengaged. When the throttle is released, the one-way clutch locks up, connecting the crankshaft to the drive pulley. Since the drivebelt is always engaged with the pulleys, the wheels remain connected to the crankshaft through the final drive, transmission, drivebelt and pulleys, and one-way clutch. This allows engine braking to occur.

8 The CVT is air cooled. The cooling air is drawn into the housing by fins on the drive pulley. The air enters a duct at the upper rear, circulates around the pulleys, and exits through another duct.

Removal

Cover and ducts

Refer to illustrations 10.10a through 10.10e, 10.11 and 10.12

9 Remove the front or rear fender and right footboard as necessary for access (see Chapter 8).

10 To remove an air duct, loosen its clamp, remove the mounting bolt(s) and separate the duct from the housing **(see illustrations)**.

11 Remove the cover mounting bolts **(see illustration)**. Tap the cover

10.10d . . . pull out the trim clips (arrows) to free the upper end of the rear duct . . .

10.10e . . . loosen the clamp at the engine and remove the short rear duct

Chapter 2 Part B Engine, clutch and transmission (2000 and later 400/450 models)   2B-9

10.11 Remove the cover bolts (arrows) and remove the cover and gasket

10.12a Remove the bearing cover (arrow) . . .

10.12b . . . and its dowels . . .

10.12c . . . the dowels go in these holes (arrows)

loose if necessary (don't pry it) and separate the cover and gasket from the engine.

12   Remove the bearing housing and locate its dowels **(see illustrations)**.

Pulleys and drivebelt

Refer to illustrations 10.13

13   Look for directional arrows on the belt **(see illustration)**. They should point in the forward direction of the belt along the top run.

14   Prevent the pulleys from turning with a holding tool (Yamaha part

10.13 Make sure there's a directional arrow visible on the belt; if not, make an arrow mark pointing in the forward direction along the top run of the belt

10.14a Remove the drive pulley nut and washer, then take off the outer half of the drive pulley

2B-10 Chapter 2 Part B Engine, clutch and transmission (2000 and later 400/450 models)

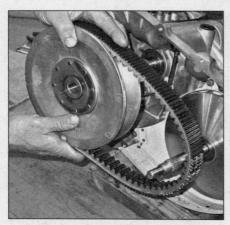

10.14b Remove the driven pulley and drivebelt . . .

10.14c . . . then remove the inner half of the drive pulley

10.16a Unbolt the cover . . .

10.16b . . . and remove the bearing cover bolts (arrows) . . .

10.16c . . . pull off the cover . . .

no. YS-01880-A, 90890-01701 or equivalent. Unscrew the nuts from the driven and drive pulleys (see illustration). Pull the drive pulley outer half off the crankshaft, then remove the drivebelt, drive pulley inner half and driven pulley (see illustrations).

Centrifugal and one-way clutches

Refer to illustrations 10.16a, 10.16b, 10.16c, 10.16d and 10.17

15 Remove the cover and pulleys as described above.

16 Unbolt the cover and centrifugal clutch housing (see illustrations). Take them off, remove the gasket and locate the dowel pins (see illustration).

17 Prevent the clutch carrier from turning with a strap wrench or similar tool. Unstake the locknut with a punch or by grinding away the staked portion (see illustration). Unscrew the locknut, then take the one-way clutch and centrifugal clutch off the crankshaft (see illustration 10.16d).

10.16d . . . and locate the dowels (A), remove the one-way clutch (B) and the centrifugal clutch (C)

10.17 Bend back the staked portion of the locknut (arrow) with a sharp punch and unscrew the nut

Chapter 2 Part B Engine, clutch and transmission (2000 and later 400/450 models)   2B-11

10.22 Remove the snap-ring (arrow) and bearing

10.23 Pry out the oil seal (arrow) and remove the snap-ring, bearing and second snap-ring from under it

10.26 Be sure the directional arrow on the one-way clutch (arrow) is visible when the one-way clutch is installed

Inspection

Cover and ducts

18 Check the cover gasket for damage or deterioration and replace it if its condition is in doubt.

19 Check the cover and ducts for damage and replace them if necessary.

Drivebelt and pulleys

20 Check the drivebelt for wear or damage and replace it if its condition is in doubt (see Chapter 1). Check along the surface that contacts the pulleys for wear, especially for cupped spots that indicate severe slippage. Also check for burn marks caused by belt slippage. If you find any problems, replace the belt. If the belt has been slipping, check the cover gasket for leaks that could allow the entry of water.

21 Check the belt contact surfaces on each pulley for wear, scoring or corrosion. Also check the moving components of each assembly for wear or damage. If there's a problem, have the pulley assembly repaired by a Yamaha dealer or other qualified repair shop.

Centrifugal and one-way clutches

Refer to illustration 10.22, 10.23, 10.26 and 10.27

22 Remove the snap-ring and take the bearing out of the centrifugal clutch housing **(see illustration)**.

23 Pry the oil seal out of the bearing housing **(see illustration)**. Remove the snap-ring from each side and remove the large bearing.

24 Spin the bearings with fingers and check for roughness, looseness or noise. Replace it if problems are found.

25 Check the one-way clutch for visible wear or damage and replace it if problems are found. If the one-way clutch needs to be replaced, the centrifugal clutch housing should also be replaced.

26 Place the one-way clutch in the centrifugal clutch housing with the arrow mark toward the clutch housing **(see illustration)**. Install the centrifugal clutch in the one-way clutch. Try to turn the centrifugal clutch clockwise. It should turn easily clockwise, but should lock up when you try to turn it counterclockwise. If not, replace the one-way clutch and housing.

27 Check the friction surfaces of the centrifugal clutch for wear or damage **(see illustration)**. Measure the depth of the clutch grooves and replaced the clutch as an assembly if they're worn to less than the value listed in this Chapter's Specifications.

28 Spin the bearing in the bearing housing with fingers and check it for roughness, looseness or noise. If problems are found, unbolt the bearing retainer, then remove the oil seal and bearing. Install a new bearing, the washer and retainer, then tighten the retainer bolt to the torque listed in this Chapter's Specifications.

Installation

Refer to illustration 10.29

29 Installation is the reverse of the removal steps, with the following additions:

a) *Use a new locknut, coated with molybdenum disulfide oil, to secure the centrifugal clutch to the crankshaft. Tighten the locknut to the torque listed in this Chapter's Specifications, then stake it in position with a hammer and punch.*

10.27 Inspect the one-way clutch's friction surface (lower arrow) and centrifugal clutch weights (upper arrow)

10.29 Thread two bolts or screws in like this and tighten to spread the pulley halves for drivebelt installation

2B-12 Chapter 2 Part B Engine, clutch and transmission (2000 and later 400/450 models)

11.2 Remove the oil line union bolts (arrows) and the sealing washers

11.5 Remove the snap-ring and slide off the oil pump driven gear

11.6a Bend back the lockwasher tab (arrow) and remove the oil pump drive gear . . .

b) Apply engine oil to the bearing inside the clutch housing and the bearing inside the bearing housing.
c) Use a new gasket between the clutch housing and engine.
d) Tighten all remaining nuts and bolts to the torques listed in this Chapter's Specifications. Use thread locking agent on the bolts that secure the cover to the clutch housing.
e) To expand the driven pulley so the drivebelt can be installed, thread two bolts or screws (6 mm X 1.0 mm thread pattern, 1-3/4 inches long into the holes provided for the purpose **(see illustration)**. Tighten the bolts or screws to push the pulley halves apart far enough so the belt can be installed.

11 External oil pipe and oil pump gears - removal and installation

Oil pipe
Refer to illustration 11.2
1 Remove the drivebelt and pulleys (see Section 10).
2 Remove the oil pipe union bolts **(see illustration)**. Take off the pipe and sealing washers.
3 Installation is the reverse of the removal steps. Tighten the union bolts to the torque listed in this Chapter's Specifications.

Oil pump gears
Refer to illustrations 11.5, 11.6a and 11.6b
4 Remove the recoil starter and alternator (see Section 8 and Chapter 9).
5 Remove the snap-ring from the driven gear **(see illustration)**. Pull the gear off the shaft.
6 Bend back the tab on the drive gear lockwasher **(see illustrations)**. Hold the gears so it won't turn and unscrew the locknut.
7 Take the drive and driven gears off their shafts.
8 Installation is the reverse of the removal steps. Use a new lockwasher. Tighten the nut to the torque listed in this Chapter's Specifications, then bend a lockwasher tab against the nut to secure it.

12 Crankcase - disassembly and reassembly

1 To examine and repair or replace the crankshaft, connecting rod, bearings and transmission components, the crankcase must be split into two parts.

Disassembly
Refer to illustrations 12.12a, 12.12b, 12.13 and 12.14
2 Remove the engine from the vehicle (see Section 4).

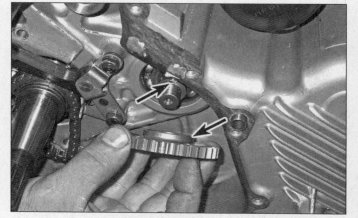

11.6b . . . the shouldered side of the gear faces the engine

3 Remove the speed sensor.
4 Remove the carburetor (see Chapter 4).
5 Remove the oil strainer and filter (see Chapter 1).
6 Remove the alternator rotor and the starter motor (see Chapter 9).
7 Remove the drivebelt, pulleys and centrifugal clutch (see Section 10).
8 Remove the shift select mechanism (see Section 7).
9 Remove the cam chain tensioner, cylinder head, cam chain, cylinder and piston (see Sections 5, 6 and 9 and Part D of this Chapter).
10 Remove the oil pump gears (see Section 11).

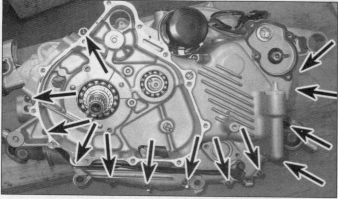

12.12a Remove the left crankcase bolts (arrows) . . .

Chapter 2 Part B Engine, clutch and transmission (2000 and later 400/450 models) 2B-13

12.12b ... and the right crankcase bolts (arrows)

12.13 Tap gently on the engine mounting bosses to separate the case halves; pry only at the pry points, not against the mating surfaces

11 Check carefully to make sure there aren't any remaining components that attach the halves of the crankcase together.
12 Loosen the crankcase bolts in two or three stages, in a criss-cross pattern (see illustrations). Remove the bolts and label them; they are different lengths.
13 Tap gently on the ends of the transmission shafts, balancer shaft and crankshaft as the case halves are being separated (see illustration). Carefully pry the crankcase apart at the pry points and lift the left half off the right half (see illustration). Don't pry against the mating surfaces or they'll develop leaks.
14 Locate the crankcase dowels (see illustration). If they aren't secure in their holes, remove them and set them aside for safekeeping.
15 Refer to Sections 13 through 15 for information on the internal components of the crankcase.

Reassembly

16 Remove all traces of old gasket and sealant from the crankcase mating surfaces with a sharpening stone or similar tool. Be careful not to let any fall into the case as this is done and be careful not to damage the mating surfaces.
17 Check to make sure the dowel pins are in place in their holes in the mating surface of the crankcase (see illustration 12.14).
18 Coat both crankcase mating surfaces with Quick Gasket (ACC-11001-05-01) or equivalent sealant.
19 Pour some engine oil over the transmission gears, balancer shaft and crankshaft bearing surfaces and the shift cam. Don't get any oil on the crankcase mating surfaces.
20 Carefully place the left crankcase half onto the right crankcase half. While doing this, make sure the transmission shafts, shift drums, crankshaft and balancer fit into their ball bearings in the left crankcase half.
21 Install the crankcase half bolts in the correct holes and tighten them so they are just snug. Then tighten them in two or three stages, in a criss-cross pattern, to the torque listed in this Chapter's Specifications.
22 Turn the transmission shafts to make sure they turn freely. Also make sure the crankshaft and balancer shaft turn freely.
23 The remainder of installation is the reverse of removal.

13 Oil pump - removal and installation

Removal

Refer to illustrations 13.2 and 13.3

1 Disassemble the crankcase (see Section 12).
2 Locate the oil pump washer (see illustration). If it came off the shaft, reinstall it.

12.14 Separate the case halves and locate the dowels (arrows)

13.2 If you're planning to disassemble the oil pump, loosen the screw (A) before removing the mounting screws (B)

2B-14 Chapter 2 Part B Engine, clutch and transmission (2000 and later 400/450 models)

13.3 Remove the oil pump and its gasket; use a new gasket on installation

13.5 On assembly, make sure the dowels (outer arrows) and drive pin (inner arrow) are in position

3 If you're planning to disassemble the pump, loosen the cover screw (see illustration 13.2). Remove the oil pump mounting screws. Take the oil pump off and remove the gasket (see illustration).

Inspection

Refer to illustration 13.5

4 Remove the cover screw (see illustration 13.2). If you haven't already done so, remove the washer and snap-ring from the oil pump shaft (see illustration 13.2).
5 Remove the shaft and pump cover from the pump body (see illustration). Remove the pin from the shaft, pull the shaft out of the pump cover, and take the rotors out of the pump body.
6 Refer to Part D of this Chapter to check the oil pump clearances.
7 Check the pump shaft for a loose fit in the cover. Replace the pump if problems are found.
8 Reassemble the pump by reversing the disassembly steps, with the following additions:

a) Before installing the cover, pack the cavities between the rotors with petroleum jelly - this will ensure the pump develops suction quickly and begins oil circulation as soon as the engine is started.
b) Make sure the cover dowels and drive pin are in position (see illustration 13.5).
c) Tighten the cover screw to the torque listed in this Chapter's Specifications.

Installation

9 Installation is the reverse of removal, with the following additions:

a) Install a new gasket (see illustration 13.2).
b) Tighten the oil pump mounting screws to the torque listed in this Chapter's Specifications.

14 Balancer and crankshaft - removal and installation

Refer to illustrations 14.2 and 14.4a through 14.4c

1 Disassemble the crankcase (see Section 12).
2 Turn the crankshaft and balancer so their alignment marks are lined up (see illustration). This is how they should align when the balancer is reinstalled.
3 Pull the balancer out of the engine.
4 Unhook the crankshaft end seals and remove them (see illustration). Mark each seal for position and direction as it is removed.
5 Refer to Part D of this Chapter to remove, inspect and reinstall the crankshaft.
6 The remainder of installation is the reverse of the removal steps.

14.2 The balancer and crankshaft marks (arrows) must be aligned as shown or severe engine vibration will occur

14.4a Remove the seal cover screws (arrows), the cover . . .

Chapter 2 Part B Engine, clutch and transmission (2000 and later 400/450 models)   2B-15

14.4b ... and its gasket (right arrow) for access to the crankshaft sealing rings (left arrows) ...

14.4c ... the ends of the rings hook together

Be sure to align the marks on the crankshaft and balancer, or severe engine vibration will occur.

15 Transmission shafts, forks and shift cam - removal, inspection and installation

Note 1: *When disassembling the transmission shafts, place the parts on a long rod or thread a wire through them to keep them in order and facing the proper direction.*
Note 2: *This section covers the low range used on some models. If the vehicle you're working on doesn't have a low range, ignore the steps that don't apply.*

Removal

Refer to illustrations 15.2, 15.3, 15.4, 15.5, 15.6, 15.7, 15.8, 15.9, 15.10, 15.11, 15.12a and 15.12b

1 Remove the engine, then separate the case halves (see Sections 4 and 11).
2 Remove the snap-ring and washer from the driven sprocket **(see illustration)**.
3 Lift off the driven sprocket and disengage it from the chain. Remove the driven sprocket needle bearing and thrust washer **(see illustration)**.
4 Remove the no. 2 clutch dog and low shift fork (if equipped) **(see**

15.2 Remove the snap-ring (arrow), washer and driven sprocket, then lift off the sprocket and disengage it from the chain

illustration). Slide the spring off the fork shaft.
5 Disengage the chain from the drive sprocket and remove it. Lift the secondary shaft out of the crankcase **(see illustration)**.

15.3 Remove the driven sprocket bearing and thrust washer

15.4 Remove the no. 2 clutch dog (right arrow), low shift fork (center arrow) and lift off the fork shaft spring (left arrow)

15.5 Lift the secondary shaft out of the crankcase

15.6 Lift out the shift cam

15.7 Remove the snap-ring (arrow), washer and low wheel gear

15.8 Remove the snap-ring, then lift off the middle driven gear and remove the snap-ring below it

15.9 Lift out the driveaxle, then lift out the fork shaft, fork, spring and washer (arrow)

6   Lift the shift cam out of the crankcase (see illustration).
7   Remove the snap-ring, washer and low wheel gear (see illustration).
8   Remove the snap-ring, middle driven gear and a second snap-ring (see illustration).
9   Lift out the driveaxle assembly and remove the fork shaft, reverse shift fork, spring and washer (see illustration).
10 Remove the snap-rings and gear components from the driveaxle (see illustration). Place them on a long rod so they can be reassembled in the same order.
11 Check the parking pawl for wear and damage (see illustration). If problems are found, remove the bolt, washer, parking pawl, spring and bushing.

15.10 Place the driveaxle components in order on a long rod

15.11 Inspect the parking pawl and remove it if there's any wear or damage

Chapter 2 Part B Engine, clutch and transmission (2000 and later 400/450 models) 2B-17

15.12a Remove the six hex bolts (not the screws) . . .

15.12b . . . and lift out the middle drive gear assembly

12 Unbolt the middle drive shaft's bearing housing from the crankcase and lift it out **(see illustrations)**. Rotate the shaft and check the bearing for rough or noisy movement. Check the drive pinion gear for wear or damage. Rotate the middle driven shaft (in the crankcase), feeling for tightness, rough spots, excessive looseness and listening for noises. Replacement of the bevel gear or shaft will require setting up the gear backlash of the middle driven gear; take the case and middle driven gear assembly to a Yamaha dealer to have this procedure done.

13 Refer to Part D of this Chapter to inspect the transmission components.

Installation

14 Installation is the basically the reverse of the removal procedure, but take note of the following points:
   a) Use new snap-rings.
   b) The shift fork marked R faces the right side of the crankcase; the shift fork marked L faces the left side.
   c) Lubricate the components with engine oil before assembling them.
   d) After assembly, check the gears to make sure they're installed correctly. Move the shift cam through the gear positions and rotate the gears to make sure they mesh and shift correctly.

Notes

Chapter 2 Part C
Engine, clutch and transmission (600 and 660 models)

Contents

	Section		Section
Balancer and crankshaft - removal and installation	17	External oil pipes - removal and installation	13
Cam chain tensioner - removal and installation	5	General information	1
Camshaft, chain and guides - removal and installation	7	Oil pump and relief valve - removal and installation	16
Compression test	See Chapter 2D	Oil pump sprockets and balancer gears (660 models) - removal, inspection and installation	14
Crankcase - disassembly and reassembly	15		
Cylinder - removal and installation	11	Operations possible with the engine in the frame	2
Cylinder head - removal and installation	8	Operations requiring engine removal	3
Cylinder head cover and rocker arms - removal, inspection and installation	6	Recoil starter - removal, inspection and installation	10
		Shift select mechanism - removal, inspection and installation	9
Drivebelt and pulleys - general information, removal, inspection and installation	12	Transmission shafts, forks and shift cam - removal, inspection and installation	18
Engine - removal and installation	4		

Specifications

600 models

General
Bore	95 mm (3.74 inches)
Stroke	84 m (3.31 inches)
Displacement	595 cc

Centrifugal clutch
Lining thickness
Standard	1.5 mm (0.08 inch)
Limit	1.0 mm (0.04 inch)

Transmission
Main axle and driveaxle runout limit	0.06 mm (0.0024 inch)

Torque specifications
Engine upper rear bracket to engine bolt	42 Nm (30 ft-lbs)
Engine upper rear bracket to frame	33 Nm (24 ft-lbs)
Cylinder head cover bolts	10 Nm (86 inch-lbs)
Cylinder head	
M6 thread bolt	10 Nm (86 ft-lbs)
M8 thread bolts	29 Nm (21 ft-lbs)
M10 thread studs	20 Nm (14 ft-lbs)
M8 nuts	22 Nm (16 ft-lbs)

600 models (continued)
Torque specifications
Cylinder
    M6 thread bolt .... 10 Nm (86 inch-lbs)
    M10 nut .... 42 Nm (30 ft-lbs)
Cam chain guide bolts .... 10 Nm (86 inch-lbs)
Camshaft sprocket bolts .... 20 Nm (14 ft-lbs)
Cam chain tensioner body bolts .... 11 Nm (96 inch-lbs)
Cam chain tensioner cap bolt .... 20 Nm (14 ft-lbs)
Shift housing bolts .... 12 Nm (104 inch-lbs)
Shift lever pivot bolt .... Not specified
Crankcase bolts
    Hex bolts (M6 thread) .... 10 Nm (86 inch-lbs)
    Allen bolts (M8 thread) .... 31 Nm (22 ft-lbs)
Crankcase bearing retainer screws .... Not specified
Oil pump mounting bolts .... 10 Nm (86 inch-lbs)
Oil pump assembly screw .... 7 Nm (61 inch-lbs)
Oil pump strainer screws .... 7 Nm (61 inch-lbs)
Oil pump relief valve screw (to oil pump) .... 7 Nm (61 inch-lbs)
Oil pump relief valve retainer bolts (to crankcase) .... Not specified
Centrifugal clutch nut .... 140 Nm (100 ft-lbs)
Centrifugal clutch housing bolts .... 10 Nm (86 inch-lbs)
Centrifugal clutch cover bolts .... 10 Nm (86 inch-lbs)
Drive and driven pulley nuts .... 100 Nm (72 ft-lbs)
Bearing housing bolts (inside pulley cover) .... Not specified
Middle driveaxle bearing retainer screws .... 29 Nm (21 ft-lbs)
Middle driveaxle bearing housing bolts .... 33 Nm (24 ft-lbs)
Middle driveaxle pinion gear nut .... 145 Nm (105 ft-lbs)

660 models
General
Bore .... 100 mm (3.94 inches)
Stroke .... 84 m (3.31 inches)
Displacement .... 660 cc

Centrifugal clutch
Lining thickness
    Standard .... 1.5 mm (0.08 inch)
    Limit .... 1.0 mm (0.04 inch)

Transmission
Main axle and driveaxle runout limit .... 0.06 mm (0.0024 inch)

Torque specifications
Engine upper rear bracket through bolt and nut .... 56 Nm (40 ft-lbs)
Engine upper rear bracket bolts .... 10 Nm (86 ft-lbs)
Engine mounting insulator nuts .... 42 Nm (30 ft-lbs)
Engine front bracket to engine bolts .... 33 Nm (24 ft-lbs)
Engine left front insulator to bracket bolt .... 10 Nm (86 inch-lbs)
Cylinder head cover bolts .... 10 Nm (86 inch-lbs)
Cylinder head
    M6 thread bolt .... 10 Nm (86 inch-lbs)
    M9 thread bolts .... 38 Nm (27 ft-lbs)
Cylinder
    M6 thread bolt .... 10 Nm (86 inch-lbs)
    M10 thread bolts .... 42 Nm (30 ft-lbs)
Cam chain guide bolts .... 8 Nm (70 inch-lbs)
Camshaft sprocket bolts .... 20 Nm (14 ft-lbs)
Cam chain tensioner body bolts .... 10 Nm (86 inch-lbs)
Cam chain tensioner cap bolt .... 7 Nm (61 inch-lbs)
External oil pipe bolts .... 18 Nm (156 inch-lbs)
Oil filter hex fitting .... 63 Nm (46 ft-lbs)
Crankcase bolts .... 10 Nm (86 inch-lbs)
Shift housing bolts .... 10 Nm (86 inch-lbs)
Shift lever pivot bolt .... 14 Nm (120 inch-lbs)
Crankcase bearing retainer bolts .... 10 Nm (86 inch-lbs)
Oil pump mounting bolts .... 10 Nm (86 inch-lbs)

Chapter 2 Part C Engine, clutch and transmission (600 and 660 models)

Torque specifications

Oil pump assembly screw	Not specified
Oil pressure relief valve bolts	10 Nm (86 inch-lbs)
Centrifugal clutch nut	160 Nm (115 ft-lbs)
Centrifugal clutch housing bolts	10 Nm (86 inch-lbs)
Drive pulley nut	120 Nm (85 ft-lbs)
Driven pulley nut	100 Nm (72 ft-lbs)
Bearing housing bolts (inside pulley cover)	10 Nm (86 inch-lbs)
Pull cover bolts	10 Nm (86 inch-lbs)
Middle driveaxle bearing retainer screws	29 Nm (21 ft-lbs)
Middle driveaxle bearing housing bolts	32 Nm (23 ft-lbs)
Middle driveaxle pinion gear nut	145 Nm (105 ft-lbs)

1 General information

The engine/transmission unit is of the air-cooed (600) or liquid-cooled (660), single-cylinder four-stroke design. The valves (two exhaust on all models; two intake on 600 models and three intake on 660 models) are operated by a chain and sprockets. The engine/transmission assembly is constructed from aluminum alloy. The crankcase is divided vertically.

The crankcase incorporates a wet sump, pressure-fed lubrication system which uses a gear-driven rotor-type oil pump, an oil filter and separate strainer screen and an oil temperature warning switch.

Power from the crankshaft is routed to the internal transmission gears via a constantly variable transmission, consisting of a drivebelt and two variable-diameter pulleys. These change the effective gear ratio automatically, so no clutch or conventional transmission gears are needed. A one-way clutch in the front pulley allows the engine to provide compression braking when the throttle is released. The internal transmission gears provide forward and reverse ranges, as well as a low range on some models.

2 Operations possible with the engine in the frame

The components and assemblies listed below can be removed without having to remove the engine from the frame. If, however, a number of areas require attention at the same time, removal of the engine is recommended.

Recoil starter
Starter motor
Starter reduction gears
Balancer gears (660 models)
Oil pump sprocket (660 models)
Starter clutch
Alternator rotor and stator
Drivebelt and pulleys
Shift select lever and linkage
Cam chain tensioner
Camshaft
Rocker arms and shafts
Cylinder head
Cylinder and piston

3 Operations requiring engine removal

It is necessary to remove the engine/transmission assembly from the frame and separate the crankcase halves to gain access to the following components:

Oil pump
Balancer
Crankshaft and connecting rod
Transmission shafts
Shift cam and forks

4 Engine - removal and installation

Note: *Engine removal and installation should be done with the aid of an assistant to avoid damage or injury that could occur if the engine is dropped. A hydraulic floor jack should be used to support and lower the engine if possible (they can be rented at low cost).*

Removal

Refer to illustrations 4.10, 4.15a and 4.15b

1 Drain the engine oil (all models) and coolant (660 models) and disconnect the spark plug wire (see Chapter 1).
2 Remove the fuel tank, carburetor, air cleaner housing and exhaust system (see Chapter 4). Plug the carburetor intake opening with rags.
3 Remove the front and rear fenders, footrests and skid plates (see Chapter 8).
4 Remove the drive pulley air ducts (see Section 12).
5 Disconnect the shift linkage at the engine and brake pedal, then unbolt the select lever housing and take it off (see Chapter 2B).
6 Remove the front driveshaft protector (see Chapter 6).
7 If you're working on a 600 model, disconnect the oil cooler hoses (see Chapter 2A). If you're working on a 660, remove the coolant reservoir and water pump (see Chapter 3).
8 Disconnect the crankcase breather hose from the air cleaner housing (see Chapter 4).
9 Disconnect the engine ground cable.
10 Free the wiring harnesses from the retainer(s) at the engine **(see illustration)**. Label and disconnect the following wires (refer to Chapters 5 or 9 for component location if necessary):

Ignition pulse generator
Alternator
Gear position switches
Oil or coolant temperature switch
Speed sensor (660 models)
Starter

4.10 Free the wiring harnesses from the retainers

2C-4 Chapter 2 Part C Engine, clutch and transmission (600 and 660 models)

4.15a Remove the front engine mount through-bolt (arrow)

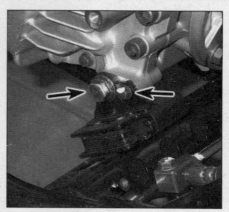

4.15b Remove the rear engine mount through-bolt (left arrow) and the rear bracket bolts (right arrow) (left bracket shown)

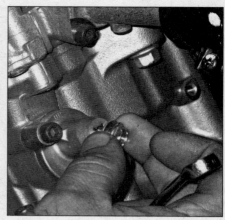

5.2 Unscrew the cam chain tensioner plug

11 Remove the rear wheels (see Chapter 7).
12 Remove the swingarm (600 models) or final drive unit (660 models) (see Chapter 6). **Note:** *On 660 models, if you don't plan to do any work on the rear final; drive unit or rear suspension, it's easier to remove the rear subframe, complete with the final drive unit, rear suspension, and rear driveshaft (see Chapter 6).*
13 Support the engine securely from below. **Note:** *Use a jack (preferably a floor jack) that can be repositioned if necessary as the engine mounting bolts are removed.*
14 If you're working on a 600 model, remove the engine mounting bolts at the upper front, lower front, upper rear and lower rear.
15 If you're working on a 660 model, remove the engine mounting bolts, nuts, insulators and brackets in the following order **(see illustrations)**:

  a) *Front rubber insulator nuts (from below)*
  b) *Upper rear engine mounting bolts*
  c) *Rear engine mount through-bolt*

16 Have an assistant help you lift the engine and remove it to the right side of the vehicle (600) or left side of the vehicle (660). If you're working on a 4WD model, pull the engine rearward to disengage the front driveshaft from the engine.
17 If necessary, remove the engine mounts and brackets from the engine and frame.
18 Slowly lower the engine to a suitable work surface.

Installation

19 Check the rubber engine supports for wear or damage and replace them with new ones if necessary before installing the engine.

600 models

20 Coat the driveshaft splines with moly-based grease. Install the engine from the right side of the vehicle and move it forward to engage the driveshaft with the engine (refer to Chapter 6 if necessary).
21 Lift the engine to align the mounting bolt holes, then install the brackets and mounting bolts, but don't tighten them yet.
22 Tighten the mounts evenly to the torques listed in this Chapter's Specifications.

660 models

23 If the front mounting brackets were removed from the engine, install them and tighten their fasteners slightly, but don't torque them yet.
24 Place the front mounting insulators in position in the frame, but don't tighten the nuts yet.
25 Install the rear mounting insulators and their nuts, but don't tighten the nuts yet.
26 Coat the driveshaft splines with moly-based grease. Install the engine from the left side of the vehicle and move it forward to engage the driveshaft with the engine (refer to Chapter 6 if necessary).
27 Lift the engine with a jack to align the mounting bolt holes, then install the following in order (don't torque them yet):

  Engine mount through-bolt and nut
  Rear mounting insulator-to-engine bolts
  Front mounting insulator nuts

28 Tighten the nuts and bolts to the torque listed in this Chapter's Specifications, in the following order:

  a) *Front bracket-to-engine bolts*
  b) *Rear mounting insulator nuts*
  c) *Rear bracket-to-engine bolts*
  d) *Rear through-bolt*
  e) *Front mounting insulator nuts*

All models

29 The remainder of installation is the reverse of the removal steps, with the following additions:

  a) *Use new gaskets at all exhaust pipe connections.*
  b) *Adjust the shift linkage following the procedures in Chapter 1.*
  c) *Fill the engine oil and coolant and check the differential oil level, also following the procedures in Chapter 1. Run the engine and check for leaks.*

5 Cam chain tensioner - removal and installation

600 models

1 This is the same as for 1993 through 1999 400 models. Refer to Part A for procedures and to this Chapter's Specifications for tightening torques.

660 models

Removal

Refer to illustration 5.2

2 Unscrew the cam chain tensioner plug **(see illustration)**. Unbolt the tensioner and take it off the engine.

Installation

Refer to illustrations 5.4a and 5.4b

3 Insert a screwdriver in the tensioner hole (the one the plug was removed from). Lightly press the tensioner piston in and turn the screwdriver clockwise to retract the piston.
4 With the piston retracted, install the tensioner on the engine **(see illustration)**. Make sure the UP mark is upright **(see illustration)**.

Chapter 2 Part C Engine, clutch and transmission (600 and 660 models)   2C-5

5.4a When the tensioner is reinstalled, the piston must be retracted as shown

5.4b Install the tensioner with the UP mark upright

6.4 Remove the camshaft end cover and O-ring; use thread locking agent on the cover bolt

5   Tighten the tensioner mounting bolts to the torque listed in this Chapter's Specifications.
6   Remove the screwdriver and listen to make sure the tensioner piston extends. Once it does, install the plug.

6 Cylinder head cover and rocker arms - removal, inspection and installation

Removal
Refer to illustrations 6.4, 6.6 and 6.7

1   Remove the seat, fuel tank, front fenders and air cleaner housing (see Chapters 4, 8 and 5).
2   Remove the shift lever housing (see Section 9).
3   Refer to *Valve clearances - check and adjustment* in Chapter 1 and place the engine at top dead center on the compression stroke.
4   Unbolt the camshaft end cover. Remove the cover, together with the oil check bolt, and its O-ring **(see illustration)**.
5   If you're working on a 660 model, remove the external oil lines from the camshaft cover (see Section 13).
6   Loosen the cover bolts evenly, in several stages, working in a diagonal sequence **(see illustration)**. Once they're all loose, remove them.
7   Lift the cover off the cylinder head **(see illustration)**. If it's stuck, tap gently with a soft-faced mallet. Don't pry the cover off or it will be damaged.
8   Locate the cover dowels (they may have stayed in the cover or the

6.6 Loosen the cover bolts (arrows) in a criss-cross pattern (660 shown; 600 similar)

cylinder head) **(see illustration 6.7)**.
9   Remove all traces of old sealant from the cover and cylinder head mating surfaces.

Inspection
Refer to illustration 6.10

10   Unscrew the rocker shaft plug **(see illustration)**.

6.7 Lift off the cover and locate the dowels (arrows)

6.10 Unscrew the rocker shaft plug from the cover

2C-6 Chapter 2 Part C Engine, clutch and transmission (600 and 660 models)

7.3 Unscrew one sprocket bolt, then rotate the sprocket and unscrew the other bolt

7.4 Lift the camshaft out

7.11 The camshaft pins must fit into the notches of the decompressor plates

11 Pull the rocker shafts out. Remove the rocker arms and wave washers from the cover. On 660 models, note that the dual intake rocker arm (the one that operates two valves) goes toward the right side of the vehicle.

12 Refer to Part D of this Chapter to inspect the rocker arms and shafts.

13 Check the camshaft bearing surfaces in the cover for wear or damage. If problems are found, remove the camshaft (see Section 7) and check the bearing surfaces in the cylinder head. Refer to Part D of this Chapter and check the camshaft journals.

Installation

14 Installation is the reverse of the removal steps, with the following additions:

a) Use new O-rings on the right exhaust rocker shaft, the intake rocker shaft and the rocker shaft plug.

b) Be sure to install a wave washer next to each rocker arm. On 600 models, the wave washers go on the inboard sides of the rocker arms (toward the center of the engine). On 660 models, the exhaust wave washers go toward the inboard sides of the rocker arms. The wave washer on the dual intake rocker arm goes toward the left side of the vehicle (the inboard side of the rocker arm). The wave washer on the single intake rocker arm also goes toward the lefty side of the vehicle (the outboard side of the rocker arm).

c) Lubricate the rocker shafts with engine oil and the camshaft contact surfaces of the rocker arms with molybdenum disulfide grease.

d) Install the rocker shafts with their bolt passages vertical.

e) Apply a thin coat of Quick Gasket or equivalent sealant to the mating surfaces of the cylinder head and cover.

f) Tighten the cover bolts evenly, in two or three stages, to the torque listed in this Chapter's Specifications.

g) If you're working on a 660 model, use new sealing washers on the external oil lines.

7   Camshaft, chain and guides - removal and installation

Removal

Refer to illustrations 7.3 and 7.4

1 Remove the cylinder head cover (see Section 6).

2 Prevent the crankshaft from turning. To do this, remove the recoil starter as described in Chapter 2A. Hold the recoil starter pulley with a clutch holder tool. If the factory tool or an equivalent isn't available, you can make your own from some steel strap, bent at the ends and bolted together in the middle **(see Illustration 7.5 in Chapter 2A)**.

3 Unbolt the cam sprocket and take it off the camshaft **(see illustration)**. Disengage the sprocket from the chain and support the chain with

7.12a The two camshaft punch marks (arrows) align with the gasket surface . . .

wire so it doesn't fall down off the crankshaft sprocket.

4 Lift the camshaft out of the cylinder head **(see illustration)**.

5 Lift the front cam chain guide out of the cylinder. The rear guide is bolted at the bottom, so the recoil starter and alternator rotor will have to be removed for access if the guide or the cam chain need to be removed.

6 Stuff clean rags into the cam chain openings so dirt, small parts or tools can't fall into them.

7 Refer to Part D of this Chapter to inspect the camshaft.

Installation

Refer to illustrations 7.11, 7.12a and 7.12b

8 Make sure the engine is still at top dead center on the compression stroke (refer to *Valve clearances check and adjustment* in Chapter 1 if necessary).

9 Reinstall the chain and rear guides if they were removed.

10 Install the camshaft in the cylinder head with the lobes downward and the small holes in the journals upward **(see illustration 7.4)**.

11 Place the decompressor cam guide plates on the cam sprocket (if they were removed). Make sure the spring lever pins align with the decompressor cam notches **(see illustration)**.

12 Engage the chain with the cam sprocket, then install the sprocket on the camshaft. Two of the three punch marks in the cam sprocket must be aligned with the mating surface; the remaining mark must be straight up **(see illustrations)**. The punch mark on the decompressor lever must also be straight up.

Chapter 2 Part C Engine, clutch and transmission (600 and 660 models)

7.12b ... and the single punch mark (arrow) goes straight up

8.2a Loosen the cylinder head Allen bolt (arrow) ...

8.2b ... the hex bolt under the intake side ...

8.2c ... the hex bolt under the exhaust side ...

8.2d ... and loosen the main head bolts (arrows) in a criss-cross pattern

13 Install the camshaft sprocket bolts and tighten them to the torque listed in this Chapter's Specifications. If the engine turns, hold it as described in Step 2.
14 The remainder or installation is the reverse of the removal steps.

8 Cylinder head - removal and installation

Removal

Refer to illustrations 8.2a, 8.2b, 8.2c, 8.2d and 8.4

1 Remove the cylinder head cover and cylinder head (see Sections 6 and 7).
2 Loosen the cylinder head bolts in the specified sequence, 1/4-turn at a time, until all are loose, then remove them. The sequence is as follows:
  a) Allen bolt on the left rear corner of the head (see illustration).
  b) Hex bolt on the underside of the head on the intake side (see illustration).
  c) Hex bolt on the underside of the head on the exhaust side (see illustration).
  d) Main head bolts (see illustration).
3 Lift the cylinder head off the cylinder. If it's stuck, don't attempt to pry it off - tap around the sides with a plastic hammer to dislodge it. On 600 models, be careful not to tap against the cooling fins; they're easily broken.

4 Locate the cylinder head dowels (see illustration). They may be in the cylinder or they may have come off with the head. Note that on 600 models, the dowel nearest the intake side has an O-ring.
5 Refer to Part D of this Chapter to inspect the cylinder head and valves.

8.4 Here are the dowel locations (left arrows); the UP mark (right arrow) goes upright when the gasket is installed

11.4a Remove the cylinder Allen bolts (arrows) . . .

11.4b . . . and the main bolts (660 models, shown) or nuts (600 models)

Installation

6 Carefully lower the cylinder head over the dowels and O-ring, guiding the cam chain through the slot in the cylinder head. It's helpful to have an assistant support the cam chain with a piece of wire so it doesn't fall and become kinked or detached from the crankshaft. When the head is resting on the cylinder, wire the cam chain to another component to keep tension on it.
7 Install the cylinder head bolts finger-tight. Tighten the bolts and nuts in the reverse of the tightening sequence (see Step 2), in two stages, to the torque listed in this Chapter's Specifications.
8 The remainder of installation is the reverse of removal.
9 Change the engine oil and adjust the valve clearances (see Chapter 1).

9 Shift select mechanism - removal, inspection and installation

These procedures are the same as for 400/450 models. Refer to Part B of this Chapter for procedures and to this Chapter's Specifications for tightening torques.

10 Recoil starter - removal, inspection and installation

These procedures are the same as for 400/450 models. Refer to Part A of this Chapter for procedures and to this Chapter's Specifications for tightening torques.

11 Cylinder - removal and installation

Removal

Refer to illustrations 11.4a, 11.4b, 11.5 and 11.6

1 Drain the engine oil and coolant (see Chapter 1). Disconnect the water pump outlet hose and remove its fitting from the cylinder (see Chapter 3).
2 Following the procedure given in Section 7, remove the cylinder head. Make sure the crankshaft is positioned at Top Dead Center (TDC).
3 Lift out the cam chain front guide.
4 Remove the two Allen bolts and four hex nuts (600) or bolts (660) that secure the cylinder (see illustrations).
5 Lift the cylinder straight up to remove it (see illustration). If it's stuck, tap around its perimeter with a soft-faced mallet. Don't attempt to pry between the cylinder and crankcase as you'll ruin the mating surfaces.
6 Locate the dowel pins (they may have come off with the cylinder or still be in the crankcase (see illustration). Be careful not to let these drop into the engine. Stuff rags around the piston and remove the base O-ring, gasket and all traces of old gasket material from the surfaces of cylinder and crankcase.
7 Refer to Part D of this Chapter to inspect the cylinder.

Installation

8 Lubricate the cylinder bore with plenty of clean engine oil. Apply a thin film of moly-based grease to the piston skirt.

11.5 Lift off the cylinder and remove the base O-ring (arrow)

11.6 Locate the cylinder base dowels (arrows) and remove the gasket

Chapter 2 Part C Engine, clutch and transmission (600 and 660 models)   2C-9

12.3 The upper end of the front air duct on 660 models is secured by a pin and grommet (arrow)

12.4 Unscrew the cover bolts (arrows) and take the cover off

9 Install the dowel pins, then lower a new cylinder base gasket over them **(see illustration 11.6)**. Install the base O-ring **(see illustration 11.5)**.

10 Attach a piston ring compressor to the piston and compress the piston rings. A large hose clamp can be used instead - just make sure it doesn't scratch the piston, and don't tighten it too much.

11 Install the cylinder and carefully lower it down until the piston crown fits into the cylinder liner **(see illustration 8.10 in Chapter 2A)**. While doing this, pull the camshaft chain up, using a hooked tool or piece of stiff wire. Push down on the cylinder, making sure the piston doesn't get cocked sideways, until the bottom of the cylinder liner slides down past the piston rings. A wood or plastic hammer handle can be used to gently tap the cylinder down, but don't use too much force or the piston will be damaged.

12 Remove the ring compressor or hose clamp, being careful not to scratch the piston.

13 The remainder of installation is the reverse of the removal steps.

12 Drivebelt and pulleys - general information, removal, inspection and installation

12.5 Remove the bearing housing bolts (arrows; two lower bolts hidden), take the bearing housing off

General information

1 Refer to Part B of this Chapter for general information on the operation of the drivebelt and pulleys.

Removal

Cover and ducts

Refer to illustrations 12.3, 12.4, 12.5 and 12.6

2 Remove the front or rear fender and right footboard as necessary for access (see Chapter 8).

3 To remove the air ducts, loosen their clamps, remove the mounting bolts and separate the ducts from the housing. On 660 models, the front duct is held in place at the top by a pin and grommet **(see illustration)**.

4 Remove the cover mounting bolts **(see illustration)**. Tap the cover loose if necessary (don't pry it) and separate the cover and gasket from the engine.

5 Remove the bearing housing and locate the cover dowels **(see illustration)**.

6 On 660 models, if necessary, remove the drivebelt and pulleys for access to the inner cover (see Chapter 2B). Remove the inner cover bolts, then take off the inner cover and gasket **(see illustrations)**.

12.6a Remove the inner cover bolts (arrows) and take the inner cover off . . .

12.6b . . . and locate the inner cover dowels

2C-10 Chapter 2 Part C Engine, clutch and transmission (600 and 660 models)

12.17 The OUT SIDE mark on the one-way clutch faces outward when the one-way clutch is installed

13.1 Remove the union bolts (arrows) to detach the oil line (660 shown, 600 similar); use new sealing washers on installation

Pulleys and drivebelt

7   This is the same as for 2000 and later Kodiak models. Refer to Part B of this Chapter.

Centrifugal and one-way clutches

8   This is the same as for 2000 and later Kodiak models. Refer to Part B of this Chapter. Note that the centrifugal clutch on Grizzly 660 models has a collar that fits over the crankshaft.

Inspection

Cover and ducts

9   Check the cover gaskets for damage or deterioration and replace if their condition is in doubt.
10   Check the cover and ducts for damage and replace them if necessary.
11   Spin the bearing in the bearing housing with fingers and check for rough or noisy movement. If problems are found, unbolt the bearing retainer, remove the bearing and pry out the oil seal. Install a new bearing and seal, then bolt the retainer in place.

Drivebelt and pulleys

12   This is the same as for 2000 and later Kodiak models. Refer to Part B of this Chapter.

Centrifugal and one-way clutches

13   Remove the snap-ring and take the bearing out of the centrifugal clutch housing (see illustration 10.22 in Chapter 2B).
14   If you're working on a 600 model, take the collar and O-ring off the clutch housing.
15   Spin the bearing in the bearing housing with fingers and check it for roughness, looseness or noise. If problems are found, unbolt the bearing retainer, then remove the bearing. Install a new bearing and the retainer, then tighten the retainer bolt to the torque listed in this Chapter's Specifications.
16   Check the oil seal in the outer side of the bearing housing for leakage. If problems are found, pry it out and drive in a new one with a bearing driver or a socket the same diameter as the seal.

Installation

Refer to illustration 12.17

17   Installation is the reverse of the removal steps, with the following additions:

  a) *Install the one-way clutch with its OUT SIDE mark facing away from the engine (see illustration).*

  b) *Use a new locknut, coated with molybdenum disulfide oil, to secure the centrifugal clutch to the crankshaft. Tighten the locknut to the torque listed in this Chapter's Specifications, then stake it in position with a hammer and punch.*
  c) *Apply engine oil to the bearing inside the clutch housing and the bearing inside the bearing housing.*
  d) *Use a new gasket between the clutch housing and engine.*
  e) *Tighten all remaining nuts and bolts to the torques listed in this Chapter's Specifications. Use thread locking agent on the bolts that secure the cover to the clutch housing.*

13 External oil pipes - removal and installation

Refer to illustrations 13.1 and 13.2

1   To remove the pipe on the right side of the engine, remove the drivebelt and pulleys (see Section 12). Remove the oil pipe union bolts **(see illustration)**. Take off the pipe and sealing washers.
2   660 models have two connected oil pipes that run from the crankcase to the cylinder head on the right side of the engine **(see illustration)**. To remove these, unscrew the union bolts, remove the sealing washers and lift the pipes off.
3   Installation is the reverse of the removal steps. Use new sealing washers. Tighten the union bolts to the torque listed in this Chapter's Specifications.

13.2 Remove the union bolts (arrows) to detach the external oil lines on 660 models; use new sealing washers on installation

Chapter 2 Part C Engine, clutch and transmission (600 and 660 models)   2C-11

14.2 The balancer marks must align like this (arrows) (660 shown; 600 similar)

14.3a Remove the snap-ring . . .

14 Oil pump sprockets and balancer gears (660 models) - removal, inspection and installation

Refer to illustrations 14.2, 14.3a, 14.3b, 14.4, 14.5 and 14.7

1   Remove the alternator (see Chapter 9).
2   Bend back the lockwasher tabs on the balancer driven gear/oil pump drive sprocket **(see illustration)**. Wedge a piece of copper or aluminum between the gear teeth to keep the gears from turning and unscrew the nut.
3   Remove the snap-ring and take the oil pump driven sprocket off the shaft **(see illustrations)**.
4   Slip the gear off the balancer shaft and disengage the oil pump chain **(see illustration)**. Locate the Woodruff key and store it where it won't be lost.
5   Remove the snap-ring and plate **(see illustration)**. Pull the outer balancer gear off the buffer boss, taking care not to lose the springs and pins.
6   Removal of the buffer boss is the same as for 1993 through 1999 400 models (see Chapter 2A). Note that there are eight springs and four pins on 660 models. **Note:** *Removal and installation of the buffer boss require special tools (see Chapter 2A). If you don't have them, have the buffer boss installed by a dealer service department or other qualified shop. The crankshaft can be removed from the crankcase without removing the buffer boss.*

14.3b . . . slip the oil pump drive sprocket off and disengage it from the chain

7   Installation is the reverse of the removal steps, with the following additions:

14.4 Remove the balancer driven gear/oil pump drive sprocket and locate the key (arrow)

14.5 Remove the snap-ring and plate from the balancer drive gear, then remove the outer part of the gear, the springs and pins

2C-12   Chapter 2 Part C Engine, clutch and transmission (600 and 660 models)

14.7 The crankshaft keyway, inner gear punch mark and outer gear punch mark (arrows) must align with each other

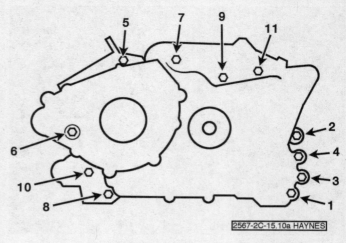

15.10a Left crankcase loosening sequence (Grizzly 600)

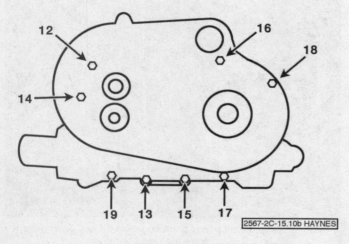

15.10b Right crankcase loosening sequence (Grizzly 600)

a) Align the punch mark on the drive gear with the punch mark on the buffer boss **(see illustration)**. Both should be aligned with the crankshaft keyway.

b) Align the marks on the balancer drive and driven gears **(see illustration 14.2)**.

15 Crankcase - disassembly and reassembly

1 To examine and repair or replace the crankshaft, connecting rod, bearings and transmission components, the crankcase must be split into two parts.

Disassembly

Refer to illustrations 15.10a through 15.10e, 15.11 and 15.12

2 Remove the engine from the vehicle (see Section 5).
3 Remove the oil strainer and filter (see Chapter 1).
4 Remove the alternator rotor and the starter motor (see Chapter 9).
5 Remove the drivebelt, pulleys and centrifugal clutch (see Section 12).

15.10c Here are the 660 left crankcase bolts (arrows; one upper bolt hidden)

15.10d Here are the 660 right crankcase bolts (arrows; one upper bolt hidden)

Chapter 2 Part C Engine, clutch and transmission (600 and 660 models)

15.10e Remove the crankshaft seal holder; unhook the seal ends to remove the seals from the holder

15.11 If necessary, use a puller like this one to separate the crankcase, but BE SURE to protect the end of the crankshaft with the crankshaft nut and a socket

6 Remove the shift select mechanism (see Section 9).
7 Remove the cam chain tensioner, cylinder head, cam chain, cylinder and piston (see Sections 5, 6, 7, 8 and 11 and Part D of this Chapter).
8 If you're working on a 660 model, remove the external oil pipe, balancer gears and oil pump sprockets (see Sections 13 and 14).
9 Check carefully to make sure there aren't any remaining components that attach the halves of the crankcase together.
10 Loosen the crankcase bolts in two or three stages in the loosening sequence (600), or in a criss-cross pattern (660) **(see illustrations)**. Remove the bolts and label them; they are different lengths. On 660 models, remove the crankshaft seal holder from the right end of the crankshaft **(see illustration)**.
11 Tap gently on the ends of the transmission shafts, balancer shaft and crankshaft as the case halves are being separated. If necessary, use a puller to push on the end of the crankshaft **(see illustration)**. Carefully pry the crankcase apart at the pry points and lift the right half off the left half. Don't pry against the case mating surfaces or they'll develop leaks. **Note:** *Yamaha specifies removing the left half of the crankcase from the right half on 660 models. However, we found that this caused transmission parts to fall on the floor, and the transmission shafts to fall partway out and become jammed. When we removed the right case half from the left half, it came off without problems.*
12 Locate the crankcase dowels **(see illustration)**. If they aren't secure in their holes, remove them and set them aside for safekeeping.
13 Refer to Sections 16 through 18 for information on the internal components of the crankcase.

Reassembly

14 Remove all traces of old sealant from the crankcase mating surfaces with a sharpening stone or similar tool. Be careful not to let any fall into the case as this is done and be careful not to damage the mating surfaces.
15 Check to make sure the dowel pins are in place in their holes in the mating surface of the crankcase **(see illustration 15.12)**.
16 Coat both crankcase mating surfaces with Quick Gasket (ACC-11001-05-01) or equivalent sealant.
17 Pour some engine oil over the transmission gears, balancer shaft and crankshaft bearing surfaces and the shift cam. Don't get any oil on the crankcase mating surfaces.
18 Carefully place the right crankcase half onto the left crankcase half. While doing this, make sure the transmission shafts, shift drums, crankshaft and balancer fit into their ball bearings in the left crankcase half.
19 Install the crankcase half bolts in the correct holes and tighten them so they are just snug. Then tighten them in two or three stages,

15.12 Locate the crankcase dowels (arrows) (660 shown; 600 similar)

in a criss-cross pattern, to the torque listed in this Chapter's Specifications.
20 Turn the transmission shafts to make sure they turn freely. Also make sure the crankshaft and balancer shaft turn freely.
21 The remainder of installation is the reverse of removal.

16 Oil pump and relief valve - removal and installation

Oil pump removal

1 Disassemble the crankcase (see Section 15).

600 models

2 Remove the snap-ring and take off the oil pump driven gear.
3 If you're planning to disassemble the pump, loosen the cover screw now, while the pump is still bolted to the crankcase. Remove the oil pump mounting bolts. Take the oil pump off and remove the gasket.

660 models

Refer to illustrations 16.4a, 16.4b and 16.4c
4 If you're planning to disassemble the pump, loosen the cover screw now, while the pump is still bolted to the crankcase **(see illustration)**. Unbolt the oil pickup screen and remove it, then remove its O-ring

16.4a Loosen the assembly screw while the pump is still bolted in; unbolt the oil pickup (arrow) . . .

16.4b . . . then detach it from the pump and remove the O-ring (arrow)

(see illustration). Remove the oil pump mounting bolts, then take the oil pump off and remove the gasket **(see illustration).**

Oil pump inspection

5 Remove the cover screw. Remove the cover, rotors, drive pins, center cover, dowel pins and shaft. On 600 models, unbolt the relief valve retainer and remove the retainer, spring and relief valve. The oil pump on 600 models has two sets of rotors; be sure not to mix these up.

6 Check all parts for visible wear and damage. Replace the oil pump if problems are found.

7 Refer to Part D of this Chapter to check the oil pump clearances.

8 Check the pump shaft for a loose fit in the cover. Replace the pump if problems are found.

9 Reassemble the pump by reversing the disassembly steps, with the following additions:

a) Before installing the cover, pack the cavities between the rotors with petroleum jelly - this will ensure the pump develops suction quickly and begins oil circulation as soon as the engine is started.
b) Make sure the cover dowels and drive pins are in position.
c) Tighten the cover screw, relief valve screws (600 models) and strainer screw to the torque listed in this Chapter's Specifications.

Oil pump installation

10 Installation is the reverse of removal, with the following additions:

a) Install a new gasket.
b) Tighten the oil pump mounting screws or bolts to the torque listed in this Chapter's Specifications.

Relief valve (660 models)

Refer to illustrations 16.11a and 16.11b

Removal

11 Unbolt the relief valve retainer from the crankcase **(see illustra-**

16.4c Unbolt the pump, lift it out and remove the gasket

16.11a Unbolt the oil pressure relief valve retainer . . .

16.11b . . . and remove the relief valve and its O-ring (arrow) from the crankcase

Chapter 2 Part C Engine, clutch and transmission (600 and 660 models) 2C-15

17.3 Lift the balancer shaft (arrow) out of the crankcase

18.10 Unbolt the middle driven gear assembly and lift it out of the crankcase

tion). Work the relief valve and O-ring free of the crankcase and pull them out **(see illustration)**.
12 Remove the snap-ring from the valve housing. Remove the spring cap, spring and valve from the valve body.

Inspection
13 Check all parts for wear and damage and replace as needed.

Installation
14 Installation is the reverse of the removal Steps. Use a new O-ring and cotter pin. Tighten the retainer bolts to the torque listed in this Chapter's Specifications.

17 Balancer and crankshaft - removal and installation

Refer to illustration 17.3
1 Disassemble the crankcase (see Section 12).
2 If you're working on a 600 model, turn the crankshaft and balancer so their alignment marks are lined up **(see illustration 14.2)**. This is how they should align when the balancer is reinstalled.
3 Pull the balancer out of the engine **(see illustration)**.
4 Refer to Part D of this Chapter to remove, inspect and reinstall the crankshaft.
5 The remainder of installation is the reverse of the removal steps. Be sure to align the marks on the crankshaft and balancer, or severe engine vibration will occur.

18 Transmission shafts, forks and shift cam - removal, inspection and installation

Note: *When disassembling the transmission shafts, place the parts on a long rod or thread a wire through them to keep them in order and facing the proper direction.*

Removal
1 Remove the engine, then separate the case halves (see Sections 4 and 13).

600 models
2 Remove the idler gear assembly.
3 Lift out the secondary shaft.
4 Remove the no. 2 clutch dog and reverse shift fork. Lift out the shift cam.

18.11 Lift the transmission shafts, forks and fork shaft out together

5 Pull out the fork shaft and remove the low shift fork, spring and cup.
6 Unbolt the middle drive shaft housing and remove the shaft from the crankcase.
7 Unbolt the middle drive shaft's bearing housing from the crankcase and lift it out. Rotate the shaft and check the bearing for rough or noisy movement. Check the drive pinion gear for wear or damage. Rotate the middle driven shaft (in the crankcase), feeling for tightness, rough spots, excessive looseness and listening for noises. Replacement of the bevel gear or shaft will require setting up the gear backlash of the middle driven gear; take the case and middle driven gear assembly to a Yamaha dealer to have this procedure done.
8 Remove the snap-rings and gear components from the driveaxle. Place them on a long rod so they can be reassembled in the same order.
9 Refer to Part D of this Chapter to inspect the transmission components.

660 models
Refer to illustrations 18.10, 18.11, 18.12, 18.13, 18.14a and 18.14b
10 Unbolt the middle driven gear assembly from the crankcase and lift it out **(see illustration)**.
11 Lift the transmission shafts and shift forks out of the crankcase together **(see illustration)**.

Chapter 2 Part C Engine, clutch and transmission (600 and 660 models)

18.12 If necessary, remove the snap-ring (arrow) and thrust washer, then remove the parking pawl and shaft

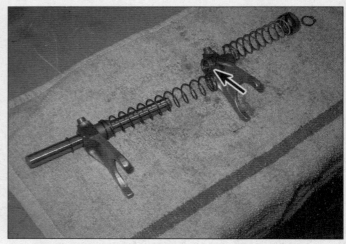

18.13 Shift fork shaft components; note that one fork has a shoulder (arrow) that fits inside the spring

18.14a Here are the driveaxle components disassembled . . .

18.14b . . . when assembled, they should look like this

12 Check the parking pawl and its shaft for wear or damage (**see illustration**). If necessary, remove the snap-ring and thrust washer and slide the pawl off the shaft. Work the shaft free of the crankcase and lift it out.

13 Remove the snap-rings and disassemble the fork shaft (**see illustration**).
14 Remove the snap-rings and disassemble the driveaxle (**see illustrations**).

Installation

600 models

15 Installation is the basically the reverse of the removal procedure, but take note of the following points:

  a) Use new snap-rings.
  b) The number mark on each shift fork faces the right side of the crankcase.
  c) Lubricate the components with engine oil before assembling them.
  d) After assembly, check the gears to make sure they're installed correctly. Move the shift cam through the gear positions and rotate the gears to make sure they mesh and shift correctly.

660 models

Refer to illustrations 18.18a, 18.18b and 18.19

16 Assemble the fork shaft components and driveaxle components (**see illustrations 18.13, 18.14a and 18.14b**).
17 If the parking pawl and shaft were removed, install them, using a new snap-ring (**see illustration 18.12**).
18 Mesh the gears and shift forks and position them in the case (see

18.18a The gears and forks engage like this when they're installed

Chapter 2 Part C Engine, clutch and transmission (600 and 660 models) 2C-17

18.18b Install the shafts and position the fork shaft to one side of its hole (arrow) . . .

18.19 . . . then install the shift cam and move the forks into engagement with the shift cam grooves; let the fork shaft drop into its hole

illustration). For the time being, place the lower end of the fork shaft to one side of its hole **(see illustration)**.

19 Install the shift cam. Slide the fork shaft over so it drops into its hole, engaging the shift fork pins with the shift cam grooves as you do so **(see illustration)**.

20 The remainder of installation is the basically the reverse of the removal procedure, but take note of the following points:

  a) *Use new snap-rings.*

  b) *The number mark on each shift fork faces the right side of the crankcase.*

  c) *Lubricate the components with engine oil before assembling them.*

  d) *After assembly, check the gears to make sure they're installed correctly. Move the shift cam through the gear positions and rotate the gears to make sure they mesh and shift correctly.*

Notes

Chapter 2 Part D
General engine overhaul procedures

Contents

	Section
Camshaft and rocker arms - inspection	5
Crankcase bearings - inspection, removal and installation	13
Crankshaft and connecting rod - removal, inspection and installation	14
Cylinder - inspection	9
Cylinder compression - check	3
Cylinder head - inspection	6
Cylinder head and valves - disassembly, inspection and reassembly	8
Engine disassembly and reassembly - general information	4

	Section
General information	1
Initial start-up after overhaul	16
Major engine repair - general note	2
Oil pump - inspection	12
Piston - removal, inspection and installation	10
Piston rings - installation	11
Recommended break-in procedure	17
Transmission components - inspection	15
Valves/valve seats/valve guides - servicing	7

Specifications

Kodiak

Rocker arms

Rocker arm inside diameter
  Standard .... 12.000 to 12.018 mm (0.4724 to 0.4731 inch)
  Limit .... 12.078 mm (0.4755 inch)
Rocker shaft outside diameter
  Standard .... 11.981 to 11.991 mm (0.4717 to 0.4721 inch)
  Limit .... 11.951 mm (0.4705 inch)
Shaft-to-arm clearance
  Standard .... 0.009 to 0.037 mm (0.0004 to 0.0015 inch)
  Limit .... 0.08 mm (0.0031 inch)

Camshaft

Lobe height
  Intake (1993 through 1998)
    Standard .... 40.29 to 40.39 mm (1.586 to 1.590 mm)
    Limit .... 40.26 mm (1.585 inch)
  Exhaust (1993 through 1998)
    Standard .... 40.28 to 40.38 mm (1.586 to 1.590 mm)
    Limit .... 40.25 mm (1.585 inch)
  Intake and exhaust (1999 and later)
    Standard .... 40.62 to 40.72 mm (1.586 to 1.590 mm)
    Limit .... Not specified
Camshaft runout limit .... 0.03 mm (0.0012 inch)

Cylinder head, valves and valve springs

Cylinder head warpage limit	0.03 mm (0.0012 inch)
Valve stem runout	0.01 mm (0.0004 inch)
Valve stem diameter	
Intake	
Standard	6.975 to 6.990 mm (0.2746 to 0.2752 inch)
Limit	6.95 mm (0274 inch)
Exhaust	
Standard	6.955 to 6.970 mm (0.2738 to 0.2744 inch)
Limit	6.915 mm (0272 inch)
Valve guide inside diameter	
Standard	7.000 to 7.012 mm (0.2756 to 0.2761 inch)
Limit	7.03 mm (0.277 inch)
Stem-to-guide clearance	
Intake	
Standard	0.010 to 0.037 mm (0.0004 to 00015 inch)
Limit	0.08 mm (0.0031 inch)
Exhaust	
Standard	0.030 to 0.057 mm (0.0012 to 0.0022 inch)
Limit	0.10 mm (0.004 inch)
Seat width	
Standard	1.2 to 1.4 mm (0.047 to 0.055 inch)
Limit	1.6 mm (0.063 inch)
Margin thickness	
Intake	1.0 to 1.4 mm (0.039 to 0.055 inch)
Exhaust	0.8 to 1.2 mm (0.031 to 0.047 inch)
Valve spring free length	
Inner spring	
Standard	39.9 mm (1.57 inch)
Limit	37.9 mm (1.49 inch)
Outer spring	
Standard	43.27 mm (1.70 inch)
Limit	41.27 mm (1.62 inch)
Valve spring bend limit	1.6 mm (0.063 inch)

Cylinder

1993 through 1999	
Bore diameter	82.97 to 83.02 mm (3.2665 to 3.2685 inch)
Out-of-round limit	0.01 mm (0.0004 inch)
Taper limit	Not specified
Measuring point	40 mm (1.57 inch) from top of bore
2000 and later	
Bore diameter	84.500 to 84.510 mm (3.3268 to 3.3272 inch)
Out-of-round limit	
400 models	0.03 mm (0.0012 inch)
450 models	0.01 mm (0.0004 inch)
Taper limit	0.05 mm (0.0016 inch)

Piston

1993 through 1999 models	
Diameter	82.92 to 82.97 mm (3.265 to 3.267 inches)
Measuring point	5.5 mm (0.217 inch) from bottom of skirt
Piston-to-cylinder clearance	0.04 to 0.06 mm (0.0016 to 0.0024 inch)
Oversize pistons and rings	
First oversize	83.50 mm (3.287 inches)
Second oversize	84.00 mm (3.307 inches)
Piston pin bore	19.004 to 19.015 mm (0.7482 to 0.7486 inch)
Piston pin outer diameter	18.990 to 18.995 mm (0.7476 to 0.7478 inch)
Piston pin-to-piston clearance	Not specified
Piston pin offset	0.5 mm (0.02 inch)
2000 and later models	
Diameter	84.445 to 84.460 mm (3.3246 to 3.3252 inches)
Measuring point	5.0 mm (0.2 inch) from bottom of skirt
Piston-to-cylinder clearance	
Standard	0.040 to 0.065 mm (0.0016 to 0.0026 inch)
Limit	0.15 mm (0.006 inch)
Piston pin bore	20.004 to 20.015 mm (0.7876 to 0.7880 inch)
Piston pin outer diameter	19.991 to 20.000 mm (0.7871 to 0.7874 inch)

Chapter 2 Part D General engine overhaul procedures

Piston pin-to-piston clearance
  Standard .... 0.004 to 0.022 mm 0.0002 to 0.0009 inch)
  Limit .... 0.07 mm (0.0028 inch)
Piston pin offset .... 0.5 mm (0.02 inch)

Piston rings
1993 through 1999 models
  Ring side clearance
    Top
      Standard .... 0.04 to 0.08 mm (0.0016 to 0.0031 inch)
      Limit .... 0.12 mm (0.0047 inch)
    Second
      Standard .... 003 to 0.07 mm (0.0012 to 0.0028 inch)
      Limit .... 0.12 mm (0.0047 inch)
  Ring end gap
    Top
      Standard .... 0.2 to 0.4 mm (0.008 to 0.018 inch)
      Limit .... 0.5 mm (0.02 inch)
    Second
      Standard .... 0.2 to 0.4 mm (0.008 to 0.018 inch)
      Limit .... 0.5 mm (0.02 inch)
    Oil
      Standard .... 0.3 to 0.9 mm (0.012 to 0.035 inch)
      Limit .... Not specified
  Ring gap measuring point .... 40 mm (1.57 inch) from top of bore
2000 and later models
  Ring side clearance (400)
    Top
      Standard .... 0.03 to 0.08 mm (0.0012 to 0.0031 inch)
      Limit .... 0.13 mm (0.0051 inch)
    Second
      Standard .... 0.03 to 0.07 mm (0.0012 to 0.0028 inch)
      Limit .... 0.13 mm (0.0051 inch)
  Ring side clearance (450)
    Top
      Standard .... 0.03 to 0.07 mm (0.0012 to 0.0028 inch)
      Limit .... 0.12 mm (0.0047 inch)
    Second
      Standard .... 0.02 to 0.06 mm (0.0008 to 0.0024 inch)
      Limit .... 0.12 mm (0.0047 inch)
  Ring end gap
    Top
      Standard .... 0.2 to 0.4 mm (0.008 to 0.018 inch)
      Limit .... 0.65 mm (0.026 inch)
    Second
      Standard .... 0.4 to 0.6 mm (0.016 to 0.024 inch)
      Limit .... 0.95 mm (0.037 inch)
    Oil
      Standard .... 0.2 to 0.7 mm (0.008 to 0.028 inch)
      Limit .... Not specified
  Ring gap measuring point .... 40 mm (1.57 inch) from top of bore

Oil pump
Inner-to-outer rotor clearance
  Standard .... 0.15 mm (0.006 inch)
  Limit .... 0.2 mm (0.008 inch)
Outer rotor-to-body clearance
  Standard .... 0.4 to 0.9 mm (0.002 to 0.004 inch)
  Limit .... Not specified

Crankshaft and connecting rod
1993 through 1999 models
  Runout limit .... 0.06 mm (0.0024 inch)
  Assembly width .... 58.95 to 59.00 mm (2.321 to 3.323 inch)
  Connecting rod big-end side clearance
    Standard .... 0.35 to 0.85 mm (0.014 to 0.033 inch)
    Limit .... 0.7 mm (0.028 inch)
  Connecting rod small-end endplay
    Standard .... 0.8 to 1.0 mm (0.0315 to 0.0394 inch)
    Limit .... 2 mm (0.0787 inch)

Crankshaft and connecting rod (continued)
2000 and later models
    Runout limit .... 0.03 mm (0.0012 inch)
    Assembly width .... 62.95 to 63.00 mm (2.478 to 2.480 inch)
    Connecting rod big-end side clearance
        Standard .... 0.25 to 0.75 mm (0.010 to 0.030 inch)
        Limit .... 1.0 mm (0.040 inch)
    Connecting rod small-end endplay
        Standard .... 0.010 to 0.025 mm (0.0004 to 0.0010 inch)
        Limit .... Not specified

Grizzly 600

Rocker arms
Rocker arm inside diameter
    Standard .... 12.000 to 12.018 mm (0.4724 to 0.4731 inch)
    Limit .... Not specified
Rocker shaft outside diameter
    Standard .... 11.985 to 11.991 mm (0.4719 to 0.4721 inch)
    Limit .... Not specified
Shaft-to-arm clearance
    Standard .... 0.009 to 0.033 mm (0.0004 to 0.0013 inch)
    Limit .... Not specified

Camshaft
Lobe height
    Intake
        Standard .... 36.47 to 36.57 mm (1.436 to 1.440 mm)
        Limit .... 36.37 mm (1.433 inch)
    Exhaust
        Standard .... 36.62 to 36.72 mm (1.442 to 1.446 mm)
        Limit .... 36.52 mm (1.438 inch)
Camshaft runout limit .... 0.03 mm (0.0012 inch)
Camshaft journal diameter
    Standard .... 22.967 to 22.980 mm (0.9042 to 0.9047 inch)
    Limit .... Not specified
Camshaft bearing diameter
    Standard .... 23.000 to 23.021 mm (0.9055 to 0.9063 inch)
    Limit .... Not specified
Journal-to-bearing clearance
    Standard .... 0.020 to 0.054 mm (0.0008 to 0.0021 inch)
    Limit .... Not specified

Cylinder head, valves and valve springs
Cylinder head warpage
    Standard .... 0.03 mm 0.0012 inch)
    Limit .... 0.10 mm (0.004 inch)
Valve stem runout .... 0.01 mm (0.0004 inch)
Valve stem diameter
    Intake
        Standard .... 6.975 to 6.990 mm (0.2746 to 0.2752 inch)
        Limit .... Not specified
    Exhaust
        Standard .... 6.955 to 6.970 mm (0.2738 to 0.2744 inch)
        Limit .... Not specified
Valve guide inside diameter
    Standard .... 7.000 to 7.012 mm (0.2556 to 0.2761 inch)
    Limit .... Not specified
Stem-to-guide clearance
    Intake
        Standard .... 0.010 to 0.037 mm (0.0004 to 00015 inch)
        Limit .... 0.08 mm (0.0031 inch)
    Exhaust
        Standard .... 0.030 to 0.057 mm (0.0012 to 0.0022 inch)
        Limit .... 0.10 mm (0.004 inch)
Seat width (intake and exhaust)
    Standard .... 1.0 to 1.2 mm (0.039 to 0.047 inch)
    Limit .... Not specified

Chapter 2 Part D General engine overhaul procedures

Margin thickness
  Intake .... 1.0 to 1.4 mm (0.039 to 0.055 inch)
  Exhaust .... 0.8 to 1.2 mm (0.031 to 0.047 inch)
Valve spring free length
  Inner spring
    Standard .... 40.1 mm (1.58 inch)
    Limit .... 37.9 mm (1.49 inch)
  Outer spring
    Standard .... 43.8 mm (1.72 inch)
    Limit .... 41.6 mm (1.64 inch)
Valve spring bend limit
  Inner spring .... 1.7 mm (0.063 inch)
  Outer spring .... 1.9 mm (0.075 inch)

Cylinder
Bore diameter .... 94.97 to 95.02 mm (3.739 to 3.741 inch)
Out-of-round limit .... 0.01 mm (0.0004 inch)
Taper limit .... Not specified
Measuring point .... 40 mm (1.57 inch) from top of bore

Piston
Diameter .... 94.915 to 94.965 mm (3.737 to 3.739 inches)
Measuring point .... 5.0 mm (0.2 inch) from bottom of skirt
Piston-to-cylinder clearance .... 0.045 to 0.065 mm (0.0018 to 0.0026 inch)
Piston pin bore .... 22.004 to 22.015 mm (0.8663 to 0.8667 inch)
Piston pin outer diameter .... 21.991 to 22.000 mm (0.8658 to 0.8661 inch)
Piston pin-to-piston clearance .... Not specified
Piston pin offset .... 2.0 mm (0.08 inch)

Piston rings
Ring side clearance
  Top
    Standard .... 0.04 to 0.08 mm (0.0016 to 0.0031 inch)
    Limit .... 0.13 mm (0.0051 inch)
  Second
    Standard .... 0.03 to 0.07 mm (0.001 to 0.002 inch)
    Limit .... 0.13 mm (0.0051 inch)
Ring end gap
  Top
    Standard .... 0.30 to 0.45 mm (0.012 to 0.018 inch)
    Limit .... 0.7 mm (0.028 inch)
  Second
    Standard .... 0.30 to 0.45 mm (0.012 to 0.018 inch)
    Limit .... 0.8 mm (0.031 inch)
  Oil
    Standard .... 0.2 to 0.2 mm (0.008 to 0.028 inch)
    Limit .... Not specified
Ring gap measuring point .... 40 mm (1.57 inch) from top of bore

Oil pump
Inner-to-outer rotor clearance
  Standard .... 0.12 mm (0.005 inch)
  Limit... 0.2 mm (0.008 inch)
Outer rotor-to-body clearance
  Standard .... 0.09 to 0.15 mm (0.004 to 0.006 inch)
  Limit... 0.22 mm (0.009 inch)

Crankshaft and connecting rod
Runout limit .... 0.03 mm (0.0012 inch)
Assembly width .... 74.95 to 75.00 mm (2.951 to 2.953 inch)
Connecting rod big-end side clearance
  Standard .... 0.35 to 0.65 mm (0.014 to 0.026 inch)
  Limit... 1.0 mm (0.040 inch)

Grizzly 660

Rocker arms
Rocker arm inside diameter
  Standard .... 12.000 to 12.018 mm (0.4724 to 0.4731 inch)
  Limit... Not specified

Rocker arms (continued)
Rocker shaft outside diameter
    Standard .... 11.976 to 11.991 mm (0.4715 to 0.4721 inch)
    Limit .... Not specified
Shaft-to-arm clearance
    Standard .... 0.009 to 0.042 mm (0.0004 to 0.0017 inch)
    Limit .... Not specified

Camshaft
Lobe height
    Intake
        Standard .... 35.69 to 35.79 mm (1.4051 to 1.4091 inch)
        Limit .... 35.59 mm (1.4012 inch)
    Exhaust
        Standard .... 36.5 to 36.6 mm (1.4370 to 1.4409 inch)
        Limit .... 36.4 mm (1.4331 inch)
Camshaft runout limit .... 0.03 mm (0.0012 inch)
Camshaft journal diameter
    Standard .... Not specified
    Limit .... Not specified
Camshaft bearing inside diameter... Not specified

Cylinder head, valves and valve springs
Cylinder head warpage limit .... 0.03 mm 0.0012 inch)
Valve stem runout .... 0.01 mm (0.0004 inch)
Valve stem diameter
    Intake
        Standard .... 5.975 to 5.990 mm (0.2352 to 0.2358 inch)
        Limit .... 5.945 mm (0.2341 inch)
    Exhaust
        Standard .... 5.960 to 5.975 mm (0.2346 to 0.2352 inch)
        Limit .... 5.930 mm (0.2335 inch)
Valve guide inside diameter
    Standard .... 6.000 to 6.012 mm (0.2362 to 0.2367 inch)
    Limit .... 6.050 mm (0.2559 inch)
Stem-to-guide clearance
    Intake
        Standard .... 0.010 to 0.037 mm (0.0004 to 00015 inch)
        Limit .... 0.08 mm (0.0031 inch)
    Exhaust
        Standard .... 0.025 to 0.052 mm (0.0010 to 0.0020 inch)
        Limit .... 0.10 mm (0.004 inch)
Seat width (intake and exhaust)
    Standard .... 0.9 to 1.1 mm (0.0354 to 0.0433 inch)
    Limit .... 1.6 mm (0.063 inch)
Margin thickness (intake and exhaust)... 0.85 to 1.15 mm (0.0335 to 0.0452 inch)
Valve spring free length
    Intake valve springs
        Standard .... 32.63 mm (1.28 inch)
        Limit .... 31.0 mm (1.22 inch)
    Exhaust valve springs
        Standard .... 34.46 mm (1.44 inch)
        Limit .... 34.6 mm (1.36 inch)
Valve spring bend limit
    Intake valve spring .... 1.4 mm (0.055 inch)
    Outer spring .... 1.6 mm (0.063 inch)

Cylinder
Bore diameter
    Standard .... 100.005 to 100.055 mm (3.9372 to 3.9392 inches)
    Limit .... 100.1 mm (3.9409 inches)
Out-of-round limit .... Not specified
Taper limit .... Not specified
Measuring point .... 50 mm (1.97 inch) from top of bore

Piston
Diameter.. 99.945 to 99.995 mm (3.9348 to 3.9368 inches)
Measuring point .... 2.5 mm (0.10 inch) from bottom of skirt
Piston-to-cylinder clearance .... 0.05 to 0.07 mm (0.0020 to 0.0028 inch)

Chapter 2 Part D General engine overhaul procedures

Piston pin bore
   Standard .... 22.004 to 22.015 mm (0.8663 to 0.8667 inch)
   Limit... 22.045 mm (0.8679 inch)
Piston pin outer diameter
   Standard .... 21.991 to 22.000 mm (0.8658 to 0.8661 inch)
   Limit... 21.971 mm (0.8650 inch)
Piston pin-to-piston clearance .... Not specified
Piston pin offset .... 1.0 mm (0.039 inch)

Piston rings
Ring side clearance
   Top
      Standard .... 0.04 to 0.08 mm (0.0016 to 0.0031 inch)
      Limit.. 0.13 mm (0.0051 inch)
   Second
      Standard .... 0.03 to 0.07 mm (0.001 to 0.002 inch)
      Limit.. 0.13 mm (0.0051 inch)
   Oil
      Standard .... 0.06 to 0.15 mm (0.0024 to 0.0059 inch)
      Limit.. Not specified
Ring end gap
   Top
      Standard .... 0.30 to 0.45 mm (0.012 to 0.018 inch)
      Limit.. 0.7 mm (0.028 inch)
   Second
      Standard .... 0.30 to 0.45 mm (0.012 to 0.018 inch)
      Limit.. 0.8 mm (0.031 inch)
   Oil
      Standard .... 0.2 to 0.7 mm (0.008 to 0.028 inch)
      Limit.. Not specified
Ring gap measuring point .... 50 mm (2.0 inches) from top of bore

Oil pump
Inner-to-outer rotor clearance
   Standard .... 0.03 to 0.10 mm (0.001 to 0.004 inch)
   Limit... 0.15 mm (0.006 inch)
Outer rotor-to-body clearance
   Standard .... 0.03 to 0.10 mm (0.001 to 0.004 inch)
   Limit... 0.15 mm (0.006 inch)
Side clearance
   Standard .... 0.03 to 0.10 mm (0.001 to 0.004 inch)
   Limit
      2002 models .... 0.12 mm (0.005 inch)
      2003 and later models .... 0.17 mm (0.007 inch)

Crankshaft and connecting rod
Runout limit .... 0.03 mm (0.0012 inch)
Assembly width .... 74.95 to 75.00 mm (2.951 to 2.953 inches)
Connecting rod big-end side clearance
   Standard .... 0.35 to 0.65 mm (0.014 to 0.026 inch)
   Limit... 1.0 mm (0.040 inch)
Small end endplay... 0.06 to 0.15 mm (0.0024 to 0.0059 inch)

Chapter 2 Part D General engine overhaul procedures

1 General information

Included in this portion of Chapter 2 are general inspection and overhaul procedures. The information includes advice concerning preparation for an overhaul and the purchase of replacement parts, as well as inspection procedures which will tell you if a part must be reconditioned or replaced.

The Specifications included in this Part are only those necessary for the inspection and overhaul procedures which follow. Refer to earlier Parts of Chapter 2 for additional Specifications.

2 Major engine repair - general note

1   It is not always easy to determine when or if an engine should be completely overhauled, as a number of factors must be considered.
2   High mileage is not necessarily an indication that an overhaul is needed, while low mileage, on the other hand, does not preclude the need for an overhaul. Frequency of servicing is probably the single most important consideration. An engine that has regular and frequent oil and filter changes, as well as other required maintenance, will most likely give many miles of reliable service. Conversely, a neglected engine, or one which has not been broken in properly, may require an overhaul very early in its life.
3   Exhaust smoke and excessive oil consumption are both indications that piston rings and/or valve guides are in need of attention. Make sure oil leaks are not responsible before deciding that the rings and guides are bad. Refer to Chapter 1 and perform a cylinder compression check to determine for certain the nature and extent of the work required.
4   If the engine is making obvious knocking or rumbling noises, the connecting rod and/or main bearings are probably at fault.
5   Loss of power, rough running, excessive valve train noise and high fuel consumption rates may also point to the need for an overhaul, especially if they are all present at the same time. If a complete tune-up does not remedy the situation, major mechanical work is the only solution.
6   An engine overhaul generally involves restoring the internal parts to the specifications of a new engine. During an overhaul the piston rings are replaced and the cylinder walls are bored and/or honed. If a rebore is done, then a new piston is also required. The crankshaft and connecting rod are permanently assembled, so if one of these components needs to be replaced both must be. Generally the valves are serviced as well, since they are usually in less than perfect condition at this point. While the engine is being overhauled, other components such as the carburetor and the starter motor can be rebuilt also. The end result should be a like-new engine that will give as many trouble-free miles as the original.
7   Before beginning the engine overhaul, read through all of the related procedures to familiarize yourself with the scope and requirements of the job. Overhauling an engine is not all that difficult, but it is time consuming. Plan on the vehicle being tied up for a minimum of two weeks. Check on the availability of parts and make sure that any necessary special tools, equipment and supplies are obtained in advance.
8   Most work can be done with typical shop hand tools, although a number of precision measuring tools are required for inspecting parts to determine if they must be replaced. Often a dealer service department or repair shop will handle the inspection of parts and offer advice concerning reconditioning and replacement. As a general rule, time is the primary cost of an overhaul so it doesn't pay to install worn or substandard parts.
9   As a final note, to ensure maximum life and minimum trouble from a rebuilt engine, everything must be assembled with care in a spotlessly clean environment.

3 Cylinder compression - check

Refer to illustration 3.5

1   Among other things, poor engine performance may be caused by leaking valves, incorrect valve clearances, a leaking head gasket, or worn piston, rings and/or cylinder wall. A cylinder compression check will help pinpoint these conditions and can also indicate the presence of excessive carbon deposits in the cylinder head.
2   The only tools required are a compression gauge and a spark plug wrench. Depending on the outcome of the initial test, a squirt-type oil can may also be needed.
3   Start the engine and allow it to reach normal operating temperature, then remove the spark plugs (see Chapter 1, if necessary). Work carefully - don't strip the spark plug hole threads and don't burn your hands.
4   Disable the ignition by disconnecting the primary (low tension) wires from the coil (see Chapter 5). Be sure to mark the locations of the wires before detaching them.
5   Install the compression gauge in the spark plug hole **(see illustration)**. Hold or block the throttle wide open.
6   Crank the engine over a minimum of four or five revolutions (or until the gauge reading stops increasing) and observe the initial movement of the compression gauge needle as well as the final total gauge reading. Compare the results to the value listed in this Chapter's Specifications.
7   If the compression built up quickly and evenly to the specified amount, you can assume the engine upper end is in reasonably good mechanical condition. Worn or sticking piston rings and worn cylinders will produce very little initial movement of the gauge needle, but compression will tend to build up gradually as the engine spins over. Valve and valve seat leakage, or head gasket leakage, is indicated by low initial compression which does not tend to build up.
8   To further confirm your findings, add a small amount of engine oil to the cylinder by inserting the nozzle of a squirt-type oil can through the spark plug hole. The oil will tend to seal the piston rings if they are leaking.
9   If the compression increases significantly after the addition of the oil, the piston rings and/or cylinder are definitely worn. If the compression does not increase, the pressure is leaking past the valves or the head gasket. Leakage past the valves may be due to insufficient valve clearances, burned, warped or cracked valves or valve seats or valves that are hanging up in the guides.
10   If compression readings are considerably higher than specified, the combustion chamber is probably coated with excessive carbon deposits. It is possible (but not very likely) for carbon deposits to raise the compression enough to compensate for the effects of leakage past rings or valves. Refer to Section 8, remove the cylinder head and carefully decarbonize the combustion chamber.

3.5 A compression gauge with a threaded fitting for the spark plug hole is preferred over the type that requires hand pressure to maintain the seal

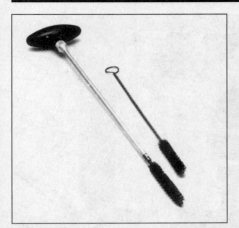

4.2 A selection of brushes is required for cleaning holes and passages in the engine components

4.3 An engine stand can be made from short lengths of lumber and lag bolts or nails

5.2a Check the cam lobes for wear - here's a good example of damage which will require replacement (or repair) of the camshaft

4 Engine disassembly and reassembly - general information

Refer to illustrations 4.2 and 4.3

1 Before disassembling the engine, clean the exterior with a degreaser and rinse it with water. A clean engine will make the job easier and prevent the possibility of getting dirt into the internal areas of the engine.

2 In addition to the precision measuring tools mentioned earlier, you will need a torque wrench, a valve spring compressor, oil gallery brushes **(see illustration)**, a piston ring removal and installation tool, a piston ring compressor and a clutch holder tool. Some new, clean engine oil of the correct grade and type, some engine assembly lube (or moly-based grease) and a tube of RTV (silicone) sealant will also be required.

3 An engine support stand make from short lengths of 2 x 4's bolted together will facilitate the disassembly and reassembly procedures **(see illustration)**. If you have an automotive-type engine stand, an adapter plate can be made from a piece of plate, some angle iron and some nuts and bolts.

4 When disassembling the engine, keep "mated" parts together (including gears, drum shifter pawls, etc.) that have been in contact with each other during engine operation. These "mated" parts must be reused or replaced as an assembly.

5 Engine/transmission disassembly should be done in the following general order with reference to the appropriate Sections.

Remove the valve cover, rocker arms and pushrods
Remove the cylinder head
Remove the cylinder
Remove the piston
Remove the clutches or drivebelt and pulleys
Remove the oil pump
Remove the cam chain tensioner and camshaft
Remove the external shift mechanism
Remove the alternator rotor and starter clutch
Separate the crankcase halves
Remove the shift drum/forks
Remove the transmission shafts/gears
Remove the crankshaft and connecting rod

6 Reassembly is accomplished by reversing the general disassembly sequence.

5 Camshaft and rocker arms - inspection

Camshaft, chain and guides

Refer to illustrations 5.2a and 5.2b

Note: *Before replacing the camshaft or the cylinder head because of damage, check with local machine shops specializing in ATV or motorcycle engine work. In the case of the camshaft; it may be possible for cam lobes to be welded, reground and hardened, at a cost far lower than that of a new camshaft. If the bearing surfaces in the cylinder head on a Grizzly model are damaged, it may be possible for them to be bored out to accept bearing inserts. Due to the cost of a new cylinder head it is recommended that all options be explored before condemning it as trash!*

1 Rotate the cam bearings (Kodiak models) and check for roughness, looseness or noise. Check the sealed side of the outer bearing for signs of leakage. Replace the bearing(s) if problems are found.

2 Check the camshaft lobes for heat discoloration (blue appearance), score marks, chipped areas, flat spots and spalling **(see illustration)**. Measure the height of each lobe with a micrometer **(see illustration)** and compare the results to the minimum lobe height listed in this Chapter's Specifications. If damage is noted or wear is excessive, the camshaft must be replaced. Check the bearing surfaces for scoring or wear. Also, be sure to check the condition of the rocker arms, as described below.

3 Except in cases of oil starvation, the camshaft chain wears very little. If the chain has stretched excessively, which makes it difficult to maintain proper tension, replace it with a new one, referring to the appropriate Part of this Chapter.

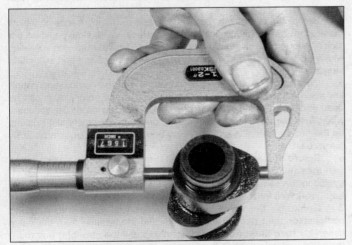

5.2b Measure the height of the cam lobes with a micrometer

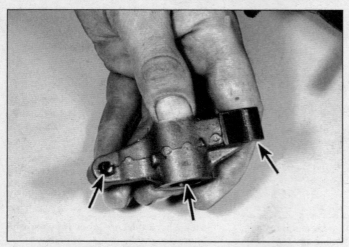

5.6 Check rocker arms for wear on the adjuster surface, inside the bore and on the cam contact surface (arrows)

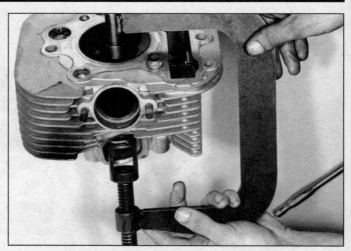

8.7a Compress the spring, remove the keepers and release the compressor

4   Check the sprocket for wear, cracks and other damage, replacing it if necessary. If the sprocket is worn, the chain is also worn, and possibly the sprocket on the crankshaft. If wear this severe is apparent, the entire engine should be disassembled for inspection.
5   Check the chain guides for wear or damage. If they are worn or damaged, replace them.

Rocker arms and shafts

Refer to illustration 5.6

6   Check the rocker arms for wear at the cam contact surfaces, inside the shaft bores and at the tips of the valve adjusting screws **(see illustration)**. Try to twist the rocker arms from side-to-side on the shafts. If they're loose on the shafts or if there's visible wear, measure the rocker arm shaft diameter and bore diameter with a micrometer and hole gauge. If the parts are worn beyond the limits listed in this Chapter's Specifications, replace them. Replace the rocker arm and shaft as a set.

6   Cylinder head - inspection

1   Check the cylinder head gasket and the mating surfaces on the cylinder head and cylinder for leakage, which could indicate warpage.
2   Clean all traces of old gasket material from the cylinder head and cylinder. Be careful not to let any of the gasket material fall into the crankcase, the cylinder bore or the bolt holes.
3   Refer to Section 8 and check the flatness of the cylinder head.

7   Valves/valve seats/valve guides - servicing

1   Because of the complex nature of this job and the special tools and equipment required, servicing of the valves, the valve seats and the valve guides (commonly known as a valve job) is best left to a professional.
2   The home mechanic can, however, remove and disassemble the head, do the initial cleaning and inspection, then reassemble and deliver the head to a dealer service department or properly equipped vehicle repair shop for the actual valve servicing. Refer to Section 8 for those procedures.
3   The dealer service department will remove the valves and springs, recondition or replace the valves and valve seats, replace the valve guides, check and replace the valve springs, spring retainers and keepers (as necessary), replace the valve seals with new ones and reassemble the valve components.
4   After the valve job has been performed, the head will be in like-new condition. When the head is returned, be sure to clean it again very thoroughly before installation on the engine to remove any metal particles or abrasive grit that may still be present from the valve service operations. Use compressed air, if available, to blow out all the holes and passages.

8   Cylinder head and valves - disassembly, inspection and reassembly

1   As mentioned in the previous Section, valve servicing and valve guide replacement should be left to a dealer service department or vehicle repair shop. However, disassembly, cleaning and inspection of the valves and related components can be done (if the necessary special tools are available) by the home mechanic. This way no expense is incurred if the inspection reveals that service work is not required at this time.
2   To properly disassemble the valve components without the risk of damaging them, a valve spring compressor is absolutely necessary. If the special tool is not available, have a dealer service department or vehicle repair shop handle the entire process of disassembly, inspection, service or repair (if required) and reassembly of the valves.

Disassembly

Refer to illustrations 8.7a and 8.7b

3   Remove the carburetor intake tube from the cylinder head (see Chapter 4).
4   Before the valves are removed, scrape away any traces of gasket material from the head gasket sealing surface. Work slowly and do not nick or gouge the soft aluminum of the head. Gasket removing solvents, which work very well, are available at most vehicle shops and auto parts stores.
5   Carefully scrape all carbon deposits out of the combustion chamber area. A hand held wire brush or a piece of fine emery cloth can be used once most of the deposits have been scraped away. Do not use a wire brush mounted in a drill motor, or one with extremely stiff bristles, as the head material is soft and may be eroded away or scratched by the wire brush.
6   Before proceeding, arrange to label and store the valves along with their related components so they can be kept separate and reinstalled in the same valve guides they are removed from (again, plastic bags work well for this).
7   Compress the valve spring(s) on the first valve with a spring compressor, then remove the keepers and the retainer from the valve assembly **(see illustration)**. Do not compress the spring(s) any more than is absolutely necessary. Carefully release the valve spring compressor and remove the spring(s), spring seat and valve from the head

Chapter 2 Part D General engine overhaul procedures

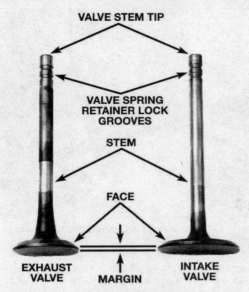

8.7b Check for valve wear at the points shown here

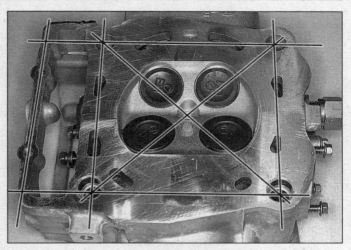

8.14 Check the gasket surface for flatness with a straightedge and feeler gauge in the directions shown

(see illustration). If the valve binds in the guide (won't pull through), push it back into the head and deburr the area around the keeper groove with a very fine file or whetstone.

8   Repeat the procedure for the remaining valves. Remember to keep the parts for each valve together so they can be reinstalled in the same location.

9   Once the valves have been removed and labeled, pull off the valve stem seals with pliers and discard them (the old seals should never be reused).

10   Next, clean the cylinder head with solvent and dry it thoroughly. Compressed air will speed the drying process and ensure that all holes and recessed areas are clean.

11   Clean all of the valve springs, keepers, retainers and spring seats with solvent and dry them thoroughly. Do the parts from one valve at a time so that no mixing of parts between valves occurs.

12   Scrape off any deposits that may have formed on the valve, then use a motorized wire brush to remove deposits from the valve heads and stems. Again, make sure the valves do not get mixed up.

Inspection

Refer to illustrations 8.14, 8.15, 8.16, 8.17, 8.18, 8.19a and 8.19b

13   Inspect the head very carefully for cracks and other damage. If cracks are found, a new head will be required. Check the cam bearing surfaces for wear and evidence of seizure. Check the camshaft for wear as well (see Section 5).

14   Using a precision straightedge and a feeler gauge, check the head gasket mating surface for warpage. Lay the straightedge lengthwise, across the head and diagonally (corner-to-corner), intersecting the head bolt holes, and try to slip a feeler gauge under it, on either side of each combustion chamber (see illustration). The feeler gauge thickness should be the same as the cylinder head warpage limit listed in this Chapter's Specifications. If the feeler gauge can be inserted between the head and the straightedge, the head is warped and must either be machined or, if warpage is excessive, replaced with a new one.

15   Examine the valve seats in each of the combustion chambers. If they are pitted, cracked or burned, the head will require valve service that is beyond the scope of the home mechanic. Measure the valve seat width (see illustration) and compare it to this Chapter's Specifications. If it is not within the specified range, or if it varies around its circumference, valve service work is required.

16   Clean the valve guides to remove any carbon buildup, then measure the inside diameters of the guides (at both ends and the center of the guide) with a small hole gauge and a micrometer (see illustration). Record the measurements for future reference. The guides are measured at the ends and at the center to determine if they are worn in a bell-mouth pattern (more wear at the ends). If they are, guide replacement is an absolute must.

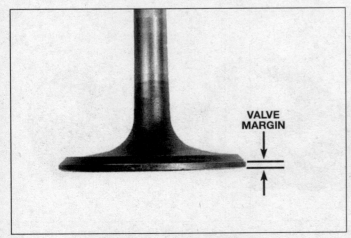

8.15 Measuring valve seat width

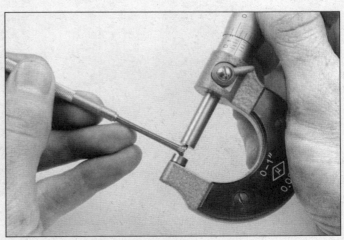

8.16 Measure the valve guide inside diameter with a hole gauge, then measure the gauge with a micrometer

Chapter 2 Part D General engine overhaul procedures

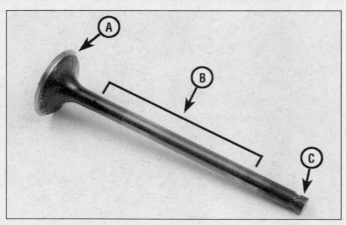

8.17 Check the valve face (A), stem (B) and keeper groove (C) for wear and damage

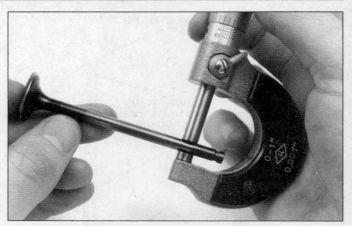

8.18 Measuring valve stem diameter

17 Carefully inspect each valve face for cracks, pits and burned spots. Check the valve stem and the keeper groove area for cracks **(see illustration)**. Rotate the valve and check for any obvious indication that it is bent. Check the end of the stem for pitting and excessive wear and make sure the bevel is the specified width. The presence of any of the above conditions indicates the need for valve servicing.

18 Measure the valve stem diameter **(see illustration)**. If the diameter is less than listed in this Chapter's Specifications, the valves will have to be replaced with new ones. Also check the valve stem for bending. Set the valve in a V-block with a dial indicator touching the middle of the stem. Rotate the valve and look for a reading on the gauge (which indicates a bent stem). If the stem is bent, replace the valve.

19 Check the end of each valve spring for wear and pitting. Measure the free length **(see illustration)** and compare it to this Chapter's Specifications. Any springs that are shorter than specified have sagged and should not be reused. Stand the spring on a flat surface and check it for squareness **(see illustration)**.

20 Check the spring retainers and keepers for obvious wear and cracks. Any questionable parts should not be reused, as extensive damage will occur in the event of failure during engine operation.

21 If the inspection indicates that no service work is required, the valve components can be reinstalled in the head.

Reassembly

Refer to illustrations 8.23, 8.24, 8.26 and 8.27

22 If the valve seats have been ground, the valves and seats should be lapped before installing the valves in the head to ensure a positive seal between the valves and seats. This procedure requires coarse and fine valve lapping compound (available at auto parts stores) and a valve lapping tool. If a lapping tool is not available, a piece of rubber or plastic hose can be slipped over the valve stem (after the valve has been installed in the guide) and used to turn the valve.

23 Apply a small amount of coarse lapping compound to the valve face **(see illustration)**, then slip the valve into the guide. **Note:** *Make sure the valve is installed in the correct guide and be careful not to get any lapping compound on the valve stem.*

24 Attach the lapping tool (or hose) to the valve and rotate the tool between the palms of your hands. Use a back-and-forth motion rather than a circular motion. Lift the valve off the seat and turn it at regular intervals to distribute the lapping compound properly. Continue the lapping procedure until the valve face and seat contact area is of uniform width and unbroken around the entire circumference of the valve face and seat **(see illustration)**. Once this is accomplished, lap the valves again with fine lapping compound.

25 Carefully remove the valve from the guide and wipe off all traces of lapping compound. Use solvent to clean the valve and wipe the seat area thoroughly with a solvent soaked cloth. Repeat the procedure for the remaining valves.

26 Lay the spring seat in place in the cylinder head, then install new valve stem seals on both of the guides **(see illustration)**. Use an appropriate size deep socket to push the seals into place until they are properly seated. Don't twist or cock them, or they will not seal properly against the valve stems. Also, don't remove them again or they will be damaged.

27 Coat the valve stems with assembly lube or moly-based grease, then install one of them into its guide. Next, install the spring seat,

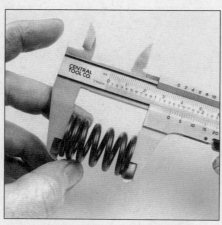

8.19a Measuring the free length of the valve springs

8.19b Checking the valve springs for squareness

8.23 Apply the lapping compound very sparingly, in small dabs, to the valve face only

Chapter 2 Part D General engine overhaul procedures

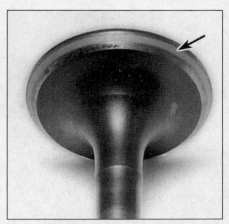

8.24 After lapping, the valve face should exhibit a uniform, unbroken contact pattern (arrow)

8.26 Push the oil seal onto the valve guide (arrow)

8.27 A small dab of grease will help hold the keepers in place on the valve while the spring compressor is released

springs and retainers, compress the springs and install the keepers. **Note:** *Install the springs with the tightly wound coils at the bottom (next to the spring seat).* When compressing the springs with the valve spring compressor, depress them only as far as is absolutely necessary to slip the keepers into place. Apply a small amount of grease to the keepers **(see illustration)** to help hold them in place as the pressure is released from the springs. Make certain that the keepers are securely locked in their retaining grooves.

28 Support the cylinder head on blocks so the valves can't contact the workbench top, then very gently tap each of the valve stems with a soft-faced hammer. This will help seat the keepers in their grooves.

29 Once all of the valves have been installed in the head, check for proper valve sealing by pouring a small amount of solvent into each of the valve ports. If the solvent leaks past the valve(s) into the combustion chamber area, disassemble the valve(s) and repeat the lapping procedure, then reinstall the valve(s) and repeat the check. Repeat the procedure until a satisfactory seal is obtained.

9 Cylinder - inspection

Refer to illustrations 9.3 and 9.6
Caution: *Don't attempt to separate the liner from the cylinder.*

1 Check the top surface of the cylinder for warpage, using the same method as for the cylinder head (see Section 8). Measure along the sides and diagonally across the stud holes.

2 Check the cylinder walls carefully for scratches and score marks.

3 Using the appropriate precision measuring tools, check the cylinder's diameter at the top, center and bottom of the cylinder bore, parallel to the crankshaft axis **(see illustration)**. Next, measure the cylinder's diameter at the same three locations across the crankshaft axis. Compare the results to this Chapter's Specifications. If the cylinder walls are tapered, out-of-round, worn beyond the specified limits, or badly scuffed or scored, have the cylinder rebored and honed by a dealer service department or an ATV repair shop. If a rebore is done, oversize pistons and rings will be required as well.

4 As an alternative, if the precision measuring tools are not available, a dealer service department or repair shop will make the measurements and offer advice concerning servicing of the cylinder.

5 If it's in reasonably good condition and not worn to the outside of the limits, and if the piston-to-cylinder clearance can be maintained properly, then the cylinder does not have to be rebored; honing is all that is necessary.

6 To perform the honing operation you will need the proper size flexible hone with fine stones as shown in *Maintenance techniques, tools and working facilities* at the front of this book, or a "bottle brush" type hone, plenty of light oil or honing oil, some shop towels and an electric drill motor. Hold the cylinder block in a vise (cushioned with soft jaws or

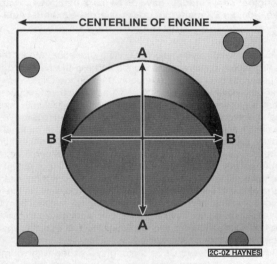

9.3 Measure the cylinder diameter at a right angle to the engine centerline (A) and along the engine centerline (B)

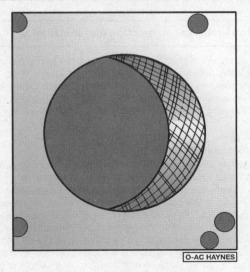

9.6 The cylinder hone should leave a smooth, crosshatch pattern with the lines intersecting at approximately a 60-degree angle

2D-14 Chapter 2 Part D General engine overhaul procedures

10.3a The arrow mark on the piston points to the exhaust side of the engine; some models have an IN mark that goes toward the intake side, an EX mark that goes toward the exhaust side or an arrow with an EX mark

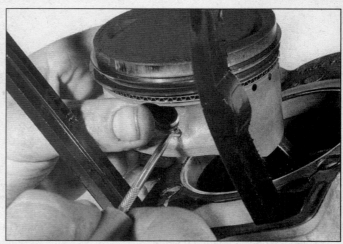

10.3b Wear eye protection and pry the circlip out of its groove with a pointed tool

wood blocks) when performing the honing operation. Mount the hone in the drill motor, compress the stones and slip the hone into the cylinder. Lubricate the cylinder thoroughly, turn on the drill and move the hone up and down in the cylinder at a pace which will produce a fine crosshatch pattern on the cylinder wall with the crosshatch lines intersecting at approximately a 60-degree angle **(see illustration)**. Be sure to use plenty of lubricant and do not take off any more material than is absolutely necessary to produce the desired effect. Do not withdraw the hone from the cylinder while it is running. Instead, shut off the drill and continue moving the hone up and down in the cylinder until it comes to a complete stop, then compress the stones and withdraw the hone. Wipe the oil out of the cylinder and repeat the procedure on the remaining cylinder. Remember, do not remove too much material from the cylinder wall. If you do not have the tools, or do not desire to perform the honing operation, a dealer service department or vehicle repair shop will generally do it for a reasonable fee.

7 Next, the cylinder must be thoroughly washed with warm soapy water to remove all traces of the abrasive grit produced during the honing operation. Be sure to run a brush through the bolt holes and flush them with running water. After rinsing, dry the cylinder thoroughly and apply a coat of light, rust-preventative oil to all machined surfaces.

10 Piston - removal, inspection and installation

1 The piston is attached to the connecting rod with a piston pin that is a slip fit in the piston and rod.
2 Before removing the piston from the rod, stuff a clean shop towel into the crankcase hole, around the connecting rod. This will prevent the circlips from falling into the crankcase if they are inadvertently dropped.

Removal
Refer to illustrations 10.3a, 10.3b and 10.4

3 The piston should have an IN mark on its crown that goes toward the intake (rear) side of the engine **(see illustration)**, or an EX mark that goes toward the front (exhaust) side of the engine, or an arrow mark that points to the front of the engine. Some models have both an arrow mark and an EX mark. If this mark is not visible due to carbon buildup, scribe an arrow into the piston crown before removal. Support the piston and pry the circlip out with a pointed tool **(see illustration)**.
4 Push the piston pin out from the opposite end to free the piston from the rod. You may have to deburr the area around the groove to enable the pin to slide out (use a triangular file for this procedure). If the pin won't come out, you can fabricate a piston pin removal tool from a long bolt, a nut, a piece of tubing and washers **(see illustration)**.

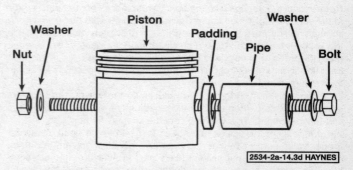

10.4 The piston pin should come out with hand pressure - if it doesn't, this removal tool can be fabricated from readily available parts

Inspection
Refer to illustrations 10.6, 10.11, 10.13, 10.14 and 10.16

5 Before the inspection process can be carried out, the pistons must be cleaned and the old piston rings removed.
6 Using a piston ring removal and installation tool, carefully remove the rings from the pistons **(see illustration)**. Do not nick or gouge the pistons in the process.
7 Scrape all traces of carbon from the tops of the pistons. A hand-held wire brush or a piece of fine emery cloth can be used once the majority of the deposits have been scraped away. Do not, under any circumstances, use a wire brush mounted in a drill motor to remove deposits from the pistons; the piston material is soft and will be eroded away by the wire brush.
8 Use a piston ring groove cleaning tool to remove any carbon deposits from the ring grooves. If a tool is not available, a piece broken off the old ring will do the job. Be very careful to remove only the carbon deposits. Do not remove any metal and do not nick or gouge the sides of the ring grooves.
9 Once the deposits have been removed, clean the pistons with solvent and dry them thoroughly. Make sure the oil return holes below the oil ring grooves are clear.
10 If the pistons are not damaged or worn excessively and if the cylinders are not rebored, new pistons will not be necessary. Normal piston wear appears as even, vertical wear on the thrust surfaces of the piston and slight looseness of the top ring in its groove. New piston rings, on the other hand, should always be used when an engine is rebuilt.
11 Carefully inspect each piston for cracks around the skirt, at the pin bosses and at the ring lands **(see illustration)**.
12 Look for scoring and scuffing on the thrust faces of the skirt, holes

Chapter 2 Part D General engine overhaul procedures

10.6 Remove the piston rings with a ring removal and installation tool

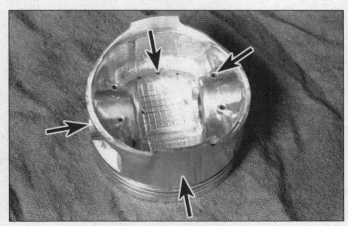

10.11 Check the piston pin bore and the piston skirt for wear, and make sure any internal holes are clear (arrows)

in the piston crown and burned areas at the edge of the crown. If the skirt is scored or scuffed, the engine may have been suffering from overheating and/or abnormal combustion, which caused excessively high operating temperatures. The oil pump should be checked thoroughly. A hole in the piston crown, an extreme to be sure, is an indication that abnormal combustion (pre-ignition) was occurring. Burned areas at the edge of the piston crown are usually evidence of spark knock (detonation). If any of the above problems exist, the causes must be corrected or the damage will occur again.

13   Measure the piston ring-to-groove clearance (side clearance) by laying a new piston ring in the ring groove and slipping a feeler gauge in beside it **(see illustration)**. Check the clearance at three or four locations around the groove. Be sure to use the correct ring for each groove; they are different. If the clearance is greater then specified, new pistons will have to be used when the engine is reassembled.

14   Check the piston-to-bore clearance by measuring the bore (see Section 11) and the piston diameter **(see illustration)**. Measure the piston across the skirt on the thrust faces at a 90-degree angle to the piston pin, at the specified distance up from the bottom of the skirt. Subtract the piston diameter from the bore diameter to obtain the clearance. If it is greater than specified, the cylinder will have to be rebored and a new oversized piston and rings installed. If the appropriate precision measuring tools are not available, the piston-to-cylinder clearance can be obtained, though not quite as accurately, using feeler gauge stock. Feeler gauge stock comes in 12-inch lengths and various thicknesses and is generally available at auto parts stores. To check the clearance, slip a piece of feeler gauge stock of the same thickness as the specified piston clearance into the cylinder along with appropriate piston. The cylinder should be upside down and the piston must be positioned exactly as it normally would be. Place the feeler gauge between the piston and cylinder on one of the thrust faces (90-degrees to the piston pin bore). The piston should slip through the cylinder (with the feeler gauge in place) with moderate pressure. If it falls through, or slides through easily, the clearance is excessive and a new piston will be required. If the piston binds at the lower end of the cylinder and is loose toward the top, the cylinder is tapered, and if tight spots are encountered as the piston/feeler gauge is rotated in the cylinder, the cylinder is out-of-round. Be sure to have the cylinder and piston checked by a dealer service department or a repair shop to confirm your findings before purchasing new parts.

15   Apply clean engine oil to the pin, insert it partway into the piston and check for freeplay by rocking the pin back-and-forth. If the pin is loose, a new piston and possibly new pin must be installed.

16   Repeat Step 15, this time inserting the piston pin into the connecting rod **(see illustration)**. If the pin is loose, measure the pin diameter and the pin bore in the rod (or have this done by a dealer or repair shop). A worn pin can be replaced separately; if the rod bore is worn, the rod and crankshaft must be replaced as an assembly.

17   Refer to Section 11 and install the rings on the pistons.

Installation

Refer to illustration 10.18

18   Install the piston with its mark toward the correct side of the engine **(see illustration 10.3a)**. Lubricate the pin and the rod bore with moly-based grease. Install a new circlips in the groove in one side of the piston (don't reuse the old circlips). Push the pin into position from the

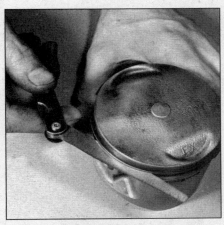

10.13 Measure the piston ring-to-groove clearance with a feeler gauge

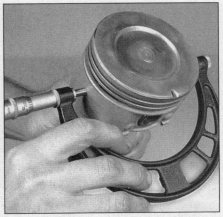

10.14 Measure the piston diameter with a micrometer

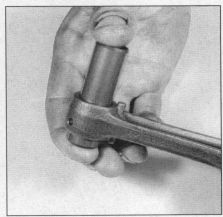

10.16 Slip the piston pin into the rod and try to rock it back-and-forth to check for looseness

10.18 Make sure both piston pin circlips are securely seated in the piston grooves

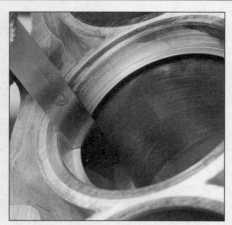
11.2 Check the piston ring end gap with a feeler gauge at the bottom of the cylinder

11.4 If the end gap is too small, clamp a file in a vise and file the ring ends (from the outside in only) to enlarge the gap slightly

opposite side and install another new circlip. Compress the circlips only enough for them to fit in the piston. Make sure the clips are properly seated in the grooves **(see illustration)**.

11 Piston rings - installation

Refer to illustrations 11.2, 11.4, 11.7a, 11.7b, 11.9a, 11.9b and 11.12

1 Before installing the new piston rings, the ring end gaps must be checked.
2 Insert the top (No. 1) ring into the bottom of the first cylinder and square it up with the cylinder walls by pushing it in with the top of the piston. The ring should be about one-half inch above the bottom edge of the cylinder. To measure the end gap, slip a feeler gauge between the ends of the ring **(see illustration)** and compare the measurement to the Specifications.
3 If the gap is larger or smaller than specified, double check to make sure that you have the correct rings before proceeding.
4 If the gap is too small, it must be enlarged or the ring ends may come in contact with each other during engine operation, which can cause serious damage. The end gap can be increased by filing the ring ends very carefully with a fine file **(see illustration)**. When performing this operation, file only from the outside in.
5 Repeat the procedure for the second compression ring (ring gap is not specified for the oil ring rails or spacer).
6 Once the ring end gaps have been checked/corrected, the rings can be installed on the piston.
7 The oil control ring (lowest on the piston) is installed first. It is composed of three separate components. Slip the spacer into the groove, then install the upper side rail **(see illustrations)**. Do not use a piston ring installation tool on the oil ring side rails as they may be damaged. Instead, place one end of the side rail into the groove between the spacer expander and the ring land. Hold it firmly in place and slide a finger around the piston while pushing the rail into the groove (taking care not to cut your fingers on the sharp edges). Next, install the lower side rail in the same manner.
8 After the three oil ring components have been installed, check to make sure that both the upper and lower side rails can be turned smoothly in the ring groove.
9 Install the no. 2 (middle) ring next **(see illustrations)**. It can be readily distinguished from the top ring by its tapered cross-section shape. Do not mix the top and middle rings.
10 To avoid breaking the ring, use a piston ring installation tool and make sure that the identification mark is facing up. Fit the ring into the middle groove on the piston. Do not expand the ring any more than is necessary to slide it into place.
11 Finally, install the no. 1 (top) ring in the same manner. Make sure the identifying mark is facing up. Be very careful not to confuse the top and second rings. Besides the different profiles, the top ring is narrower than the second ring.
12 Once the rings have been properly installed, stagger the end gaps, including those of the oil ring side rails **(see illustration)**.

11.7a Installing the oil ring expander - make sure the ends don't overlap

11.7b Installing an oil ring side rail - don't use a ring installation tool to do this

11.9a Install the middle ring with its identification mark up

Chapter 2 Part D General engine overhaul procedures

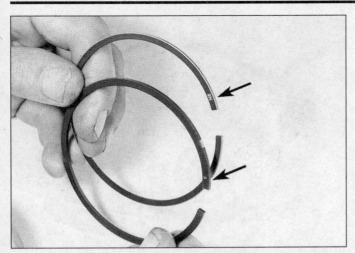

11.9b The top and middle rings have identification marks (arrows) - these must be up when the rings are installed

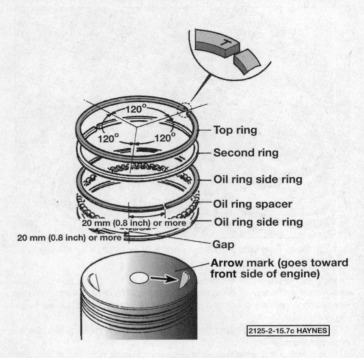

11.12 Ring details

12 Oil pump - inspection

Refer to illustrations 12.3a, 12.3b and 12.3c

1 Remove and disassemble the pump, referring to the appropriate Part of this Chapter.
2 Wash all of the pump components n solvent, then dry them off. Check the pump body, the rotors and the cover for scoring and wear. If any damage or excessive or uneven wear is evident, replace the pump. If you are rebuilding the engine, it's a good idea to install a new oil pump.
3 Place the rotors in the pump cover. Measure the clearance between the outer rotor and body, and between the inner and outer rotors, with a feeler gauge **(see illustrations)**. Place a straightedge across the pump body and rotors and measure the gap with a feeler gauge **(see illustration)**. If any of the clearances are beyond the limits listed in the Chapter's Specifications, replace the pump.

13 Crankcase bearings - inspection, removal and installation

Refer to illustration 13.3

1 Separate the crankcase and remove the following:
  a) Transmission shafts and gears
  b) Middle drive gear
  c) Crankshaft and main bearings
  d) Shift cam and forks

2 Clean the crankcase halves thoroughly with new solvent and dry them with compressed air. All oil passages should be blown out with compressed air and all traces of old gasket sealant should be removed from the mating surfaces. **Caution:** *Be very careful not to nick or gouge the crankcase mating surfaces or leaks will result. Check both crankcase sections very carefully for cracks and other damage.*
3 Check the bearings in the case halves **(see illustration)**. If they don't turn smoothly, replace them. For bearings that aren't accessible from the outside, a blind hole puller will be needed for removal. Drive the remaining bearings out with a bearing driver or a socket having an outside diameter slightly smaller than that of the bearing outer race. Before installing the bearings, allow them to sit in the freezer overnight, and about fifteen-minutes before installation, place the case half in an oven, set to about 200-degrees F, and allow it to heat up. The bearings are an interference fit, and this will ease installation. **Warning:** *Before*

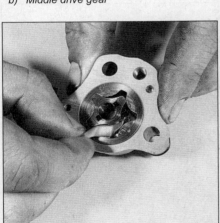

12.3a Use a feeler gauge to measure the inner-to-outer rotor clearance . . .

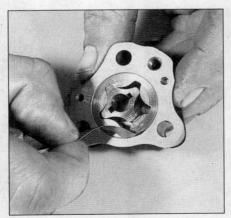

12.3b . . . and the outer rotor-to-body clearance

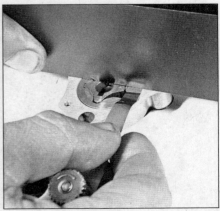

12.3c Lay a straightedge across the rotors and pump body and measure the gap with a feeler gauge

2D-18 Chapter 2 Part D General engine overhaul procedures

13.3 Case bearings may be a shrink fit or held in by retainers

14.2a The crankshaft should stay in the left case half like this (early Kodiak 400 shown)...

heating the case, wash it thoroughly with soap and water so no explosive fumes are present. Also, don't use a flame to heat the case. Install the bearings with a socket or bearing driver that bears against the bearing outer race.

4 If any damage is found that can't be repaired, replace the crankcase halves as a set.

5 Assemble the case halves and check to make sure the crankshaft and the transmission shafts turn freely.

14 Crankshaft and connecting rod - removal, inspection and installation

Note: *The procedures in this section require special tools. If you don't have the necessary equipment or suitable substitutes, have the crankshaft removed and installed by a Yamaha dealer.*

Removal

Refer to illustrations 14.2a and 14.2b

1 Remove the engine and separate the crankcase halves. The transmission shafts need not be removed.

2 On 1993 through 1999 Kodiak 400 models, the crankshaft should stay in the left half of the case when the right half is lifted off. However, if the right bearing is tight enough, the crankshaft may stay in the right case half **(see illustration)**. If this happens, have the crankshaft

removed from the case half by a Yamaha dealer or other repair shop.

3 The crankshaft may be loose enough in its bearing that you can lift it out of the crankcase half that it stayed in. If not, push it out with a Yamaha puller or equivalent.

Inspection

Refer to illustrations 14.4, 14.6 and 14.7

4 Measure the side clearance between connecting rod and crankshaft with a feeler gauge **(see illustration)**. If it's more than the limit listed in this Chapter's Specifications, replace the crankshaft and connecting rod as an assembly.

5 Set up the crankshaft in V-blocks with a dial indicator contacting the big end of the connecting rod. Move the connecting rod side-to-side against the indicator pointer and compare the reading to the value listed in this Chapter's Specifications. If it's beyond the limit, the crankshaft can be disassembled and the needle roller bearing replaced. However, this is a specialized job that should be done by a Yamaha dealer or qualified machine shop.

6 Check the crankshaft splines, the cam chain sprocket, the ball bearing at the sprocket end of the crankshaft and the bearing journals for visible wear or damage **(see illustration)**. Yamaha lists the ball bearing end of the crankshaft as a separately available part, but check with your dealer first; it may be more practical to replace the entire crankshaft if the ball bearing or cam sprocket is worn or damaged. Replace the crankshaft if any of the other conditions are found.

14.2b ...but if it stays in the right case half like this, have it removed by a Yamaha dealer

14.4 Check the connecting rod side clearance with a feeler gauge

Chapter 2 Part D General engine overhaul procedures

14.6 Check the cam chain sprocket and the ball bearing on the end of the crankshaft

7 Set the crankshaft in a lathe or a pair of V-blocks, with a dial indicator contacting each end **(see illustration)**. Rotate the crankshaft and note the runout. If the runout at either end is beyond the limit listed in this Chapter's Specifications, replace the crankshaft and connecting rod as an assembly.
8 Measure the assembly width of the crankshaft **(see illustration 14.7)**. If it exceeds the limit listed in this Chapter's Specifications, replace the crankshaft.

Installation

Refer to illustration 14.9

9 Start the crankshaft into the left case half. If it doesn't go in easily, pull it in the rest of the way with a Yamaha puller or equivalent **(see illustration)**.
10 The remainder of installation is the reverse of the removal steps.

15 Transmission components - inspection

1 Inspect the shift fork grooves in the gears, the middle driven gear holder and the dog clutch. If a groove is worn or scored, replace the affected part and inspect its corresponding shift fork.
2 Check the shift forks for distortion and wear, especially at the fork ears. If they are discolored or severely worn they are probably bent.

Inspect the guide pins for excessive wear and distortion and replace any defective parts with new ones.
3 Check the shift fork guide bars evidence of wear, galling and other damage. Make sure the shift forks move smoothly on the guide bars. If the shafts are worn or bent, replace them with new ones.
4 Check the edges of the grooves in the shift cam(s) for signs of excessive wear.
5 Hold the inner race of the shift cam bearing with fingers and spin the outer race. Replace the bearing if it's rough, loose or noisy. If you're working on a 1993 through 1999 model, replace the segment on the no. 1 shift cam if it's worn or damaged.
6 Check the gear teeth for cracking and other obvious damage. Check the bushing surface in the inner diameter of the freewheeling gears for scoring or heat discoloration. Replace damaged parts.
7 Inspect the engagement dogs and dog holes on gears so equipped for excessive wear or rounding off. Replace the paired gears as a set if necessary.
8 Check the transmission shaft bearings in the crankcase for wear or heat discoloration and replace them if necessary (see Section 13).

16 Initial start-up after overhaul

1 Make sure the engine oil level is correct, then remove the spark plug from the engine. Place the engine kill switch in the Off position and unplug the primary (low tension) wires from the coil.
2 Turn on the key switch and crank the engine over with the starter several times to build up oil pressure. Reinstall the spark plug, connect the wires and turn the switch to On.
3 Make sure there is fuel in the tank, then operate the choke.
4 Start the engine and allow it to run at a moderately fast idle until it reaches operating temperature. **Caution:** *If the oil temperature light (if equipped) doesn't go off, or it comes on while the engine is running, stop the engine immediately.*
5 Check carefully for oil leaks and make sure the transmission and controls, especially the brakes, function properly before road testing the machine. Refer to Section 17 for the recommended break-in procedure.
6 Upon completion of the road test, and after the engine has cooled down completely, recheck the valve clearances (see Chapter 1).

17 Recommended break-in procedure

1 Any rebuilt engine needs time to break-in, even if parts have been installed in their original locations. For this reason, treat the machine

14.7 Measure runout on each side of the crankshaft (A); if the assembly width (B) is greater than specified, replace the crankshaft

14.9 These tools are used to pull the crankshaft into the left case half

2D-20 Chapter 2 Part D General engine overhaul procedures

gently for the first few miles to make sure oil has circulated throughout the engine and any new parts installed have started to seat.

2 Even greater care is necessary if the cylinder has been rebored or a new crankshaft has been installed. In the case of a rebore, the engine will have to be broken in as if the machine were new. This means greater use of the transmission and a restraining hand on the throttle for the first few operating days. There's no point in keeping to any set speed limit - the main idea is to vary the engine speed, keep from lugging (laboring) the engine and to avoid full-throttle operation. These recommendations can be lessened to an extent when only a new crankshaft is installed. Experience is the best guide, since it's easy to tell when an engine is running freely.

3 If a lubrication failure is suspected, stop the engine immediately and try to find the cause. If an engine is run without oil, even for a short period of time, irreparable damage will occur.

Chapter 3
Cooling system

Contents

	Section		Section
Coolant hoses - replacement	7	Radiator - removal and installation	5
Coolant reservoir - removal and installation	3	Radiator cap - check	2
Cooling fan and thermostat switch - check and replacement	6	Thermostat - removal, check and installation	4
General information	1	Water pump - removal, inspection and installation	8

Specifications

General
Coolant type	See Chapter 1
Mixture ratio	See Chapter 1
Cooling system capacity	See Chapter 1
Radiator cap pressure rating	13 psi

Thermostat
  Opening temperature
    Kodiak .... 63.5 to 66.5-degrees C (147 to 152-degrees F)
    Grizzly .... 50 to 54-degrees C (122 to 158-degrees F)
  Opening
    Kodiak .... 3 mm (1/8-inch)
    Grizzly .... 8 mm (5/16-inch)

Fan switch ratings
  Kodiak
    Heating up
      Below 86+/-3-degrees C (187+/-5-degrees F) .... No continuity
      Above 86+/-3-degrees C (187+/-5-degrees F) .... Continuity
    Cooling down
      Above 80+/-3-degrees C (176+/-5-degrees F) .... Continuity
      Below 80+/-3-degrees C (176+/-5-degrees F) .... No continuity
  Grizzly
    Heating up
      Below 75+/-3-degrees C (167+/-5-degrees F) .... No continuity
      Above 75+/-3-degrees C (167+/-5-degrees F) .... Continuity
    Cooling down
      Above 68+/-3-degrees C (154+/-5-degrees F) .... Continuity
      Below 68+/-3-degrees C (154+/-5-degrees F) .... No continuity

Tightening torques
Fan switch	28 Nm (20 ft-lbs)
Thermostat housing bolts	10 Nm (86 inch-lbs)
Water pipe bolt	10 Nm (86 inch-lbs)
Water pump mounting bolts	10 Nm (86 inch-lbs)
Water pump cover and drain bolts	Not specified

1 General information

2000 and later Kodiak models and all Grizzly 660 models use a liquid cooling system. The system utilizes a water/antifreeze mixture to carry away excess heat produced during the combustion process. The cylinder is surrounded by a water jacket, through which the coolant is circulated by the water pump. The coolant passes through the cylinder head to the radiator.

There's a thermostat in the coolant passage from the cylinder. When the engine is warm, the thermostat opens and allows coolant to flow to the radiator.

In the radiator, the coolant is cooled by passing air, then routed through another hose back to the water pump, where the cycle is repeated. The water pump is mounted in the crankcase casting on the left side of the engine.

An electric fan, mounted on the radiator and automatically controlled by a thermostatic switch, provides a flow of cooling air through the radiator when the vehicle is standing still or moving slowly.

The entire system is sealed and pressurized. The pressure is controlled by a valve which is part of the radiator cap. By pressurizing the coolant, the boiling point is raised, which prevents premature boiling of the coolant. An overflow hose, connected between the radiator and reservoir tank, directs coolant to the tank when the radiator cap valve is opened by excessive pressure. The coolant is automatically siphoned back to the radiator as the engine cools. **Warning 1:** *Do not allow antifreeze to come in contact with your skin or painted surfaces of the vehicle. Rinse off spills immediately with plenty of water. Antifreeze is highly toxic if ingested. Never leave antifreeze lying around in an open container or in puddles on the floor; children and pets are attracted by its sweet smell and may drink it. Check with local authorities about disposing of used antifreeze. Many communities have collection centers which will see that antifreeze is disposed of safely.* **Warning 2:** *Do not remove the pressure cap from the radiator when the engine and radiator are hot. Scalding hot coolant and steam may blow out under pressure, which could cause serious injury. To open the pressure cap, let the engine cool. When the engine has cooled, place a thick rag, such as a towel, over the radiator cap; slowly rotate the cap counterclockwise to the first stop. This procedure allows any residual pressure to escape. When the steam has stopped escaping, press down on the on cap while turning counterclockwise and remove it.*

2 Radiator cap - check

If problems such as overheating and loss of coolant occur, check the entire system as described in Chapter 1. The radiator cap opening pressure should be checked by a dealer service department or service station equipped with the special tester required to do the job. If the cap is defective, replace it with a new one.

3 Coolant reservoir - removal and installation

Removal

Refer to illustration 3.2

1   Disconnect the breather hose and coolant hose from the reservoir and catch any escaped coolant. Plug the end of the reservoir hose so it doesn't siphon coolant from the system.
2   Remove the reservoir mounting bolts and lift it out **(see illustration)**.
3   Check the reservoir for cracks, especially if it has required repeated topping up. If cracks are found, replace the reservoir.

Installation

4   Installation is the reverse of the removal steps.

4 Thermostat - removal, check and installation

Warning: *The engine must be completely cool before beginning this procedure.*

Removal

Refer to illustrations 4.3a, 4.3b, 4.4a and 4.4b

1   Remove the seat and take the trim panel off the right side of the fuel tank (see Chapter 8).
2   Drain the cooling system (see Chapter 1).
3   Disconnect the radiator inlet hose from the thermostat housing **(see illustrations)**.
4   Unbolt the thermostat housing from the cylinder head and take out the thermostat **(see illustrations)**.

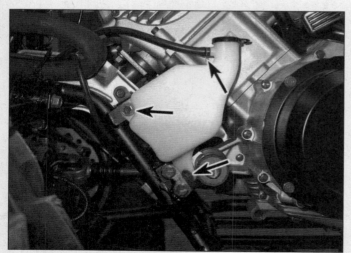

3.2 Disconnect the overflow hose (upper arrow) and remove the mounting bolts (lower arrows) to detach the reservoir tank

4.3a On Kodiaks, disconnect the coolant hose and unscrew the bolts (left arrows); on installation, push the hose against the stop on the fitting (right arrow)

Chapter 3 Cooling system

4.3b On Grizzly models, disconnect the coolant hose and unscrew the bolts (left arrows; on installation, push the hose against the stop on the fitting (right arrow)

Inspection

5   Remove any coolant deposits, then visually check the thermostat for corrosion, cracks and other damage. If it was open when it was removed, the thermostat is defective.

6   To check the thermostat operation, submerge it in a pan of water along with a thermometer. The thermostat should be suspended so it does not touch the sides of the container. **Warning:** *Antifreeze is poisonous. DO NOT use a cooking pan to test the thermostat!*

7   Gradually heat the water in the pan with a hot plate or stove and check the temperature when the thermostat just starts to open. Compare the opening temperature to the value listed in this Chapter's Specifications.

8   When the water reaches the fully open temperature listed in this Chapter's Specifications, the thermostat should be open about 5/16 inch.

9   If these specifications are not met, or if the thermostat doesn't open when the water is heated, install a new one.

Installation

10   Install the thermostat in the housing with its air bleed hole upward. On Kodiak models, the air bleed hole should align with the cast projec-

4.4a Here's the Kodiak thermostat; on installation, align the air bleed hole (lower arrow) with the cast mark (upper arrow)

tion on the thermostat housing.

11   Install the thermostat housing, using a new seal if necessary. Tighten its bolts securely.

12   Connect the hose to the housing.

13   Refill the cooling system (see Chapter 1).

5   Radiator - removal and installation

Warning: *The engine must be completely cool before beginning this procedure.*

Removal

Refer to illustrations 5.4 and 5.6

1   Drain the cooling system (see Chapter 1).

2   Remove the seat, side panels, left footrest, front cargo rack, front bumper and front fenders (see Chapter 8). If you're working on a Grizzly, remove the handlebar cover and fuel tank cover.

3   Follow the wiring harnesses from the fan and temperature sensor to the connectors and disconnect them.

4   Disconnect the siphon hose from the radiator at the filler neck **(see illustration)**. If you're going to remove the siphon hose, follow it and note how it's routed.

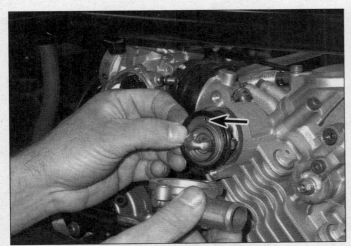

4.4b Here's the Grizzly thermostat; on installation, position the air bleed hole upward (arrow)

5.4 Disconnect the reservoir hose (arrow) . . .

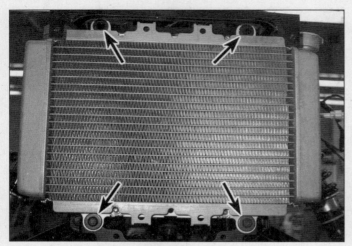

5.6 ... loosen the mounting bolts (lower arrows) and slip the radiator off the pegs (upper arrows)

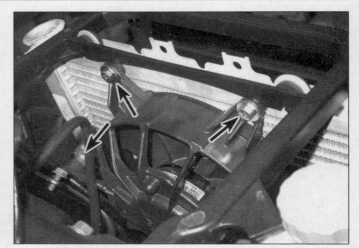

6.4 Disconnect the fan switch (left arrow) and remove the mounting screws (right arrows) (upper screws shown)

5 Disconnect the coolant hoses from the radiator.
6 Remove the radiator mounting bolts and slip the radiator off its upper mounting pegs **(see illustration)**. Lift the radiator out.

Installation

7 Installation is the reverse of the removal steps, with the following additions:
   a) *Don't forget to connect the fan switch and fan wires.*
   b) *Fill the cooling system with the recommended coolant (see Chapter 1).*

6 Cooling fan and switch - check and replacement

Check

Refer to illustration 6.4

1 If the engine is overheating and the cooling fan doesn't come on, first check the main fuse (see Chapter 9). If the fuse is blown, check the fan circuit for shorts to ground (see the *Wiring diagrams* at the end of this book). Check that the battery is fully charged. Locate the circuit breaker in the fan wiring harness and check it with an ohmmeter or continuity tester. It should have continuity at room temperature (20-degrees C/68-degrees F). If not, replace it.
2 If the fuse and battery are good, follow the wiring harness from the fan motor to the electrical connector and disconnect the connector. Using two jumper wires, apply battery voltage to the terminals in the fan motor side of the connector (refer to the wiring diagrams at the end of the manual to identify the power and ground wires). If the fan doesn't work, replace the motor.
3 If the fan does come on, the problem lies in the fan switch or the wiring that connects the components.
4 Disconnect the electrical connector from the switch on the left side of the radiator **(see illustration)**. Bypass the switch by connecting a short jumper wire between the terminals in the harness side of the switch connector. The fan should now run. If it does, the fan wiring is good and the switch is defective.
5 If the fan still doesn't run when the switch is bypassed, check the ground side of the circuit. Leave the short jumper wire in place to bypass the switch. Disconnect the electrical connector from the fan motor. Connect a jumper wire between the power wire terminals, one in the harness side of the connector and one in the fan motor side. Connect another jumper wire between the ground wire terminal in the fan motor side of the connector and a good ground (bare metal on the engine or frame). If the fan now runs, look for a break or bad connection in the ground wire side of the circuit. If it still doesn't run, look for a break or bad connection in the power side of the circuit.

Replacement

6 Remove the radiator (see Section 5).

Fan motor

7 Unbolt the fan and take it off the radiator **(see illustration 6.4)**.
8 Installation is the reverse of the removal steps.

Fan switch

9 Prepare the new switch by coating the threads with Three Bond Sealock no. 10 or equivalent. **Caution:** *Don't drop the switch or it will be ruined.*
10 Disconnect the electrical connector from the switch and unscrew the switch from the radiator.
11 Install the new switch, tightening it to the torque listed in this Chapter's Specifications.
12 Connect the electrical connector to the switch. Check the coolant level and top up if necessary (see Chapter 1).

7 Coolant hoses - replacement

Refer to illustrations 7.1a, 7.1b and 7.1c
Warning: *The engine must be completely cool before beginning this procedure.*

1 The coolant hoses are attached to the engine at the cylinder and

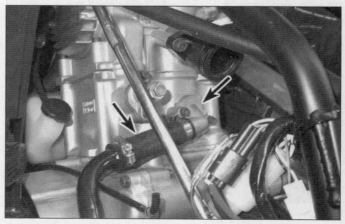

7.1a The Kodiak hose fitting (right arrow) and hose (left arrow) are on the intake side of the cylinder

Chapter 3 Cooling system

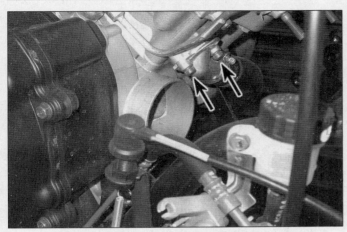

7.1b The Grizzly hose fitting is on the exhaust side; remove its screws (arrows) . . .

7.1c . . . and loosen the clamp at the water pump to remove the hose (arrow)

water pump inlet pipe **(see illustrations)**.

2   To remove and install hoses, first drain the cooling system (see Chapter 1). Loosen the clamps and work the hoses free of the fittings. Note the positions of any retainers.

3   Installation is the reverse of the removal steps. Replace any cut tie-wraps with new ones.

8 Water pump - removal, inspection and installation

Warning: *The engine must be completely cool before beginning this procedure.*

Removal

Refer to illustrations 8.5a, 8.5b and 8.5c

1   If you're working on a Kodiak, remove the seat, left fuel tank panel and left engine cover (see Chapter 8).

2   If you're working on a Grizzly, remove the seat and right fuel tank panel.

3   Drain the cooling system (see Chapter 1).

4   Disconnect the coolant hoses from the water pump (see Section 7).

5   Unbolt the outlet pipe from the water pump **(see illustrations)**. Work the pipe free of the pump and remove the O-ring **(see illustration)**.

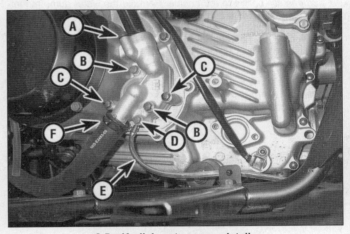

8.5a Kodiak water pump details

A	Coolant pipe bolt	D	Drain bolt
B	Cover bolts	E	Weep hole hose
C	Mounting bolts	F	Coolant hose clamp

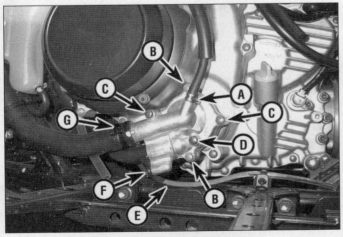

8.5b Grizzly water pump details

A	Relief hose clamp	E	Weep hole hose
B	Cover bolts	F	Coolant pipe bolt
C	Mounting bolts	G	Coolant hose clamp
D	Drain bolt		

8.5c Don't forget to install the coolant pipe O-ring (Kodiak shown)

8.7a Unscrew the impeller . . .

8.7b . . . and check the mechanical seal for signs of leakage

6 **Note:** *If you're planning to remove the cover bolts, loosen them while the pump is still bolted to the engine. Also, if you're going to remove the impeller, remove the cover and loosen the impeller while the pump is still bolted to the engine.* Remove the water pump mounting bolts, take the pump off the engine and remove its O-ring. If you're working on a Grizzly, disconnect the breather hose from the water pump after the pump has been removed from the engine.

Inspection
Refer to illustrations 8.7a and 8.7b

7 Remove the pump drain bolt and cover bolts. Separate the cover from the housing and disassemble the pump **(see illustrations)**.

8 Check the rubber damper on the impeller shaft for wear or damage. If there was oil or coolant in the hose connected to the weep hole fitting, the mechanical seal is leaking. Check for engine oil in the coolant or coolant in the engine oil. Spin the bearing with fingers and check for rough or noisy movement. If any of these problems are found, have the water pump overhauled by a dealer service department or other qualified shop.

9 If the pump is in good condition, reassemble it, using a new gasket. Use a new sealing washer on the drain bolt.

Installation

10 Installation is the reverse of the removal steps. Use new O-rings on the water pump and coolant pipe. Tighten the pump mounting bolts to the torque listed in this Chapter's Specifications.

Chapter 4
Fuel and exhaust systems

Contents

	Section		Section
Air cleaner housing - removal and installation	10	Fuel level - check and adjustment	9
Carburetor - disassembly, cleaning and inspection	7	Fuel tank - cleaning and repair	3
Carburetor - reassembly and float height check	8	Fuel tank - removal and installation	2
Carburetor - removal and installation	6	General information	1
Carburetor overhaul - general information	5	Idle fuel/air mixture adjustment	4
Choke cable - removal and installation	12	Throttle cables - removal, installation and adjustment	11
Exhaust system - removal and installation	13		

Specifications

General
Fuel type.. Unleaded gasoline subject to local regulations; minimum octane 91 RON (86 pump octane)

Carburetor

1993 through 1998 Kodiak 400
Main jet
  1993 through 1995 .... 122.5
  1996 through 1998 105
Jet needle/clip position 5H26/3
Needle jet N-8
Pilot jet 45
Pilot screw setting (turns out from lightly seated position)
  1993 through 1995 2
  1996 through 1998 .... 3-1/4
Float height .... 11.4 to 13.4 mm (29/64 to 17/32 inch)
Fuel level .... 1.0 to 2.0 mm (0.04 to 0.08 inch)

1999 Kodiak 400
Main jet
  California models 112.5
  Except California 115
Jet needle/clip position
  California .... 4DHY17/not adjustable
  Except California 4DHY13-3
Needle jet P-0M (823)
Pilot jet 42.5
Pilot screw setting (turns out from lightly seated position)
  California 2-1/2
  1996 through 1998 2
Float height .... 12 to 14 mm (0.47 to 0.55 inch)
Fuel level .... 2.0 to 3.0 mm (0.08 to 0.12 inch)

Carburetor

2000 to 2001 Kodiak 400
Main jet	
California models	130
Except California	132.5
Jet needle/clip position	
California	5EP11-55/not adjustable
Except California	5EP7-55-3
Needle jet	P-0M (823)
Pilot jet	17.5
Pilot screw setting (turns out from lightly seated position)	Not specified
Float height	13 mm (0.51 inch)
Fuel level	2.0 to 3.0 mm (0.08 to 0.12 inch)

2002 Kodiak 400
Main jet	130
Jet needle/clip position	5EP3-55-3
Needle jet	P-0M
Pilot jet	17.5
Pilot screw setting (turns out from lightly seated position)	Not specified
Float height	13 mm (0.51 inch)
Fuel level	3.0 to 4.0 mm (0.12 to 0.16 inch)

2003 and later Kodiak 400/450
Main jet	
400 models	132.5
450 models	131.3
Jet needle/clip position	5EP13-55-3
Needle jet	P-0M
Pilot jet	17.5
Pilot screw setting (turns out from lightly seated position)	Not specified
Float height	13 mm (0.51 inch)
Fuel level	4.0 to 5.0 mm (0.16 to 0.20 inch)

Grizzly 600
Main jet	
California	143.8
Except California	145
Jet needle/clip position	
California	6HH23-94-1
Except California	6HH23-94-3
Needle jet	Y-0M
Pilot jet	42.5
Pilot screw setting (turns out from lightly seated position)	Not specified
Float height	14.7 mm (0.58 inch)
Fuel level	1.5 mm (0.06 inch)

Grizzly 660
Main jet	153.8
Jet needle/clip position	6JP9-53-2
Needle jet	O-0M
Pilot jet	40
Pilot screw setting (turns out from lightly seated position)	Not specified
Float height	13 mm (0.51 inch)
Fuel level	4.5 mm (0.18 inch)

Tightening torques

1993 through 1999 Kodiak 400
Muffler/silencer to frame	27 Nm (19 ft-lbs)
Muffler/silencer clamp bolts	20 Nm (168 inch-lbs)
Exhaust pipe holder nuts	12 Nm (104 inch-lbs)

2000 and later Kodiak 400/450
Muffler/silencer to frame	25 Nm (18 ft-lbs)
Muffler/silencer clamp bolts	15 Nm (123 inch-lbs)
Exhaust pipe holder nuts	20 Nm (168 inch-lbs)

Chapter 4 Fuel and exhaust systems

Grizzly 600
Muffler/silencer to frame.. 26 Nm (19 ft-lbs)
Muffler/silencer clamp bolts.. Not specified
Exhaust pipe holder nuts .... 12 Nm (104 inch-lbs)

Grizzly 660
Muffler/silencer to frame.. 20 Nm (168 inch-lbs)
Muffler/silencer clamp bolts.. 20 Nm (168 inch-lbs)
Exhaust pipe holder nuts .... 14 Nm (120 inch-lbs)
Exhaust pipe to bracket bolt.. 15 Nm (132 inch-lbs)

1 General information

The fuel system consists of the fuel tank, fuel tap, filter screen, carburetor and connecting lines, hose and control cables.

A Mikuni flat-slide carburetor is used on 1993 through 1998 Kodiak models. A choke knob on the carburetor operates the enrichment circuit.

A Mikuni CV carburetor is used on 1999 and later Kodiak and all Grizzly models. A choke lever operates the enrichment circuit through a cable. On all models, a thumb lever on the right handlebar operates the throttle.

The exhaust system consists of a pipe and a muffler/silencer.

Many of the fuel system service procedures are considered routine maintenance items and for that reason are included in Chapter 1.

2 Fuel tank - removal and installation

Warning: *Gasoline is extremely flammable, so take extra precautions when you work on any part of the fuel system. Don't smoke or allow open flames or bare light bulbs near the work area, and don't work in a garage where a gas-type appliance (such as a water heater or clothes dryer) is present. Since gasoline is carcinogenic, wear protective gloves when there's a possibility of being exposed to fuel, and, if you spill any fuel on your skin, rinse it off immediately with soap and water. Mop up any spills immediately and do not store fuel-soaked rags where they could ignite. When you perform any kind of work on the fuel system, wear safety glasses and have a fire extinguisher suitable for a class B type fire (flammable liquids) on hand.*

1 The fuel tank is secured to a bracket by two bolts at the rear. At the front, the tank is supported by a bolt and rubber grommet on each side.

Removal
Refer to illustrations 2.3a and 2.3b

2 Remove the seat, and where necessary for access, the side covers. Remove the fuel tank cover (see Chapter 8).
3 Remove the fuel tank mounting bolts **(see illustrations)**.
4 Disconnect the fuel line from the fuel tap.
5 Pull the fuel tank backward off the front mounting bracket. Pull the breather hose out of its hole in the forward panel and lift the tank off the vehicle together with the fuel tap.

Installation
6 Before installing the tank, check the condition of the rubber mounting dampers - if they're hardened, cracked, or show any other signs of deterioration, replace them.
7 When installing the tank, reverse the removal procedure. Don't pinch any control cables or wires.

3 Fuel tank - cleaning and repair

1 The fuel tank is plastic and can't be repaired by traditional welding or brazing techniques. All repairs to the fuel tank should be carried out by a professional who has experience in this critical and potentially dangerous work. Even after cleaning and flushing of the fuel system, explosive fumes can remain and ignite during repair of the tank.
2 If the fuel tank is removed from the vehicle, it should not be placed in an area where sparks or open flames could ignite the fumes coming out of the tank. Be especially careful inside garages where a gas-type appliance is located, because it could cause an explosion.

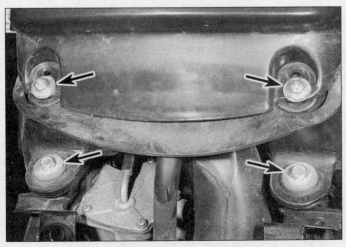

2.3a Remove the fuel tank cover screws (upper arrows) and rear mounting bolts (lower arrows) . . .

2.3b . . . and one front mounting bolt from each side of the tank

4-4 Chapter 4 Fuel and exhaust systems

4.4 The pilot screw (arrow) adjusts idle fuel/air mixture (early carburetor shown; later models similar)

4 Idle fuel/air mixture adjustment

1993 through 1998 Kodiak models

1   Fuel/air mixture adjustment is part of the routine idle speed adjustment procedure described in Chapter 1.

1999 Kodiak and 1998 through 2001 Grizzly models

Refer to illustration 4.4

2   Idle fuel/air mixture on these vehicles is preset at the factory and should not need adjustment unless the carburetor is overhauled or the pilot screw, which controls the mixture adjustment, is replaced.
3   The engine must be properly tuned up before making the adjustment (valve clearances set to specifications, spark plug in good condition and properly gapped).
4   To make an initial adjustment, turn the pilot screw clockwise until it seats lightly, then back it out the number of turns listed in this Chapter's Specifications **(see illustration)**. **Caution:** *Turn the screw just far enough to seat it lightly. If it's bottomed hard, the screw or its seat may be damaged, which will make accurate mixture adjustments impossible.*
5   Warm up the engine to normal operating temperature. Shut it off and connect a tune-up tachometer, following the tachometer manufacturer's instructions.
6   Restart the engine and compare idle speed to the value listed in the Chapter 1 Specifications. Adjust it if necessary.

2000 and later Kodiak, 2002 and later Grizzly models

7   Fuel/air mixture is adjusted by turning the pilot screw. Yamaha doesn't specify a standard pilot screw setting.

5 Carburetor overhaul - general information

1   Poor engine performance, hesitation, hard starting, stalling, flooding and backfiring are all signs that major carburetor maintenance may be required.
2   Keep in mind that many so-called carburetor problems are really not carburetor problems at all, but mechanical problems within the engine or ignition system malfunctions. Try to establish for certain that the carburetor is in need of maintenance before beginning a major overhaul.
3   Check the fuel tap and its strainer screen, the fuel line, the intake manifold clamps and Allen bolts, the O-ring between the intake manifold and cylinder head, the air filter element, the cylinder compression, the spark plug and the ignition timing before assuming that a carburetor overhaul is required. If the vehicle has been unused for more than a month, refer to Chapter 1, drain the float chamber and refill the tank with fresh fuel.
4   Most carburetor problems are caused by dirt particles, varnish and other deposits which build up in and block the fuel and air passages. Also, in time, gaskets and O-rings shrink or deteriorate and cause fuel and air leaks which lead to poor performance.
5   When the carburetor is overhauled, it is generally disassembled completely and the parts are cleaned thoroughly with a carburetor cleaning solvent and dried with filtered, unlubricated compressed air. The fuel and air passages are also blown through with compressed air to force out any dirt that may have been loosened but not removed by the solvent. Once the cleaning process is complete, the carburetor is reassembled using new gaskets, O-rings and, generally, a new inlet needle valve and seat.
6   Before disassembling the carburetors, make sure you have a carburetor rebuild kit (which will include all necessary O-rings and other parts), some carburetor cleaner, a supply of rags, some means of blowing out the carburetor passages and a clean place to work.

6 Carburetor - removal and installation

Warning: *Gasoline (petrol) is extremely flammable, so take extra precautions when you work on any part of the fuel system. Don't smoke or allow open flames or bare light bulbs near the work area, and don't work in a garage where a gas-type appliance (such as a water heater or clothes dryer) is present. Since gasoline is carcinogenic, wear protective gloves when there's a possibility of being exposed to fuel, and, if you spill any fuel on your skin, rinse it off immediately with soap and water. Mop up any spills immediately and do not store fuel-soaked rags where they could ignite. When you perform any kind of work on the fuel system, wear safety glasses and have a fire extinguisher suitable for a class B type fire (flammable liquids) on hand.*

Removal

1   Remove the fuel tank (see Section 2). Remove the rubber cover (if equipped) from under the tank.
2   Refer to Section 11 and disconnect the throttle cable. On all except 1993 through 1998 Kodiak models, disconnect the choke cable (see Section 12).

1993 through 1998 Kodiak models

Refer to illustration 6.4

3   Loosen the clamping bands on the air cleaner duct and lift it out.
4   Remove the nuts and detach the carburetor from the intake mani-

6.4 On 1993 through 1998 models, remove the nuts (left arrows) to detach the carburetor from the manifold; remove the Allen bolts (right arrows) to detach the manifold

Chapter 4 Fuel and exhaust systems

6.5 Carburetor mounting details (later models)
- A Clamp screws
- B Intake manifold bolts (Kodiak)
- C Vent hose and fitting

6.6 Grizzly intake manifolds have four bolts (arrows; 660 shown)

fold **(see illustration)**. Lift out the carburetor, then disconnect the throttle cable.

All except 1993 through 1998 Kodiak models
Refer to illustration 6.5
5 Loosen the carburetor clamping band and work the carburetor free of the intake manifold **(see illustration)**.

All models
Refer to illustrations 6.6 and 6.7
6 If you plan to replace the manifold gasket or O-ring(s), unbolt the manifold from the cylinder **(see illustration 6.4, 6.5 or the accompanying illustration)**.
7 Check the intake manifold and air cleaner duct for cracks, deterioration or other damage **(see illustration)**. Replace the O-ring(s) if its condition is in doubt. Since very small defects in an O-ring may affect carburetor performance, it's a good idea to replace the O-ring(s) whenever it's removed.
8 After the carburetor has been removed, stuff clean rags into the intake port in the cylinder head to prevent the entry of dirt or other objects.

Installation
9 Installation is the reverse of the removal steps, with the following addition: Adjust throttle lever freeplay (see Chapter 1).

7 Carburetor - disassembly, cleaning and inspection

Warning: *Gasoline is extremely flammable, so take extra precautions when you work on any part of the fuel system. Don't smoke or allow open flames or bare light bulbs near the work area, and don't work in a garage where a gas-type appliance (such as a water heater or clothes dryer) is present. Since gasoline is carcinogenic, wear protective gloves when there's a possibility of being exposed to fuel, and, if you spill any fuel on your skin, rinse it off immediately with soap and water. Mop up any spills immediately and do not store fuel-soaked rags where they could ignite. When you perform any kind of work on the fuel system, wear safety glasses and have a fire extinguisher suitable for a class B type fire (flammable liquids) on hand.*

Disassembly
1 Remove the carburetor from the machine as described in Section 6. Set it on a clean working surface.

6.7 The O-ring(s) should be replaced whenever the manifold is removed

1993 through 1998 Kodiak models
Refer to illustrations 7.2a through 7.2o
2 Refer to the accompanying illustrations to disassemble the carburetor **(see illustrations)**.

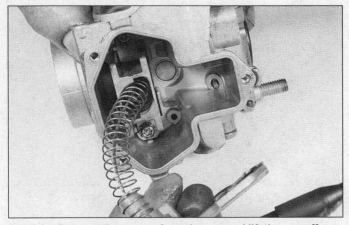

7.2a Remove the screws from the cap and lift the cap off, together with the spring, cable and jet needle components

Chapter 4 Fuel and exhaust systems

7.2b Remove the screws and take off the float chamber . . .

7.2c . . . remove the main jet ring . . .

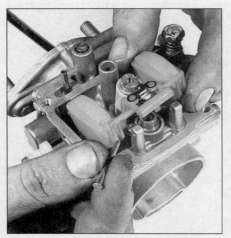

7.2d . . . pull out the float pivot pin . . .

7.2e . . . and unhook the needle valve; bend the tang (arrow) if necessary to change float level

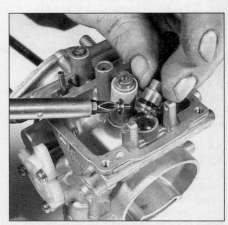

7.2f Remove the retainer screw and lift out the needle valve seat with its O-ring; the O-ring should be replaced whenever it's removed

7.2g Remove the main jet and washer . . .

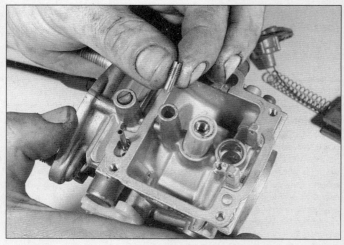

7.2h . . . the pilot jet . . .

Chapter 4 Fuel and exhaust systems

4-7

7.2i ... and the pilot screw, together with its spring, washer and O-ring

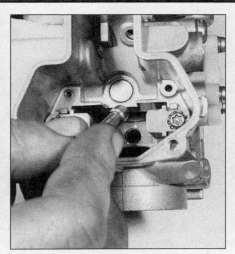

7.2j Remove the main nozzle ...

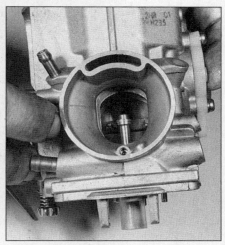

7.2k ... on installation, the shouldered end is up

7.2l Unscrew the choke knob (or choke plunger on models equipped with a choke lever)

7.2m Remove the coasting enricher cover screws (arrows) ...

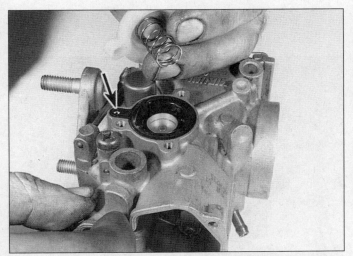

7.2n ... and lift out the spring and diaphragm; the locating tab (arrow) fits into the notch on installation

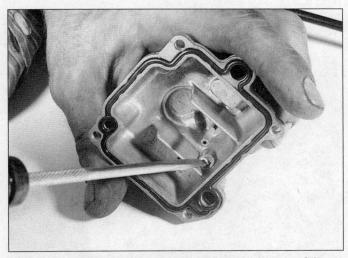

7.2o Unscrew the choke (starter) jet from the bottom of the float chamber

4-8   Chapter 4   Fuel and exhaust systems

7.3a   Remove the screws, lift off the cap, remove the throttle piston and spring . . .

7.3b   . . . and, if equipped, the O-ring that's held down by a tab (arrows)

7.3c   Lift out the jet needle holder and spring, then the jet needle

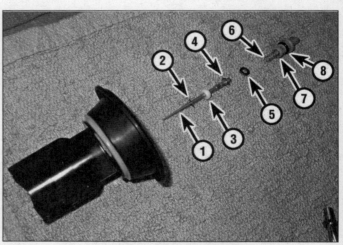

7.3d   Jet needle details

1	Jet needle	5	Thick metal washer
2	Thin metal washer	6	Spring
3	Nylon washer	7	Needle holder
4	Clip	8	O-ring

All except 1993 through 1998 Kodiak models
Refer to illustrations 7.3a through 7.3p

3   Refer to the accompanying illustrations to disassemble the carburetor **(see illustrations)**.

7.3e   Remove the cover screws . . .

7.3f   . . . and lift off the cover; the pins (arrows) align the cover on installation

Chapter 4 Fuel and exhaust systems

7.3g Make sure the passage inside the cover is clear

7.3h The post (upper arrow) fits in the hole (lower arrow) on installation

7.3i Remove the float chamber screws (arrows), then lift off the float chamber and its O-ring

7.3j Lift off the float, together with the needle valve

A Idle mixture screw
B Pilot jet
C Starter (choke) jet
D Main jet and needle jet
E Needle valve seat retaining screw
F Float
G Needle valve

7.3k Remove the needle valve seat retaining screw . . .

7.3l . . . and work the needle valve and its O-ring (arrow) free of the carburetor, taking care not to damage it

7.3m Unscrew the starter (choke) jet

7.3n Hold the needle jet with an open-end wrench, unscrew the main jet . . .

7.3o . . . and separate the main jet from the needle jet, then unscrew the needle jet and remove its O-ring (arrow)

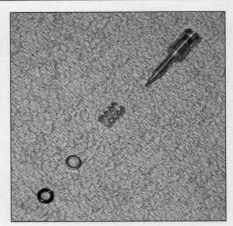
7.3n Unscrew the mixture screw and remove its spring, washer and O-ring

Cleaning

Caution: *Use only a carburetor cleaning solution that is safe for use with plastic parts (be sure to read the label on the container).*

4 Submerge the metal components in the carburetor cleaner for approximately thirty minutes (or longer, if the directions recommend it).

5 After the carburetor has soaked long enough for the cleaner to loosen and dissolve most of the varnish and other deposits, use a brush to remove the stubborn deposits. Rinse it again, then dry it with compressed air. Blow out all of the fuel and air passages in the main and upper body. **Caution:** *Never clean the jets or passages with a piece of wire or a drill bit, as they will be enlarged, causing the fuel and air metering rates to be upset.*

Inspection

6 Check the operation of the choke plunger. If it doesn't move smoothly, replace it, along with the return spring. If the plunger O-ring is deteriorated or damaged, replace it.

7 Check the tapered portion of the pilot screw for wear or damage. Replace the pilot screw if necessary.

8 Check the carburetor body, float chamber and top cover for cracks, distorted sealing surfaces and other damage. If any defects are found, replace the faulty component, although replacement of the entire carburetor will probably be necessary (check with your parts supplier for the availability of separate components).

9 Check the jet needle for straightness by rolling it on a flat surface (such as a piece of glass). Replace it if it's bent or if the tip is worn.

10 Check the tip of the fuel inlet valve needle. If it has grooves or scratches in it, it must be replaced. Push in on the rod in the other end of the needle, then release it - if it doesn't spring back, replace the valve needle.

11 Check the float chamber O-ring and the drain plug (in the float chamber). Replace them if they're damaged.

12 Operate the throttle shaft to make sure the throttle butterfly valve opens and closes smoothly. If it doesn't, replace the carburetor.

13 Check the floats for damage. This will usually be apparent by the presence of fuel inside one of the floats. If the floats are damaged, they must be replaced.

14 Check the coasting enricher diaphragm for splits, holes and general deterioration. Holding it up to a light will help to reveal problems of this nature.

15 Check the piston valve in the carburetor body for wear or damage. If it's worn or damaged, replace the carburetor.

8 Carburetor - reassembly and float height check

Refer to illustration 8.6

1 Reassembly is the reverse of disassembly, with the following additions. **Caution:** *When installing the jets, be careful not to over-tighten them - they're made of soft material and can strip or shear easily.* **Note:** *When reassembling the carburetor, be sure to use the new O-rings, gaskets and other parts supplied in the rebuild kit.*

2 Install the clip on the jet needle if it was removed. Place it in the needle groove listed in this Chapter's Specifications.

3 Install the pilot screw (if removed) along with its spring, washer and O-ring, turning it in until it seats lightly. Now, turn the screw out the number of turns listed in this Chapter's Specifications.

4 Install the coasting enricher valve into the carburetor body. Seat the bead of the diaphragm into the groove in the carburetor body, making sure the diaphragm isn't distorted or kinked. If you're working on a 1999 or later Kodiak or any Grizzly, install the throttle diaphragm in the same way.

5 Reverse the disassembly steps to install the jets.

6 Invert the carburetor. Attach the fuel inlet valve needle to the float. Set the float into position in the carburetor, making sure the valve needle seats correctly. Install the float pivot pin. To check the float height, hold the carburetor so the float hangs down, then tilt it back until the valve needle is just seated. Measure the distance from the float chamber gasket surface to the top of the float and compare your measurement to the float height listed in this Chapter's Specifications **(see illustration)**. If it isn't as specified, bend the tang on the float to change it.

7 Install the O-ring into the groove in the float chamber. Place the float chamber on the carburetor and install the screws, tightening them securely.

8.6 Hold the carburetor upside down and measure float height from the O-ring surface

Chapter 4 Fuel and exhaust systems

9.2 A ruler and a clear plastic tube like this one can be used to measure fuel level if you don't have the special tool

10.2 Loosen the clamp screws (arrows) and disconnect the ducts

10.3a On early models, remove the housing bolts (arrows) . . .

9 Fuel level - check and adjustment

Refer to illustration 9.2

Warning: *Gasoline (petrol) is extremely flammable, so take extra precautions when you work on any part of the fuel system. Don't smoke or allow open flames or bare light bulbs near the work area, and don't work in a garage where a gas-type appliance (such as a water heater or clothes dryer) is present. Since gasoline is carcinogenic, wear protective gloves when there's a possibility of being exposed to fuel, and, if you spill any fuel on your skin, rinse it off immediately with soap and water. Mop up any spills immediately and do not store fuel-soaked rags where they could ignite. When you perform any kind of work on the fuel system, wear safety glasses and have a fire extinguisher suitable for a class B type fire (flammable liquids) on hand.*

1   Park the vehicle on a level surface and make sure the carburetor is level. If necessary, adjust its position slightly by placing a floor jack under the engine and raising it.
2   Attach Yamaha service tool YM-01312-A to the drain fitting on the bottom of the carburetor float bowl. This is a clear plastic tube graduated in millimeters. An alternative is to use a length of clear plastic tubing and an accurate ruler **(see illustration)**. Hold the graduated tube (or the free end of the clear plastic tube) vertically against the float chamber cover.
3   Unscrew the drain screw at the bottom of the float chamber a couple of turns, then start the engine and let it idle - fuel will flow into the tube. Wait for the fuel level to stabilize, then note how far the fuel level is below the line on the float chamber cover.
4   Measure the distance between the line and the top of the fuel in the tube or gauge. This distance is the fuel level.
5   Compare your reading to the value listed in this Chapter's Specifications. If the fuel level is not correct, remove the float chamber cover and bend the float tang up or down as necessary, then recheck the fuel level.

10 Air cleaner housing - removal and installation

Removal

Refer to illustrations 10.2, 10.3a and 10.3b

1   Refer to Section 2 and remove the fuel tank.
2   Loosen the clamps and detach the carburetor tube from the air cleaner housing **(see illustration 6.5 and the accompanying illustration)**. On 1993 through 1998 Kodiak models, disconnect the intake tube as well.
3   If you're working on a 1993 through 1998 Kodiak, remove the air cleaner housing bolts **(see illustration)**. On all other models, remove the screws and detach the housing pins (if equipped) from the grommets **(see illustration)**. On some models, a breather hose runs through a retainer on the intake duct; free the hose from the retainer. Lift the air cleaner housing out of the frame.

Installation

4   Installation is the reverse of the removal steps.

11 Throttle cables - removal, installation and adjustment

Refer to illustrations 11.2a through 11.2e, 11.3a, 11.3b and 11.4

1   Loosen the throttle cable at the handlebar adjuster as much as possible.
2   Remove the cover screws and lift the cover from the cable housing on the carburetor **(see illustrations)**. Rotate the throttle pulley and

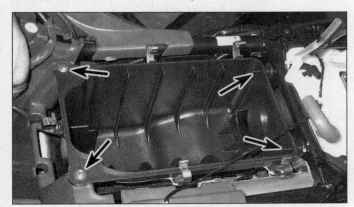

10.3b . . . on later models, the housing is secured by screws; Grizzly models also use two pins and grommets (arrows)

11.2a Remove the cover from the carburetor (this is an early model) . . .

Chapter 4 Fuel and exhaust systems

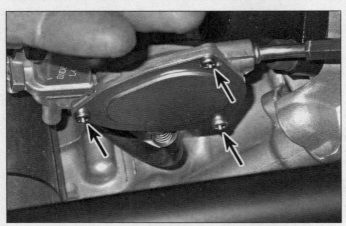

11.2b . . . the cover on later models looks like this

11.2c Rotate the throttle pulley to create slack in the cable (this is an early model) . . .

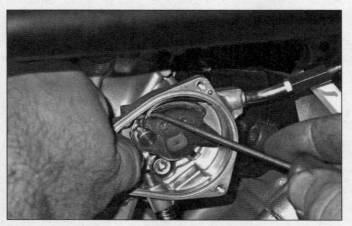

11.2d . . . and this is a later model . . .

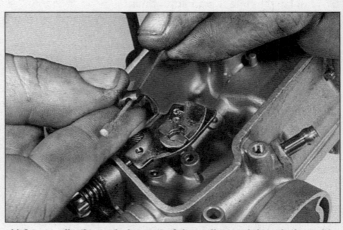

11.2e . . . slip the end plug out of the pulley and detach the cable from the plug

detach the cable from the lever **(see illustrations)**.
3 Remove the cover from the throttle housing on the handlebar, remove the lever components and disconnect the cable **(see illustrations)**. Free the cable from any retainers, noting how it's routed.
4 If necessary, remove the throttle housing clamp screws and detach the throttle housing from the handlebar **(see illustration)**.

Installation

5 If the throttle housing was removed, install it on the handlebar and tighten its clamp screws loosely. Position the housing so its protrusion is aligned with the notch in the handlebar spacer **(see illustration 11.4)**. Install the clamp and screws and tighten them securely.
6 Route the cable into place. Make sure it doesn't interfere with any

11.3a Remove the cover screws (arrows) . . .

11.3b . . . and lift off the cover for access to the lever and cable

Chapter 4 Fuel and exhaust systems

11.4 Align the throttle lever housing protrusion with the notch in the spacer (arrow)

12.1a Unscrew the choke cable fitting from the side of the carburetor (arrow) . . .

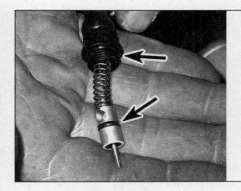

12.1b . . . pull out the cable, choke plunger and O-rings (arrows); detach the plunger from the cable if necessary

other components and isn't kinked or bent sharply.
7   Lubricate the end of the cable with multi-purpose grease and connect it to the slider in the throttle housing. Do the same with the two carburetor cables.
8   Reverse the disconnection steps to connect the throttle cable to the handlebar lever. Operate the lever and make sure it returns to the idle position by itself under spring pressure. **Warning:** *If the lever doesn't return by itself, find and solve the problem before continuing with installation. A stuck lever can lead to loss of control of the vehicle.*

Adjustment

9   Follow the procedure outlined in Chapter 1, *Throttle operation/grip freeplay - check and adjustment*, to adjust the cable.
10 Turn the handlebar back and forth to make sure the cables don't cause the steering to bind.
11 Once you're sure the cables operate properly, install the covers on the throttle lever housing and cable housing.
12 With the engine idling, turn the handlebar through its full travel (full left lock to full right lock) and note whether idle speed increases. If it does, the cable is routed incorrectly. Correct this dangerous condition before riding the vehicle.
13 Install the fuel tank and front fender.

12 Choke cable - removal and installation

Refer to illustrations 12.1a and 12.1b
1   Unscrew the choke (starter plunger) from the carburetor and disconnect the cable **(see illustrations)**.
2   Disconnect the upper end of the choke cable from the lever on the left handlebar. Free the cable from any retainers and remove it from the vehicle.
3   Installation is the reverse of the removal Steps.

13.1a Unscrew the exhaust pipe nuts (late Kodiak shown; one nut hidden)

13 Exhaust system - removal and installation

Refer to illustration 13.1a and 13.1b
1   Remove the exhaust pipe holder nuts and slide the holder off the mounting studs **(see illustrations)**.

13.1b Grizzly models have dual exhaust pipes (660 shown)

2   If necessary, unbolt the heat shield and remove it from the exhaust pipe.
3   Remove the muffler/silencer mounting bolts.
4   Pull the exhaust system forward, separate the pipe from the cylinder head and remove the system from the machine.

5   Installation is the reverse of removal, with the following additions:
   a) *Be sure to install a new gasket at the cylinder head.*
   b) *Tighten the muffler mounting bolts, clamp bolts and holder nuts to the torques listed in this Chapter's Specifications.*

Chapter 5
Ignition system

Contents

	Section		Section
Engine kill switch - check, removal and installation	See Chapter 9	Ignition (main) switch and key lock cylinder - check, removal and installation	See Chapter 9
General information	1	Ignition system - check	2
Ignition coil - check, removal and installation	3	Ignition timing - general information and check	6
Ignition control module (ICM) - harness check, removal and installation	5	Pulse generator - check, removal and installation	4
		Spark plug replacement	See Chapter 1

Specifications

1993 through 1998 Kodiak
Spark plug cap resistance	10 k-ohms
Ignition coil primary resistance	0.36 to 0.48 ohms
Ignition coil secondary resistance	5.44 to 7.36 k-ohms
Pickup coil resistance (red and white wires)	171 to 209 ohms
Source coil resistance (brown and green wires)	270 to 330 ohms

1999 through 2001 Kodiak 400
Spark plug cap resistance	10 k-ohms
Ignition coil primary resistance	0.18 to 0.28 ohms
Ignition coil secondary resistance	6.32 to 9.48 k-ohms
Pickup coil resistance (white/red and white/green wires)	459 to 561 ohms
Source coil resistance (brown and green wires)	270 to 330 ohms

2002 Kodiak 400
Spark plug cap resistance	10 k-ohms
Ignition coil primary resistance	0.18 to 0.28 ohms
Ignition coil secondary resistance	6.32 to 9.48 k-ohms
Pickup coil resistance (white/red and white/green wires)	459 to 561 ohms
Rotor rotation/direction sensing coil resistance (red/white and blue wires)	0.104 to 0.127 ohms

2003 and later Kodiak 400/450
Spark plug cap resistance	10 k-ohms
Ignition coil primary resistance	0.18 to 0.28 ohms
Ignition coil secondary resistance	6.32 to 9.48 k-ohms
Pickup coil resistance (white/red and white/green wires)	459 to 561 ohms
Rotor rotation/direction sensing coil resistance (red/white and blue wires)	0.085 to 0.105 ohms

Grizzly 600
Spark plug cap resistance	10 k-ohms
Ignition coil primary resistance	0.18 to 0.28 ohms
Ignition coil secondary resistance	6.32 to 9.48 k-ohms
Pickup coil resistance (red and white wires)	459 to 561 ohms
Source coil resistance (brown and green wires)	270 to 330 ohms

Grizzly 660
Spark plug cap resistance	10 k-ohms
Ignition coil primary resistance	0.18 to 0.28 ohms
Ignition coil secondary resistance	6.32 to 9.48 k-ohms
Pickup coil resistance (white/red and white/green wires)	459 to 561 ohms
Rotor rotation/direction sensing coil resistance (red/white and blue wires)	0.104 to 0.127 ohms

Torque specifications
Pickup coil screws or Allen bolts*
1993 through 1998 Kodiak 400	5 Nm (43 inch-lbs)
1999 and later Kodiak 400/450	7 Nm (61 inch-lbs)
Grizzly 600	7 Nm (61 inch-lbs)
Grizzly 660	10 Nm (86 inch-lbs)
Timing hole cap	See Chapter 1

*Apply non-permanent thread locking agent to the bolt threads.

1 General information

These vehicles are equipped with a battery operated, fully transistorized, breakerless ignition system. The system consists of the following components:

CDI magneto
CDI unit
Battery and fuse
Ignition coil
Spark plug
Engine kill (stop) and main (key) switches
Primary and secondary (HT) circuit wiring

The transistorized ignition system functions on the same principle as a breaker point ignition system with the CDI magneto and CDI unit performing the tasks previously associated with breaker points and a mechanical advance system. As a result, adjustment and maintenance of ignition components is eliminated (with the exception of spark plug replacement).

Because of their nature, the individual ignition system components can be checked but not repaired. If ignition system troubles occur, and the faulty component can be isolated, the only cure for the problem is to replace the part with a new one. Keep in mind that most electrical parts, once purchased, can't be returned. To avoid unnecessary expense, make very sure the faulty component has been positively identified before buying a replacement part.

2 Ignition system - check

Refer to illustrations 2.5 and 2.13

Warning: *Because of the very high voltage generated by the ignition system, extreme care should be taken when these checks are performed.*

1 If the ignition system is the suspected cause of poor engine performance or failure to start, a number of checks can be made to isolate the problem.
2 Make sure the ignition kill (stop) switch is in the Run or On position.

Engine will not start

3 Refer to Chapter 1 and disconnect the spark plug wire. Connect the wire to a spare spark plug and lay the plug on the engine with the threads contacting the engine. If necessary, hold the spark plug with an insulated tool. Crank the engine over and make sure a well-defined, blue spark occurs between the spark plug electrodes. **Warning:** *Don't remove the spark plug from the engine to perform this check - atomized fuel being pumped out of the open spark plug hole could ignite, causing severe injury!*
4 If no spark occurs, the following checks should be made:
5 Unscrew the spark plug cap from the plug wire and check the cap resistance with an ohmmeter **(see illustration)**. If the resistance is infinite, replace it with a new one.
6 Make sure all electrical connectors are clean and tight. Check all wires for shorts, opens and correct installation.
7 Check the battery voltage with a voltmeter. If the voltage is less than 12-volts, recharge the battery.
8 Check the ignition fuse and the fuse connections (see Chapter 9). If the fuse is blown, replace it with a new one; if the connections are loose or corroded, clean or repair them.
9 Refer to Section 3 and check the ignition coil primary and secondary resistance.

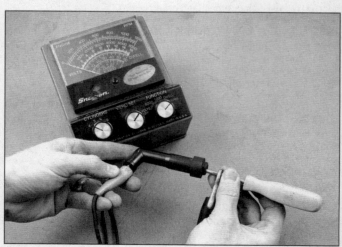

2.5 Unscrew the spark plug cap from the plug wire and measure its resistance with an ohmmeter

Chapter 5 Ignition system

2.13 A simple spark gap testing fixture can be made from a block of wood, two nails, a large alligator clip, a screw and a piece of wire

3.10 The ignition coil is secured by two bolts (arrows)

10 Refer to Section 4 and check the pulse generator resistance.
11 If the preceding checks produce positive results but there is still no spark at the plug, refer to Section 5 and check the CDI unit.

Engine starts but misfires

12 If the engine starts but misfires, make the following checks before deciding that the ignition system is at fault.
13 The ignition system must be able to produce a spark across a seven millimeter (1/4-inch) gap (minimum). A simple test fixture **(see illustration)** can be constructed to make sure the minimum spark gap can be jumped. Make sure the fixture electrodes are positioned seven millimeters apart.
14 Connect one of the spark plug wires to the protruding test fixture electrode, then attach the fixture's alligator clip to a good engine ground (earth).
15 Crank the engine over with the key in the On position and see if well-defined, blue sparks occur between the test fixture electrodes. If the minimum spark gap test is positive, the ignition coil is functioning properly. If the spark will not jump the gap, or if it is weak (orange colored), refer to Steps 5 through 11 of this Section and perform the component checks described.

3 Ignition coil - check, removal and installation

Check

1 In order to determine conclusively that the ignition coils are defective, they should be tested by an authorized Yamaha dealer service department which is equipped with the special electrical tester required for this check.
2 However, the coil can be checked visually (for cracks and other damage) and the primary and secondary resistances can be measured with an ohmmeter. If the coil is undamaged, and if the resistances are as specified, it is probably capable of proper operation.
3 To check the coil for physical damage, it must be removed (see Step 9). To check the resistance, remove the fuel tank (see Chapter 4), unplug the primary circuit electrical connectors from the coil and remove the spark plug wire from the spark plug. Mark the locations of all wires before disconnecting them.
4 To check the coil primary resistance, attach one ohmmeter lead to the primary terminals and the other ohmmeter lead to the coil base where the mounting bolts pass through it.
5 Place the ohmmeter selector switch in the Rx1 position and compare the measured resistance to the value listed in this Chapter's Specifications.

6 If the coil primary resistance is not as specified, check the coil secondary resistance by disconnecting the meter leads and attaching them between the spark plug terminal and the primary terminal.
7 Place the ohmmeter switch in the Rx1000 position and compare the measured resistance to the values listed in this Chapter's Specifications.
8 If the resistances are not as specified, unscrew the spark plug cap from the plug wire and check the resistance between the primary terminal and the end of the plug wire. If it is now within specifications, the spark plug cap is bad. If it's still not as specified, the coil is probably defective and should be replaced with a new one.

Removal and installation
Refer to illustration 3.10
9 Remove the fuel tank and disconnect the spark plug wire from the plug if you haven't already done so (see Chapters 1 and 4)
10 Support the coil with one hand and remove the coil mounting bolts, then lift the coil out **(see illustration)**. Note that on some models one bolt secures a coil primary wire.
11 Installation is the reverse of the removal Steps.

4 CDI magneto - check, removal and installation

Check

1 Disconnect the CDI unit electrical connector(s). If necessary, refer to the wiring diagrams at the end of the manual to identify the connectors by wire color.
2 Set the ohmmeter to Rx100. **Note:** *During the next steps, connect the ohmmeter to the side of the connector that leads back to the engine, not to the wiring harness side.*
3 Identify the two source coil wires, referring to the wiring diagrams at the end of the manual. Also identify the two pickup coil wires or charging/rotor direction coil wires.
4 Connect an ohmmeter between the pairs of wires and check the readings. Compare them to the values listed in this Chapter's Specifications.
5 If any of the readings is incorrect, the coil(s) must be replaced. They're supplied as a set with the alternator stator assembly, so the stator must be replaced as well (see Chapter 9).

5 CDI unit - check and replacement

Check

1 The CDI unit can only be checked by process of elimination; that is,

after all other possible causes of ignition problems have been checked and eliminated, the CDI unit is probably at fault.

2   Perform the checks in Sections 2 through 4 to test other parts of the ignition system. If all of these test OK, the CDI unit is probably at fault. However, since a new CDI unit can't be returned once purchased, it's a good idea to have a dealer service department or other qualified shop check the ignition system before buying a new unit.

Replacement

Refer to illustration 5.3

3   Disconnect the electrical connector from the CDI unit **(see illustration)**. Remove its mounting screws and take it off the frame.
4   Installation is the reverse of the removal Steps.

6   Ignition timing - general information and check

General information

1   Ignition timing need be checked only if you're troubleshooting a problem such as loss of power. Since the ignition timing can't be adjusted and since none of the ignition system parts is subject to mechanical wear, there's no need for regular checks.
2   The ignition timing is checked with the engine running, both at idle and at a higher speed listed in this Chapter's Specifications. Inexpensive neon timing lights should be adequate in theory, but in practice may produce such dim pulses that the timing marks are hard to see. If possible, one of the more precise xenon timing lights should be used, powered by an external source of the appropriate voltage. *Note: Don't use the vehicle's own battery as an incorrect reading may result from stray impulses within the electrical system.*

Check

3   Warm the engine to normal operating temperature, make sure the transmission is in Neutral, then shut the engine off.
4   Refer to *Valve clearance - check and adjustment* in Chapter 1 and remove the timing window cap.
5   Connect the timing light and a tune-up tachometer to the engine,

5.3 The CDI unit on early models is mounted under the front fender at the center of the vehicle; on later models, it's under the left rear fender

following the manufacturer's instructions.
6   Start the engine. Make sure it idles at the speed listed in the Chapter 1 Specifications. Adjust if necessary.
7   Point the timing light into the timing window. At idle, the line next to the F mark on the alternator rotor should align with the notch at the side of the timing window.
8   Raise engine speed by turning the throttle stop screw (see Chapter 1). The timing mark on the alternator rotor should move in relation to the notch.
9   If the timing is incorrect and all other ignition components have tested as good, the CDI unit may be defective. Have it tested by a dealer service department or other qualified shop.
10 When the check is complete, grease the timing window O-ring, then install the O-ring and cap and disconnect the test equipment.

Chapter 6
Steering, suspension and final drive

Contents

	Section
Driveaxles - CV joint and boot replacement	10
Driveaxles - removal and installation	9
Driveshaft universal joints - replacement	19
Front differential and driveshaft - removal, inspection and installation	11
General information	1
Handlebar - removal, inspection and installation	2
Knuckles - removal, inspection, and installation	6
Middle driven gear and transfer case (1993 through 1998 models) - removal, inspection and installation	12
Rear axle (swingarm models) - removal, inspection and installation	13

	Section
Rear driveshaft (swingarm models) - removal, inspection and installation	18
Rear final drive unit - removal, inspection and installation	14
Rear stabilizer bar (IRS models) - removal and installation	20
Shock absorbers - removal, installation and adjustment	4
Steering knuckle bearing and seal replacement	7
Steering shaft - removal, inspection, bushing/bearing replacement and installation	3
Suspension arms - removal, inspection and installation	8
Swingarm - removal and installation	16
Swingarm bearings - check	15
Swingarm bearings or bushings - replacement	17
Tie-rods - removal, inspection and installation	5

Specifications

Tie-rod balljoint spacing
   1993 through 1999 Kodiak .... 344.5 mm (13.6 inches)
   All other models .... Not specified
Rear axle runout, swingarm models (maximum) .... 1.5 mm (0.06 inch)

Torque specifications

Handlebar bracket bolts
   1993 through 2002 Kodiak, all Grizzly models .... 20 Nm (168 in-lbs)
   2003 and later Kodiak .... 23 Nm (17 ft-lbs)
Tie-rod nuts
   1993 and later Kodiak, Grizzly 600 .... 25 Nm (18 ft-lbs)
   Grizzly ....
Tie-rod locknuts
   1993 through 1999 Kodiak .... 30 Nm (22 ft-lbs)
   2000 through 2002 Kodiak, all Grizzly models .... 15 Nm (11 ft-lbs)
   2003 and later Kodiak .... 40 Nm (29 ft-lbs)
Steering shaft nut
   1993 through 1998 Kodiak .... 30 Nm (22 ft-lbs)
   1999 Kodiak .... 35 Nm (25 ft-lbs)
   2000 through 2002 Kodiak .... 110 Nm (80 ft-lbs)
   2003 and 2004 Kodiak .... 130 Nm (94 ft-lbs)
   2005 Kodiak .... 190 Nm (140 ft-lbs)
   Grizzly 600 .... 84 Nm (61 ft-lbs)
   Grizzly 660 .... 180 Nm (130 ft-lbs)

Torque specifications (continued)

Steering shaft upper bracket bolts
    1993 through 1988 Kodiak .... 20 Nm (14 ft-lbs)
    1999 and later Kodiak, all Grizzly models .... 23 Nm (17 ft-lbs)
Front shock absorbers
    All except Grizzly 600 .... 45 Nm (32 ft-lbs)
    Grizzly 600
        To steering knuckle .... 115 Nm (85 ft-lbs)
        To frame .... 55 Nm (40 ft-lbs)
Rear shock absorber(s)
    1993 through 1998 Kodiak .... 50 Nm (36 ft-lbs)
    1999 Kodiak, all Grizzly 600 .... 59 Nm (43 ft-lbs)
    2000 through 2004 Kodiak .... 82 Nm (60 ft-lbs)
    2005 Kodiak, all Grizzly 660 .... 45 Nm (32 ft-lbs)
Front suspension arm pivot bolts .... 45 Nm (32 ft-lbs)
Upper balljoint nut
    1993 through 2002 Kodiak .... 25 Nm (18 ft-lbs)
    2003 and later Kodiak .... 30 Nm (22 ft-lbs)
    Grizzly 600 .... 48 Nm (35 ft-lbs)
    Grizzly 660 .... 25 Nm (18 ft-lbs)
Lower balljoint pinch bolt and nut
    1993 through 1998 Kodiak .... 35 Nm (25 ft-lbs)
    1999 through 2002 Kodiak, all Grizzly models .... 48 Nm (35 ft-lbs)
Lower balljoint nut (2003 and later Kodiak) .... 30 Nm (22 ft-lbs)
Front differential
    1993 through 1999 Kodiak
        Side or front mounting bolts .... 55 Nm (40 ft-lbs)
        Rear mounting bolts .... 23 Nm (17 ft-lbs)
    2000 and later Kodiak, all Grizzly models .... 55 Nm (40 ft-lbs)
Transfer case bolts (1993 through 1998 Kodiak)
    M6 bolts .... 10 Nm (84 In-lbs)
    M8 bolts .... 25 Nm (18 ft-lbs)
Rear final drive unit
    1993 through 1999 Kodiak
        Nuts .... 45 Nm (32 ft-lbs)
        Bolts .... 23 Nm (17 ft-lbs)
    2000 and 2001 Kodiak
        Bolts .... 63 Nm (45 ft-lbs)
        Nuts .... 57 Nm (41 ft-lbs)
    2003 and 2004 Kodiak
        Bolts .... 63 Nm (45 ft-lbs)
        Nuts .... 63 Nm (45 ft-lbs)
    2005 Kodiak .... 45 Nm (32 ft-lbs)
    Grizzly 600
        Bolts .... 63 Nm (45 ft-lbs)
        Nuts .... 57 Nm (41 ft-lbs)
    Grizzly 660 .... 55 Nm (40 ft-lbs)
Swingarm
    1993 through 1998 Kodiak
        Pivot shafts .... 6 Nm (51 inch-lbs)
        Pivot shaft locknuts .... 130 Nm (94 ft-lbs)
    1999 Kodiak
        Right pivot shaft .... 6 Nm (51 inch-lbs)
        Right locknut .... 130 Nm (94 ft-lbs)
        Left pivot shaft .... 130 Nm (94 ft-lbs)
    2000 and 2001 Kodiak .... 59 Nm (43 ft-lbs)
    2003 and 2004 Kodiak .... 82 Nm (59 ft-lbs)
    Grizzly 600
        Left pivot shaft .... 6 Nm (51 inch-lbs)
        Left locknut .... 130 Nm (94 ft-lbs)
        Right pivot shaft .... 130 Nm (94 ft-lbs)
Rear suspension arm pivot bolts and nuts (IRS) .... 45 Nm (32 ft-lbs)
Rear knuckle mounting bolts (IRS) .... 45 Nm (32 ft-lbs)
Rear stabilizer bar bolts (IRS) .... 30 Nm (22 ft-lbs)
Rear stabilizer bar link nuts (IRS)
    Kodiak .... 55 Nm (40 ft-lbs)
    Grizzly .... 48 Nm (35 ft-lbs)

Chapter 6 Steering, suspension and final drive

2.4 On some models, the lower bracket halves can be removed from the steering shaft; place the protrusion in the hole in the steering shaft bracket on installation

2.6a Place the punch mark (arrow) on each upper bracket half toward the front of the vehicle

1 General information

The front suspension on all models except the Grizzly 600 uses an upper and lower control arm on each side of the vehicle, connected by knuckles which support the wheel hubs. A shock absorber with a concentric coil spring is installed between each upper suspension arm and the frame.

The front suspension on Grizzly 600 models consists of a lower control arm and shock absorber with concentric coil spring on each side of the vehicle.

Front final drive on all models is by a driveshaft, solidly mounted differential, and driveaxles with constant velocity joints, which connect the differential to the wheel hubs.

The rear suspension on Kodiak 400/450 models through 2004, as well as Grizzly 600 models, consists of a single shock absorber with a concentric coil spring and a steel swingarm. Final drive is by a shaft, which passes through an integral tube on the swingarm.

The rear suspension on 2005 Kodiak models, as well as all Grizzly 660 models, is an independent design, using an upper and lower control arm, knuckle and a shock absorber with concentric coil spring on each side of the vehicle. Final drive on all models is by a shaft, solidly mounted final drive unit (swingarm models) or driveaxles with constant velocity joints, which connect the differential to the rear wheel hubs (IRS models).

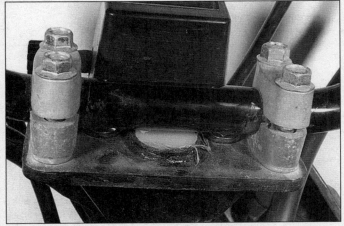

2.6b Tighten the front bracket bolts first, then the rear brackets; tighten the bolts to Specifications and don't try to close the gap at the rear edge of each bracket

The steering system consists of knuckles mounted at the outer ends of the front suspension and connected to a steering shaft by tie-rods. The steering shaft is turned by a one-piece handlebar.

2 Handlebar - removal, inspection and installation

1 The handlebar is a one-piece tube. The tube fits into a bracket, which is integral with the steering shaft. If the handlebar must be removed for access to other components, such as the steering shaft, simply remove the bolts and slip the handlebar off the bracket. It's not necessary to disconnect the cables, wires or brake hose (4WD), but it is a good idea to support the assembly with a piece of wire or rope, to avoid unnecessary strain on the cables, wires and the brake hose.

2 If the handlebar is to be removed completely, refer to Chapter 3 for the throttle housing removal procedure, Chapter 6 for the master cylinder removal procedure and Chapter 8 for the switch removal procedure.

Removal
Refer to illustration 2.4

3 Lift the indicator bulb housing off the handlebar (see Chapter 9).
4 Remove the handlebar bracket bolts and lift off the brackets (**see illustration**). Separate the upper and lower halves and take the handlebar out of the brackets.

Inspection

5 Check the handlebar and brackets for cracks and distortion and replace them if any undesirable conditions are found.

Installation
Refer to illustrations 2.6a and 2.6b

6 Installation is the reverse of the removal steps, with the following additions:
   a) When installing the handlebar to the brackets, place the punch mark on each upper bracket half toward the front of the vehicle (**see illustration**).
   b) Tighten the bracket bolts to the torques listed in this Chapter's Specifications, leaving a gap between the rear of each upper bracket half and the corresponding lower bracket half (**see illustration**).

Caution: *DO NOT try to close the gap at the rear by overtightening the bolts, or you'll break the brackets.*

3.6a Bend back the lockwasher tabs and remove the bolts and clamp . . .

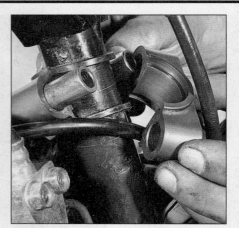
3.6b . . . to expose the bushing and seals

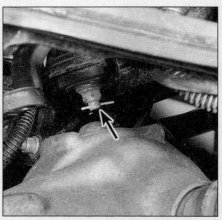
3.8 Remove the cotter pin and nut (arrow) from the bottom end of the steering shaft

3 Steering shaft - removal, inspection, bushing/bearing replacement and installation

Removal

Refer to illustrations 3.6a, 3.6b and 3.8

1 Remove the handlebars and their brackets (see Section 2).
2 Remove the seat, front cargo rack and front fender (see Chapter 8).
3 Remove the fuel tank (see Chapter 4).
4 Remove the odometer/speedometer (see Chapter 9).
5 On models so equipped, remove the cover from beneath the lower end of the steering shaft.
6 Unbolt the steering shaft bracket from the frame to expose the upper bushing and seals **(see illustrations)**.
7 Refer to Section 5 and disconnect the inner ends of the tie-rods.
8 Remove the cotter pin and nut from the bottom of the steering shaft **(see illustration)**.
9 Remove the steering shaft from the vehicle.

Inspection

10 Clean all the parts with solvent and dry them thoroughly, using compressed air, if available.
11 Check the steering shaft bushings and seals for wear, deterioration or damage. Replace them if there's any doubt about their condition.
12 Check the steering shaft and its steering arm for bending or other signs of damage. On all except 1993 through 1999 Kodiak 400 models, the steering arm can be removed from the shaft if it's worn or damaged. On 1993 through 1999 Kodiaks, the arm is an integral part of the shaft. Do not attempt to repair any steering components. Replace them with new parts if defects are found.
13 Insert a finger into the steering shaft bearing and turn the inner race. If it's rough, loose or noisy, replace it as described below.

Bearing replacement

Refer to illustration 3.14

14 Pry the upper and lower grease seals out of the bearing housing in the frame **(see illustration)**.
15 Unscrew the bearing retainer with Yamaha tool YM-01327 or equivalent. Remove the bearing through the top of the housing. The tool is a motorcycle damper rod holder with a 30 mm hex, usually used to prevent the damper rod from turning when disassembling the front forks on a motorcycle. The tool or equivalent is commonly available at motorcycle dealers.
16 Pack a new bearing with high-quality grease (preferably a moly-based grease). Position the bearing in the housing, screw in the retainer with the Yamaha special tool and tighten it to the torque listed in this Chapter's Specifications.

3.14 Pry out the seal (arrow)

17 Coat the lips of new upper and lower grease seals with grease, then tap them into the housing with a seal driver or a socket the same diameter as the seal.

Installation

18 Installation is the reverse of removal, with the following additions:
   a) Lubricate the steering shaft bushings with grease.
   b) Use new locknuts and cotter pins and tighten all fasteners to the torque listed in this Chapter's Specifications.

4 Shock absorbers - removal, installation and adjustment

Removal and installation

Front shock absorbers

Refer to illustrations 4.3a and 4.3b

1 Securely block both rear wheels so the vehicle won't roll. Refer to Chapter 7 and remove the front wheels.
2 Support the outer ends of the front suspension with jackstands so they won't drop when the shock absorbers are removed.
3 On all except Grizzly 600 models, remove the nuts and bolts at the upper and lower ends of the shock absorber **(see illustrations)**. Separate the shock absorber from the frame and suspension arm and lift it out. On Grizzly 600 models, remove the snap-ring and nut at the upper end of the shock absorber, then unbolt the lower end from the steering knuckle and lift it out.

Chapter 6 Steering, suspension and final drive

4.3a Remove the nut and bolt at the upper end of the shock absorber . . .

4.3b . . . and at the lower end

4.7 Remove the cotter pin (A), withdraw the pivot pin and remove the thrust washers; the adjuster (B) is shown on the softest setting

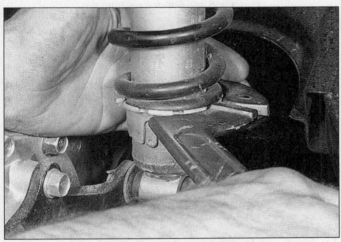

4.9 Turn the adjuster to change the setting

5.2 Remove the cotter pin and undo the locknut (4WD shown)

A	Cotter pin and locknut	D	Upper balljoint cotter pin and locknut
B	Toe-in adjusting flat		
C	Tie-rod locknut	E	Lower balljoint pinch bolt

4 Check the shock absorber for signs of wear or damage such as oil leaks, bending, a weak spring and worn bushings. Replace both shock absorbers as a pair if any problems are found.

5 Installation is the reverse of the removal steps. Tighten the nuts and bolts to the torque listed in this Chapter's Specifications.

Rear shock absorbers

Refer to illustration 4.7

6 Securely block both front wheels so the vehicle can't roll. Jack up the rear end and support it securely with the rear wheels off the ground.

7 Remove the mounting bolt and nut at the top of the shock, then the cotter pin and pivot pin at the bottom **(see illustration)**. Lift the shock out of the vehicle. If you're working on a model with independent rear suspension, remove the opposite shock in the same way.

8 Installation is the reverse of the removal steps, with the following additions:

a) Tighten the nut(s) and bolt(s) to the torque listed in this Chapter's Specifications.
b) Use a new cotter pin.

Adjustment

Refer to illustration 4.9

9 The shock absorbers on all except Grizzly 600 models are adjusted by turning the ring at the bottom of the shock with a spanner wrench **(see illustration)**.

10 The rear shock absorber on Grizzly 600 models is adjusted by sliding the adjuster lever. Grizzly 600 front shock absorbers are not adjustable.

5 Tie-rods - removal, inspection and installation

Removal

Refer to illustration 5.2

1 Look for a white paint mark on the right-hand tie-rod. If you don't see one, make your own so the tie-rods don't get mixed up when both are removed.

2 Remove the cotter pin from the nut at the outer end of the tie-rod **(see illustration)**.

3 Undo the nut. Separate the tie-rod stud from the knuckle with a bearing puller, power steering pump puller or "pickle-fork" balljoint separator. **Caution:** *It's very easy to damage the rubber boot on the tie-rod with a pickle-fork separator. If you're going to use the tie-rod again, it's best to use another type of tool.*

4 Repeat Steps 1 and 2 to disconnect the inner end of the tie rod **(see illustration 23.11b in Chapter 1)**.

Inspection

5   Check the tie-rod shaft for bending or other damage and replace it if any problems are found. Don't try to straighten the shaft.
6   Check the tie-rod balljoint boots for cracks or deterioration. Twist and rotate the threaded studs. They should move easily, without roughness or looseness. If a boot or stud show any problems, unscrew the tie-rod end from the tie-rod and install a new one.

Installation

7   Thread the tie-rod ends onto the tie-rods until the length between stud centerlines is as listed in this Chapter's Specifications. The length of exposed threads on each end of the tie-rod must be even. The flat on the tie-rod used to adjust toe-in goes at the outer end of the tie-rod **(see illustration 23.11a in Chapter 1)**.
8   The remainder of installation is the reverse of the removal steps, with the following additions:

   a) Use new cotter pins and bend them to hold the nuts securely.
   b) Check front wheel toe-in and adjust as necessary (see Chapter 1).

6   Knuckles - removal, inspection, and installation

Steering knuckles

Removal

Refer to illustration 6.5

1   If you're working on a 2000 or later model, remove the front fenders (see Chapter 8) and the front air duct. Securely block both rear wheels so the vehicle won't roll. Loosen the front wheel nuts with the tires still on the ground, then jack up the front end, support it securely on jackstands and remove the front wheels.
2   Refer to Section 5 and disconnect the outer end of the tie-rod from the knuckle.
3   Remove the front brake panel (drum brakes) or caliper, disc and splash shield (disc brakes) (see Chapter 7). The front brake hose can be left connected, but be careful not to twist it and be sure to support the panel or caliper with wire or rope so it doesn't hang by the brake hose.
4   Separating the balljoint(s) from the knuckle requires a separator tool. Equivalent automotive tools can be rented, but they must be small enough for use on these vehicles. If the correct special tool isn't available, the knuckle can be removed as an assembly with the upper and lower suspension arms. This assembly can then be taken to a Yamaha dealer for balljoint removal (and knuckle bearing replacement, if necessary).
5   Remove the cotter pin and nut from the upper balljoint **(see illustration)**.
6   Separate the balljoints from the knuckle. Pull the knuckle off the end of the driveaxle.

6.5 The upper balljoint is threaded and secured to the steering knuckle by a nut; the lower balljoint is secured to the knuckle by a pinch bolt and nut or a balljoint nut

Inspection

Refer to illustration 6.9

7   Check the knuckle carefully for cracks, bending or other damage. Replace it if any problems are found.
8   If the vehicle has been in a collision or has been bottomed hard, it's a good idea to have the knuckle magnafluxed by a machine shop to check for hidden cracks.
9   If you're working on a 4WD model, turn the inner race of each knuckle bearing with a finger **(see illustration)**. If it's rough, loose or noisy, refer to Section 7 and replace it.
10   Replace the bearing grease seals if they show signs of leakage or wear.

Installation

11   Installation is the reverse of the removal steps, with the following additions: Use new cotter pins and tighten the nuts to the torque listed in this Chapter's Specifications.

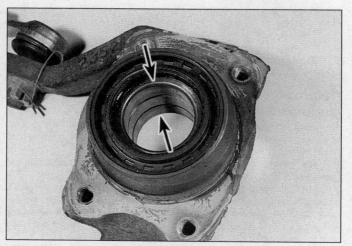

6.9 Turn the bearing inner races (arrows) with a finger to check for roughness

6.14a Remove the hub, unscrew the knuckle nuts (arrows) and remove the pivot bolts . . .

Chapter 6 Steering, suspension and final drive

6.14b ... and pull the knuckle off the end of the driveaxle

6.15a Pry off the grease seals and remove the pivot bushings for inspection

Rear knuckles (IRS models)
Removal
Refer to illustrations 6.14 and 6.14b
12 Remove the rear wheels and hubs (see Chapter 7).
13 Unbolt the driveaxle protector (if equipped).
14 Unbolt the knuckle from the upper and lower suspension arms **(see illustration)**. Pull it off the end of the driveaxle **(see illustration)**.

Inspection
Refer to illustrations 6.15a and 6.15b
15 Check the knuckle grease seals and pivot bushings for wear and damage and replace them if necessary **(see illustration)**. Inspect the bearings as described in Step 10 above and replace them if necessary as described in Section 7. Note that the rear knuckle bearings are secured by a snap-ring **(see illustration)**.

Installation
16 Installation is the reverse of the removal steps. Tighten all fasteners to the torque listed in this Chapter's Specifications.

7 Steering knuckle bearing and seal replacement

Bearing replacement
Refer to illustrations 7.1 and 7.2
1 Pry out the bearing grease seals **(see illustration)**.
2 Insert a drift through the knuckle and place it against the bearing on the opposite side **(see illustration)**. Tap around the circumference of the bearing to drive the bearing out of the knuckle, then remove the spacer and drive the other bearing out from the opposite side.
3 Pack a new bearing with grease, then drive it in with a bearing driver or socket that bears against the outer race of the bearing. **Caution:** *Don't apply pressure to the inner race or the bearing may be damaged.* Seat the bearing securely, then install the snap-ring and make sure it fits completely into its groove.
4 Install the spacer, then install the remaining bearing as described in Step 2.
5 Tap in new grease seals with a bearing driver or socket the same diameter as the seals. Make sure the seals seat squarely in their bores, then lubricate the seal lips with grease.

8 Suspension arms - removal, inspection and installation

Note: This procedure describes removal and installation of the upper and lower suspension arms on models so equipped. If you plan to remove only the upper or lower arm, ignore the steps which don't apply.

Front suspension arms
Removal
Refer to illustration 8.6
1 Securely block both rear wheels so the vehicle won't roll. Loosen the front wheel nuts with the tires still on the ground, then jack up the

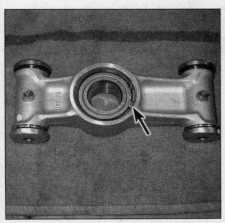

6.15b If the bearing needs to be replaced, remove the snap-ring (arrow)

7.1 Pry the seals from the knuckle

7.2 Tap out the bearings with a hammer and drift and remove the spacer

6-8 Chapter 6 Steering, suspension and final drive

8.6 Remove the pivot nuts and bolts to separate the suspension arm from the frame

8.12 Remove the pivot bolts and, if necessary, the shock absorber lower bolt (arrows)

front end, support it securely on jackstands and remove the front wheels.

Grizzly 600 models
2 Unbolt the shock absorber from the knuckle. Remove the pivot bolts and nuts and take the suspension arm out.

All except Grizzly 600 models
3 Refer to Section 6 and remove the steering knuckle.
4 Unbolt the bottom end of the shock absorber from the upper suspension arm (see Section 4).
5 Detach the brake fluid hose from the upper suspension arm.
6 Remove the nuts and bolts at the inner end of the suspension arm **(see illustration 4.3b and the accompanying illustration)** and pull the suspension arms out.

Inspection
7 Check the suspension arm(s) for bending, cracks or other damage. Replace damaged parts. Don't attempt to straighten them.
8 Check the rubber bushings at the inner end of the suspension arm for cracks, deterioration or wear of the metal insert. Check the pivot bolts for wear as well. Replace the suspension arm if any problems are visible.
9 Check the balljoint boot for cracks or deterioration. Twist and rotate the threaded stud. It should move easily, without roughness or looseness. The balljoints can't be replaced separately from the suspension arm. If the boot or stud show any problems, replace the suspension arm together with the balljoint.

Installation
10 Installation is the reverse of the removal steps, with the following addition: Tighten the nuts and bolts slightly while the vehicle is jacked up, then tighten them to the torque listed in this Chapter's Specifications while the vehicle's weight is resting on the wheels.

Rear suspension arms (IRS models)
Removal
Refer to illustration 8.12
11 Securely block both rear wheels so the vehicle won't roll. Loosen the front wheel nuts with the tires still on the ground, then jack up the front end, support it securely on jackstands and remove the front wheels.
12 Unbolt the suspension arm from the knuckle **(see illustration)**. If you're working on a lower suspension arm, unbolt the shock absorber as well.
13 Remove the suspension arm pivot bolts **(see illustration 8.12)**. Work the suspension arm free of the mounts and take it off the vehicle.

14 Check the suspension arm bushings for wear, damage or deterioration. Replace them if problems are found. If the bushings won't come out, have them pressed out by a dealer or machine shop.
15 Check the knuckle bolt holes and shock absorber bolt holes for oval wear or cracks. Replace the suspension arm if these are found.

Installation
16 Installation is the reverse of the removal steps. Tighten all fasteners to the torque listed in this Chapter's Specifications.

9 Driveaxles - removal and installation

Note: *This section applies to the front driveaxles on 4WD models and the rear driveaxles on models with independent rear suspension.*

1 Remove the front or rear wheels (see Chapter 7).

Front driveaxles
Removal
Refer to illustrations 9.5a and 9.5b
2 Remove the front brake panel (drum brakes) or caliper, disc and splash shield (see Chapter 7).
3 On 1993 through 1999 Kodiak models, separate the lower suspension arm from the steering knuckle (see Section 6). Swing the steering knuckle outward and pull the end off the driveaxle out. **Note:** *If you can't*

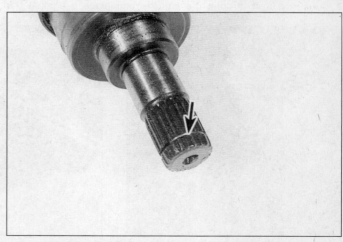

9.5a This circlip holds the inner end of the driveaxle in the differential . . .

Chapter 6 Steering, suspension and final drive

9.5b ... pull on the joint (not on the shaft) to free the circlip from the differential

9.8 The driveaxle can be removed together with the hub and knuckle; just be sure to pry the inner joint out of the final drive unit so it isn't pulled apart

pull the steering knuckle out far enough, remove the shock absorber.
4   On 2000 and later Kodiak models and all Grizzly models, remove the steering knuckles (see Section 6).
5   The inner end of the driveaxle is held in the front differential unit by a circlip **(see illustration)**. With the outer end of the driveaxle free of the knuckle, grasp the joint at the inner end firmly so it won't be pulled apart, then pull the driveaxle out of the differential **(see illustration)**. **Caution:** *Pull the driveaxle straight out (don't let it tilt up, down or sideways) to prevent damage to the oil seal in the differential.*

Installation

6   Installation is the reverse of the removal steps. After installing the driveaxle in the differential, tug it outward to make sure the circlip is locked in place.

Rear driveaxles

Removal

Refer to illustrations 9.8 and 9.9
7   Unbolt the driveaxle protector (if equipped).
8   Remove the rear hub and knuckle (see Chapter 7 and Section 6).
Note: *If you're removing the driveaxle to work on other components (such as the rear final drive unit), you can leave the knuckle attached to the driveaxle and remove them together* **(see illustration)**.
9   Detach the driveaxle from the differential as described in Step 5

above **(see illustration)**.
10   Installation is the reverse of the removal steps. After installing the driveaxle in the differential, tug it outward to make sure the circlip is locked in place.

10   Driveaxles - CV joint and boot replacement

1   This section applies to the front driveaxles on 4WD models and the rear driveaxles on models with independent rear suspension.

Inner CV joint and boot

Disassembly

Refer to illustrations 10.3, 10.4, 10.6 and 10.8
2   Remove the driveaxle from the vehicle (see Section 9). Mount the driveaxle in a vise. The jaws of the vise should be lined with wood or rags to prevent damage to the driveaxle.
3   Pry the boot clamp retaining tabs up with a small screwdriver and slide the clamps off the boot **(see illustration)**.
4   Slide the boot back on the axleshaft and pry the wire ring ball retainer from the outer race **(see illustration)**.
5   Pull the outer race off the inner bearing assembly.
6   Remove the snap-ring from the groove in the axleshaft with a pair of snap-ring pliers **(see illustration)**.

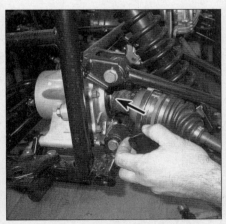

9.9 The inner end of the driveaxle is secured by a clip (arrow)

10.3 Pry the boot clamp retaining tabs (arrow) up with a small screwdriver, open the clamps and slide them off the boot

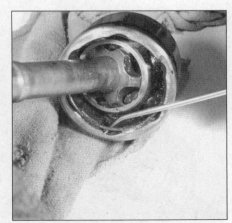

10.4 Pry the wire ring ball retainer out of the outer race

Chapter 6 Steering, suspension and final drive

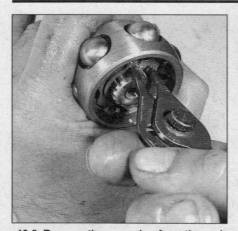

10.6 Remove the snap-ring from the end of the axle

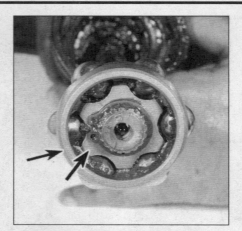

10.8 Apply match marks on the bearing (arrows) to identify which side faces out during reassembly

10.10 Wrap the splined area of the axle with tape to prevent damage to the boot when installing it

7   Slide the inner bearing assembly off the axleshaft.
8   Make match marks on the inner and outer portions of the bearing to identify which side faces out on assembly **(see illustration)**.

Inspection

9   Clean the components with solvent to remove all traces of grease. Inspect the cage, balls and races for pitting, score marks, cracks and other signs of wear and damage. Shiny, polished spots are normal and will not adversely affect CV joint performance.

Reassembly

Refer to illustrations 10.10, 10.16, 10.17a and 10.17b

10 Wrap the axleshaft splines with tape to avoid damaging the boot. Slide the small boot clamp and boot onto the axleshaft, then remove the tape **(see illustration)**.
11 Install the inner bearing assembly on the axleshaft with the previously made matchmarks facing out.
12 Install the snap-ring in the groove. Make sure it's completely seated by pushing on the inner bearing assembly.
13 Fill the outer race and boot with CV joint grease (normally included with the new boot kit). Pack the inner bearing assembly with grease, by hand, until grease is worked completely into the assembly.
14 Slide the outer race down onto the inner race and install the wire ring retainer.
15 Wipe any excess grease from the axle boot groove on the outer race. Seat the small diameter of the boot in the recessed area on the axleshaft. Push the other end of the boot onto the outer race.

16 Equalize the pressure in the boot by inserting a dull screwdriver between the boot and the outer race **(see illustration)**. Don't damage the boot with the tool.
17 Install the boot clamps **(see illustrations)**.
18 Install a new circlip on the inner CV joint stub axle.
19 Install the driveaxle as described in Section 9.

Outer CV joint and boot

Disassembly

Refer to illustration 10.21

20 Following Steps 1 through 8, remove the inner CV joint from the axleshaft.
21 Remove the outer CV joint boot clamps, using the technique described in Step 3. Slide the boot off the axleshaft **(see illustration)**.

Inspection

Refer to illustration 10.23

22 Thoroughly wash the inner and outer CV joints in clean solvent and blow them dry with compressed air, if available. **Note:** *Because the outer joint cannot be disassembled, it is difficult to wash away all the old grease and to rid the bearing of solvent once it's clean. But it is imperative that the job be done thoroughly, so take your time and do it right.*
23 Bend the outer CV joint housing at an angle to the driveaxle to expose the bearings, inner race and cage **(see illustration)**. Inspect the bearing surfaces for signs of wear. If the bearings are damaged or worn, replace the driveaxle.

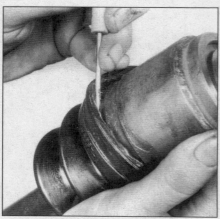

10.16 Equalize the pressure inside the boot by inserting a small, dull screwdriver between the boot and the outer race

10.17a To install the new clamps, bend the tang down and . . .

10.17b . . . fold the tabs over to hold it in place

Chapter 6 Steering, suspension and final drive

10.21 Slide the boot away from the joint and off the axleshaft

10.23 After the old grease has been rinsed away and the solvent has been blown out with compressed air, rotate the outer joint housing through its full range of motion and inspect the bearing surfaces for wear and damage - if any of the balls, the race or the cage look damaged, replace the driveaxle and outer joint assembly

Reassembly

24 Slide the new outer boot onto the driveaxle. It's a good idea to wrap vinyl tape around the shaft splines to prevent damage to the boot **(see illustration 10.10)**. When the boot is in position, add the specified amount of grease (included in the boot replacement kit) to the outer joint and the boot (pack the joint with as much grease as it will hold and put the rest into the boot). Slide the boot on the rest of the way and install the new clamps **(see illustrations 10.17a and 10.17b)**.

25 Proceed to clean and install the inner CV joint and boot by following Steps 9 through 18, then install the driveaxle as outlined in Section 9.

11 Front differential and driveshaft - removal, inspection and installation

Removal

Refer to illustrations 11.4a, 11.4b, 11.7a, 11.7b, 11.8 and 11.9

1 Refer to Section 9 and remove both front driveaxles.
2 Remove the seat, front cargo rack, front fenders and front skid plate (see Chapter 8).
3 On all except Grizzly 600 models, remove the lower suspension arms (see Section 8).
4 On 1993 through 1999 Kodiak models, unbolt the front driveshaft cover and lift it off **(see illustration)**. Unbolt the rear driveshaft protector, but leave it in place for now **(see illustration)**.
5 On Grizzly 600 models, remove the oil cooler hose retainer and the lower oil cooler mounting bolts. Unbolt the front driveshaft protector.

11.4a Remove the bolt at the rear of the driveshaft front protector (right arrow) and two more bolts at the front (left arrow)

6 Remove the differential drain plug(s) and drain the oil (see Chapter 1).
7 If the vehicle is equipped with electrically selectable 4WD, disconnect the electrical connector(s) **(see illustration)**. Disconnect the differential breather hose **(see illustration)**. **Note:** *This may be easier once*

11.4b Unbolt the driveshaft rear protector (arrows); the lower bolt secures a wiring harness retainer

11.7a Disconnect the differential wiring connectors (if equipped)

Chapter 6 Steering, suspension and final drive

11.7b Breather hose and mounting bolts (arrows)
(late Kodiak and Grizzly)

11.8 Unbolt the differential from the mounting bracket on each side

the differential has been partially removed.

8 Remove the differential mounting bolts **(see illustration 11.7b and the accompanying illustration)**.

9 Pull the differential forward to disengage the front driveshaft (from the differential on 1993 through 1999 Kodiak models; from the coupling gear at the engine on all other models) **(see illustration)**. Lift the differential and remove it from the vehicle.

10 If you're working on a 1993 through 1999 Kodiak, pull the rubber boot on the rear end of the driveshaft forward, then pull the driveshaft out. On all other models, the driveshaft is removed together with the differential. Pull it out of the differential if necessary. Note that on 2002 Grizzly 660 models, the spring fits between the driveshaft and differential. On later Grizzly 660 models, it's between the driveshaft and engine.

Inspection

Refer to illustration 11.12

11 Check the driveshaft for bending and for worn or damaged splines. Replace it if these conditions are found.

12 Check the rubber boots on the driveshaft and at the engine **(see illustration 11.9 and the accompanying illustration)**.

13 Check the oil seals at the driveaxle holes and the driveshaft hole for signs of leakage **(see illustration 11.8)**. Look into the driveaxle holes and check for obvious signs of wear and for damage such as broken gear teeth. Turn the universal joint by hand to rotate the gears so they can be inspected.

14 Differential overhaul is a complicated procedure that requires several special tools, for which there are no readily available substitutes. If there's visible wear or damage, or if the differential's rotation is rough or noisy, take it to a Yamaha dealer for disassembly and further inspection.

Installation

15 Lubricate the lips of the driveaxle seals, as well as the splines of the universal joint, with multi-purpose grease.

16 Lubricate the splines at the rear of the driveshaft and slide it into position, then pull the rubber boot into position. Make sure the spring and spring seat are in place in the front end of the driveshaft.

17 Place the differential in the frame from the right side and position it slightly forward of its installed position. Slide the differential back and slip the driveshaft into the universal joint.

18 Bolt the differential to the mounting brackets and tighten its bolts to the torque listed in this Chapter's Specifications. Install the driveaxles (see Section 9).

19 Fill the differential with the recommended type and amount of oil (see Chapter 1).

20 The remainder of installation is the reverse of the removal steps.

11.9 Pull the differential forward to disengage the driveshaft; note the location of the driveshaft spring (later Kodiak shown)

11.12 Inspect the rubber boot at the engine or driveshaft (Grizzly 660 shown)

Chapter 6 Steering, suspension and final drive

12.4 Remove the upper cover Allen bolts (the two forward bolts have copper washers and the upper bolt secures a wiring harness retainer) . . .

12.5 . . . and the four hex bolts at the rear (lower left bolt hidden)

12 Middle driven gear and transfer case (1993 through 1998 models) - removal, inspection and installation

Removal
Refer to illustrations 12.4, 12.5 and 12.6

1 Remove the rear cargo rack, rear fender and the skid plate from under the engine (see Chapter 8).
2 Remove the exhaust system (see Chapter 3).
3 Remove the rear final drive unit and swingarm (see Sections 14 and 16). The differential and swingarm can be removed as a unit if they're only being removed for access to the transfer case.
4 Remove the middle gear case Allen bolts, noting the locations of the copper washers, wiring harness retainer and driveshaft rear cover **(see illustration)**. Don't try to remove the middle gear case yet.
5 Remove the four bolts that secure the middle driven gear to the middle gear case and crankcase **(see illustration)**.
6 Pull the middle driven gear back and sideways, disengaging the middle driven gear bearings from the crankcase, and take the assembly out of the frame **(see illustration)**.

Inspection
Refer to illustrations 12.7a and 12.7b

7 Check the teeth on the middle driven gear and the middle drive gear (in the crankcase) for wear or damage **(see illustrations)**.

12.6 Take the middle driven gear (and the transfer case on 4WD models) out of the engine

Replacement of the gears requires disassembly of the middle driven gear. This is a complicated procedure involving the use of a press and special Yamaha tools, and should be only be done by a Yamaha dealer or qualified ATV shop.

12.7a Inspect the bearing, spring and bevel gear . . .

12.7b . . . and the corresponding bevel gear in the engine

A Bevel gear   B Dowels

6-14   Chapter 6 Steering, suspension and final drive

13.3 Place the hub and nut on the end of the axle and tap it gently to free it from the final drive unit

13.4 Install a new O-ring on the axle

13.6 If the bearing comes out with the axle, inspect it and replace it if necessary

8   Rotate the middle driven gear bearings and check for roughness, looseness or noise **(see illustration 12.7a)**. Hold one side of each universal joint and try to rotate the other side while checking for looseness. If problems are found, take the middle driven gear to a dealer or ATV shop for repairs.
9   If the middle driven gear is disassembled for repair, the backlash of the drive and driven gears will have to be adjusted by changing the number of shims. This procedure should be done, and the middle driven gear installed in the engine, by the same shop that does the repairs.

Installation
10   Installation is the reverse of the removal steps, with the following additions:
a) *Install the same number of shims that were removed (unless the gear has been repaired).*
b) *Lubricate the driveshaft splines with multipurpose grease.*
c) *Be sure the gear case dowels are reinstalled* **(see illustration 12.7b)**.
d) *Tighten the bearing housing assembly bolts and the case Allen bolts to the torques listed in this Chapter's Specifications.*
e) *Fill the engine (and transfer case on 4WD models) with the recommended amount and type of oil (see Chapter 1).*

13 Rear axle (swingarm models) - removal, inspection and installation

Removal
Refer to illustration 13.3
1   Securely block the front wheels so the vehicle won't roll. Loosen the rear wheel nuts with the vehicle on the ground. Jack up the rear end and support it securely, positioning the jackstands so they won't obstruct removal of the axle. Remove the rear wheels.
2   Remove the rear wheel hubs and the complete rear brake assembly (see Chapter 7). Remove the trailer hitch bracket.
3   Clean any foreign material from the left side of the axle (2000 and later Kodiak models) or right side (1993 through 1999 Kodiak and all Grizzly 600 models) so it won't be pulled into the final drive unit during removal. Slip a socket over the end of the axle to protect the threads. Tap on the left end of the axle (Kodiak models) or the right end (Grizzly 600 models) with a soft faced hammer to free it, then pull it out of the axle housing **(see illustration)**.

Inspection
Refer to illustrations 13.4 and 13.6
4   Check the axle for obvious damage, such as step wear of the splines or bending, and replace it as necessary. Remove the axle O-ring and install a new one **(see illustration)**.
5   Place the axle in V-blocks and set up a dial indicator to contact each of the outer ends in turn. Rotate the axle and compare runout to the value listed in this Chapter's Specifications. If runout is excessive, replace the axle.
6   If the axle bearing comes out with the axle, check it for roughness, looseness or noise and replace it as necessary **(see illustration)**. If the bearing is difficult to remove from the axle shaft, have it pressed off by a Yamaha dealer or machine shop.

Installation
7   Lubricate the axle splines and the lip of the differential oil seal with multipurpose grease. Install the axle from the right side of the vehicle (2000 and later Kodiak models) or the left side (1993 through 1999 Kodiak and all Grizzly 600 models). Place the hub on the axle and thread the hub nut on until it's flush with the end of the axle shaft, then tap the axle into position, aligning the splines of the axle with those of the final drive unit.
8   Install the rear brake assembly (see Chapter 7).
9   The remainder of installation is the reverse of the removal steps.
10   Check oil level in the final drive unit and add oil as necessary (see Chapter 1).

14 Rear final drive unit - removal, inspection and installation

Removal
Swingarm models
Refer to illustrations 14.3a and 14.3b
1   Remove the axle shaft (see Section 13).
2   Unbolt the skid plate and remove it from under the final drive unit.
3   Disconnect the breather tube. Unbolt the final drive unit from the axle housing and remove the nuts that secure the final drive unit to the swingarm **(see illustrations)**. Pull the unit rearward to detach it and lift it away from the swingarm.
4   If you're working on a 1993 through 1999 Kodiak, refer to Section 18 if necessary to remove the driveshaft.

Independent rear suspension models
Refer to illustrations 14.6a, 14.6b, 14.7c, 14.7a and 14.7b
5   Remove the rear knuckles, lower rear suspension arms and rear driveaxles (see Sections 6, 8 and 9). If you're working on a Grizzly 660, remove the rear brake caliper (see Chapter 7).
6   Disconnect the breather hose from the final drive unit **(see illustrations)**. Remove the mounting bolts, then pull the final drive unit

Chapter 6 Steering, suspension and final drive

14.3a Disconnect the breather tube (upper arrow) and remove the four axle housing-to-final drive bolts (lower arrows) (two upper bolts shown)

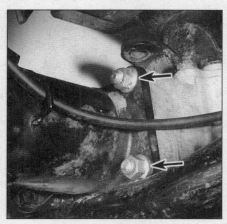

14.3b Remove the four nuts and detach the final drive unit from the swingarm

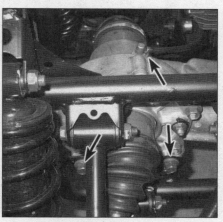

14.6a Rear differential mounting bolts and breather hose (arrows) (Kodiak with independent rear suspension)

14.6b Rear differential mounting bolts and breather hose (arrows) (Grizzly 660)

14.6c Pull the differential rearward to disengage the driveshaft

rearward to detach the driveshaft (**see illustration**). On Grizzly 660 models, if the driveshaft separates from the engine, remove the final drive unit and driveshaft together.

7 On Grizzly 660 models, remove the rubber plug at the rear end of the driveshaft and the spring that fits between the driveshaft and engine (**see illustrations**).

Inspection

Refer to illustrations 14.8a and 14.8b

8 Look into the axle holes and check for obvious signs of wear and for damage such as broken splines (**see illustrations**). Also check the seals for signs of leakage. Turn the pinion by hand (temporarily install the driveshaft and use it as a handle if necessary).

14.7a There's a rubber plug at the rear end of the driveshaft on Grizzly 660 models . . .

14.7b . . . as well as a spring at the front end (arrow)

14.8a Remove the dust seal to check the bearing; if it's worn or damaged, have it replaced

Chapter 6 Steering, suspension and final drive

14.8b Look inside the final drive unit for visible wear or damage

16.7 Loosen the clamp screws

16.8 Remove the plastic cap from each side of the swingarm . . .

9 Final drive overhaul is a complicated procedure that requires several special tools, for which there are no readily available substitutes. If there's visible wear or damage, or if rotation is rough or noisy, take it to a Yamaha dealer for disassembly and further inspection.

Installation

10 Make sure the driveshaft spring (if equipped) is in place in the driveshaft. Clean all old sealant from the mating surfaces of the final drive unit and swingarm.
11 The remainder of installation is the reverse of the removal steps. Tighten all fasteners to the torques listed in this Chapter's Specifications.
12 Fill the final drive unit with the amount and type of oil recommended in Chapter 1.

15 Swingarm bearings - check

1 Refer to Chapter 7 and remove the rear wheels, then refer to Section 4 and remove the rear shock absorber.
2 Grasp the rear of the swingarm with one hand and place your other hand at the junction of the swingarm and the frame. Try to move the rear of the swingarm from side-to-side. Any wear (play) in the bearings or bushings should be felt as movement between the swingarm and the frame at the front. The swingarm will actually be felt to move forward and backward at the front (not from side-to-side). If any play is noted, the bearings or bushings should be replaced with new ones (see Section 17).
3 Next, move the swingarm up and down through its full travel. It should move freely, without any binding or rough spots. If it does not move freely, refer to Section 16 for servicing procedures.

16 Swingarm - removal and installation

1 If the swingarm is being removed just for bearing replacement or driveshaft removal, the brake assembly, final drive and rear axle need not be removed from the swingarm.

Removal

Refer to illustrations 16.7, 16.8, 16.9, and 16.10

2 Raise the rear end of the vehicle off the ground with a jack. Support the vehicle securely so it can't be knocked over while it's jacked up.
3 Remove the rear wheels (see Chapter 7).
4 Refer to Section 4 and detach the lower end of the shock absorber from the swingarm.
5 Disconnect the rear brake lever cable and the pedal rod/cable (see Chapter 7).

6 If you're planning to remove the rear axle, final drive unit or brake assembly, do it now (see Section 13, Section 14 or Chapter 7).
7 Loosen the clamps that secure the rubber boot to the swingarm **(see illustration)**.
8 Pry the plastic pivot cap from each side of the swingarm **(see illustration)**.
9 On 1993 through 1998 Kodiak models, unscrew the locknut and pivot bolt from each side of the swingarm **(see illustration)**. On 1999 Kodiak models, unscrew the pivot bolt and locknut from the right side and the pivot shaft from the left side. On 2002 and later Kodiak models, unscrew the pivot bolt nut and remove the pivot bolt on each side. On Grizzly 600 models, unscrew the pivot bolt and locknut from the left side and the pivot shaft from the right side.
10 Pull the swingarm back and away from the vehicle, separating the driveshaft from the middle driven gear as you pull **(see illustration)**.
11 Check the pivot bearings or bushings in the swingarm for dryness or deterioration (see Section 17). If they're in need of lubrication or replacement, refer to Section 17.

Installation

12 If the driveshaft was removed from the swingarm, install it. Lubricate the driveshaft splines with molybdenum disulfide grease.
13 If the boot was removed from the swingarm, install it with one of its tabs down.
14 Lift the swingarm into position in the frame. Align the splines of the driveshaft with those of the output gear and align the pivot bolt holes in the swingarm with those in the frame.

1993 through 1998 Kodiak models

15 Install the right pivot shaft and tighten it to the torque listed in this Chapter's Specifications. Install the locknut on the right pivot shaft and tighten it to the torque listed in this Chapter's Specifications.
16 Install the left pivot shaft and tighten it until it contacts the oil seal collar, then tighten it to the torque listed in this Chapter's Specifications. Install the locknut on the left pivot shaft and tighten it to the torque listed in this Chapter's Specifications.

1999 Kodiak and all Grizzly 600 models

17 Install both pivot shafts to hold the swingarm in the frame, but don't tighten them yet.
18 Tighten the pivot bolt without a locknut to the torque listed in this Chapter's Specifications.
19 Tighten the pivot bolt with a locknut to the torque listed in this Chapter's Specifications with an Allen wrench. Tighten the pivot bolt's locknut to the torque listed in this Chapter's Specifications.

2000 and later Kodiak and all Grizzly 660 models

20 Install the swingarm pivot bolts. Install the nuts on the bolts and tighten them to the torque listed in this Chapter's Specifications.

Chapter 6 Steering, suspension and final drive

16.9 . . . unscrew the locknuts, then unscrew the pivot bolts with an Allen wrench

16.10 A spring fits inside the driveshaft (arrow) on some models

17.3 Remove the collar and pry out the seal for access to the bearing (arrow)

All models
21   Raise and lower the swingarm several times, moving it through its full travel to seat the bearings or bushings and pivot bolts.
22   Slip the boot into position and tighten the clamp.
23   The remainder of installation is the reverse of the removal steps.

17 Swingarm bearings or bushings - replacement

1993 through 1999 Kodiak, all Grizzly 600
Refer to illustration 17.3
1   The swingarm pivot shafts ride on two tapered roller bearings.
2   Remove the swingarm (see Section 16).
3   Remove the collar and pry the seal from each side of the swingarm **(see illustration)**. Take the bearings out of the swingarm and clean them thoroughly with solvent.
4   Check the bearings for roughness, looseness or play. If there's any doubt about bearing condition, replace the bearings as a set.
5   Insert a long drift from the opposite side of the swingarm so it rests against the inside of the bearing outer race. Tap against the drift to remove the bearing outer race. Work around the circumference of the outer race as you tap so the bearing doesn't tilt sideways and jam.
6   Tap new outer races into position with a bearing driver or socket just slightly smaller than the diameter of the outer race.
7   Pack the bearings with waterproof lithium-based wheel bearing grease.

2000 through 2004 Kodiak
8   Check the swingarm bushings for wear and damage and replace them if necessary. If the bushings won't come out easily, have them pressed out by a dealer service department or machine shop.

18 Rear driveshaft (swingarm models) - removal, inspection and installation

Removal
Refer to illustrations 18.2a and 18.2b
1   Refer to Section 16 and remove the swingarm.
2   Pull the driveshaft (and spring, if equipped) out of the swingarm, then pull the coupling spline out of the final drive unit **(see illustrations)**.

Inspection
3   Check the shaft for bending or other visible damage such as step wear of the splines. If the shaft is bent or the splines are worn, replace it.
4   Make sure the snap-ring is securely installed in its groove. If not, remove it and install a new one.

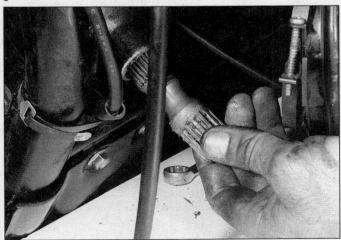

18.2a Pull out the driveshaft . . .

18.2b . . . and disengage the coupling spline from the final drive unit; on some models there's a spring inside the rear end of the driveshaft (arrow)

Chapter 6 Steering, suspension and final drive

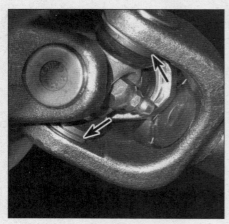

19.2 Remove the snap-rings (arrows)

20.2a The connected stabilizer link looks like this

20.2b Hold the flats on the stud with an open-end wrench so you can unscrew the nut

Installation

5   Installation is the reverse of the removal procedure. Make sure the snap-ring (and spring, if equipped) are in place.

19 Driveshaft universal joints - replacement

Refer to illustration 19.2

1   Place the U-joint in a sturdy vise and remove the snap-rings from the spider. Place the universal joint in position on either an arbor press or a workbench equipped with a large vise.
2   Remove the snap-rings **(see illustration)**.
3   Place a piece of pipe or a large socket over one of the bearing cups (the pipe or socket should be large enough that the bearing cup will fit inside it when pressed out of the yoke). Position a socket of slightly smaller diameter than the cup on the opposite bearing and use the press or vise to force the cup out (inside the pipe or large socket), stopping just before it comes completely out of the yoke. Use the vise or large pliers to work the cup the rest of the way out.
4   Transfer the socket to the other side and press out the opposite bearing cup, then remove the remaining two bearings in the same way.
5   Separate the spider and yoke. If it's necessary to remove the yoke half from the engine or differential, hold the yoke half so it won't turn and unscrew the retaining nut, then take the yoke half out of the engine or differential.

20 Rear stabilizer bar (IRS models) - removal and installation

Removal

Refer to illustrations 20.2a, 20.2b, 20.3a and 20.3b

1   Remove the rear wheels (see Chapter 7).
2   Remove the stabilizer link nuts and separate the stabilizer links from the knuckle and stabilizer **(see illustrations)**.
3   Remove the stabilizer mounting bolts and take off the mounting clamps **(see illustrations)**. Note that the left mounting clamp on Grizzly 660 models supports a brake hose retainer.
4   Check the mounting bushings for cracks or deterioration and replace them as needed. Check the stabilizer, links and mounting clamps for damage and replace as needed.
5   Installation is the reverse of the removal steps. Tighten all fasteners to the torques listed in this Chapter's Specifications.

20.3a Stabilizer bar mounting clamp bolts (Kodiak)

20.3b Stabilizer bar mounting clamp bolts (Grizzly)

Chapter 7
Brakes, wheels and tires

Contents

	Section		Section
Brake fluid level check and fluid change	See Chapter 1	Front drum brakes - removal, inspection and installation	2
Brake hoses and lines - inspection and replacement	14	General information	1
Brake lining wear and system check	See Chapter 1	Rear brake disc - inspection, removal and installation	10
Brake pedal, rear brake lever and cables - removal and installation	15	Rear brake master cylinder - removal and installation	12
Brake system bleeding	13	Rear disc brake - pad replacement	8
Drum brake wheel cylinders - overhaul	3	Rear disc brake caliper - removal, overhaul and installation	9
Front brake discs and shields - inspection, removal and installation	7	Rear drum brake - removal, inspection and installation	4
Front brake master cylinder - removal and installation	11	Tires - general information	17
Front disc brakes - caliper removal, overhaul and installation	6	Tires and wheels - general check	See Chapter 1
Front disc brakes - pad replacement	5	Wheel hubs - removal and installation	18
		Wheels - inspection, removal and installation	16

Specifications

Brakes

Brake fluid type	See Chapter 1
Brake shoe lining minimum thickness	See Chapter 1
Brake pad lining minimum thickness	See Chapter 1
Brake pedal height	See Chapter 1
Drum diameter (front and rear)	
Standard	160 mm (6.30 inches)*
Limit	161 mm (6.34 inches)*
Disc thickness	
All, except Grizzly 660 rear	3.5 mm (0.14 inch)*
Grizzly 660 rear	
Standard	8.5 mm (0.33 inch)*
Minimum	8.0 mm (0.31 inch)*
Rear disc runout limit	
Kodiak	Not specified
Grizzly	0.1 mm (0.004 inch)
Front pad wear limit	See Chapter 1

*Refer to marks cast into the drum or disc (they supersede numbers printed here).

Wheels and tires

Tire pressures	See Chapter 1
Tire tread depth	See Chapter 1

Chapter 7 Brakes, wheels and tires

Torque specifications

Front hub nuts
    1993 through 1998 .... 130 Nm (94 ft-lbs)
    1999 and later Kodiak, Grizzly 600 .... 150 Nm (110 ft-lbs)
    Grizzly 660
        2002 .... 200 Nm (145 ft-lbs)
        2003 and later .... 260 Nm (190 ft-lbs)
Rear hub nuts
    1993 through 2004 Kodiak .... 150 Nm (110 ft-lbs)
    2005 Kodiak .... 260 Nm (190 ft-lbs)
    Grizzly 600 .... 150 Nm (110 ft-lbs)
    Grizzly 660
        2002 .... 200 Nm (145 ft-lbs)
        2003 and later .... 260 Nm (190 ft-lbs)
Front drum brake hydraulic system (1993 through 1998 Kodiak)
    Wheel cylinder bolts/nuts .... 10 Nm (86 inch-lbs)
    Brake panel mounting bolts .... 25 Nm (18 ft-lbs)
    Brake hose union bolts .... 27 Nm (19 ft-lbs) (1)
    Brake hose joint mounting bolt .... 20 Nm (14 ft-lbs)
    Brake pipe flare nuts .... 18 Nm (156 inch-lbs) (2)
    Wheel cylinder bleed valve .... 6 Nm (52 inch-lbs)
    Master cylinder cover screws .... Not specified
    Master cylinder clamp bolts .... 10 Nm (86 inch-lbs)
Rear drum brake (1993 through 1999 Kodiak)
    Rear brake panel mounting bolts .... 28 Nm (20 ft-lbs)
    Rear brake lever to cam pinch bolt .... 9 Nm (75 inch-lbs)
    Rear brake drum mounting nuts .... 55 Nm (40 ft-lbs)
Rear drum brake (2003 and 2004 Kodiak 400)
    Rear brake panel mounting bolts .... 28 Nm (20 ft-lbs) (3)
    Rear brake lever to cam pinch bolt .... 9 Nm (75 inch-lbs)
    Rear brake drum cover bolts .... 28 Nm (20 ft-lbs) (3)
Rear drum brake (Grizzly 600)
    Rear brake panel mounting bolts .... 28 Nm (20 ft-lbs) (3)
    Rear brake lever to cam pinch bolt .... 10 Nm (86 inch-lbs)
Front disc brake (1999 and later Kodiak, all Grizzly 600)
    Caliper mounting bolts .... 30 Nm (22 ft-lbs)
    Disc-to-hub bolts .... 30 Nm (22 ft-lbs) (3)
    Disc splash shield bolts .... 7 Nm (61 inch-lbs)
    Brake tube flare nuts .... 18 Nm (156 inch-lbs)
    Brake hose union bolt .... 27 Nm (19 ft-lbs)
    Caliper bleed valve .... 6 Nm (52 inch-lbs)
    Master cylinder clamp bolts .... 7 Nm (61 inch-lbs) (3)
Front disc brake (Grizzly 660)
    Brake pad pins .... 18 Nm (13 ft-lbs)
    Caliper mounting bolts .... 23 Nm (17 ft-lbs)
    Disc-to-hub bolts .... 30 Nm (22 ft-lbs) (3)
    Disc splash shield bolts .... 7 Nm (61 inch-lbs)
    Brake tube flare nuts .... 18 Nm (156 inch-lbs)
    Brake hose union bolt .... 27 Nm (19 ft-lbs)
    Caliper bleed valve .... 6 Nm (52 inch-lbs)
    Master cylinder clamp bolts .... 7 Nm (61 inch-lbs) (3)
Rear disc brake (2000 through 2002 Kodiak 400)
    Brake pad pins .... 18 Nm (13 ft-lbs) (3)
    Caliper mounting bolts .... 30 Nm (22 ft-lbs)
    Disc-to-hub bolts .... 28 Nm (20 ft-lbs (3)
    Brake hose union bolt .... 30 Nm (22 ft-lbs)
    Caliper bleed valve .... 6 Nm (52 inch-lbs)
    Master cylinder mounting bolts .... 23 Nm (17 ft-lbs)
Rear disc brake (2003 and 2004 Kodiak 450)
    Brake pad pins .... 18 Nm (13 ft-lbs) (3)
    Caliper mounting bolts .... 30 Nm (22 ft-lbs)
    Disc-to-hub bolts .... 30 Nm (22 ft-lbs) (3)
    Brake hose union bolt .... 30 Nm (22 ft-lbs)
    Caliper bleed valve .... 6 Nm (52 inch-lbs)
    Master cylinder mounting bolts .... 23 Nm (17 ft-lbs)

Chapter 7 Brakes, wheels and tires

Rear disc brake hydraulic system (2005 Kodiak 400/450)
- Brake pad pins .... 17 Nm (12 ft-lbs) (3)
- Caliper mounting bolts .... 30 Nm (22 ft-lbs)
- Disc-to-hub bolts .... 30 Nm (22 ft-lbs) (3)
- Brake hose union bolt .... 30 Nm (22 ft-lbs)
- Caliper bleed valve .... 6 Nm (52 inch-lbs)
- Master cylinder mounting bolts .... 23 Nm (17 ft-lbs)
- Disc splash shield bolts .... 7 Nm (61 inch-lbs)

Rear disc brake hydraulic system (Grizzly 660)
- Brake pad pins .... 18 Nm (13 ft-lbs)
- Caliper mounting bolts .... 40 Nm (29 ft-lbs)
- Disc bolts and nuts .... 30 Nm (22 ft-lbs)
- Brake hose union bolt .... 30 Nm (22 ft-lbs)
- Caliper bleed valve .... 6 Nm (52 inch-lbs)
- Master cylinder mounting bolts .... 23 Nm (17 ft-lbs)

(1) *Use new sealing washers each time the bolts are removed.*
(2) *Replace the brake pipe with a new one each time the flare nuts are disconnected.*
(3) *Apply non-permanent thread locking agent to the bolt threads.*

1 General information

The vehicles covered by this manual include several different brake designs:

1993 through 1998 Kodiak: hydraulically actuated drum brakes at the front
All 1999 and later models: hydraulically actuated disc brakes at the front
1993 through 1999 Kodiak: single cable-actuated rear drum brake, located at the right end of the rear axle
2000 through 2002 and 2005 Kodiak: single hydraulically controlled rear disc brake
2003 and 2004 Kodiak: single cable-actuated rear drum brake
Grizzly 600: single cable-actuated rear drum brake
Grizzly 660: single hydraulically controlled rear disc brake

The rear brake on all models except the Grizzly 660 is located at one end of the rear axle. On Grizzly 660 models, the rear brake disc is mounted on the pinion gear shaft of the rear final drive unit.

The front brakes on all models are controlled by a lever on the right handlebar. The rear brake has two means of control: a lever on the left handlebar, which can be locked to provide a parking brake, and a pedal on the right side of the vehicle. On rear drum brake models, the pedal and lever are connected to the rear brake assembly by a cable (lever) and rod/cable (pedal). On rear disc brake models, the pedal is connected directly to the rear master cylinder and the lever is connected to the pedal through a cable. Pulling the lever operates the pedal, which in turn operates the rear master cylinder.

All models are equipped with steel wheels, which require very little maintenance and allow tubeless tires to be used. **Caution:** *Brake components rarely require disassembly. Do not disassemble components unless absolutely necessary. If any hydraulic brake line connection in the system is loosened, the entire system should be disassembled, drained, cleaned and then properly filled and bled upon reassembly. Do not use solvents on internal hydraulic brake components. Solvents will cause seals to swell and distort. Use only clean brake fluid for cleaning. Use care when working with brake fluid as it can injure your eyes and it will damage painted surfaces and plastic parts.*

2 Front drum brakes - removal, inspection and installation

Warning: *If a front wheel cylinder indicates the need for an overhaul (usually due to leaking fluid or sticky operation), ALL FOUR front wheel cylinders should be overhauled and all old brake fluid flushed from the system. Also, the dust created by the brake system is harmful to your health. Never blow it out with compressed air and don't inhale any of it. An approved filtering mask should be worn when working on the brakes. Do not, under any circumstances, use petroleum-based solvents to clean brake parts. Use clean brake fluid or brake system cleaner only!*

Removal

Refer to illustrations 2.3, 2.5, 2.6, 2.7 and 2.9

1   Loosen the front wheel nuts. Securely block the rear wheels so the vehicle can't roll. Jack up the front end and support it securely on jackstands.
2   Remove the front wheel.

Chapter 7 Brakes, wheels and tires

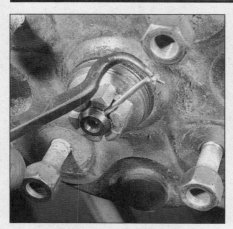

2.3 Bend back the cotter pin and pull it out

2.5 Rotate the ends of the retainer pins to align with the slot in the pin holder, then take the pin holders off

2.6 Pull the shoes apart until the ends clear the wheel cylinders, then take them off the brake panel

Brake drum

3 Remove the cotter pin from the front hub nut **(see illustration)**. Remove the nut with a socket and breaker bar.

4 Pull the brake drum and hub off the driveaxle. The hubs are integral; the drum and hub can't be separated.

Brake shoes

5 Compress the shoe holders, turn the pins 1/4 turn to align their ends with the holder slots, then remove the holders and pins **(see illustration)**.

6 Pull the ends of the brake shoes out of the wheel cylinders **(see illustration)**. Remove the shoes and springs from the brake panel.

Brake panel

7 If you're planning to remove the wheel cylinders, remove the brake hose union bolt and sealing washers from the brake panel **(see illustration)**. Place the end of the hose in a container so the brake fluid can drain or else wrap a plastic bag over the end of the hose with a rubber band to prevent loss of brake fluid. If you're removing the brake panel for access to another component such as the driveaxle, the brake hose can be left connected.

8 Remove the four brake panel bolts and lift it off the knuckle together with the wheel cylinders.

Wheel cylinders

9 Unscrew the brake pipe fittings from the back side of the brake panel with a flare nut wrench **(see illustration)**. **Note:** *Yamaha recommends replacing the brake pipe with a new one once it's removed.*

10 Unscrew the bleed valve (this will be easier to do while the wheel cylinder is bolted to the brake panel).

11 Remove the wheel cylinder mounting bolts and take the cylinders off the panel.

Inspection

12 Check the linings for wear, damage and signs of contamination from road dirt or water. If the linings are visibly defective, replace them.

13 Measure the thickness of the lining material (just the lining material, not the metal backing) and compare with the value listed in the Chapter 1 Specifications. Replace the shoes if the material is worn to the minimum or less.

14 Check the ends of the shoes where they contact the wheel cylinders and replace them if they're worn or damaged.

15 Pull back the rubber cups on the wheel cylinders. Slight moisture inside the cups is normal, but if fluid runs out, overhaul the wheel cylinders as described below.

16 Check the brake drum for wear or damage. Measure the diameter at several points with a drum micrometer (or have this done by a Yamaha dealer). Very small scratches can be polished away with fine emery cloth (polish the whole drum surface evenly). If the measurements are uneven (indicating that the drum is out-of-round) or if there are scratches deep enough to snag a fingernail, replace the drum. The drum must also be replaced if the diameter is greater than the maximum listed in this Chapter's Specifications. Yamaha doesn't recommend resurfacing the brake drums on these vehicles.

2.7 If you remove the brake hose union bolt, be sure to use a new sealing washer on each side of the bolt during assembly

2.9 Wheel cylinder mounting details

A Wheel cylinder bolts
B Brake pipe flare nuts
C Bleed valve

Chapter 7 Brakes, wheels and tires

4.2a Bend back the cotter pin and pull it out, unscrew the nut and remove the washer

4.2b Pull the drum off and inspect the waterproof seal (arrow)

4.6 Fold the shoes toward each other and lift them off

17 Check the waterproof seal on the edge of the brake panel for wear (caused by rubbing against the brake drum). Also check for damage such as cuts and tears. If the seal is worn or damaged, replace it.

Installation

18 Apply high temperature grease to the ends of the springs and to the ends of the shoes where they contact the adjusters and wheel cylinder pistons. Apply a thin smear of grease to each of the brake shoe contact points on the brake panel.
19 Hook the springs to the shoes (see illustration 2.6).
20 Pull the shoes apart and position their ends in the wheel cylinders and adjusters.
21 Install the pin holders and pins. Compress the holders and turn the pins 90-degrees so the pins secure the holders (see illustration 2.5).
22 The remainder of installation is the reverse of the removal steps, with the following additions:
a) Tighten all fasteners to the torques listed in this Chapter's Specifications.
b) Replace the metal brake pipe with a new one whenever it's removed and use new sealing washers on the brake hose union bolt.
c) Lubricate the drum seal with high temperature brake grease. Be sure not to get any grease on the inside of the drum; if you do, clean it off with a non-residue solvent such as brake cleaner or lacquer thinner.
d) Tighten the hub nut to the torque listed in this Chapter's Specifications and install a new cotter pin. If necessary, tighten the nut to align the hole in the spindle with the slots in the nut. Don't loosen the nut. Once the nut is tightened properly, bend the cotter pin to secure it.
e) Refer to Chapter 1 and adjust the brakes.

3 Drum brake wheel cylinders - overhaul

1 Remove the boot(s) from the cylinder(s). Remove the adjuster lock spring and pull the adjuster out of the other end of the cylinder.
2 Push the piston out of the cylinder.
3 Check the piston and cylinder bore for wear, scratches and corrosion. If there's any doubt about their condition, replace the cylinder as an assembly. Even barely visible flaws can reduce braking performance.
4 The piston cups and boots are available separately and should be replaced whenever the wheel cylinders are overhauled. Work the cup(s) off the piston(s). Dip new ones in clean brake fluid and carefully install them without stretching or damaging them. The wide side of the piston cup faces into the cylinder bore.
5 Check the adjuster components for wear or damage and replace as necessary.
6 Assembly is the reverse of the disassembly steps, with the following additions:
a) Coat the cylinder bore with clean brake fluid. Install the piston with the wide side of the piston cup entering the bore first. Be sure not to turn back the lip of the cup.
b) Lubricate the adjuster wheel(s) with high temperature brake grease.

4 Rear drum brake - removal, inspection and installation

Removal

Refer to illustrations 4.2a, 4.2b, 4.6, 4.7a and 4.7b
1 Securely support the rear end of the vehicle on jackstands and remove the right rear wheel.
2 Remove the cotter pin, hub nut and washer, then pull the brake drum off the axle (see illustrations).
3 Unscrew the wingnuts from the end of the brake rod and cable. Separate the rod and cable from the end pins, then take the pins out of the adjusters and remove the springs.
4 Disconnect the breather hose from the brake panel.
5 Remove the O-ring and plain washer from the axle end.
6 Fold the brake shoes into a V and remove them from the brake panel (see illustration). Disengage the springs from the shoes.
7 If necessary, unbolt the brake panel retainer, then take the retainer, O-ring and brake panel off the axle (see illustrations).

4.7a Remove the bolts and take off the brake panel retainer . . .

Inspection

8 If you removed the brake panel, clean all traces of sealant from the brake panel and the end of the axle.

9 Inspection is the same as for front drum brakes, described in Section 3. The anchor pin is integral with the brake panel and can't be replaced separately.

Installation

10 Installation is the reverse of the removal steps, with the following additions:

a) If you remove the brake panel from the hub, use silicone sealant when reinstalling it. Use non-permanent thread locking agent on the bolt threads and tighten the bolts to the torque listed in this Chapter's Specifications.

b) If you removed the brake cam, apply a thin coat of multipurpose grease to the shaft. Don't forget to reinstall its O-ring and washer.

c) Apply a thin film of high-temperature brake grease to the brake cam and the pivot areas of the anchor pin, as well as to the shoe contact areas on the brake panel. Be sure not to get any grease on the brake drum or linings.

d) Place the shoes on the brake panel with their flat ends against the brake cam and their rounded ends over the anchor pin.

e) Lubricate the drum seal with high temperature brake grease. Be sure not to get any grease on the inside of the drum; if you do, clean it off with a non-residue solvent such as brake cleaner or lacquer thinner.

f) Tighten the hub nut to the torque listed in this Chapter's Specifications and install a new cotter pin. If necessary, tighten the nut further to align the cotter pin hole in the axle with the slots in the nut. Don't loosen the nut.

g) Once the nut is tightened properly, bend the cotter pin to secure it.

h) Refer to Chapter 1 and adjust the brakes.

5 Front disc brakes - pad replacement

Refer to illustrations 5.2, 5.3a, 5.3b, 5.4a, 5.4b and 5.4c

Warning: *The dust created by the brake system is harmful to your health. Never blow it out with compressed air and don't inhale any of it. An approved filtering mask should be worn when working on the brakes.*

1 Support the front of the vehicle securely on jackstands and remove the front wheels.

2 Loosen the pad pins while the caliper is still bolted to the steering knuckle **(see illustration)**. Leave the caliper hose connected unless you plan to remove the caliper for overhaul.

3 Remove the caliper mounting bolts and lift the caliper off **(see illustration)**. If the inner disc cover is in the way, you can unbolt it and move it aside enough to provide removal clearance for the caliper. If the inner disc cover bolts are difficult to remove, leave the inner disc cover

4.7b ... then remove the O-ring (arrow) and the brake panel

5.2 Loosen - but don't remove - the brake pad pins while the caliper is still bolted to the knuckle

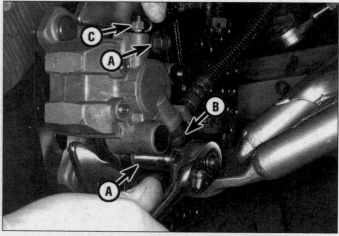

5.3a Front caliper mounting details

A Caliper mounting bolts
B Brake hose union bolt
C Bleed valve

5.3b You may need to remove the hub nut and slide the hub off part way so the caliper will clear the inner cover

Chapter 7 Brakes, wheels and tires

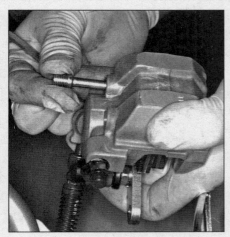

5.4a Remove the caliper, then unscrew the pad pins and pull them out

5.4b Remove the outer brake pad . . .

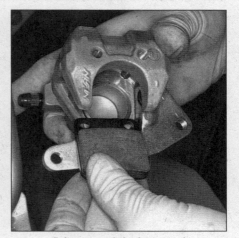

5.4c . . . and the inner pad

bolted in place and instead remove the hub nut (see Section 18) and pull the hub off just enough to clear the caliper **(see illustration)**.

4 Once the caliper is lifted off, unscrew the pad pins and pull out the pads, together with the shim on the inner pad **(see illustrations)**. Remove the pad spring from the caliper.

5 Inspect the pad spring and replace it if it's rusted or damaged. Refer to Chapter 1 and inspect the pads.

6 Check the condition of the brake disc (see Section 11). If it's in need of machining or replacement, follow the procedure in that Section to remove it. If it's okay, deglaze it with sandpaper or emery cloth, using a swirling motion.

7 Remove the cover from the master cylinder reservoir and siphon out some fluid. Push the piston into the caliper as far as possible, while checking the master cylinder reservoir to make sure it doesn't overflow. If you can't depress the pistons with thumb pressure, try using a C-clamp. If the piston sticks, remove the caliper and overhaul it as described in Section 10.

8 Install the spring and new pads. The arrow mark on the pad shim must point in the forward rotating direction of the brake disc. Install the retaining pins and tighten them slightly.

9 Install the caliper on the steering knuckle, sliding the brake disc between the pads. Install the caliper mounting bolts and tighten them to the torque listed in this Chapter's Specifications, then tighten the pad pins to the torque listed in this Chapter's Specifications.

10 Install the wheels and lower the vehicle. Tighten the wheel nuts to the torque listed in this Chapter's Specifications. Operate the right brake lever several times to seat the pads. Check the operation of the brakes carefully before riding the vehicle.

6 Front disc brakes - caliper removal, overhaul and installation

Warning: *If a caliper indicates the need of an overhaul (usually due to leaking fluid or sticky operation), all old brake fluid must be flushed from the system. Also, the dust created by the brake system is harmful to your health. Never blow it out with compressed air and don't inhale any of it. An approved filtering mask should be worn when working on the brakes. Do not, under any circumstances, use petroleum-based solvents to clean brake parts. Use brake cleaner or denatured alcohol only!*

Removal

1 Securely support the front end of the vehicle on jackstands and remove the front wheels. **Note:** *If you're planning to disassemble the caliper, read through the overhaul procedure, paying particular attention to the steps involved in removing the piston with compressed air. If you don't have access to an air compressor, you can use the vehicle's hydraulic system to force the piston out instead. To do this, remove the pads and pump the brake lever. The hydraulic pressure will push the piston out of the bore. Push one piston most of the way out, push the opposite piston all the way out, then grip the first piston and pull it out.*

2 Remove the brake hose fitting bolt and disconnect the brake hose from the caliper **(see illustration 5.2)**. Wrap the end of the hose in a plastic bag, tightly secured with a rubber band, to prevent excess fluid loss and contamination.

3 Unscrew the caliper mounting bolts and lift it off the steering knuckle **(see illustration 5.2)**. If you need to separate the caliper from the bracket, pry the rubber cap off the pin bolt, then unscrew the pin bolt from the caliper. This isn't necessary for caliper overhaul.

Overhaul

Refer to illustrations 6.5a, 6.5b and 6.6

4 Remove the brake pads and anti-rattle spring from the caliper (see Section 2, if necessary). Clean the exterior of the caliper with denatured alcohol or brake system cleaner.

5 Pack a shop rag into the space that holds the brake pads. Use compressed air, directed into the caliper fluid inlet, to remove the piston. Use only enough air pressure to ease the piston out of the bore **(see illustrations)**. If the piston is blown out forcefully, even with the rag in place, it may be damaged. **Warning:** *Never place your fingers in front of the piston in an attempt to catch or protect it when applying compressed air, as serious injury could occur.*

6.5a Carefully blow compressed air into the fluid outlet to push the piston out; keep your fingers out of the way to prevent injury

Chapter 7 Brakes, wheels and tires

6.5b Remove the piston from the bore

6.6 Remove the rubber dust seal and piston seal from their grooves with a toothpick

7.6a Bend back the cotter pin and pull it out

6 Using a wood or plastic tool, remove the piston seals (**see illustration**). Metal tools may cause bore damage.
7 Clean the pistons and bores with denatured alcohol, clean brake fluid or brake system cleaner and blow them dry with filtered, unlubricated compressed air.
8 Inspect the surface of the piston for nicks and burrs and loss of plating. Check the caliper bore, too. If surface defects are present, the caliper must be replaced. If the caliper is in bad shape, the master cylinder should also be checked.
9 Lubricate the piston seal with clean brake fluid and install it in its groove in the caliper bore. Make sure the seal seats completely and isn't twisted.
9 Lubricate the dust seal with brake fluid and install it in its groove, making sure it seats correctly.
10 Lubricate the piston with clean brake fluid and install it into the caliper bore. Using your thumbs, push the piston all the way in, making sure it doesn't get cocked in the bore.

Installation

11 Installation is the reverse of the removal steps, with the following additions:

a) *Space the pads apart so the disc will fit between them.*
b) *Use new sealing washers on the brake hose fitting.*
c) *Tighten the caliper mounting bolts and the brake hose union bolt to the torques listed in this Chapter's Specifications.*

12 Fill the master cylinder with the recommended brake fluid (see Chapter 1) and bleed the system (see Section 5). Check for leaks.
13 Check the operation of the brakes carefully before riding the vehicle.

---

7 Front brake discs and shields - inspection, removal and installation

---

Inspection

1 Securely support the front of the vehicle on jackstands and remove the front wheels.
2 Visually inspect the surface of the disc for score marks and other damage. Light scratches are normal after use and won't affect brake operation, but deep grooves and heavy score marks will reduce braking efficiency and accelerate pad wear. If the discs are badly grooved they must be machined or replaced.
3 To check disc runout, mount a dial indicator to the steering knuckle, with the plunger on the indicator touching the surface of the disc about 1/2-inch from the outer edge. Slowly turn the wheel and watch the indicator needle, comparing your reading with the limit listed in this Chapter's Specifications. If the runout is greater than allowed, check the hub bearings for play (see Chapter 1). If the bearings are worn, replace them and repeat this check. If the disc runout is still excessive, the disc will have to be replaced.
4 The disc must not be machined or allowed to wear down to a thickness less than the allowable minimum listed in this Chapter's Specifications. The thickness of the disc can be checked with a micrometer. If the thickness of the disc is less than the minimum allowable, it must be replaced. The minimum thickness is normally stamped into the disc.

Removal

Refer to illustrations 7.6a, 7.6b and 7.8
5 Remove the front wheel (see Section 16).
6 Remove the cotter pin, then have an assistant apply the front brake while you loosen the hub nut (**see illustrations**). Remove the hub nut and washer.
7 Remove the front brake caliper (see Section 6). It isn't necessary to disconnect the hose from the caliper. Set the caliper aside and support it with wire or rope so it doesn't hang by the brake hose.
8 Pull the hub off the spindle. If it's stuck, remove it with a puller (**see illustration**).
9 Mark the relationship of the disc to the hub, so it can be reinstalled in the same position. Remove the bolts that retain the disc to the hub. Loosen the bolts a little at a time, in a criss-cross pattern, to avoid distorting the disc.
10 If necessary, unbolt the disc shield from the knuckle.

7.6b Have someone firmly apply the front brakes while you crack the hub nut loose

Chapter 7 Brakes, wheels and tires

7.8 You may need a slide hammer and adapter to pull the hub off the spindle

8.2 Loosen - but don't remove - the brake pad pins while the caliper is still bolted to the vehicle

Installation

11 Clean off all grease from the brake disc using acetone or brake system cleaner. Position the disc on the hub, aligning the previously applied matchmarks (if you're reinstalling the original disc).
12 Clean the bolt threads and apply non-permanent thread locking agent to the bolt threads. Install the bolts, tightening them a little at a time in a criss-cross pattern, to the torque listed in this Chapter's Specifications.
13 Install the caliper and wheel.
14 Operate the brake lever several times to bring the pads into contact with the disc. Check the operation of the brakes carefully before riding the vehicle.

8 Rear disc brake - pad replacement

Warning: *The dust created by the brake system is harmful to your health. Never blow it out with compressed air and don't inhale any of it. An approved filtering mask should be worn when working on the brakes.*

1 Support the rear of the vehicle securely on jackstands and remove the left rear wheel.

Kodiak models

Refer to illustrations 8.2 and 8.3a through 8.3e

2 Loosen the pad pins while the caliper is still bolted to the vehicle **(see illustration)**.

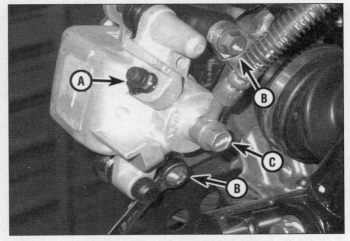

8.3a Kodiak rear caliper mounting details (IRS shown)

A Bleed valve
B Mounting bolts
C Brake hose union bolt

3 Remove the caliper mounting bolts and lift the caliper off **(see illustration)**. Unscrew the pad pins and pull out the pads, together with their shims **(see illustrations)**. Remove the pad spring from the caliper **(see illustration)**.

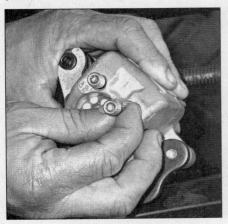

8.3b Unscrew the pad pins and pull them out . . .

8.3c . . . remove the outer pad . . .

8.3d . . . the inner pad . . .

Chapter 7 Brakes, wheels and tires

8.3e ... and the pad spring

8.11 On Grizzly 660 models, unscrew the pad pin plug ...

8.12a ... unscrew the pad pin ...

8.12b ... press down the pad spring and pull the pin out ...

8.13 ... then remove the pads (one from each side of the disc)

4 Inspect the pad spring and replace it if it's rusted or damaged.
5 Refer to Chapter 1 and inspect the pads.
6 Check the condition of the brake disc (see Section 7). If it's in need of machining or replacement, follow the procedure in Section 10 to remove it. If it's okay, deglaze it with sandpaper or emery cloth, using a swirling motion.
7 Remove the cover from the rear master cylinder reservoir and siphon out some fluid. Push the piston into the caliper as far as possible, while checking the master cylinder reservoir to make sure it doesn't overflow. If you can't depress the piston with thumb pressure, try using a C-clamp. If the piston sticks, remove the caliper and overhaul it as described in Section 6.
8 Install the spring and new pads. The arrow mark on the pad shim must point in the forward rotating direction of the brake disc. Install the retaining pins and tighten them slightly.
9 Install the caliper, sliding the brake disc between the pads. Install the caliper mounting bolts and tighten them to the torque listed in this Chapter's Specifications, then tighten the pad pins to the torque listed in this Chapter's Specifications.
10 Install the wheel and lower the vehicle. Tighten the wheel nuts to the torque listed in this Chapter's Specifications. Operate the brake pedal several times to seat the pads. Check the operation of the brakes carefully before riding the vehicle.

Grizzly models

Refer to illustrations 8.11, 8.12, 8.13 and 8.18

11 Unscrew the pad pin plug **(see illustration)**.
12 Unscrew the pad pin, then push down on the spring and pull the pin out **(see illustrations)**.
13 Pull the pads out **(see illustration)**.

14 Inspect the pad spring and replace it if it's rusted or damaged.
15 Refer to Chapter 1 and inspect the pads.
16 Check the condition of the brake disc (see Section 7). If it's in need of machining or replacement, follow the procedure in Section 10 to remove it. If it's okay, deglaze it with sandpaper or emery cloth, using a swirling motion.
17 Remove the cover from the rear master cylinder reservoir and siphon out some fluid. Push the pistons into the caliper as far as possi-

8.18 The Grizzly 660 caliper has two bleed valves (upper arrows); the brake hose union bolt is at the bottom (lower arrow)

Chapter 7 Brakes, wheels and tires

9.3 Remove the mounting bolts (arrows) and take the caliper off the final drive unit

10.6 Hold the bolts with an Allen wrench and unscrew the self-locking nuts from the other side

ble, while checking the master cylinder reservoir to make sure it doesn't overflow. If you can't depress the pistons with thumb pressure, try using a C-clamp. If the piston sticks, remove the caliper and overhaul it as described in Section 9.

18 Install the new pads. Place the spring on them, then press it in and slide the pin into position **(see illustration)**. Tighten the pin, then the plug, to the torque listed in this Chapter's Specifications.

19 Install the wheel and lower the vehicle. Tighten the wheel nuts to the torque listed in this Chapter's Specifications. Operate the brake pedal several times to seat the pads. Check the operation of the brakes carefully before riding the vehicle.

9 Rear disc brake caliper - removal, overhaul and installation

Refer to illustration 9.3

1 Securely support the rear end of the vehicle on jackstands and remove the rear wheels. **Note:** *If you're planning to disassemble the caliper, read through the overhaul procedure, paying particular attention to the steps involved in removing the piston with compressed air. If you don't have access to an air compressor, you can use the vehicle's hydraulic system to force the piston out instead. To do this, remove the pads and pump the brake lever. The hydraulic pressure will push the piston out of the bore.*

2 Remove the brake hose fitting bolt and disconnect the brake hose from the caliper **(see illustration 8.3a or 8.18)**. Wrap the end of the hose in a plastic bag, tightly secured with a rubber band, to prevent excess fluid loss and contamination.

3 Unscrew the caliper mounting bolts and lift it off the vehicle **(see illustration 8.3a or the accompanying illustration)**. On all except Grizzly 660 models, if you need to separate the caliper from the bracket, pull it off. This isn't necessary for caliper overhaul.

Overhaul

4 This is basically the same as for front calipers (see Section 6). Grizzly 660 models have four caliper pistons, so piston removal is slightly different. Use compressed air or the vehicle's hydraulic system to force the pistons partway out. If one or more pistons doesn't want to come out, block the other pistons with a block of wood or similar tool while you force the stuck piston out. Note that once one piston comes all the way out, you won't be able to use the vehicle's hydraulic system to force out the remaining pistons.

Installation

5 Installation is the reverse of the removal steps, with the following additions:

a) *Space the pads apart so the disc will fit between them.*
b) *Use new sealing washers on the brake hose fitting.*
c) *Tighten the caliper mounting bolts and the brake hose union bolt to the torques listed in this Chapter's Specifications.*

6 Fill the master cylinder with the recommended brake fluid (see Chapter 1) and bleed the system (see Section 13). Check for leaks.

7 Check the operation of the brakes carefully before riding the vehicle.

10 Rear brake disc - inspection, removal and installation

Inspection

1 Inspection is the same as for front disc brakes (see Section 7). Refer to this Chapter's Specifications for wear limits.

Removal

2 Remove the rear caliper (see Section 9).

All except Grizzly 660 models

3 Remove the rear hub (see Section 18). On some models the brake disc is bolted directly to the hub and will come off with it. On others, the disc is bolted to an adapter, which fits on the end of the axle. On these models, pull the adapter and disc off.

4 Unbolt the disc from the hub or adapter.

Grizzly 660 models

Refer to illustration 10.6

5 Remove the rear final drive unit (see Chapter 6).

6 Unbolt the plate and disc from the final drive unit **(see illustration)**.

All models

7 Installation is the reverse of the removal steps. Tighten the bolts to the torque listed in this Chapter's Specifications.

11 Front brake master cylinder - removal and installation

1 If the master cylinder is leaking fluid, or if the lever doesn't produce a firm feel when the brake is applied and bleeding the brakes does not help, master cylinder replacement is recommended.

2 **Note:** *To prevent damage to the finish from spilled brake fluid, always cover the fuel tank and front fender when working on the master cylinder.*

7-12 Chapter 7 Brakes, wheels and tires

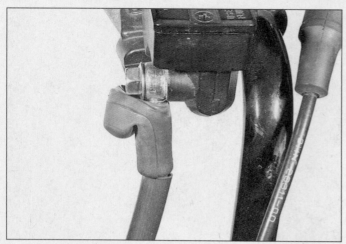

11.4 Pull back the rubber boot and remove the brake hose union bolt; use a new sealing washer on each side of the bolt during assembly

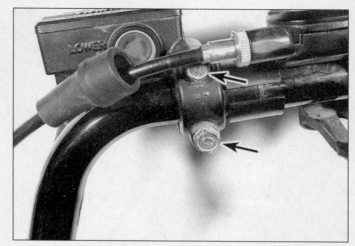

11.5 Remove the master cylinder clamp bolts (arrows); the UP mark on the clamp must be upright on installation

Removal

Refer to illustrations 11.4 and 11.5

3 Loosen, but do not remove, the screws holding the reservoir cover in place.

4 Place rags beneath the master cylinder to protect the finish in case of brake fluid spills. Remove the union bolt **(see illustration)** and separate the brake hose from the master cylinder. Wrap the end of the hose in a clean rag and suspend the hose in an upright position or bend it down carefully and place the open end in a clean container. The objective is to prevent excess loss of brake fluid, fluid spills and system contamination.

5 Remove the master cylinder mounting bolts **(see illustration)** and separate the master cylinder from the handlebar.

Installation

Refer to illustration 11.6

6 Attach the master cylinder to the handlebar. Align the protrusion on the master cylinder body with the notch in the handlebar spacer **(see illustration)**.

7 Make sure the arrow and the word UP on the master cylinder clamp are pointing up, then tighten the bolts to the torque listed in this Chapter's Specifications **(see illustration 4.5)**. Tighten the top bolt fully, then tighten the lower bolt. **Caution:** *Don't try to close the gap at the lower bolt mating surface or the clamp may break.*

8 Connect the brake hose to the master cylinder, using new sealing washers. Tighten the union bolt to the torque listed in this Chapter's Specifications.

9 Refer to Section 8 and bleed the air from the system.

12 Rear brake master cylinder - removal and installation

1 If the master cylinder is leaking fluid, or if the pedal doesn't produce a firm feel when the brake is applied and bleeding the brakes does not help, master cylinder replacement is recommended. **Caution:** *To prevent damage to the finish from spilled brake fluid, place rags between the master cylinder and bodywork.*

Removal

Refer to illustration 12.3

2 Loosen, but do not remove, the screws holding the reservoir cover in place.

3 Remove the union bolt **(see illustration)** and separate the brake hose from the master cylinder. Wrap the end of the hose in a clean rag and suspend the hose in an upright position or bend it down carefully

11.6 Position the master cylinder protrusion in the notch of the handlebar spacer

12.3 Rear master cylinder mounting details

A Brake hose union bolt
B Mounting bolts
C Cotter pin, washer and clevis pin

Chapter 7 Brakes, wheels and tires

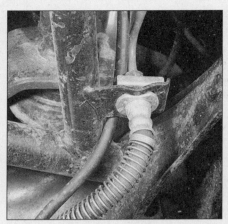

14.2 Check the hoses for cracks; pay special attention to the points where they meet the metal fittings

14.4a Some hose retainers are bolted . . .

14.4b . . . while others are secured by plastic pins

and place the open end in a clean container. The objective is to prevent excess loss of brake fluid, fluid spills and system contamination.
4   Remove the master cylinder mounting bolts **(see illustration 12.3)** and separate the master cylinder from the bracket.

Installation

5   Attach the master cylinder to the mounting bracket and tighten the bolts to the torque listed in this Chapter's Specifications **(see illustration 12.3)**.
6   Connect the brake hose to the master cylinder, using new sealing washers. Tighten the union bolt to the torque listed in this Chapter's Specifications.
7   Connect the pedal pivot to the master cylinder pushrod, using a new cotter pin **(see illustration 12.3)**.
8   Refer to Section 8 and bleed the air from the system.
9   Refer to Chapter 1 and check brake pedal freeplay, as well as the adjustment of the parking brake and shift lockout cables.

13 Brake system bleeding

1   Bleeding the hydraulic brakes on models so equipped is simply the process of removing all the air bubbles from the brake fluid reservoir, the lines and the wheel cylinders or calipers. Bleeding is necessary whenever a brake system hydraulic connection is loosened, when a component or hose is replaced, or when the master cylinder, wheel cylinders or calipers are overhauled. Leaks in the system may also allow air to enter, but leaking brake fluid will reveal their presence and warn you of the need for repair.
2   To bleed the brake, you will need some new, clean brake fluid of the recommended type (see Chapter 1), a length of clear vinyl or plastic tubing, a small container partially filled with clean brake fluid, some rags and a wrench to fit the brake bleed valve.
3   Cover the fuel tank and other painted components to prevent damage in the event that brake fluid is spilled.
4   Remove the reservoir cap and slowly pump the brake lever a few times, until no air bubbles can be seen floating up from the holes at the bottom of the reservoir. Doing this bleeds the air from the master cylinder end of the line. Reinstall the reservoir cap.
5   Attach one end of the clear vinyl or plastic tubing to the wheel cylinder or caliper bleed valve **(see illustration 2.9, 5.3a, 8.3a or 8.18)** and submerge the other end in the brake fluid in the container.
6   Check the fluid level in the reservoir. Do not allow the fluid level to drop below the lower mark during the bleeding process.
7   Carefully pump the brake lever three or four times and hold it while opening the bleed valve. When the valve is opened, brake fluid will flow out of the wheel cylinder or caliper into the clear tubing and the lever will move toward the handlebar.
8   Retighten the bleed valve, then release the brake lever gradually.

Repeat the process until no air bubbles are visible in the brake fluid leaving the wheel cylinder or caliper, and the lever is firm when applied. Remember to add fluid to the reservoir as the level drops. Use only new, clean brake fluid of the recommended type. Never reuse the fluid lost during bleeding.
9   If you're working on a Grizzly 660 rear caliper, bleed the remaining valve in the same manner as for the first valve.
10 On front brakes, repeat this procedure at the other wheel. Be sure to check the fluid level in the master cylinder reservoir frequently.
11 Replace the reservoir cap, wipe up any spilled brake fluid and check the entire system for leaks. **Note:** *If bleeding is difficult, it may be necessary to let the brake fluid in the system stabilize for a few hours (it may be aerated). Repeat the bleeding procedure when the tiny bubbles in the system have floated out.*

14 Brake hoses and lines - inspection and replacement

Inspection

Refer to illustration 14.2
1   Once a week, or if the vehicle is used less frequently, before every use, check the condition of the brake hoses.
2   Twist and flex the rubber hoses while looking for cracks, bulges and seeping fluid. Check extra carefully around the areas where the hoses connect with metal fittings, as these are common areas for hose failure **(see illustration)**.

Replacement

Refer to illustrations 14.4a and 14.4b
3   Brake hoses connect the master cylinder directly to the wheel cylinders or caliper(s) or to metal brake lines. **Note:** *Yamaha recommends that all metal brake pipes, as well as the clips that attach the metal pipes to the fittings where they join the flexible hoses, be replaced with new ones whenever they're removed.*

Flexible hoses

4   Cover the surrounding area with plenty of rags and unscrew the union bolt or flare nut. Pull out the clip or detach the hose from any retainers that may be present and remove the hose **(see illustration 6.2 and the accompanying illustrations)**.
5   Position the new hose, making sure it isn't twisted or otherwise strained, between the two components. Make sure the metal tube portion of the banjo fitting at the brake panel is located between the stoppers on the panel. Install the union bolts, using new sealing washers on both sides of the fittings, and tighten them to the torque listed in this Chapter's Specifications. If the hose is connected by a flare nut, hold it with one wrench and tighten the flare nut with another wrench.

Chapter 7 Brakes, wheels and tires

15.1 Align the slots in the adjuster and lockwheel, rotate the cable out of the slots, then drop the cable end out of the lever

15.2 Detach the cable from the bracket on the swingarm

15.3 Remove the cotter pin, washer and clevis pin (arrow) to disconnect the lower end of the cable

Metal pipes

6 Unscrew the flare nut fitting at each end of the metal pipe with a flare nut wrench. Thread the fittings of the new pipe in with fingers so they won't be cross-threaded, then tighten them with the flare nut wrench.

7 Flush the old brake fluid from the system, refill the system with the recommended fluid (see Chapter 1) and bleed the air from the system (see Section 13). Check the operation of the brakes carefully before riding the vehicle.

15 Brake pedal, rear brake lever and cables - removal and installation

Lever-operated cables

Removal

Refer to illustrations 15.1, 15.2 and 15.3

1 Loosen the lockwheel at the handlebar brake lever, then loosen the adjuster all the way. Line up the adjuster slot with the slots in the lever and bracket, then rotate the cable out of the slots and lower the cable end out of the lever **(see illustration)**.

2 If the vehicle has a rear drum brake, unscrew the cable adjusting nut at the brake assembly all the way off the end of the cable. Pull the cable out of the pin and lift it out of its bracket on the swingarm **(see illustration)**. Thread the pin and wing nut back onto the cable so they won't be lost.

3 If the vehicle has a rear disc brake, remove the cotter pin, washer and clevis pin and disconnect the lower end of the cable from the brake pedal lever **(see illustration)**.

Installation

4 Installation is the reverse of the removal steps, with the following additions:
  a) Lubricate the cable ends with multi-purpose grease.
  b) Make sure the cables are secure in their slots and retainers.
  c) On disc brake models, use a new cotter pin.
  d) Adjust brake pedal and lever play as described in Chapter 1.

Pedal rod (rear drum brake models)

Removal

5 Unscrew the pedal adjusting wing nut all the way off the rod **(see illustration 8.2a in Chapter 1)**.

6 At the brake pedal, remove the cotter pin and washer, then remove the clevis pin and detach the rod from the brake pedal. Pull the rod forward out of the pin at the rear wheel and remove it.

Installation

7 Installation is the reverse of the removal steps, with the following additions:
  a) Lubricate the clevis pin and the rear end of the rod/cable with multi-purpose grease.
  b) Adjust brake pedal height and freeplay as described in Chapter 1.

Brake pedal

Removal (drum brake models)

Refer to illustration 15.9

8 Disconnect the rod/cable from the pedal as described above. Unhook the pedal return spring and the drive select spring **(see illustration 8.2a in Chapter 1)**.

9 Pry off the clip, remove the washer and slide the pedal off the pivot shaft **(see illustration)**.

Removal (disc brake models)

10 Remove the brake pedal cover if you haven't already done so.

11 Unhook the brake light switch spring, lockout cable spring and pedal return spring **(see illustration 15.3)**. Remove the cotter pins, washers and clevis pins that attach the parking brake cable and master cylinder to the pedal. Pry off the clip, remove the washer and slide the pedal off the pivot shaft.

Chapter 7 Brakes, wheels and tires

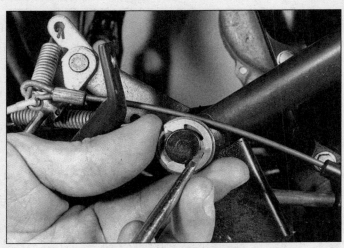

15.9 Pry the clip out of its groove

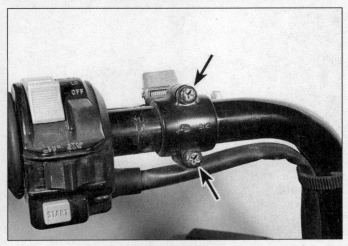

15.14 Remove the clamp screws (arrows)

Installation

12 Installation is the reverse of the removal steps, with the following additions:
  a) Lubricate the pedal shaft with multi-purpose grease.
  b) Refer to Chapter 1 and adjust brake pedal height and freeplay.

Parking brake lever

Removal

Refer to illustration 15.14

13 On all other models, disconnect the cable from the brake lever as described above.
14 Remove the lever mounting screws and take it off the handlebar **(see illustration)**.

Installation

15 Installation is the reverse of the removal steps.
16 Refer to Chapter 1 and adjust brake lever freeplay.

16 Wheels - inspection, removal and installation

Inspection

1 Clean the wheels thoroughly to remove mud and dirt that may interfere with the inspection procedure or mask defects. Make a general check of the wheels and tires as described in Chapter 1.
2 The wheels should be visually inspected for cracks, flat spots on the rim and other damage. Since tubeless tires are involved, look very closely for dents in the area where the tire bead contacts the rim. Dents in this area may prevent complete sealing of the tire against the rim, which leads to deflation of the tire over a period of time.
3 If damage is evident, the wheel will have to be replaced with a new one. Never attempt to repair a damaged wheel.

Removal

4 Securely block the wheels at the opposite end of the vehicle from the wheel being removed, so it can't roll.
5 Loosen the lug nuts on the wheel being removed. Jack up one end of the vehicle and support it securely on jackstands.
6 Remove the lug nuts and pull the wheel off.

Installation

Refer to illustration 16.7

7 Position the wheel on the studs. Make sure the directional arrow on the tire points in the forward rotating direction of the wheel **(see illustration)**.
8 Install the wheel nuts with their tapered sides toward the wheel.

This is necessary to locate the wheel accurately on the hub.
9 Snug the wheel nuts evenly in a criss-cross pattern.
10 Remove the jackstands, lower the vehicle and tighten the wheel nuts, again in a criss-cross pattern, to the torque listed in this Chapter's Specifications.

17 Tires - general information

1 Tubeless tires are used as standard equipment on this vehicle. Unlike motorcycle tires, they run at very low air pressures and are completely unsuited for use on pavement. Inflating ATV tires to excessive pressures will rupture them, making replacement of the tire necessary.
2 The force required to break the seal between the rim and the bead of the tire is substantial, much more than required for motorcycle tires, and is beyond the capabilities of an individual working with normal tire irons or even a normal bead breaker. A special bead breaker is required for ATV tires; it produces a great deal of force and concentrates it in a relatively small area.
3 Also, repair of the punctured tire and replacement on the wheel rim requires special tools, skills and experience that the average do-it-do-it-yourselfer lacks.
4 For these reasons, if a puncture or flat occurs with an ATV tire, the wheel should be removed from the vehicle and taken to a dealer service department or a repair shop for repair or replacement of the tire. The accompanying illustrations can be used as a guide to tire replacement in an emergency, provided the necessary bead breaker is available.

16.7 Be sure the directional arrow points in the forward rotating direction of the tire

TIRE CHANGING SEQUENCE

Deflate the tire and remove the valve core. Release the bead on the side opposite the tire valve with an ATV bead breaker, following the manufacturer's instructions. Make sure you have the correct blades for the tire size (using the wrong size blade may damage the wheel, the tire or the blade). Lubricate the bead with water before removal (don't use soap or any type of lubricant).

Turn the tire over and release the other bead.

If one side of the wheel has a smaller flange, remove and install the tire from that side. Use two tire levers to work the bead over the edge of the rim.

Before installing, ensure that the tire is suitable for wheel. Take note of any sidewall markings such as direction of rotation arrows, then work the first bead over the rim flange.

Use tire levers to start the second bead over the rim flange.

Hold the bead while you work the last section of it over the rim flange. Install the valve core and inflate the tire, making sure not to overinflate it.

Chapter 7 Brakes, wheels and tires

18.3 Remove the cotter pin, unscrew the nut, remove the washer and pull the hub off

18.4 If the hub nut is staked, bend back the staked portion (arrow) with a sharp punch, then unscrew the nut

18 Wheel hubs - removal and installation

Removal
Refer to illustrations 18.3 and 18.4
1   Front hubs on drum brake models are integral with the brake drums.
2   Refer to Section 16 and remove the rear wheel(s).
3   If the hub nut is secured with a cotter pin, straighten the cotter pin and pull it out **(see illustration)**.
4   If the hub nut is staked, bend back the staked portion of the nut with a sharp punch or similar tool **(see illustration)**.
5   Unscrew the hub nut and remove the washer.
6   Pull the hub off the axle shaft.

Installation
7   Installation is the reverse of the removal steps, with the following additions:
  a) *Lubricate the axle shaft and hub splines with multi-purpose grease.*
  b) *Tighten the hub nut to the torque listed in this Chapter's Specifications. If necessary, tighten it an additional amount to align the cotter pin slots. Don't loosen the nut to align the slots.*
  c) *Install a new cotter pin and bend it to secure the nut.*

Note

Chapter 8
Bodywork and frame

Contents

	Section		Section
Footrests - removal and installation	7	Rear subrame (Kodiak IRS models) - removal and installation	9
Frame - general information, inspection and repair	10	Seat - removal and installation	2
Front cargo rack and fender - removal and installation	4	Side panels and fuel tank cover - removal and installation	3
General information	1	Skidplates - removal and installation	6
Rear cargo rack and fender - removal and installation	5	Trailer hitch - removal and installation	8

1 General information

This Chapter covers the procedures necessary to remove and install the fenders and other body parts. Since many service and repair operations on these vehicles require removal of the fenders and/or other body parts, the procedures are grouped here and referred to from other Chapters.

In the case of damage to the fenders or other body parts, it is usually necessary to remove the broken component and replace it with a new (or used) one. The material that the fenders and other plastic body parts is composed of doesn't lend itself to conventional repair techniques. There are, however, some shops that specialize in "plastic welding," so it would be advantageous to check around first before throwing the damaged part away. **Note:** *When attempting to remove any body panel, first study the panel closely, noting any fasteners and associated fittings, to be sure of returning everything to its correct place on installation. In most cases, the aid of an assistant will be required when removing panels, to help avoid damaging the surface. Once the visible fasteners have been removed, try to lift off the panel as described but DO NOT FORCE the panel - if it will not release, check that all fasteners have been removed and try again. Where a panel engages another by means of lugs and grommets, be careful not to break the lugs or to damage the bodywork. Remember that a few moments of patience at this stage will save you a lot of money in replacing broken panels!*

2 Seat - removal and installation

Refer to illustrations 2.1 and 2.2

1   Lift the seat latch **(see illustration)** and lift the back end of the seat.
2   Disengage the front end of the seat from the brackets **(see illustration)** and lift the seat off the vehicle.
3   Installation is the reverse of removal.

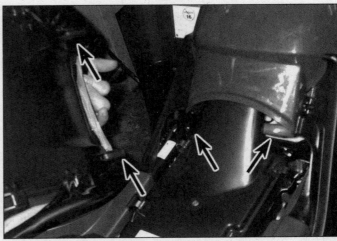

2.1 Lift the seat latch . . .

2.2 . . . lift the seat and disengage the hooks (left arrows) from the brackets (right arrows)

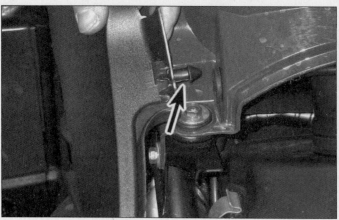

3.2 Pull the side panel post (arrow) out of the grommet . . .

3.3 . . .and disengage the tabs at the front edge of the panel

3.4a Remove two bolts at the rear (arrows) and two at the front . . .

3.4b . . . and disengage the front edge of the cover from the fender

3 Side panels and fuel tank cover - removal and installation

Refer to illustrations 3.2, 3.3, 3.4a and 3.4b

Note: *This procedure applies to 2000 and later Kodiaks and all Grizzly 660 models.*

1 If you're working on a Grizzly 660, remove the trim cover from the handlebars.
2 Carefully pull the side panel away from the vehicle to disengage the post from the grommet **(see illustration)**.
3 Disengage the hooks and tabs at the front edge of the panel and remove it from the vehicle **(see illustration)**.
4 Remove the two bolts at the rear of the fuel tank cover and the two clips or screws at the front **(see illustration)**. Lift the cover off, disengaging the tabs at the front as you do so **(see illustration)**.
5 Installation is the reverse of the removal Steps.

4 Front cargo rack and fender - removal and installation

Refer to illustrations 4.3, 4.4a, 4.4b, 4.4c, 4.6, 4.7, 4.8a and 4.8b

1 The front fender is a one-piece unit that spans the front of the vehicle and covers both front tires. A separate flap is attached to each side of the center unit.
2 On all except 1993 through 1999 Kodiak and Grizzly 600 models, remove the fuel tank side panels and cover (see Section 3).
3 Remove the cargo rack mounting bolts and lift the cargo rack off, taking care not to scratch the plastic fender **(see illustration)**.
4 If you're working on a 2000 or later Kodiak or a Grizzly 660, remove the upper trim panel **(see illustrations)**.
5 Disconnect the electrical connectors located beneath the fender.

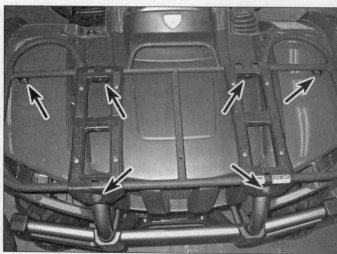

4.3 Typical cargo rack bolts (some are beneath the fender)

Chapter 8 Bodywork and frame

4.4a The rear corners of the front trim panel are secured by plastic fasteners (arrow) . . .

4.4b . . . unscrew the fasteners so the expanded portion can be pulled through the panel

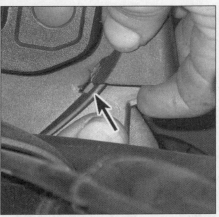

4.4c Be very careful not to damage the tabs when disengaging the panel

4.6 Remove the front bumper bolts (arrows) (Grizzly 660 shown)

4.7 The lower front of the grille (either a separate panel or integral with the fenders) is secured by two screws or bolts

6 Remove the front bumper **(see illustration)**.
7 On vehicles with a separate front grille, remove it **(see illustration)**.
8 Remove the fender mounting bolts and screws and lift the fender off the vehicle **(see illustrations)**. Have an assistant support one side if necessary, so the fender can be lifted off without scratching it. Tilt the fender forward and lift it off, taking care not to snag the fender on the odometer/speedometer.

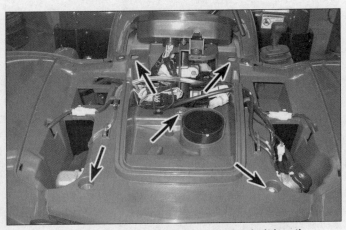

4.8a Here are typical front fender mounting bolt locations

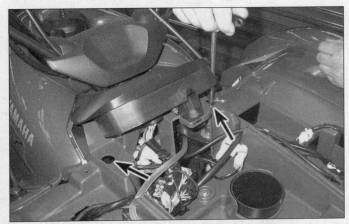

4.8b The rear bolts on Grizzly 660 models are accessible through holes (arrows)

8-4   Chapter 8 Bodywork and frame

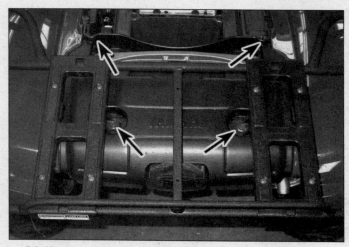

5.3 Here are typical rear cargo rack mounting bolt locations

5.4a Be sure to check carefully for rear fender bolts - some are inconspicuous

9 Installation is the reverse of removal. On vehicles with a separate front grille, use non-hardening thread locking agent on the upper grille screws.

5 Rear cargo rack and fender - removal and installation

Refer to illustrations 5.3, 5.4a and 5.4b

1 Remove the seat (see Section 2).
2 Remove the battery (see Chapter 9). Working near the battery box, remove electrical components as necessary so you can pass their connectors through the hole in the fender as it's removed.
3 Remove the rear cargo rack's mounting bolts and lift the cargo rack off the vehicle **(see illustration)**.
4 Remove the fender bolts, nuts and screws **(see illustration)**.
5 Installation is the reverse of removal.

6 Skidplates - removal and installation

1 Skidplates are secured to the underside of the vehicle by bolts. To remove a skidplate, unscrew its bolts, lower it clear and take it out.
2 Installation is the reverse of the removal steps.

7 Footrests - removal and installation

Refer to illustration 7.1

1 To remove the footrest, remove its mounting bolts **(see illustration)**.
2 Install the footrest, then install the mounting bolts and tighten them securely.

8 Trailer hitch - removal and installation

Refer to illustration 8.1

1 To remove the trailer hitch, remove its mounting bolts **(see illustration)**.
2 Install the hitch, then install the mounting bolts and tighten them securely.

9 Rear subframe (Kodiak IRS models) - removal and installation

Refer to illustrations 9.3, 9.6a, 9.6b, 9.7a and 9.7b

1 The rear subframe on Kodiak models with independent rear sus-

5.4b Some rear fender bolts are beneath the fender (arrow)

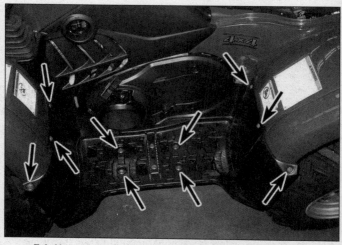

7.1 Here are typical footboard mounting bolt locations

Chapter 8 Bodywork and frame

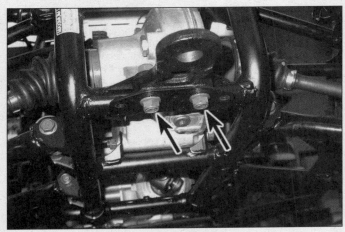

8.1 The trailer hitch is secured to the swingarm or rear frame by bolts and nuts (arrows)

9.3 Unbolt the caliper, leaving the hose connected, and place it out of the way (arrow)

9.6a Support the main frame securely and remove the left lower bolt (arrow) . . .

9.6b . . . and the right lower bolt (arrow)

pension can be removed as a unit, complete with the rear suspension and final drive unit. For some procedures, such as engine removal, this may be the easiest way to separate the rear driveshaft.
2   Remove the rear cargo rack and fender (see Section 5).
3   Unbolt the rear brake caliper and place it out of the way **(see illustration)** (refer to Chapter 7 if necessary).
4   Unbolt the rear stabilizer bar from the links (see Chapter 6).

5   Disconnect the electrical connector for the regulator/rectifier (see Chapter 9).
6   Support the engine securely with a jack and block of wood and remove the subframe lower mounting bolt on each side of the vehicle **(see illustrations)**.
7   Have an assistant help you support the subframe. Remove the upper mounting bolts, pull the subframe back to separate the rear driveshaft and remove it from the vehicle **(see illustrations)**.

9.7a Separate the lower mounts (lower arrow) and remove the upper bolts (upper arrows) . . .

9.7b . . . the driveshaft will separate like this (arrows)

10 Frame - general information, inspection and repair

1 All models use a double-cradle frame made of cylindrical steel tubing.

2 The frame shouldn't require attention unless accident damage has occurred. In most cases, frame replacement is the only satisfactory remedy for such damage. A few frame specialists have the jigs and other equipment necessary for straightening the frame to the required standard of accuracy, but even then there is no simple way of assessing to what extent the frame may have been overstressed.

3 After the machine has accumulated a lot of miles, the frame should be examined closely for signs of cracking or splitting at the welded joints. Corrosion can also cause weakness at these joints. Loose engine mount bolts can cause ovaling or fracturing to the engine mounting points. Minor damage can often be repaired by welding, depending on the nature and extent of the damage.

4 Remember that a frame that is out of alignment will cause handling problems. If misalignment is suspected as the result of an accident, it will be necessary to strip the machine completely so the frame can be thoroughly checked.

Chapter 9
Electrical system

Contents

	Section
Alternator charging coils and rotor - check and replacement	23
Battery - charging	4
Battery - check	See Chapter 1
Battery - inspection and maintenance	3
Brake switches - check and replacement	10
Carburetor heating system - check	25
Charging system - output test	22
Charging system testing - general information and precautions	21
Electric 4WD system - check	26
Electrical troubleshooting	2
Fuse and circuit breaker - check and replacement	5
Gear position switches - check and replacement	16
General information	1
Handlebar switches - check	14
Handlebar switches - removal and installation	15

	Section
Headlight aim - check and adjustment	8
Headlight bulb - replacement	7
Ignition main (key) switch - check and replacement	13
Indicator bulbs and odometer/speedometer - replacement	11
Lighting system - check	6
Regulator/rectifier - check and replacement	24
Starter circuit - check and component replacement	17
Starter clutch and reduction gears - removal, inspection and installation	20
Starter motor - disassembly, inspection and reassembly	19
Starter motor - removal and installation	18
Tail light and brake light bulbs - replacement	9
Temperature warning system - check and switch replacement	12
Wiring diagrams	27

Specifications

Battery
Type
    1993 through 1999 Kodiak .... 12V 14 Ah, fillable
    1999 through 2002 Kodiak .... 12V 18 Ah, maintenance free
    2003 and later Kodiak 400 .... 12V 12 Ah, maintenance free
    Kodiak 450, all Grizzly .... 12V 18 Ah, maintenance free

Bulbs
Headlights
    1993 through 1998 Kodiak .... 25/25 watts
    1999 and later Kodiak, all Grizzly .... 30/30 watts
Tail/brake light
    1993 through 2001 Kodiak .... 7.5 watts
    2002 and later Kodiak, all Grizzly .... 5/21 watts
Instrument light
    1993 through 1998 Kodiak .... 3.4 watts
    2003 and later Kodiak 400 .... 3 watts
Indicator lights
    1993 through 1998 Kodiak .... 3.4 watts
    1999 and later Kodiak 400, Grizzly 600 .... 1.7 watts
    Kodiak 450, Grizzly 660 .... LE

Charging system
Charging output voltage
- 1993 through 1998 Kodiak .... 12.0 volts at 3000 rpm
- 1999 through 2001 Kodiak .... 14.0 volts at 3000 rpm
- 2003 and later Kodiak 400 .... 14.0 volts at 5000 rpm
- Kodiak 450, Grizzly 600 .... 14.0 volts at 3000 rpm
- Grizzly 660 .... 14.0 volts at 5000 rpm

Charging output amperage
- 1993 through 1998 Kodiak models .... 17 amps at 3000 rpm
- 1999 Kodiak .... 15 amps at 3000 rpm
- 2000 and 2001 Kodiak .... 12 amps at 3000 rpm
- 2002 Kodiak .... 15 amps at 3000 rpm
- 2003 and later Kodiak 400 .... 17.5 amps at 5000 rpm
- Kodiak 450 .... 14 amps at 3000 rpm
- Grizzly 600 .... 12 amps at 3000 rpm
- Grizzly 660 .... 21 amps at 5000 rpm

Stator coil resistance
- 1993 through 2002 Kodiak .... 0.70 to 0.86 ohms at 20-degrees C (68-degrees F)
- 2003 and later Kodiak 400 .... 0.46 to 0.62 ohms at 20-degrees C (68-degrees F)
- Kodiak 450 .... 0.41 to 0.61 ohms at 20-degrees C (68-degrees F)
- Grizzly 600 .... 0.702 to 0.858 ohms at 20-degrees C (68-degrees F)
- Grizzly 660 .... 0.32 to 0.42 ohms at 20-degrees C (68-degrees F)

Starting system
Brush length
- 1993 through 1999 Kodiak
  - Standard .... 12.0 mm (0.47 inch)
  - Minimum .... 8.5 mm (0.33 inch)
- 2000 through 2002 Kodiak
  - Standard .... 10.0 mm (0.39 inch)
  - Minimum .... 5.0 mm (0.20 inch)
- 2003 and later Kodiak, all Grizzly
  - Standard .... 12.5 mm (0.49 inch)
  - Minimum .... 5.0 mm (0.20 inch)

Commutator diameter
- Standard .... 28 mm (1.10 inch)
- Minimum .... 27 mm (1.06 inch)

Mica depth
- 1993 through 1999 Kodiak .... 0.6 mm (0.024 inch)
- 2000 and later Kodiak, all Grizzly .... 0.7 mm (0.028 inch)

Neutral and starting circuit cut-off relay resistance
(1993 through 1998 Kodiak) .... 72 to 88 ohms

Fuse and circuit breaker rating
1993 through 1999 Kodiak
- Main fuse .... 30 amps
- Fan circuit breaker (1993 through 1998 Kodiak) .... 20 amps
- Accessory fuse (1999 Kodiak) .... 10 amps

2000 and later Kodiak
- Main fuse .... 30 amps
- Headlight fuse .... 15 amps
- Ignition fuse .... 10 amps
- Auxiliary power jack fuse .... 10 amps
- 4WD fuse .... 3 amps
- Signaling system fuse (450 models) .... 10 amps
- Odometer back-up fuse (450 models) .... 10 amps
- Spare fuses .... 30, 15, 10 and 3 amps

Grizzly 600
- Main fuse .... 30 amps
- Accessory fuse .... 10 amps
- Spare fuses .... 30 and 10 amps

Grizzly 660
- Main fuse .... 30 amps
- Headlight fuse .... 15 amps
- Ignition fuse .... 10 amps
- Auxiliary power jack fuse .... 10 amps
- 4WD fuse .... 3 amps
- Signaling system fuse .... 10 amps
- Odometer back-up fuse .... 10 amps
- Spare fuses .... 30, 15, 10 and 3 amps

Chapter 9 Electrical system

Torque specifications

Alternator cover bolts	10 Nm (84 in-lbs)
Alternator cover thrust washer screws (1999 Kodiak)	7 Nm (61 inch-lbs)
Alternator cover bearing retainer screws (2000 and later Kodiak)	7 Nm (61 inch-lbs)
Alternator rotor bolt	
All Kodiak, Grizzly 600	50 Nm (36 ft-lbs)
Grizzly 660	55 Nm (40 ft-lbs)
Charging coil/CDI magneto screws	
1993 through 1998 Kodiak	8 Nm (70 inch-lbs)*
1999 and later Kodiak, Grizzly 600	7 Nm (61 inch-lbs)*
Grizzly 660	10 Nm (84 inch-lbs)*
Starter motor mounting bolts	
1993 through 1999 Kodiak	10 Nm (84 inch-lbs)
2000 through 2002 Kodiak	8 Nm (70 inch-lbs)
2003 and later Kodiak	10 Nm (84 inch-lbs)
Grizzly 600	Not specified
Grizzly 660	8 Nm (70 inch-lbs)
Starter clutch Torx bolts	
Grizzly 600	Not specified
All others	30 Nm (22 ft-lbs)*

*Apply non-permanent thread locking agent to the threads.

1 General information

The machines covered by this manual are equipped with a 12-volt electrical system. The components include a three-phase permanent magnet alternator and a regulator/rectifier unit. The regulator/rectifier unit maintains the charging system output within the specified range to prevent overcharging and converts the AC (alternating current) output of the alternator to DC (direct current) to power the lights and other components and to charge the battery.

An electric starter mounted to the engine case behind the cylinder is standard equipment. A recoil (pull rope) starter is also used (see Chapter 2). The starting system includes the motor, the battery, the starter relay and starting circuit cut-off relay and the various wires and switches. If the engine kill switch and the main key switch are both in the On position, the cut-off relay allows the starter motor to operate only if the transmission is in Neutral. **Note:** *Keep in mind that electrical parts, once purchased, can't be returned. To avoid unnecessary expense, make very sure the faulty component has been positively identified before buying a replacement part.*

2 Electrical troubleshooting

A typical electrical circuit consists of an electrical component, the switches, relays, etc. related to that component and the wiring and connectors that hook the component to both the battery and the frame. To aid in locating a problem in any electrical circuit, wiring diagrams are included at the end of this Chapter.

Before tackling any troublesome electrical circuit, first study the appropriate diagrams thoroughly to get a complete picture of what makes up that individual circuit. Trouble spots, for instance, can often be narrowed down by noting if other components related to that circuit are operating properly or not. If several components or circuits fail at one time, chances are the fault lies in the fuse or ground/earth connection, as several circuits often are routed through the same fuse and ground/earth connections.

Electrical problems often stem from simple causes, such as loose or corroded connections or a blown fuse. Prior to any electrical troubleshooting, always visually check the condition of the fuse, wires and connections in the problem circuit.

If testing instruments are going to be utilized, use the diagrams to plan where you will make the necessary connections in order to accurately pinpoint the trouble spot.

The basic tools needed for electrical troubleshooting include a test light or voltmeter, a continuity tester (which includes a bulb, battery and set of test leads) and a jumper wire, preferably with a circuit breaker incorporated, which can be used to bypass electrical components. Specific checks described later in this Chapter may also require an ammeter or ohmmeter.

Voltage checks should be performed if a circuit is not functioning properly. Connect one lead of a test light or voltmeter to either the negative battery terminal or a known good ground/earth. Connect the other lead to a connector in the circuit being tested, preferably nearest to the battery or fuse. If the bulb lights, voltage is reaching that point, which means the part of the circuit between that connector and the battery is problem-free. Continue checking the remainder of the circuit in the same manner. When you reach a point where no voltage is present, the problem lies between there and the last good test point. Most of the time the problem is due to a loose connection. Since these vehicles are designed for off-road use, the problem may also be water or corrosion in a connector. Keep in mind that some circuits only receive voltage when the ignition key is in the On position.

One method of finding short circuits is to remove the fuse and connect a test light or voltmeter in its place to the fuse terminals. There should be no load in the circuit. Move the wiring harness from side-to-side while watching the test light. If the bulb lights, there is a short to ground/earth somewhere in that area, probably where insulation has rubbed off a wire. The same test can be performed on other components in the circuit, including the switch.

A ground/earth check should be done to see if a component is grounded/earthed properly. Disconnect the battery and connect one lead of a self-powered test light (such as a continuity tester) to a known good ground/earth. Connect the other lead to the wire or ground/earth connection being tested. If the bulb lights, the ground/earth is good. If the bulb does not light, the ground/earth is not good.

A continuity check is performed to see if a circuit, section of circuit or individual component is capable of passing electricity through it. Disconnect the battery and connect one lead of a self-powered test light (such as a continuity tester) to one end of the circuit being tested and the other lead to the other end of the circuit. If the bulb lights, there is continuity, which means the circuit is passing electricity through it properly. Switches can be checked in the same way.

Remember that all electrical circuits are designed to conduct electricity from the battery, through the wires, switches, relays, etc. to the electrical component (light bulb, motor, etc.). From there it is directed to the frame (ground/earth) where it is passed back to the battery. Electrical problems are basically an interruption in the flow of electricity from the battery or back to it.

Chapter 9 Electrical system

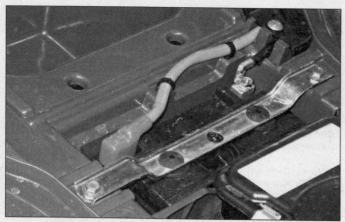

3.2 Typical battery cables - the positive cable should have a plastic cover to prevent accidental shorts

5.1a The fuse holder on early models is located inside this rubber cover . . .

3 Battery - inspection and maintenance

Refer to illustration 3.2

1 Most battery damage is caused by heat, vibration, and/or low electrolyte levels, so keep the battery securely mounted, check the electrolyte level frequently and make sure the charging system is functioning properly. The battery used on 1993 through 1998 Kodiak models is a fillable type. The electrolyte level should be checked periodically as described in Chapter 1. The battery used on all other models is a maintenance free (sealed) type and therefore doesn't require the addition of water. However, the following checks should still be regularly performed. **Warning:** *Always disconnect the negative cable first and connect it last to prevent sparks which could the battery to explode.*

2 Remove the battery. If you're working on a 1993 through 1998 Kodiak, see Chapter 1. On all other models, remove the seat. Disconnect the negative cable, then the positive cable **(see illustration)**. Lift the battery out of the holder.

3 Check around the base inside of the battery for sediment, which is the result of sulfation caused by low electrolyte levels. These deposits will cause internal short circuits, which can quickly discharge the battery. Look for cracks in the case and replace the battery if either of these conditions is found.

4 Check the battery terminals and cable ends for tightness and corrosion. If corrosion is evident, disconnect the cables from the battery, disconnecting the negative (-) terminal first, and clean the terminals and cable ends with a wire brush or knife and emery paper. Reconnect the cables, connecting the negative cable last, and apply a thin coat of petroleum jelly to the cables to slow further corrosion.

5 The battery case should be kept clean to prevent current leakage, which can discharge the battery over a period of time (especially when it sits unused). Wash the outside of the case with a solution of baking soda and water. Do not get any baking soda solution in the battery cells. Rinse the battery thoroughly, then dry it.

6 If acid has been spilled on the frame or battery box, neutralize it with a baking soda and water solution, then touch up any damaged paint. Make sure the battery vent tube (if equipped) is directed away from the frame and is not kinked or pinched.

7 If the vehicle sits unused for long periods of time, disconnect the cables from the battery terminals. Refer to Section 4 and charge the battery approximately once every month. Maintenance chargers, which are designed to keep a battery charged over long periods of storage, are available at motorcycle and ATV dealers.

4 Battery - charging

1 If the machine sits idle for extended periods or if the charging system malfunctions, the battery can be charged from an external source.

2 To properly charge the battery, you will need a charger of the correct rating, a hydrometer, a clean rag and a syringe for adding distilled water to the battery cells.

3 The maximum charging rate for any battery is 1/10th of the rated amp-hour capacity. As an example, the maximum charge rate for a 14 amp/hour battery would be 1.4 amps. If the battery is charged at a higher rate, it could overheat, causing the plates inside the battery to buckle.

4 Do not allow the battery to be subjected to a so-called quick charge (high charge rate over a short period of time) unless you are prepared to buy a new battery.

5 When charging the battery, always remove it from the machine and be sure to check the electrolyte level before hooking up the charger. Add distilled water to any cells that are low.

6 Loosen the cell caps, hook up the battery charger leads (positive lead to battery positive terminal, negative lead to battery negative terminal), cover the top of the battery with a clean rag, then, and only then, plug in the battery charger. **Warning:** *The hydrogen gas escaping from a charging battery is explosive, so keep open flames and sparks well away from the area. Also, the electrolyte is extremely corrosive and will damage anything it comes in contact with.*

7 Allow the battery to charge until the specific gravity is as specified (refer to Chapter 1 for the specific gravity checking procedure). The charger must be unplugged and disconnected from the battery when making specific gravity checks. If the battery overheats or gases excessively, the charging rate is too high. Either disconnect the charger or lower the charging rate to prevent damage to the battery.

8 If one or more of the cells do not show an increase in specific gravity after a long slow charge, or if the battery as a whole does not seem to want to take a charge, it's time for a new battery.

9 When the battery is fully charged, unplug the charger first, then disconnect the leads from the battery. Install the cell caps and wipe any electrolyte off the outside of the battery case.

10 If the recharged battery discharges rapidly when left disconnected, it's likely that an internal short caused by physical damage or sulfation has occurred. A new battery will be required. A sound battery will tend to lose its charge at about 1-percent per day.

5 Fuse and circuit breaker - check and replacement

Fuse(s)

1993 through 1999 Kodiak

Refer to illustrations 5.1a and 5.1b

1 These models use a single 30 amp fuse, located under the seat

Chapter 9 Electrical system

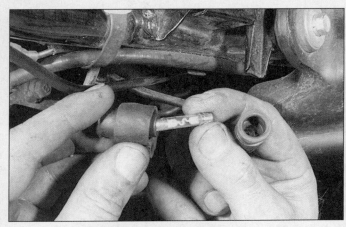

5.1b ... pull the cover apart for access to the fuse

5.3a On later Kodiak models, remove the cover and retaining band (arrows) for access to the electrical components

on the right side of the vehicle (see illustration). The fuse is mounted in a plastic holder, which is contained in a rubber cover. A spare fuse is mounted behind the fuse holder. The fuse can be removed and checked visually. Pull open the rubber cover and pull the fuse out (see illustration). A blown fuse is easily identified by a break in the element.

Grizzly 600

2   These models use a single 30-amp main fuse of the bayonet type, located in a fuse box under the left rear fender, as well as an auxiliary fuse to protect the auxiliary DC circuit. The fuse can be checked visually without removing it from its holder; just open the box and look through the plastic to see if the metal element inside is broken. If so, pull the fuse out and push a new one in.

All other models

Refer to illustrations 5.3a, 5.3b and 5.3c

3   The fuses are located in a fuse box or in individual holders under the seat near the battery (see illustrations). Fuse ratings and applications are listed in this Chapter's Specifications.

All models

4   If the fuse blows, be sure to check the wiring harnesses very carefully for evidence of a short circuit. Look for bare wires and chafed, melted or burned insulation. If a fuse is replaced before the cause is located, the new fuse will blow immediately.
5   Never, under any circumstances, use a higher rated fuse or bridge the fuse terminals, as damage to the electrical system - or even a fire - could result.
6   Occasionally a fuse will blow or cause an open circuit for no obvious reason. Corrosion of the fuse ends and fuse holder terminals may occur and cause poor fuse contact. If this happens, remove the corrosion with a wire brush or emery paper, then spray the fuse end and terminals with electrical contact cleaner.

Circuit breaker

7   Early models use a circuit breaker to protect the auxiliary DC accessory terminal.
8   To reset the circuit breaker, switch off the main key switch and any equipment connected to the accessory terminal. Wait 30 seconds, then push in the knob on the circuit breaker (it's located next to the fuse holder).
9   Turn on the main key switch and the equipment connected to the accessory terminal. If the circuit breaker trips again, check the wiring for breaks or poor connections, referring to the wiring diagrams at the end of the book. The circuit breaker will also trip if equipment connected to the accessory terminal draws too much current.

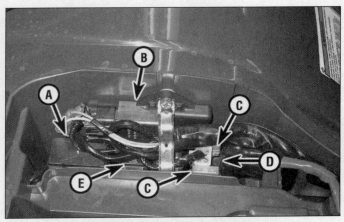

5.3b Electrical components (later Kodiak models)

A	Fuse box	D	Starter relay
B	CDI unit	E	4WD relays 1 and 2
C	Main fuse and spare		(hidden)
	main fuse		

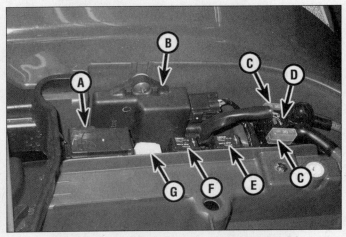

5.3c Electrical components (later Grizzly models)

A	Fuse box	D	Starter relay
B	CDI unit	E	4WD relay 1
C	Main fuse and spare	F	4WD relay 2
	main fuse	G	4WD relay 3

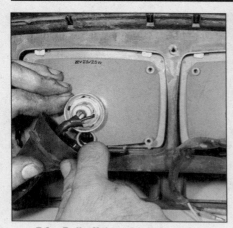
7.2a Pull off the rubber cover . . .

7.2b . . . turn the bulb socket counterclockwise and remove it from the case . . .

7.3 . . . then pull the bulb out of the socket without touching the glass

6 Lighting system - check

1 The battery provides power for operation of the headlights, tail light, brake light (if equipped) and instrument cluster lights. If none of the lights operate, always check battery voltage before proceeding. Low battery voltage indicates either a faulty battery, low battery electrolyte level or a defective charging system. Refer to Chapter 1 and Section 3 of this Chapter for battery checks and Sections 21 through 24 for charging system tests. Also, check the condition of the fuse and replace it with a new one if it's blown.

Headlights

2 If both of the headlight bulbs are out with the headlight switch in Lo or Hi and the main key switch On, check the fuse (see Section 5).
3 If only one headlight is out, try installing the bulb from the working headlight. If this solves the problem, replace the defective bulb. If not, test further as described below.
4 Disconnect the electrical connector from the bulb that doesn't light. Connect the negative lead of a voltmeter to the ground wire terminal in the wiring harness. Turn the main key switch On and connect the positive lead to the low beam terminal, then to the high beam terminal (see the wiring diagrams at the end of the manual to identify the terminals). The voltmeter should indicate 12 volts or more.
 a) If there's voltage at the terminals, the bulb is burned out or the bulb socket is corroded.
 b) If there's no voltage, the problem lies in the wiring or one of the switches in the circuit. Refer to Sections 13 and 14 for the switch testing procedures, and also the wiring diagrams at the end of this Chapter.

Taillight

5 If the taillight fails to work, check the bulb and the bulb terminals first.
6 If the bulb and terminals are good, disconnect the taillight electrical connector. Connect a voltmeter negative lead to the ground wire in the wiring harness and the positive lead to the power wire. With the main key switch and lighting switch On, the voltmeter should indicate 12 volts or more.
 a) If there's voltage at the terminals, the bulb is burned out or the bulb socket is corroded.
 b If there's no voltage, the problem lies in the wiring or one of the switches in the circuit. Refer to Sections 13 and 14 for the switch testing procedures, and also the wiring diagrams at the end of this Chapter.
7 If no voltage is indicated, check the ground wire and the wiring between the tail light and the lighting switch, then check the switch.

Brake light

8 If the machine is equipped with a brake light, see Section 10 for the brake light circuit checking procedure.

Gear position indicator light(s)

9 If a gear position indicator light fails to operate when the transmission is in the appropriate gear, check the fuse and the bulb (see Section 11 for bulb removal procedures). If the bulb and fuse are in good condition, check for battery voltage at the wire attached to the neutral switch on the left side of the engine. If battery voltage is present, refer to Section 16 for the switch check and replacement procedures.
10 If no voltage is indicated, check the wiring to the bulb, to the switch and between the switch and the bulb for open circuits and poor connections.

7 Headlight bulb - replacement

Warning: *If the headlight has just burned out, give the bulb time to cool before changing the bulb to avoid burning your fingers.*

1993 through 1999 Kodiak

Refer to illustrations 7.2a, 7.2b and 7.3
1 Remove the headlight cover screws (one at the top center and one at each bottom outer corner) and take off the cover.
2 Pull the rubber cover off the bulb. Twist the bulb socket counterclockwise and remove it from the headlight case **(see illustrations)**.
3 Pull the bulb out without touching the glass **(see illustration)**.

2000 and later Kodiak

Refer to illustrations 7.5a, 7.5b and 7.6
4 Working under the fender, remove the cover from the back of the headlight assembly.
5 Twist the socket and remove it from the headlight assembly, together with the bulb **(see illustrations)**.
6 Lift the bulb retaining tab with a small screwdriver or similar tool **(see illustration)**. Pull the bulb out of the socket without touching the glass.

Grizzly 600

7 Working beneath the fender, disconnect the headlight electrical connector. Remove the headlight assembly screws and take the assembly out of the fender.
8 Remove the screw that secures the headlight cover and take it off the assembly.
9 Remove the bulb as described in Steps 2 and 3 above.

Chapter 9 Electrical system

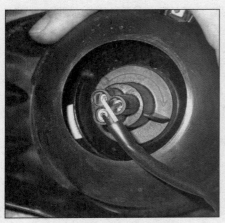

7.5a Twist the socket to disengage the tabs . . .

7.5b . . . and remove it from the housing . . .

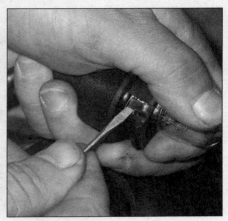

7.6 . . . lift up the tab to free the bulb

7.10 Pull the cover out of the back of the housing . . .

7.11 . . . remove the rubber cover and socket . . .

7.12 . . . and remove the bulb without touching the glass

Grizzly 660

Refer to illustrations 7.10, 7.11 and 7.12

10 Working beneath the fender, pull the cover off the back of the headlight housing **(see illustration)**.
11 Remove the rubber cover from the back of the headlight **(see illustration)**. Twist the bulb socket counterclockwise and remove it from the headlight case.
12 Pull the bulb out without touching the glass **(see illustration)**.

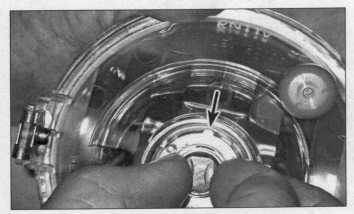

7.13 Align the tab on the bulb with the notch in the socket

All models

Refer to illustration 7.13

13 Installation is the reverse of the removal procedure, with the following additions:

a) *Be sure not to touch the bulb with your fingers - oil from your skin will cause the bulb to overheat and fail prematurely. If you do touch the bulb, wipe it off with a clean rag dampened with rubbing alcohol.*
b) *Align the tab on the metal bulb flange or the tabs on the plastic bulb socket with the slot(s) in the headlight case* **(see illustration 7.6 or the accompanying illustration)**.
c) *Make sure the arrow mark on the headlight cover (if equipped) is facing up.*

8 Headlight aim - check and adjustment

Refer to illustrations 8.3a, 8.3b and 8.3c

1 An improperly adjusted headlight may cause problems for oncoming traffic or provide poor, unsafe illumination of the terrain ahead. Before adjusting the headlight, be sure to consult with local traffic laws and regulations. Yamaha doesn't provide specifications for headlight adjustment.
2 The headlight beam can be adjusted vertically. Before performing the adjustment, make sure the fuel tank is at least half full, and have an assistant sit on the seat.

Chapter 9 Electrical system

8.3a On early models, the headlight adjusting screw is mounted below each headlight (arrow)

8.3b Here's a typical adjusting screw location on later models (arrow)

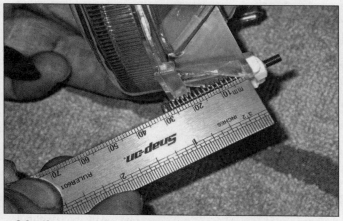

8.3c If you're going to disassemble the adjuster, measure the length of the spring first

9.1a On early models, remove the lens screws and take off the lens . . .

3   Insert a Phillips screwdriver into the vertical adjuster screw (**see illustrations**), then turn the adjuster as necessary to raise or lower the beam. **Note:** *If you're planning to disassemble the headlight housing, measure the length of the adjuster spring beforehand* (**see illustration**). *Returning it to the same length on assembly will give you a starting point for adjustment.*

9   Tail light and brake light bulbs - replacement

Tail light

Refer to illustrations 9.1a, 9.1b, 9.2a and 9.2b

1   If the taillight lens has external screws, remove them and take off the lens (**see illustration**). If it doesn't, twist the bulb socket and remove it from the taillight housing (**see illustration**).

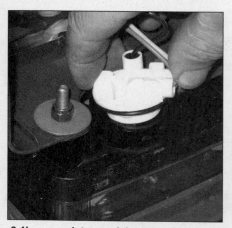

9.1b . . . on later models, twist the socket to align the tabs, then remove the socket and O-ring

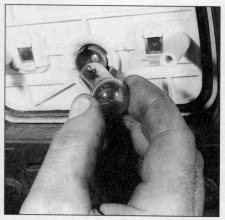

9.2a . . . press the bulb into the socket, turn it counterclockwise and pull it out; this is an early model . . .

9.2b . . . and this is a later model

Chapter 9 Electrical system

10.8 Left handlebar switch details
A Brake switch retaining prong
B Switch housing screws

10.10 Turn the nut (arrow) to adjust the rear brake light switch

2 Press the bulb into its socket and turn it counterclockwise to remove **(see illustrations)**.
3 Check the socket terminals for corrosion and clean them if necessary.
4 Press the bulb into its socket, turn counterclockwise to engage the pins, then release the bulb.
5 Install the lens and tighten the screws securely, but not enough to crack the plastic.

10 Brake switches - check and replacement

1 All models use an electrical switch at the left brake lever. The switch is part of the starting circuit. The starting system is designed so the starter won't operate unless the machine is in neutral and the drive select lever is in forward, or the left brake lever is pulled in. The purpose of the switch is to indicate to the starting system that the lever is pulled in.
2 Some models are equipped with a brake light. On these models, the light is operated by switches at the brake lever and right handlebar.
3 Before checking any electrical circuit, check the fuses (see Section 5).
4 Using a test light connected to a good ground/earth, check for voltage to the wire at the brake light switch. If there's no voltage present, check the wire between the switch and the ignition switch (see the wiring diagrams at the end of the book).
5 If voltage is available, touch the probe of the test light to the other terminal of the switch, then pull the brake lever or depress the brake pedal - if the test light doesn't light up, replace the switch.
6 If the test light does light, check the wiring between the switch and the brake lights (see the wiring diagrams at the end of the book).

Switch replacement

Brake lever switch
Refer to illustration 10.8
7 Unplug the electrical connector from the switch.
8 Press in on the prong that secures the switch to the lever **(see illustration)**. Slip the switch out and push a new one in until the prong engages with its hole.

Brake pedal switch

Adjustment
Refer to illustration 10.10
9 Remove the cover from the switch (it's mounted behind the right front fender and is secured by a single screw or bolt).

10 Hold the switch body so it won't turn, and rotate the nut (not the switch body) to change the switch adjustment **(see illustration)**. The brake light should come on just before the rear brake takes effect.

Replacement
11 Unplug the electrical connector in the switch harness.
12 Disconnect the spring from the brake pedal switch **(see illustration 10.10)**.
13 Hold the adjuster nut from turning and rotate the switch body all the way up until it clears the nut threads, then lift it out.
14 Install the switch by reversing the removal procedure.

11 Indicator bulbs and odometer/speedometer - replacement

Refer to illustrations 11.1, 11.2a and 11.2b

Indicator bulbs

Note: *This section applies to light bulbs used in the instrument cluster on early models. Light-emitting diodes (LEDs) used on later models can't be replaced separately. If an LED is defective, the instrument cluster must be replaced as an assembly.*

1 Pull the plastic bulb cluster clips free of the handlebar and turn it over to expose the bulb sockets **(see illustration)**.

11.1 Free the bulb housing from the handlebar and turn it over . . .

Chapter 9 Electrical system

11.2a . . . pull the bulb socket out of the rubber housing . . .

11.2b . . . press the bulb into the socket and turn counterclockwise (anti-clockwise) to remove

11.5 Pull out the clips and remove the mounting dampers to free the odometer/speedometer (odometer shown)

　　A　Cable nut　　　　B　Clips

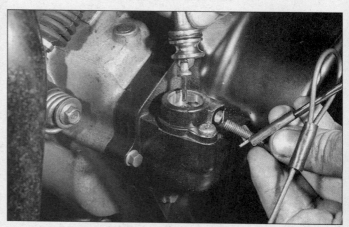

11.6 Remove the screw completely and pull the cable out of the clutch cover

2   To replace a bulb, pull the appropriate rubber socket out of the handlebar cover **(see illustration)**. Press the bulb into its socket, turn it counterclockwise and pull the bulb out of the socket **(see illustration)**.
3   If the socket contacts are dirty or corroded, they should be scraped clean and sprayed with electrical contact cleaner before new bulbs are installed.
4   Push the new bulb into its socket, turn it clockwise and release it. Install the bulb cluster on the handlebar.

Odometer/speedometer (early models)
Cable
Refer to illustrations 11.5 and 11.6
5   Unscrew the nut and pull the upper end of the cable out of the odometer or speedometer **(see illustration)**.
6   Remove the retaining screw completely (don't just loosen it) from the clutch cover at the lower end of the cable and pull the cable out **(see illustration)**.
7   Detach the cable from any retainers or clips and remove it from the machine.
8   Installation is the reverse of the removal steps. Be sure to reinstall the retainer for the reverse lockout release cable when you install the retaining screw.

Gauge
9   Disconnect the cable from the gauge as described above.
10 Pull out the retaining clips and remove the dampers, then lift the

11.13a Remove the screw (arrow) and retainer

gauge off the bracket **(see illustration 11.5)**.
11 Installation is the reverse of the removal steps.

Gears
Refer to illustrations 11.13a and 11.13b
12 Remove the clutch cover from the right side of the engine (see Chapter 2).
13 Remove the screw and retainer from the clutch cover, then remove the gears **(see illustrations)**.
14 Installation is the reverse of the removal steps.

Chapter 9 Electrical system

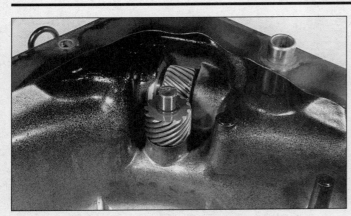

11.13b The gears are accessible from inside the clutch cover

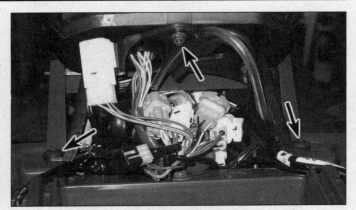

11.16a On later Kodiak models, disconnect the connectors, remove the hose retainer (upper arrow) and the mounting screws (lower arrows) to detach the cluster

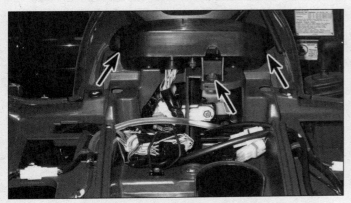

11.16b On later Grizzly models, disconnect the connectors, remove the nut (lower arrow) and the mounting screws (upper arrows, hidden) to detach the cluster

Instrument cluster (later models)

Refer to illustrations 11.16a and 11.16b

15 Remove the trim cover from the handlebars (if equipped). Remove the side cover, fuel tank cover and front trim cover (see Chapter 8).
16 Disconnect the electrical connectors **(see illustrations)**. Remove the cluster fasteners and take the cluster off the vehicle.
17 Installation is the reverse of the removal Steps.

12 Temperature warning system - check and switch replacement

Check

1993 through 1999 Kodiak

1 These models are equipped with an oil temperature warning system that turns on an indicator light on the handlebars when the oil overheats. The system consists of an oil temperature switch mounted on the left side of the engine, a thermistor and a warning indicator light in the handlebar cover. The indicator light should come on for a few seconds when the engine is first started, then turn off. **Caution:** *If the light comes on while the engine is running, shut it off immediately and let it cool for at least 10 minutes. Continued operation with overheated oil can cause serious engine damage.*
2 If the oil temperature warning light doesn't come on at all, check the bulb and replace it if it's burned out.
3 If the light doesn't come on (with a good bulb) or doesn't turn off, locate the thermistor. It's mounted beneath the rear end of the seat and can be identified by its two wires, one brown and one black.
4 Disconnect the thermistor electrical connector and connect the thermistor in series with the vehicle's battery and the oil temperature indicator bulb, using lengths of wire. The bulb should light, then go out. The time required varies according to temperature; it may be a minute or more.
5 If the bulb lights and goes out as described, the thermistor is good. Check the wiring in the oil warning circuit for breaks or poor connections.
6 If the wiring is good and the system still doesn't perform properly, the oil temperature switch is probably defective. Since the switch can't be returned once it's purchased, it's a good idea to have the system tested by a Yamaha dealer or substitute a known good switch before buying a new one.

Grizzly 600 models

7 If the oil temperature warning light doesn't come on at all, check the bulb and replace it if it's burned out.
8 If the light doesn't come on (with a good bulb), locate the temperature switch. It's mounted beneath the rear end of the seat and can be identified by its two wires, one white/green and one black.
9 **Warning:** *This procedure requires heating oil to a very high temperature. Take care not to touch it. Be sure the pan is securely supported so it can't spill. Have a working fire extinguisher nearby.* Place the switch in a pan of engine oil, supporting it with wire so it doesn't touch the sides or bottom of the pan. Connect an ohmmeter to the switch terminals. Heat the oil to 300-degrees F (150-degrees C). The ohmmeter should indicate 307 to 339 ohms, gradually dropping to 209 to 231 ohms when the temperature reaches 425-degrees F (220-degrees C).
10 If the switch doesn't perform as described, replace it as described below.

Liquid-cooled models

Refer to illustrations 12.11a and 12.11b

11 Locate the switch on the engine **(see illustrations)**.

12.11a Here's the coolant temperature switch on liquid-cooled Kodiak models (arrow)

12.11b The coolant temperature switch on liquid-cooled Grizzly models

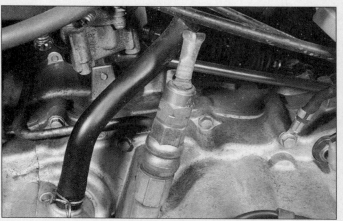

12.14 The early Kodiak oil temperature switch is located on the left side of the engine

12 Unscrew the switch. Place the switch in a pan of antifreeze and water (50/50 mixture), supporting it with wire so it doesn't touch the sides or bottom of the pan. Connect an ohmmeter to the switch terminals. Heat the coolant to 300-degrees F (150-degrees C). The ohmmeter should indicate 307 to 339 ohms, gradually dropping to 209 to 231 ohms when the temperature reaches 425-degrees F (220-degrees C).
13 If the switch doesn't perform as described, replace it as described below.

Switch replacement

Refer to illustration 12.14

14 Locate the switch **(see illustration 12.11a, 12.11b or the accompanying illustration)**. Disconnect its electrical connector, unscrew the switch and remove the sealing washer (if equipped).
15 If the switch doesn't have a sealing washer, coat the threads of the new switch with Three Bond Sealock no.10 or equivalent. If it does have a sealing washer, use a new one. Install the switch, tighten it securely and connect the electrical connector.

13 Ignition main (key) switch - check and replacement

Check

1 Follow the wiring harness from the ignition switch to the connector and unplug the connector.
2 Using an ohmmeter, check the continuity of the terminal pairs indicated in the wiring diagrams at the end of this book. Continuity should

13.4 Remove the plastic nut (arrow) to detach the ignition main (key) switch from the fender

exist between the terminals connected by a solid line when the switch is in the indicated position.
3 If the switch fails any of the tests, replace it.

Replacement

Refer to illustration 13.4

4 The ignition switch is secured to the front fender by a plastic nut **(see illustration)**.
5 If you haven't already done so, unplug the switch electrical connector. Unscrew the nut and lower the switch out of the fender.
6 Installation is the reverse of the removal procedure.

14 Handlebar switches - check

1 Generally speaking, the switches are reliable and trouble-free. Most troubles, when they do occur, are caused by dirty or corroded contacts, but wear and breakage of internal parts is a possibility that should not be overlooked. If breakage does occur, the entire switch and related wiring harness will have to be replaced with a new one, since individual parts are not usually available.
2 The switches can be checked for continuity with an ohmmeter or a continuity test light. Always disconnect the battery negative cable, which will prevent the possibility of a short circuit, before making the checks.
3 Trace the wiring harness of the switch in question and unplug the electrical connectors.
4 Using the ohmmeter or test light, check for continuity between the terminals of the switch harness with the switch in the various positions. Refer to the continuity diagrams contained in the wiring diagrams at the end of the book. Continuity should exist between the terminals connected by a solid line when the switch is in the indicated position.
5 If the continuity check indicates a problem exists, refer to Section 15, disassemble the switch and spray the switch contacts with electrical contact cleaner. If they are accessible, the contacts can be scraped clean with a knife or polished with crocus cloth. If switch components are damaged or broken, it will be obvious when the switch is disassembled.

15 Handlebar switches - removal and installation

Refer to illustration 15.1

1 The handlebar switches are composed of two halves that clamp around the bars. They are easily removed for cleaning or inspection by taking out the clamp screws and pulling the switch halves away from the handlebars **(see illustration 10.8 and the accompanying illustration)**.

Chapter 9 Electrical system

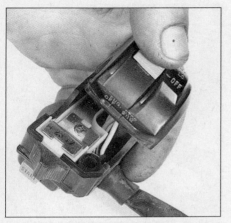

15.1 The handlebar switches are mounted in the left handlebar housing

16.1a The neutral switch is located on the left side of the engine near the shift pedal shaft

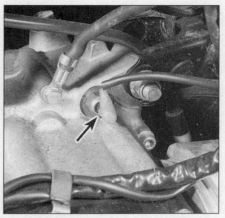

16.1b The reverse switch (arrow) is located on the left side of the engine above the middle gear case

16.1c Here are the Grizzly 660 neutral switch (lower arrow) and reverse switch (upper arrow)

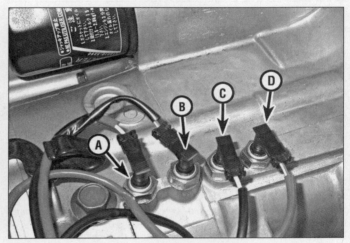

16.8 Late Kodiak models have up to four gear position switches; their functions can be identified by their wire colors

- A Low range switch
- B High range switch
- C Neutral switch
- D Reverse switch

2 To completely remove the switches, the electrical connectors in the wiring harness must be unplugged and the harness separated from the tie wraps and retainers.

3 When installing the switches, make sure the wiring harness is properly routed to avoid pinching or stretching the wires.

16 Gear position switches - check and replacement

1993 through 1998 Kodiak, all Grizzly

Refer to illustrations 16.1a, 16.1b and 16.1c

1 Disconnect the electrical connector from the switch being tested **(see illustrations)**.

2 Connect one lead of an ohmmeter to a good ground and the other lead to the terminal post on the switch being tested.

3 When the transmission is in neutral, the ohmmeter should read 0 ohms between the neutral switch and ground - in any other gear, the meter should read infinite resistance.

4 When the shift select lever is in reverse, the ohmmeter should read infinite resistance between the reverse switch and ground - in High or Low forward, the meter should read 0 ohms.

5 If the switch doesn't check out as described, replace it.

6 Wrap the threads of the switch with Teflon tape or apply a thin coat of RTV sealant to them. Install the switch in the case with a new sealing washer and tighten it to the torque listed in this Chapter's Specifications.

7 Reconnect the switch wires.

2000 and later Kodiak

Refer to illustration 16.8

8 These models use up to four gear position switches to indicate Neutral, Reverse, High range and Low range (if equipped). They're mounted on the right side of the crankcase, forward of the oil filter **(see illustration)**.

9 Follow the harness from the switch to its connector. Disconnect the connector.

10 Connect one lead of an ohmmeter to a good ground and the other lead to the connector terminal of the switch being tested (the switch side of the connector, not the wiring harness side).

11 Place the transmission in gear (neutral, reverse, high range or low range, depending on the switch being tested). When the shifter is in the specified gear, the ohmmeter should show continuity (little or no resistance) between the wire's terminal and ground. In any other gear position, the ohmmeter should show no continuity (infinite resistance).

12 If the switch doesn't perform as described, unscrew it and install a new one, using a new sealing washer.

Chapter 9 Electrical system

17.5 The starter relay on early models is located forward of the battery

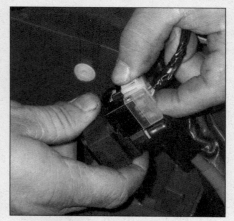

17.6 On later models, it's in the rear fender; lift it out for easier access to the wires

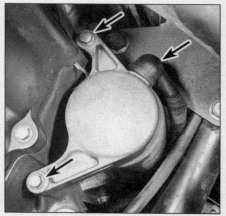

18.2a Starter motor mounting details (early Kodiak models)

17 Starter circuit - check and component replacement

1 Depending on the procedure, it may be necessary to remove the seat, rear cargo rack or rear fender for access to other parts (see Chapter 8).
2 Make sure the vehicle's battery is fully charged. Charge it from an external source if necessary (see Section 4).
3 Check the main fuse (see Section 5).
4 Check all wiring in the starter for breaks or poor connections, referring to the wiring diagrams at the end of this book. This includes the battery cables. Check the terminals for corrosion.

Starter relay

Check

Refer to illustrations 17.5 and 17.6

Warning: *Make sure the transmission is in Neutral before performing this test.*

5 Locate the starter relay at the left rear of the vehicle near the battery **(see illustrations 5.3b, 5.3c or the accompanying illustration)**.
6 Disconnect the electrical connector for the two thin wires connected to the relay **(see illustration)**. Refer to the wiring diagrams at the end of this book to identify the positive and negative wires.
7 Connect a length of wire from the positive wire's terminal in the connector to the battery positive terminal (the side of the connector that runs to the relay, not the harness side). Connect another length of wire from the battery negative terminal to the negative wire's terminal in the connector. The starter should crank the engine. If it doesn't, the problem may be in the starter itself (refer to Sections 18 and 19 for removal and inspection procedures), in the electrical cables between the battery and starter relay, or in the starter relay. If the starter is good and the cables are in good condition and properly connected, the relay is probably at fault.

Replacement

8 Disconnect the negative cable from the battery.
9 Pull back the rubber covers from the terminal nuts, remove the nuts and disconnect the starter relay cables. Disconnect the remaining electrical connector from the starter relay.
10 Pull the relay's rubber mount off the metal bracket and pull the relay out of the mount.
11 Installation is the reverse of removal. Reconnect the negative battery cable after all the other electrical connections are made.

Starter switch

12 The starter switch is part of the switch assembly on the left handlebar. Refer to Section 14 for checking and replacement procedures.

18.2b Starter motor mounting details (typical later model)

18 Starter motor - removal and installation

Removal

Refer to illustrations 18.2a and 18.2b

1 Disconnect the cable from the negative terminal of the battery.
2 Pull back the rubber boot and remove the nut retaining the starter cable to the starter **(see illustrations)**. Remove the starter mounting bolts.
3 Lift the outer end of the starter up a little bit and slide the starter out of the engine case. **Caution:** *Don't drop or strike the starter - its magnets may be demagnetized, which will ruin it.*
4 Check the condition of the O-ring on the end of the starter that fits into the engine and replace it if necessary

Installation

5 Remove any corrosion or dirt from the mounting lugs on the starter and the mounting points on the crankcase.
6 Apply a little engine oil to the O-ring and install the starter by reversing the removal procedure.

19 Starter motor - disassembly, inspection and reassembly

1 Remove the starter motor (see Section 18).

Chapter 9 Electrical system

19.2 Position of the through-bolts is indicated by alignment marks (arrow)

19.3 Remove the through-bolts and pull the cover off

19.4 Pull the bracket and brush plate off the housing; the housing tab, brush plate slot and bracket slot (arrows) must be aligned on assembly

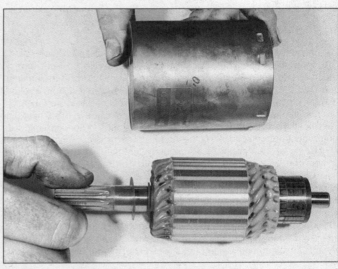

19.5 Pull the armature out of the housing and note the location of the shims on each end

Disassembly

Refer to illustrations 19.2, 19.3, 19.4 and 19.5

2   One of the through-bolts should be centered between alignment marks **(see illustration)**. Make your own marks if they aren't visible.
3   Unscrew the two through-bolts, then remove the cover with its O-ring from the motor **(see illustration)**.
4   Remove the bracket with its O-ring and the brush set from the motor **(see illustration)**.
5   Slide off the insulating washer and shim(s) from the armature, noting their locations, and withdraw the armature from the housing **(see illustration)**.

Inspection

Refer to illustrations 19.6, 19.8, 19.9a, 19.9b and 19.15

Note: *Check carefully which components are available as replacements before starting overhaul procedures.*

6   Lift the brush springs and slide the brushes out of their holders **(see illustration)**.
7   The parts of the starter motor that most likely will require attention are the brushes. If one brush must be replaced, replace both of them. The brushes are replaced together with the terminal bolt and the brush plate. Brushes must be replaced if they are worn excessively, cracked, chipped, or otherwise damaged. Measure the length of the brushes and compare the results to the brush length listed in this Chapter's Specifications. If either of the brushes is worn beyond the specified limits, replace them both.

19.6 Detach the positive brush from the brush plate and lift the plate out

Chapter 9 Electrical system

19.8 Check the commutator for cracks and discoloring, then measure the diameter and compare it with the minimum diameter listed in this Chapter's Specifications

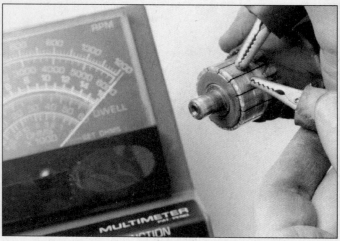

19.9a Continuity should exist between the commutator bars

8   Inspect the commutator for scoring, scratches and discoloration. The commutator can be cleaned and polished with 600-grit emery paper, but do not remove copper from the commutator. After cleaning, clean out the grooves and wipe away any residue with a cloth soaked in an electrical system cleaner or denatured alcohol. Measure the commutator diameter and compare it to the diameter listed in this Chapter's Specifications **(see illustration)**. If it's less than the service limit, the motor must be replaced with a new one.

9   Using an ohmmeter or a continuity test light, check for continuity between the commutator bars **(see illustration)**. Continuity should exist between each bar and all of the others. Also, check for continuity between the commutator bars and the armature shaft **(see illustration)**. There should be no continuity between the commutator and the shaft. If the checks indicate otherwise, the armature is defective.

10 Check the undercut of the mica between the commutator bars. If it isn't deep enough, carefully scrape away mica with a broken-off piece of hacksaw blade until the undercut is as listed in this Chapter's Specifications.

11 Check the seal in the cover for wear or damage. Check the bearing on the armature for roughness, looseness or loss of lubricant. Check with a motorcycle shop or Yamaha dealer to see if the seal and bearing can be replaced separately; if this isn't possible, replace the starter motor.

12 Inspect the bushing in the bracket. Replace the starter motor if the bushing is worn or damaged.

13 Check the starter pinion for worn, chipped or broken teeth. If the gear is damaged or worn, replace the starter motor.

14 Inspect the insulating washers and shims for signs of damage and replace if necessary.

15 Check the magnets inside the starter housing for damage or loss of magnetism **(see illustration)**. Replace the starter motor if the magnets are damaged.

Reassembly

Refer to illustration 19.18

16 Lift the brush springs and slide the brushes back into position in their holders.

17 Make sure the shim(s) are in place on the bracket end of the armature.

18 Install the brush plate in the bracket, making sure its notch is correctly aligned with the housing notch **(see illustration)**. Insert the terminal bolt through the bracket, then install the O-ring, insulator and nut on the terminal bolt.

19 Insert the armature in the housing, locating the brushes to the commutator bars **(see illustration 19.18)**. Check that each brush is securely pressed against the commutator by its spring and is free to move easily in its holder.

20 Install the large O-ring and housing on the bracket; make sure the tab on the housing aligns with the notches in the brush plate and bracket **(see illustration 19.4)**.

19.9b There should be no continuity between each commutator bar and the armature shaft

19.15 Replace the starter if the magnets inside the housing are damaged or weak

Chapter 9 Electrical system

19.18 Align the brush plate and bracket notches (arrow)

20.2a Pull off the starter wheel gear (arrow) . . .

20.2b . . . then remove the needle roller bearing and washer

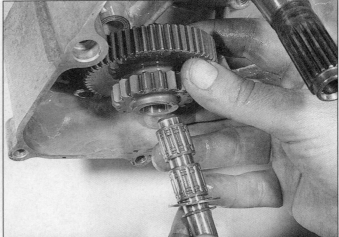

20.3 The idle gear shaft should pull out of the crankcase easily; if not, remove the snap-ring and washer, then slide the gear and two needle roller bearings off the shaft

21 Apply a smear of grease to the cover seal lip.
22 Slide the shim(s) onto the front end of the armature shaft. Fit the large O-ring to the housing and carefully slide the front cover into position, aligning the marks on each side of the through-bolt hole (see illustration 19.2).
23 Fit the through-bolts and tighten them securely.

20 Starter clutch and reduction gears - removal, inspection and installation

Removal

1 Refer to Section 23 and remove the alternator cover(s) and rotor.

1993 through 1999 Kodiak

Refer to illustrations 20.2a, 20.2b and 20.3

2 Pull the starter wheel gear off the end of the crankshaft, then remove the needle roller bearing and washer (see illustrations).
3 Support the starter idle gear and pull its shaft out of the crankcase, together with the snap-ring, washer and needle roller bearings (see illustration).

All other models

Refer to illustrations 20.4a, 20.4b, 20.4c, 20.5a and 20.5b

4 Pull the starter wheel gear off the end of the crankshaft, then remove the washer (see illustrations).

20.4a Starter reduction gear details (2000 and later Kodiak)

A Wheel gear   B Idle gear   C Starter pinion

9-18   Chapter 9   Electrical system

20.4b   Pull off the wheel gear and remove the washer

20.4c   Starter reduction gear details (Grizzly 660)

    A   Wheel gear   B   Idle gear   C   Starter pinion

5   On all except Grizzly 600 models, support the starter idle gear and pull its shaft out of the crankcase, together with the snap-ring (if equipped), washer and needle roller bearing(s) **(see illustrations)**. On Grizzly 600 models, remove the starter driven gear unit and its thrust washer.

Inspection

Refer to illustration 20.8

6   Check the gears for worn or broken teeth. Check the shafts and the friction surface on the gears for wear or damage and replace any parts that show defects.

7   Since needle roller bearing wear is difficult to see, the bearings should be replaced if there's any doubt about their condition.

8   Check the starter clutch in the back of the alternator rotor for visible wear and damage and replace it as described below if problems are found **(see illustration)**.

9   Place the alternator rotor in the starter clutch. Hold the alternator rotor with one hand so its open side is toward you and the starter wheel gear is away from you. Try to rotate the starter wheel gear with the other hand. The gear should rotate counterclockwise (anti-clockwise) smoothly, but not rotate clockwise at all.

10   If the gear rotates both ways or neither way, or if its movement is rough, remove the Torx bolts and separate the starter clutch from the

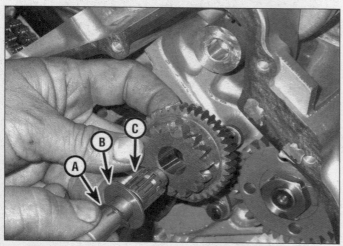

20.5a   On later Kodiak models, remove the shaft, snap-ring, washer, needle roller bearing and idle gear

    A   Snap-ring   C   Needle roller bearing
    B   Washer

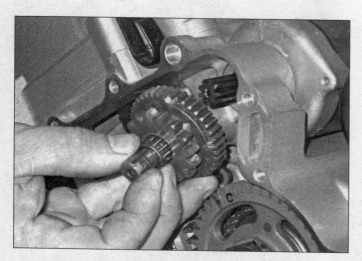

20.5b   On Grizzly 660 models, remove the shaft, needle roller bearing and idle gear

20.8   Check the starter clutch for visible wear and damage

Chapter 9 Electrical system

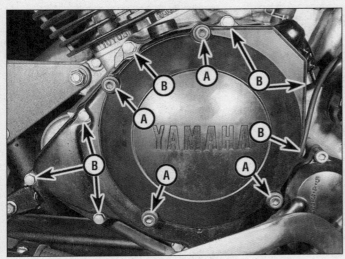

23.6a Alternator cover details (early Kodiak models)

A Allen bolts   B Hex bolts

23.6b On Grizzly 660 models, remove the recoil starter and outer cover (shown with oil filler cap access cover removed)

alternator rotor.

11 Install the starter clutch in the alternator rotor with its arrow mark facing away from the rotor. Before you tighten the Torx bolts, place the starter wheel gear on the rotor and try to turn it both ways. It should turn counterclockwise but not clockwise, as described in Step 9. If the gear turns the wrong way, the starter clutch is installed backwards.

12 Apply non-permanent thread locking agent to the threads of the Torx bolts and tighten them to the torque listed in this Chapter's Specifications.

Installation

13 Installation is the reverse of the removal steps, with the following addition: Lubricate the gears, bearings and shafts with clean engine oil.

21 Charging system testing - general information and precautions

1 If the performance of the charging system is suspect, the system as a whole should be checked first, followed by testing of the individual components (the alternator and the regulator/rectifier). **Note:** *Before beginning the checks, make sure the battery is fully charged and that all system connections are clean and tight.*

2 Checking the output of the charging system and the performance of the various components within the charging system requires the use of an ohmmeter; voltmeter or ammeter (depending on model); or the equivalent multimeter.

3 When making the checks, follow the procedures carefully to prevent incorrect connections or short circuits, as irreparable damage to electrical system components may result if short circuits occur.

4 If the necessary test equipment is not available, it is recommended that charging system tests be left to a dealer service department or a reputable ATV repair shop.

22 Charging system - output test

1 If a charging system problem is suspected, perform the following checks. Start by checking the fuse (see Section 5) and battery (see Section 3 and Chapter 1). If necessary, charge the battery (see Section 4).

2 Find the charging system output (voltage at engine speed) for your vehicle listed in this Chapter's Specifications.

3 Start the engine and let it warm up to normal operating temperature.

4 With the engine idling, attach the positive lead of a 0 to 20 volt voltmeter to the positive (+) battery terminal and the negative lead to the battery negative (-) terminal.

5 Slowly increase the engine speed to the rpm value listed in this Chapter's Specifications and note the voltmeter reading.

6 If the output is as specified, the alternator is functioning properly.

7 Low voltage may be the result of damaged windings in the alternator stator coils or wiring problems. The alternator rotor magnets may also be weak. Make sure all electrical connections are clean and tight, then refer to the following Sections to check the alternator stator coils and the regulator/rectifier.

8 Output above the specified range indicates a defective voltage regulator/rectifier. Refer to Section 24 for regulator testing and replacement procedures.

9 Disconnect the test equipment.

23 Alternator charging coils and rotor - check and replacement

Charging coil check

1 Locate and disconnect the coil connector on the left side of the vehicle frame. The connector can be identified by its three white wires.

2 Connect an ohmmeter between each of the terminals in the side of the connector that runs back to the engine (connect the positive lead to one of the terminal and the negative lead to each of the two remaining terminals in turn). If the readings are outside the range listed in this Chapter's Specifications, replace the charging coils as described below.

3 Connect the ohmmeter between a good ground on the vehicle and each of the connector terminals in turn. The meter should indicate infinite resistance (no continuity). If not, replace the charging coils.

Charging coil and CDI magneto replacement

Refer to illustrations 23.6a, 23.6b, 23.7a, 23.7b, 23.8a, 23.8b, 23.8c, 23.8d, 23.9a, 23.9b and 23.9c

4 Drain the engine oil (see Chapter 1).

5 If the vehicle has a recoil starter, remove it (see Chapter 2).

6 If you're working on a 1993 through 1999 Kodiak or a Grizzly 660, remove the outer cover from the left crankcase cover **(see illustrations)**.

7 If the vehicle does not have a recoil starter, remove the bolt that

9-20   Chapter 9 Electrical system

23.7a On models without a recoil starter, remove the outer bolt . . .

23.7b . . . then pull out the rotor that fits in the seal

23.8a On early Kodiak models, the upper rear bolt secures a wiring harness retainer and the lower rear bolt has a copper washer (arrows)

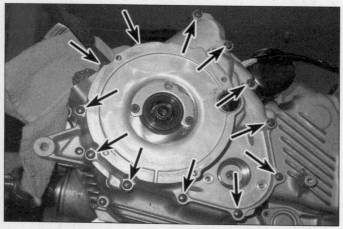

23.8b Alternator cover bolts (2000 and later Kodiak)

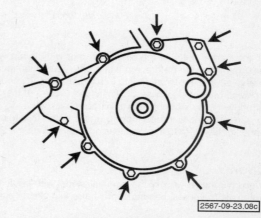

23.8c Alternator cover bolts (Grizzly 600 models)

secures the rotor to the alternator rotor. Hold the rotor so it won't turn with a large open end or adjustable wrench (see illustration). Pull the rotor out of the cover (see illustration).

8 Remove the cover bolts (see illustration 23.6a and the accompanying illustrations). Pull the cover off the engine. You may need to pull firmly to overcome the resistance of the rotor magnets, but don't use excessive force. If the cover seems to be stuck, check to make sure all fasteners have been removed.

9 Remove the charging coil screws and the CDI magneto screws (see illustrations), then remove the charging coils and CDI magneto

23.8d Alternator cover bolts (Grizzly 660 models)

23.9a The charging coils and CDI magneto (early Kodiak shown; Grizzly 600 similar) (arrows)

Chapter 9 Electrical system

23.9b The charging coils and CDI magneto (later Kodiak) (arrows)

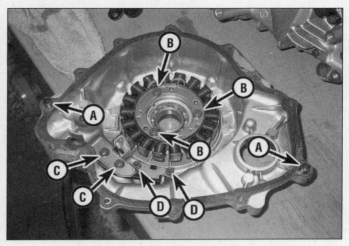

23.9c The charging coils and CDI magneto (Grizzly 660) (arrows)
- a Dowels
- b Charging coil screws
- c Harness cover screws
- d CDI magneto screws

together (they're replaced as a unit).

10 Check the seal in the cover for wear or damage. Spin the bearing inner race with a finger and check for roughness, looseness or noise. If the bearing or seal needs to be replaced, remove the Torx screws, take off the retainer, pry out the seal and remove the bearing **(see illustration 23.7a)**. Note that on some models, only two screws are used, even though the retainer has three holes.

11 Installation is the reverse of the removal steps, with the following additions:

a) Apply non-permanent thread locking agent to the threads of the charging coil and CDI magneto screws, then tighten them to the torque listed in this Chapter's Specifications.
b) Remove all old gasket material from the alternator cover and crankcase. Use a new gasket on the alternator cover.
c) Make sure the cover dowels are in position.
d) If you're working on a 1993 through 1999 Kodiak, use a new copper washer on the lower rear cover bolt **(see illustration 23.8a)**. Install the wiring harness retainer on the upper rear cover bolt. Tighten the cover bolts evenly, in a criss-cross pattern, to the torque listed in this Chapter's Specifications.

Rotor replacement

Removal

Refer to illustrations 23.14 and 23.16

Note: To remove the alternator rotor, the special Yamaha puller (part no. YM-01404) or an aftermarket equivalent will be required. Don't try to remove the rotor without the proper puller, as it's almost sure to be damaged. Pullers are readily available from motorcycle dealers and aftermarket tool suppliers.

12 Remove the alternator cover as described above for access to the rotor.
13 Hold the alternator rotor with a strap wrench.
14 Thread the outer portion of the puller onto the rotor **(see illustration)**. Hold the flats of the outer portion with a wrench and turn the bolt with another wrench to separate the rotor from the crankshaft.
15 Pull the rotor off, together with the starter clutch.
16 Check the rotor Woodruff key; if it's not secure in its slot, pull it out and set it aside for safekeeping **(see illustration)**. A convenient method is to stick the Woodruff key to the magnets inside the rotor, but be certain not to forget it's there, as serious damage to the rotor and charging coils will occur if the engine is run with anything stuck to the magnets.

Installation

17 Degrease the center of the rotor and the end of the crankshaft.
18 Make sure the Woodruff key is positioned securely in its slot.
19 Align the rotor slot with the Woodruff key. Place the rotor, together with the starter clutch, on the crankshaft.

23.14 Thread the rotor puller onto the threaded portion of the rotor (arrow) and hold the flats (arrow) with a wrench while turning the puller bolt to free the rotor

23.16 Pull off the rotor, together with the starter clutch, and locate the Woodruff key (arrow)

Chapter 9 Electrical system

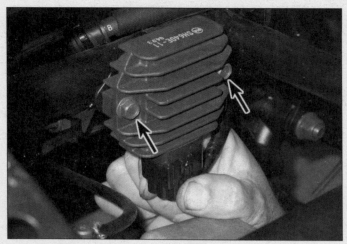

24.3a Unplug the electrical connector and remove the mounting bolt(s) (arrows) . . .

24.3b . . . some models use a single bolt and a tab on the frame (arrow)

20 Take a look to make sure there isn't anything stuck to the inside of the rotor.
21 The remainder of installation is the reverse of the removal steps.

24 Regulator/rectifier - check and replacement

Check

1 The regulator/rectifier is tested by process of elimination (when all other possible causes of charging system failure have been checked and eliminated, the rectifier/regulator is defective). Since it's easy to miss a problem, it's a good idea to have the charging system tested by a Yamaha dealer or substitute a known good unit before buying a new one.

Replacement

Refer to illustrations 24.3a and 24.3b
2 Where necessary for access, remove the rear fender (see Chapter 8).
3 Disconnect the rectifier/regulator electrical connector **(see illustrations)**. Remove the mounting bolts and lift it off the frame.
4 Installation is the reverse of the removal steps.

26.3 Here are the Kodiak 4WD relay locations

A Relay 1   B Relay 2

25 Carburetor heating system - check

1 If the carburetor heater doesn't seem to be working, follow the wiring harness from the heater element on the bottom of the carburetor and disconnect it (refer to Chapter 3 for heater location if necessary).
2 Connect an ohmmeter between the terminals in the heater element side of the connector. It should indicate 6 to 12 ohms. If not, replace the heater element.
3 If the heater element is good, locate the thermo switch in the wiring harness (two yellow wires). Remove the thermo switch, connect an ohmmeter to its terminals and heat it in a pan of water. With the water cold (below about 60-degrees F/16-degrees C), there should be continuity. At higher temperatures, there should be no continuity. If the thermo switch doesn't perform correctly, replace it.

26 Electric 4WD system - check

Refer to illustration 26.3
1 If the electrically selectable 4WD system used on later models doesn't work, check the main and 4WD fuses (see Section 5). Replace the fuse(s) if necessary.
2 Make sure the battery is fully charged.
3 Locate the three 4WD relays. On Kodiak models, relays 1 and 2 are in the left side of the rear fender under the seat **(see illustration)**. Relay 3 is under the right front fender. You'll need to remove the seat for access to relays 1 and 2 and the front cargo rack and fenders for access to relay 3 (see Chapter 8). On Grizzly models, all three relays are in the left side of the rear fender under the seat **(see illustration 5.3c)**.
4 Test relay 1, using an ohmmeter and a 12-volt battery (the vehicle's battery will work if it's fully charged). Disconnect the relay, look at the relay terminals and note which terminal connects to each wire color in the harness. Make the test connections (to the terminals in the relay, not the terminals in the wiring harness) as follows:

   a) Without the battery connected; connect ohmmeter positive to brown/black, ohmmeter negative to black - there should be continuity
   b) With the battery connected (battery positive to brown/red, battery negative to blue/green); connect ohmmeter positive to brown/black, ohmmeter negative to brown/red - there should be continuity

If the ohmmeter doesn't show continuity in both cases, replace the relay.
5 Test relay 2, using the ohmmeter and 12-volt battery used to test relay 1. Disconnect the relay, look at the relay terminals and note which

Chapter 9 Electrical system   9-23

terminal connects to each wire color in the harness. Make the test connections (to the terminals in the relay, not the terminals in the wiring harness) as follows:

a) *Without the battery connected; connect ohmmeter positive to black/yellow, ohmmeter negative to black - there should be continuity*

b) *With the battery connected (battery positive to brown/red, battery negative to blue/red); connect ohmmeter positive to black/yellow, ohmmeter negative to brown/red - there should be continuity*

If the ohmmeter doesn't show continuity in both cases, replace the relay.

6   Test relay 3, using the ohmmeter and 12-volt battery used to test relays 1 and 2. Disconnect the relay, look at the relay terminals and note which terminal connects to each wire color in the harness. Make the test connections (to the terminals in the relay, not the terminals in the wiring harness) as follows:

a) *Without the battery connected; connect ohmmeter positive to brown/red, ohmmeter negative to black - there should be continuity*

b) *With the battery connected (battery positive to brown/red, battery negative to yellow/black); connect ohmmeter positive to blue/red, ohmmeter negative to gray - there should be continuity*

If the ohmmeter doesn't show continuity in both cases, replace the relay.

7   Test the switch (see Section 14) and replace it if necessary.

8   To test the motor, disconnect its electrical connectors **(see illustration 11.7a in Chapter 6)**. Remove the Allen bolts that secure the motor to the differential and take it out.

9   Connect a pair of 1.5-volt "C" batteries together and connect them, using a pair of wires, to the upper two pins in the 5-pin connector socket on the motor. The motor should turn. When the wire connections are reversed, the motor should turn in the opposite direction. If not, replace it.

10 Inspect the shift fork sliding gear in the differential (the flat gear that the motor pinion rides in). If it's worn or damaged, have the differential overhauled by a dealer service department or other qualified shop.

27 Wiring diagrams

Prior to troubleshooting a circuit, check the fuses to make sure they're in good condition. Make sure the battery is fully charged and check the cable connections.

When checking a circuit, make sure all connectors are clean, with no broken or loose terminals or wires. When unplugging a connector, don't pull on the wires - pull only on the connector housings.

Notes

Chapter 10 Wiring diagrams

Wiring diagram color codes

BLK	Black	GRN/WHT	Green/white
BLK/RED	Black/red	GRN/YEL	Green/yellow
BLK/WHT	Black/white	ORG	Orange
BLU	Blue	PNK	Pink
BLU/BLK	Blue/black	RED	Red
BRN	Brown	WHT	White
BRN/BLU	Brown/blue	WHT/BLK	White/black
BRN/RED	Brown/red	WHT/BLU	White/blue
GRN	Green	WHT/GRN	White/green
GRN/BLU	Green/blue	YEL	Yellow

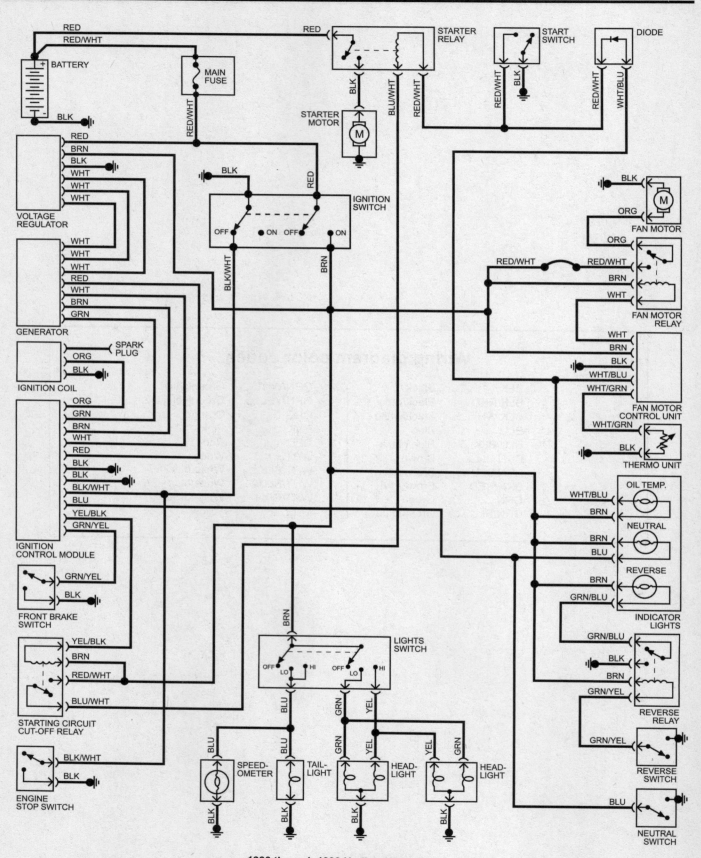

1993 through 1999 Kodiak 400 - typical

Chapter 10 Wiring diagrams

10-3

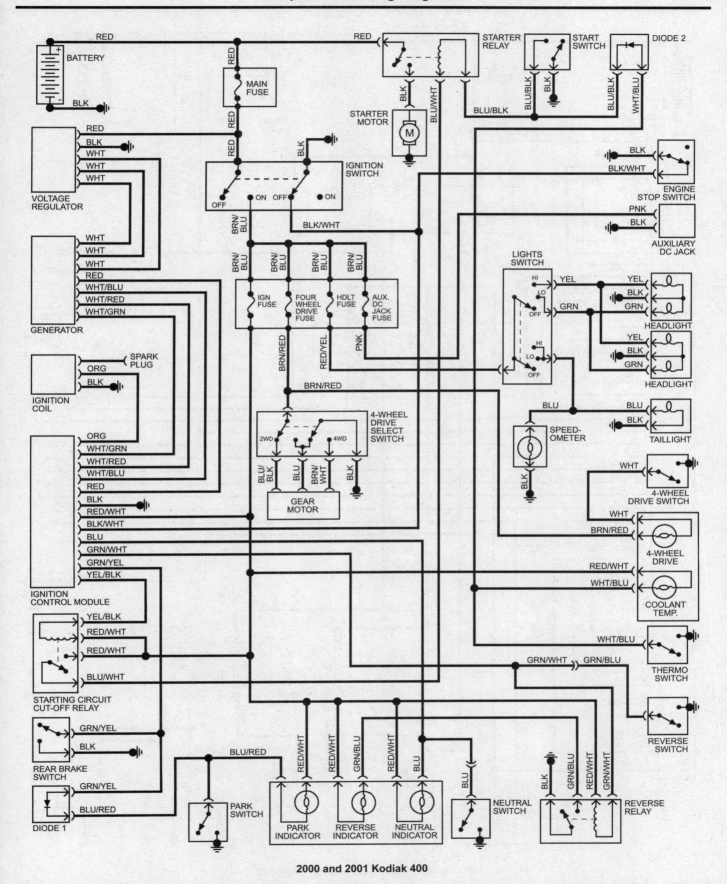

2000 and 2001 Kodiak 400

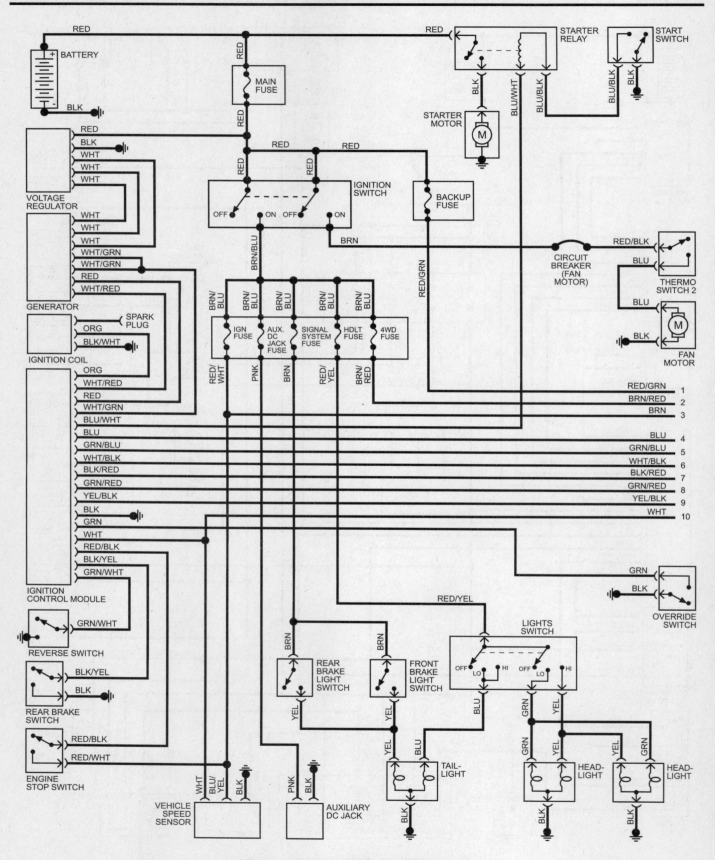

2003 and later Kodiak 450 - typical (page 1 of 2)

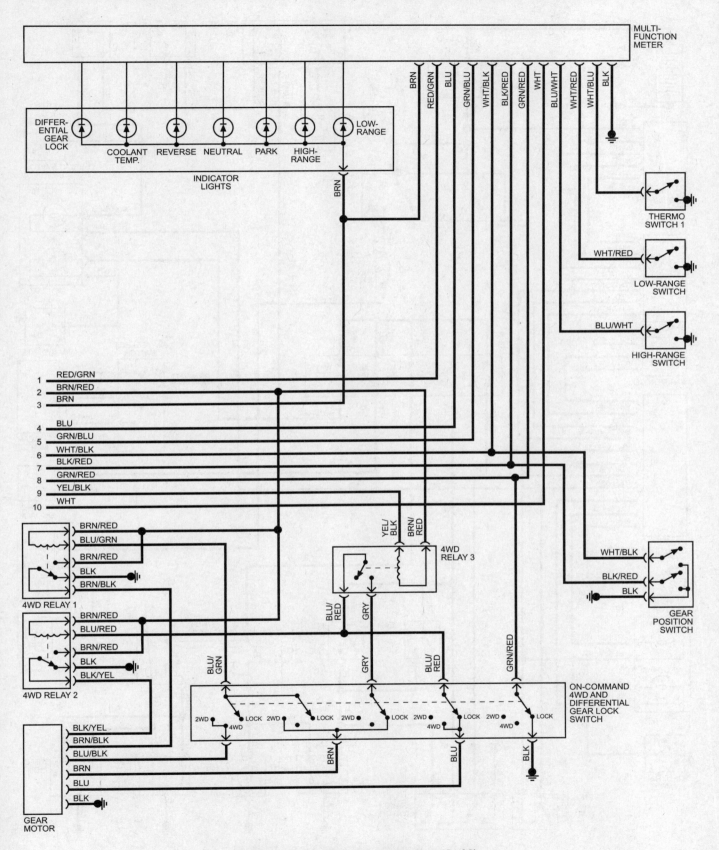

Chapter 10 Wiring diagrams

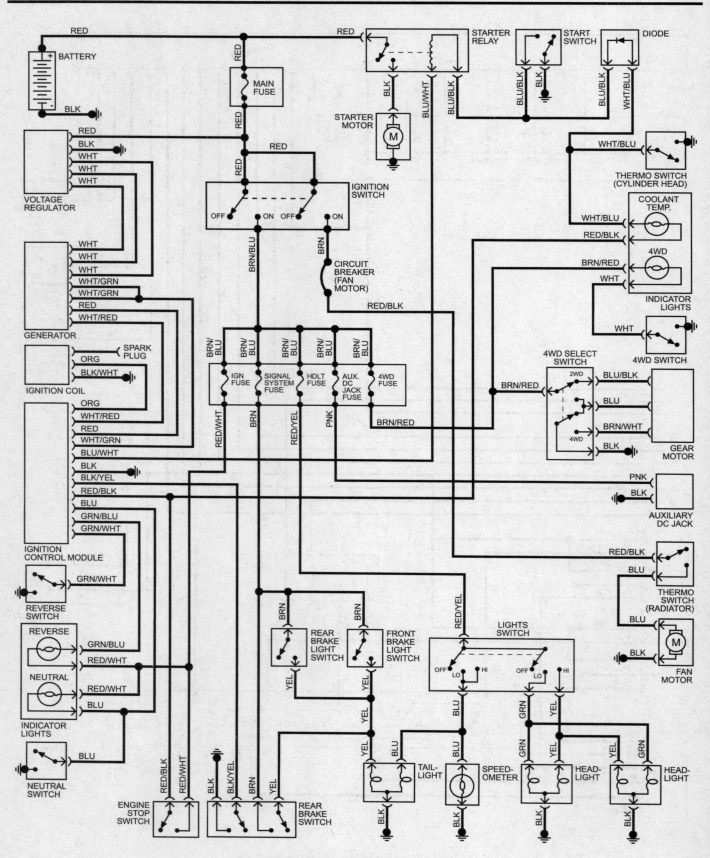

2002 and later Kodiak 400 - typical

Chapter 10 Wiring diagrams

10-7

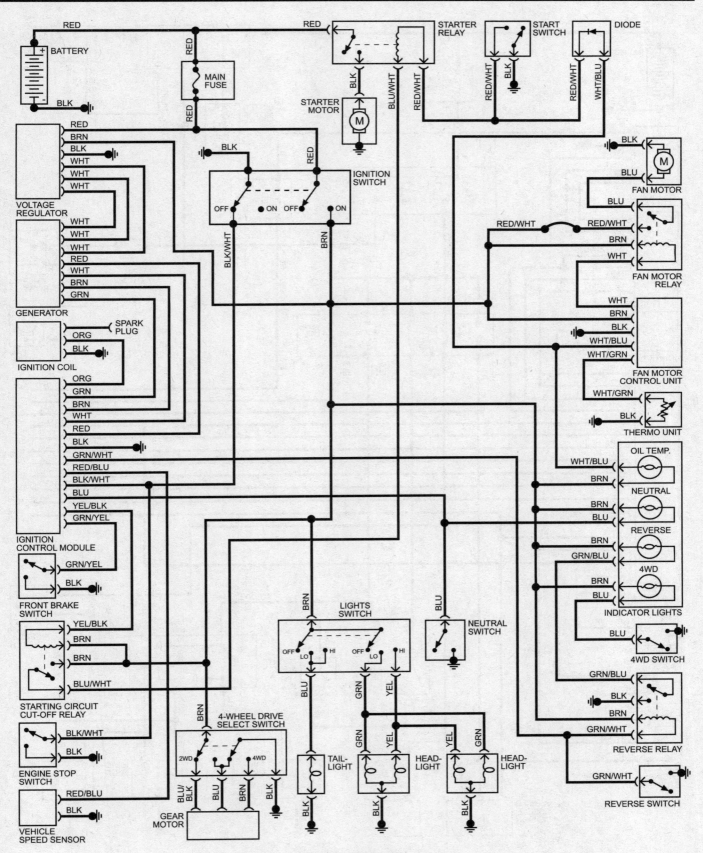

1998 through 2001 Grizzly 600 - typical

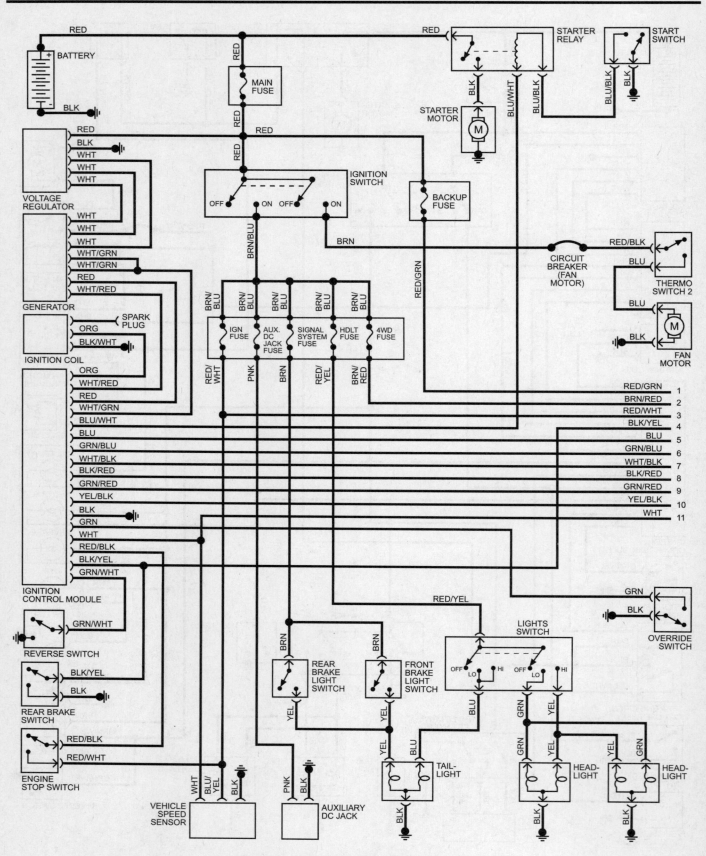

2002 and later Grizzly 660 - typical (page 1 of 2)

Chapter 10 Wiring diagrams

10-9

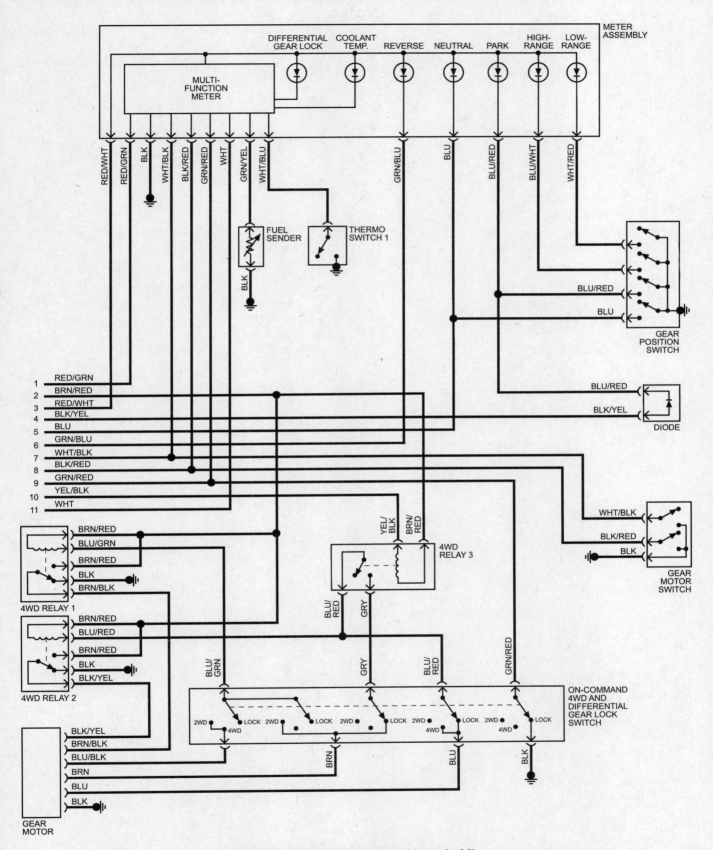

2002 and later Grizzly 660 - typical (page 2 of 2)

Notes

Conversion factors

Length (distance)
Inches (in)	X	25.4	= Millimeters (mm)	X 0.0394	= Inches (in)
Feet (ft)	X	0.305	= Meters (m)	X 3.281	= Feet (ft)
Miles	X	1.609	= Kilometers (km)	X 0.621	= Miles

Volume (capacity)
Cubic inches (cu in; in^3)	X	16.387	= Cubic centimeters (cc; cm^3)	X 0.061	= Cubic inches (cu in; in^3)
Imperial pints (Imp pt)	X	0.568	= Liters (l)	X 1.76	= Imperial pints (Imp pt)
Imperial quarts (Imp qt)	X	1.137	= Liters (l)	X 0.88	= Imperial quarts (Imp qt)
Imperial quarts (Imp qt)	X	1.201	= US quarts (US qt)	X 0.833	= Imperial quarts (Imp qt)
US quarts (US qt)	X	0.946	= Liters (l)	X 1.057	= US quarts (US qt)
Imperial gallons (Imp gal)	X	4.546	= Liters (l)	X 0.22	= Imperial gallons (Imp gal)
Imperial gallons (Imp gal)	X	1.201	= US gallons (US gal)	X 0.833	= Imperial gallons (Imp gal)
US gallons (US gal)	X	3.785	= Liters (l)	X 0.264	= US gallons (US gal)

Mass (weight)
Ounces (oz)	X	28.35	= Grams (g)	X 0.035	= Ounces (oz)
Pounds (lb)	X	0.454	= Kilograms (kg)	X 2.205	= Pounds (lb)

Force
Ounces-force (ozf; oz)	X	0.278	= Newtons (N)	X 3.6	= Ounces-force (ozf; oz)
Pounds-force (lbf; lb)	X	4.448	= Newtons (N)	X 0.225	= Pounds-force (lbf; lb)
Newtons (N)	X	0.1	= Kilograms-force (kgf; kg)	X 9.81	= Newtons (N)

Pressure
Pounds-force per square inch (psi; lbf/in^2; lb/in^2)	X	0.070	= Kilograms-force per square centimeter (kgf/cm^2; kg/cm^2)	X 14.223	= Pounds-force per square inch (psi; lbf/in^2; lb/in^2)
Pounds-force per square inch (psi; lbf/in^2; lb/in^2)	X	0.068	= Atmospheres (atm)	X 14.696	= Pounds-force per square inch (psi; lbf/in^2; lb/in^2)
Pounds-force per square inch (psi; lbf/in^2; lb/in^2)	X	0.069	= Bars	X 14.5	= Pounds-force per square inch (psi; lbf/in^2; lb/in^2)
Pounds-force per square inch (psi; lbf/in^2; lb/in^2)	X	6.895	= Kilopascals (kPa)	X 0.145	= Pounds-force per square inch (psi; lbf/in^2; lb/in^2)
Kilopascals (kPa)	X	0.01	= Kilograms-force per square centimeter (kgf/cm^2; kg/cm^2)	X 98.1	= Kilopascals (kPa)

Torque (moment of force)
Pounds-force inches (lbf in; lb in)	X	1.152	= Kilograms-force centimeter (kgf cm; kg cm)	X 0.868	= Pounds-force inches (lbf in; lb in)
Pounds-force inches (lbf in; lb in)	X	0.113	= Newton meters (Nm)	X 8.85	= Pounds-force inches (lbf in; lb in)
Pounds-force inches (lbf in; lb in)	X	0.083	= Pounds-force feet (lbf ft; lb ft)	X 12	= Pounds-force inches (lbf in; lb in)
Pounds-force feet (lbf ft; lb ft)	X	0.138	= Kilograms-force meters (kgf m; kg m)	X 7.233	= Pounds-force feet (lbf ft; lb ft)
Pounds-force feet (lbf ft; lb ft)	X	1.356	= Newton meters (Nm)	X 0.738	= Pounds-force feet (lbf ft; lb ft)
Newton meters (Nm)	X	0.102	= Kilograms-force meters (kgf m; kg m)	X 9.804	= Newton meters (Nm)

Vacuum
Inches mercury (in. Hg)	X	3.377	= Kilopascals (kPa)	X 0.2961	= Inches mercury
Inches mercury (in. Hg)	X	25.4	= Millimeters mercury (mm Hg)	X 0.0394	= Inches mercury

Power
Horsepower (hp)	X	745.7	= Watts (W)	X 0.0013	= Horsepower (hp)

Velocity (speed)
Miles per hour (miles/hr; mph)	X	1.609	= Kilometers per hour (km/hr; kph)	X 0.621	= Miles per hour (miles/hr; mph)

Fuel consumption*
Miles per gallon, Imperial (mpg)	X	0.354	= Kilometers per liter (km/l)	X 2.825	= Miles per gallon, Imperial (mpg)
Miles per gallon, US (mpg)	X	0.425	= Kilometers per liter (km/l)	X 2.352	= Miles per gallon, US (mpg)

Temperature
Degrees Fahrenheit = (°C x 1.8) + 32   Degrees Celsius (Degrees Centigrade; °C) = (°F − 32) x 0.56

*It is common practice to convert from miles per gallon (mpg) to liters/100 kilometers (l/100km), where mpg (Imperial) x l/100 km = 282 and mpg (US) x l/100 km = 235

Fraction/Decimal/Millimeter Equivalents

DECIMALS TO MILLIMETERS | FRACTIONS TO DECIMALS TO MILLIMETERS

Decimal	mm	Decimal	mm	Fraction	Decimal	mm	Fraction	Decimal	mm
0.001	0.0254	0.500	12.7000	1/64	0.0156	0.3969	33/64	0.5156	13.0969
0.002	0.0508	0.510	12.9540	1/32	0.0312	0.7938	17/32	0.5312	13.4938
0.003	0.0762	0.520	13.2080	3/64	0.0469	1.1906	35/64	0.5469	13.8906
0.004	0.1016	0.530	13.4620						
0.005	0.1270	0.540	13.7160						
0.006	0.1524	0.550	13.9700	1/16	0.0625	1.5875	9/16	0.5625	14.2875
0.007	0.1778	0.560	14.2240						
0.008	0.2032	0.570	14.4780						
0.009	0.2286	0.580	14.7320	5/64	0.0781	1.9844	37/64	0.5781	14.6844
		0.590	14.9860	3/32	0.0938	2.3812	19/32	0.5938	15.0812
0.010	0.2540			7/64	0.1094	2.7781	39/64	0.6094	15.4781
0.020	0.5080								
0.030	0.7620								
0.040	1.0160	0.600	15.2400	1/8	0.1250	3.1750	5/8	0.6250	15.8750
0.050	1.2700	0.610	15.4940						
0.060	1.5240	0.620	15.7480						
0.070	1.7780	0.630	16.0020	9/64	0.1406	3.5719	41/64	0.6406	16.2719
0.080	2.0320	0.640	16.2560	5/32	0.1562	3.9688	21/32	0.6562	16.6688
0.090	2.2860	0.650	16.5100	11/64	0.1719	4.3656	43/64	0.6719	17.0656
		0.660	16.7640						
0.100	2.5400	0.670	17.0180						
0.110	2.7940	0.680	17.2720	3/16	0.1875	4.7625	11/16	0.6875	17.4625
0.120	3.0480	0.690	17.5260						
0.130	3.3020								
0.140	3.5560								
0.150	3.8100			13/64	0.2031	5.1594	45/64	0.7031	17.8594
0.160	4.0640	0.700	17.7800	7/32	0.2188	5.5562	23/32	0.7188	18.2562
0.170	4.3180	0.710	18.0340	15/64	0.2344	5.9531	47/64	0.7344	18.6531
0.180	4.5720	0.720	18.2880						
0.190	4.8260	0.730	18.5420						
		0.740	18.7960	1/4	0.2500	6.3500	3/4	0.7500	19.0500
0.200	5.0800	0.750	19.0500						
0.210	5.3340	0.760	19.3040						
0.220	5.5880	0.770	19.5580	17/64	0.2656	6.7469	49/64	0.7656	19.4469
0.230	5.8420	0.780	19.8120	9/32	0.2812	7.1438	25/32	0.7812	19.8438
0.240	6.0960	0.790	20.0660	19/64	0.2969	7.5406	51/64	0.7969	20.2406
0.250	6.3500								
0.260	6.6040								
0.270	6.8580	0.800	20.3200	5/16	0.3125	7.9375	13/16	0.8125	20.6375
0.280	7.1120	0.810	20.5740						
0.290	7.3660	0.820	21.8280						
		0.830	21.0820	21/64	0.3281	8.3344	53/64	0.8281	21.0344
0.300	7.6200	0.840	21.3360	11/32	0.3438	8.7312	27/32	0.8438	21.4312
0.310	7.8740	0.850	21.5900	23/64	0.3594	9.1281	55/64	0.8594	21.8281
0.320	8.1280	0.860	21.8440						
0.330	8.3820	0.870	22.0980						
0.340	8.6360	0.880	22.3520	3/8	0.3750	9.5250	7/8	0.8750	22.2250
0.350	8.8900	0.890	22.6060						
0.360	9.1440								
0.370	9.3980			25/64	0.3906	9.9219	57/64	0.8906	22.6219
0.380	9.6520			13/32	0.4062	10.3188	29/32	0.9062	23.0188
0.390	9.9060	0.900	22.8600	27/64	0.4219	10.7156	59/64	0.9219	23.4156
0.400	10.1600	0.910	23.1140						
0.410	10.4140	0.920	23.3680						
0.420	10.6680	0.930	23.6220	7/16	0.4375	11.1125	15/16	0.9375	23.8125
0.430	10.9220	0.940	23.8760						
0.440	11.1760	0.950	24.1300						
0.450	11.4300	0.960	24.3840	29/64	0.4531	11.5094	61/64	0.9531	24.2094
0.460	11.6840	0.970	24.6380	15/32	0.4688	11.9062	31/32	0.9688	24.6062
0.470	11.9380	0.980	24.8920	31/64	0.4844	12.3031	63/64	0.9844	25.0031
0.480	12.1920	0.990	25.1460						
0.490	12.4460	1.000	25.4000	1/2	0.5000	12.7000	1	1.0000	25.4000

Trail rules

Just when you're ready to have some fun out in the dirt you get slapped with more rules. But by following these rules you'll ensure everyone's enjoyment, not just your own. It's important that all off-roaders follow these rules, as it will help to keep the trails open and keep us in good standing with other trail users. Really, these rules are no more than common sense and common courtesy.

- **Don't ride where you're not supposed to.** Stay off private property and obey all signs marking areas that are off limits to motorized vehicles. Also, as much fun as it might be, don't ride in State or Federal wilderness areas.

- **Leave the land as you found it.** When you've left the area, the only thing you should leave behind are your tire tracks. Use good judgement - if the ground is muddy, don't ride; you'll make deep ruts which will eventually harden and leave a rough (and possibly hazardous) surface. Stay on the trails, too. There are plenty of trails to ride on without blazing new ones. Be sure to carry out all litter that you create (and if you want to do a good deed, pick up any litter that you come across). Be sure to leave gates as you found them, or if the gate has a sign on it, comply with whatever the sign says (some people don't close gates after passing through them. Others may close gates when the landowner actually wants to keep them open).

- **Give other trail users the right-of-way.** There has been an ongoing dispute amongst trail users as to who belongs there and who doesn't. If the off-roading community shows respect and courtesy to hikers and equestrians, we stand a far better chance of being able to enjoy our sport in the years to come, and to keep the trails open for our children. When you ride up behind hikers or horses, give them plenty of room and pass slowly so as not to startle them. When you approach an equestrian from the opposite direction, stop your machine when the horse nears you so it won't get frightened and bolt.

- **Don't scare the animals!** Whether it be horses, cattle or wild animals like deer, rabbits or coyotes, leave them alone. Remember, you're visiting their home, so treat them with respect. Besides, startling animals can be dangerous. Loud noises or your sudden appearance can trigger an animal's defensive instinct, which could mean bad news for you.

- **Don't ride "over your head."** Sometimes the trails start to resemble ski runs, with a few irresponsible riders going so fast that they're barely able to maintain control of their vehicles. They'd never be able to stop to avoid another trail user if they had to. Most collisions on the trail are caused by such individuals and the results are occasionally tragic. You should only ride fast in areas where you can clearly see a good distance ahead - never on trails with blind corners or rises high enough that prevent you from seeing what's on the other side.

- **Be prepared.** Carry everything you think you may need to make minor repairs should your machine break down. Know how to make basic repairs and keep your ATV in good mechanical condition to minimize the chances of becoming stranded. Always let someone know where you're going, and ride with a friend whenever possible.

Service record

Date	Mileage/hours	Work performed

Index

A

About this manual, 0-5
Acknowledgements, 0-2
Air cleaner
    filter element and drain tube cleaning, 1-19
    housing, removal and installation, 4-11
Alternator charging coils and rotor, check and replacement, 9-19
ATV chemicals and lubricants, 0-15
Axle, rear (swingarm models), removal, inspection and installation, 6-14

B

Balancer and crankshaft, removal and installation
    2000 and later 400/450 models, 2B-14
    600 and 660 models, 2C-15
Balancer gears, removal, inspection and installation, 1993 through 1999 400 models, 2A-14
Battery
    charging, 9-4
    electrolyte level/specific gravity, check, 1-9
    inspection and maintenance, 9-4
Bodywork and frame, 8-1 through 8-6
Boot replacement, CV joint, 6-9
Brake
    caliper, removal, overhaul and installation
        front, 7-7
        rear, 7-11
    disc, inspection, removal and installation
        front, 7-8
        rear, 7-11
    drum brakes, removal, inspection and installation
        front, 7-3
        rear, 7-5
    hoses and lines, inspection and replacement, 7-13
    lever and pedal freeplay, check and adjustment, 1-11
    light bulbs, replacement, 9-8
    master cylinder, removal and installation
        front, 7-11
        rear, 7-12
    pad replacement
        front, 7-6
        rear, 7-9
    pedal, rear brake lever and cables, removal and installation, 7-14
    switches, check and replacement, 9-9
    system bleeding, 7-13
    system, general check, 1-10
    wheel cylinders, overhaul, 7-5
Brakes, wheels and tires, 7-1 through 7-18
Bulb replacement
    indicator and odometer/speedometer, 9-9
    tail light and brake light, 9-8
Buying parts, 0-6

C

Cable, removal and installation
    choke, 4-13
    throttle, 4-11
Caliper, removal, overhaul and installation
    front, 7-7
    rear, 7-11
Cam chain tensioner, removal and installation
    1993 through 1999 400 models, 2A-4
    2000 and later 400/450 models, 2B-3
    600 and 660 models, 2C-4
Camshaft and rocker arms, inspection, 2D-9
Camshaft, removal and installation,
    1993 through 1999 400 models, 2A-4
    2000 and later 400/450 models, 2B-4
    600 and 660 models, 2C-6
Capacities, lubricants and fluids, 1-4
Carburetor
    disassembly, cleaning and inspection, 4-5
    fuel level, check and adjustment, 4-11

heating system, check, 9-22
overhaul, general information, 4-4
reassembly and float height check, 4-10
removal and installation, 4-4

Cargo rack and fender, removal and installation
front, 8-2
rear, 8-4

CDI magneto, check, removal and installation, 5-3
CDI unit, check and replacement, 5-3
Charging system
alternator charging coils and rotor, check and
    replacement, 9-19
output test, 9-19
regulator/rectifier, check and replacement, 9-22
testing, general information and precautions, 9-19

Chemicals and lubricants, 0-15
Choke
cable, removal and installation, 4-13
operation check, 1-15

Circuit breaker, check and replacement, 9-4
Clutch, check and freeplay adjustment, 1-14
Coil, ignition, check, removal and installation, 5-3
Coolant
hoses, replacement, 3-4
reservoir, removal and installation, 3-2
draining, flushing and refilling, 1-25

Cooling fan and switch, check and replacement, 3-4
Cooling system, 3-1 through 3-6
Crankcase bearings, inspection, removal and installation, 2D-17
Crankcase, disassembly and reassembly
1993 through 1999 400 models, 2A-19
2000 and later 400/450 models, 2B-12
600 and 660 models, 2C-12

Crankshaft and connecting rod, removal, inspection and installation, 2D-18
CV joint and boot replacement, 6-9
Cylinder compression, check, 2D-8
Cylinder head and valves, disassembly, inspection and reassembly, 2D-10
Cylinder head cover and rocker arms, removal, inspection and installation
600 and 660 models, 2C-5

Cylinder head, removal and installation
1993 through 1999 400 models, 2A-4
2000 and later 400/450 models, 2B-4
600 and 660 models, 2C-7

Cylinder head, inspection, 2D-10
Cylinder
inspection, 2D-13
removal and installation
    1993 through 1999 400 models, 2A-7
    2000 and later 400/450 models, 2B-7
    600 and 660 models, 2C-8

D

Diagnosis, 0-16
Differential and driveshaft, removal, inspection and installation, front, 6-11

Disc brake
caliper removal, overhaul and installation, 7-7
inspection, removal and installation
    rear, 7-11
    front, 7-8
pad replacement
    front, 7-6
    rear, 7-9

Driveaxles
CV joint and boot replacement, 6-9
removal and installation, 6-8

Drivebelt and pulleys, general information, removal, inspection and installation
2000 and later 400/450 models, 2B-7
600 and 660 models, 2C-9

Drivebelt, inspection, 1-24
Driveshaft
removal and installation
    front, 6-11
    rear (swingarm models), 6-17
universal joints, replacement, 6-18

Drum brake
removal, inspection and installation
    front, 7-3
    rear, 7-5
wheel cylinders, overhaul, 7-5

E

Electric 4WD system, check, 9-22
Electrical system, 9-1 through 9-24
Electrical troubleshooting, 9-3
Engine disassembly and reassembly, general information, 2D-9
Engine, clutch and transmission (1993 through 1999 400 models), 2A-1 through 2A-24
balancer gears, removal, inspection and installation, 2A-14
cam chain tensioner, removal and installation, 2A-4
crankcase, disassembly and reassembly, 2A-19
cylinder head, camshaft and rocker arms, removal, inspection and installation, 2A-4
cylinder, removal and installation, 2A-7
engine, removal and installation, 2A-3
external oil pipe and oil cooler, removal and installation, 2A-8
external shift mechanism, removal, inspection and installation, 2A-17
major engine repair, general note, 2A-2
oil pipe and pump, removal, inspection and installation, 2A-16
operations possible with the engine in the frame, 2A-2
operations requiring engine removal, 2A-2
primary clutch, removal, inspection and installation, 2A-8
recoil starter, removal, inspection and installation, 2A-17
reverse shift mechanism, removal, inspection and installation, 2A-13
secondary clutch and release mechanism, removal, inspection and installation, 2A-10
transmission shafts, balancer shaft and shift cam, removal, inspection and installation, 2A-21

Index

Engine, clutch and transmission (2000 and later 400/450 models), 2B-1 through 2B-18
- balancer and crankshaft, removal and installation, 2B-14
- cam chain tensioner, removal and installation, 2B-3
- crankcase, disassembly and reassembly, 2B-12
- cylinder head, camshaft and rocker arms, removal, inspection and installation, 2B-4
- cylinder, removal and installation, 2B-7
- drivebelt and pulleys, general information, removal, inspection and installation, 2B-7
- engine, removal and installation, 2B-2
- external oil pipe and oil pump gears, removal and installation, 2B-12
- oil pump, removal and installation, 2B-13
- operations possible with the engine in the frame, 2B-2
- operations requiring engine removal, 2B-2
- recoil starter, removal, inspection and installation, 2B-7
- shift select mechanism, removal, inspection and installation, 2B-5
- transmission shafts, forks and shift cam, removal, inspection and installation, 2B-15

Engine, clutch and transmission (600 and 660 models), 2C-1 through 2C-18
- balancer and crankshaft, removal and installation, 2C-15
- cam chain tensioner, removal and installation, 2C-4
- camshaft, chain and guides, removal and installation, 2C-6
- crankcase, disassembly and reassembly, 2C-12
- cylinder head cover and rocker arms, removal, inspection and installation, 2C-5
- cylinder head, removal and installation, 2C-7
- cylinder, removal and installation, 2C-8
- drivebelt and pulleys, general information, removal, inspection and installation, 2C-9
- engine, removal and installation, 2C-3
- external oil pipes, removal and installation, 2C-10
- oil pump and relief valve, removal and installation, 2C-13
- oil pump sprockets and balancer gears (660 models), removal, inspection and installation, 2C-11
- operations possible with the engine in the frame, 2C-3
- operations requiring engine removal, 2C-3
- recoil starter, removal, inspection and installation, 2C-8
- shift select mechanism, removal, inspection and installation, 2C-8
- transmission shafts, forks and shift cam, removal, inspection and installation, 2C-15

Engine, removal and installation
- 1993 through 1999 400 models, 2A-3
- 2000 and later 400/450 models, 2B-2
- 600 and 660 models, 2C-3

Engine/transfer case oil/filter and differential oil, change, 1-16

Exhaust system
- inspection, 1-20
- removal and installation, 4-13

External oil pipes, removal and installation
- and oil cooler, 1993 through 1999 400 models, 2A-8
- and oil pump gears, 2000 and later 400/450 models, 2B-12
- 600 and 660 models, 2C-10

External shift mechanism, removal, inspection and installation, 1993 through 1999 400 models, 2A-17

F

Fasteners, check, 1-23
Fault finding, 0-16
Fender, removal and installation
- front, 8-2
- rear, 8-4

Final drive unit, rear, removal, inspection and installation, 6-14
Fluid levels, check, 1-7
Fluids and lubricants, recommended, 1-4
Footrests, removal and installation, 8-4
Four-wheel drive system, electric, check, 9-22
Frame, general information, inspection and repair, 8-6
Front brake
- discs and shields, inspection, removal and installation, 7-8
- master cylinder, removal and installation, 7-11

Front cargo rack and fender, removal and installation, 8-2
Front differential and driveshaft, removal, inspection and installation, 6-11
Front disc brakes
- caliper removal, overhaul and installation, 7-7
- pad replacement, 7-6

Front drum brakes, removal, inspection and installation, 7-3
Fuel
- carburetor
  - disassembly, cleaning and inspection, 4-5
  - overhaul, general information, 4-4
  - reassembly and float height check, 4-10
  - removal and installation, 4-4
- idle fuel/air mixture adjustment, 4-4
- level, carburetor, check and adjustment, 4-11
- system, check and filter cleaning, 1-19
- tank
  - cleaning and repair, 4-3
  - cover, removal and installation, 8-2
  - removal and installation, 4-3

Fuel and exhaust systems, 4-1 through 4-14
Fuse and circuit breaker, check and replacement, 9-4

G

Gear position switches, check and replacement, 9-13
General engine overhaul procedures, 2D-1 through 2D-20
- camshaft and rocker arms, inspection, 2D-9
- crankcase bearings, inspection, removal and installation, 2D-17
- crankshaft and connecting rod, removal, inspection and installation, 2D-18
- cylinder compression, check, 2D-8
- cylinder head and valves, disassembly, inspection and reassembly, 2D-10
- cylinder head, inspection, 2D-10
- cylinder, inspection, 2D-13
- engine disassembly and reassembly, general information, 2D-9
- initial start-up after overhaul, 2D-19
- major engine repair, general note, 2D-8

oil pump, inspection, 2D-17
piston rings, installation, 2D-16
piston, removal, inspection and installation, 2D-14
recommended break-in procedure, 2D-19
transmission components, inspection, 2D-19
valves/valve seats/valve guides, servicing, 2D-10
General specificiations, 0-7

H

Handlebar switches
check, 9-12
removal and installation, 9-12
Handlebar, removal, inspection and installation, 6-3
Headlight
aim, check and adjustment, 9-7
bulb, replacement, 9-6
Hitch, removal and installation, 8-4
Hubs, wheel, removal and installation, 7-17

I

Identification numbers, 0-6
Idle fuel/air mixture adjustment, 4-4
Idle speed, check and adjustment, 1-23
Ignition
CDI magneto, check, removal and installation, 5-3
CDI unit, check and replacement, 5-3
coil, check, removal and installation, 5-3
main (key) switch, check and replacement, 9-12
system, check, 5-2
timing, general information and check, 5-4
Ignition system, 5-1 through 5-4
Indicator bulbs and odometer/speedometer, replacement, 9-9
Initial start-up after overhaul, 2D-19
Introduction to the Yamaha Kodiak and Grizzly, 0-5
Introduction to tune-up and routine maintenance, 1-7

K

Knuckle, steering
bearing and seal replacement, 6-7
removal, inspection, and installation, 6-6

L

Lighting system, check, 9-6
Lubricants and chemicals, 0-15
Lubricants and fluids, recommended, 1-4
Lubrication, general, 1-15

M

Magneto, check, removal and installation, 5-3
Maintenance intervals, 1-6
Maintenance techniques, tools and working facilities, 0-8
Maintenance, routine, 1-1 through 1-26
Major engine repair, general note, 2D-8
Master cylinder, brake, removal and installation
front, 7-11
rear, 7-12
Middle driven gear and transfer case (1993 through 1998 models), removal, inspection and installation, 6-13

O

Oil pump, removal and installation
1993 through 1999 400 models, 2A-16
2000 and later 400/450 models, 2B-13
600 and 660 models, 2C-13
Oil pump, inspection, 2D-17
Oil/filter, engine, change, 1-16
Operations possible with the engine in the frame
1993 through 1999 400 models, 2A-2
2000 and later 400/450 models, 2B-2
600 and 660 models, 2C-3
Operations requiring engine removal
1993 through 1999 400 models, 2A-2
2000 and later 400/450 models, 2B-2
600 and 660 models, 2C-3

P

Piston rings, installation, 2D-16
Piston, removal, inspection and installation, 2D-14
Primary clutch, removal, inspection and installation, 1993 through 1999 400 models, 2A-8

R

Radiator cap, check, 3-2
Radiator, removal and installation, 3-3
Rear axle (swingarm models), removal, inspection and installation, 6-14
Rear brake
disc, inspection, removal and installation, 7-11
master cylinder, removal and installation, 7-12
Rear cargo rack and fender, removal and installation, 8-4
Rear disc brake
caliper, removal, overhaul and installation, 7-11
pad replacement, 7-9
Rear driveshaft (swingarm models), removal, inspection and installation, 6-17
Rear drum brake, removal, inspection and installation, 7-5
Rear final drive unit, removal, inspection and installation, 6-14

Rear stabilizer bar (IRS models), removal and installation, 6-18
Rear subframe (Kodiak IRS models), removal and installation, 8-4
Recoil starter, removal, inspection and installation
    1993 through 1999 400 models, 2A-17
    2000 and later 400/450 models, 2B-7
    600 and 660 models, 2C-8
Recommended break-in procedure, 2D-19
Recommended lubricants and fluids, 1-4
Regulator/rectifier, check and replacement, 9-22
Reverse shift mechanism, removal, inspection and installation, 1993 through 1999 400 models, 2A-13
Routine maintenance, 1-1 through 1-26
    intervals, 1-6

S

Safety first!, 0-14
Scheduled maintenance intervals, 1-6
Seat, removal and installation, 8-1
Secondary clutch and release mechanism, removal, inspection and installation, 1993 through 1999 400 models, 2A-10
Shift linkage, check and adjustment, 1-13
Shift select mechanism, removal, inspection and installation
    2000 and later 400/450 models, 2B-5
    600 and 660 models, 2C-8
Shock absorbers, removal, installation and adjustment, 6-4
Side panels and fuel tank cover, removal and installation, 8-2
Skidplates, removal and installation, 8-4
Spark plug
    replacement, 1-20
    torque, 1-3
    type and gap, 1-1
Stabilizer bar, rear (IRS models), removal and installation, 6-18
Starter
    circuit, check and component replacement, 9-14
    clutch and reduction gears, removal, inspection and installation, 9-17
    motor
        disassembly, inspection and reassembly, 9-14
        removal and installation, 9-14
Steering
    knuckle
        bearing and seal replacement, 6-7
        removal, inspection, and installation, 6-6
    shaft, removal, inspection, bushing/bearing replacement and installation, 6-4
    system, inspection and toe-in adjustment, 1-23
    suspension and final drive, 6-1 through 6-18
Subframe, rear (Kodiak IRS models), removal and installation, 8-4
Suspension arms, removal, inspection and installation, 6-7
Suspension, check, 1-23
Swingarm
    bearings, check, 6-16
    bearings or bushings, replacement, 6-17
    removal and installation, 6-16

T

Tail light and brake light bulbs, replacement, 9-8
Temperature warning system, check and switch replacement, 9-11
Thermostat, removal, check and installation, 3-2
Throttle
    cables, removal, installation and adjustment, 4-11
    freeplay and speed limiter, check and adjustment, 1-14
Tie-rods, removal, inspection and installation, 6-5
Timing, ignition, general information and check, 5-4
Tires, general information, 7-15
Tires/wheels, general check, 1-12
Tools and working facilities, 0-8
Trailer hitch, removal and installation, 8-4
Transfer case and middle driven gear (1993 through 1998 models), removal, inspection and installation, 6-13
Transmission components, inspection, 2D-19
Transmission shafts, balancer shaft and shift cam, removal, inspection and installation, 1993 through 1999 400 models, 2A-21
Transmission shafts, forks and shift cam, removal, inspection and installation
    2000 and later 400/450 models, 2B-15
    600 and 660 models, 2C-15
Troubleshooting, 0-16
Tune-up and routine maintenance, 1-1 through 1-26

V

Valve clearances, check and adjustment, 1-21
Valves/valve seats/valve guides, servicing, 2D-10

W

Water pump, removal, inspection and installation, 3-5
Wheel cylinders, brake, overhaul, 7-5
Wheel hubs, removal and installation, 7-17
Wheels, inspection, removal and installation, 7-15
Wiring diagrams, 10-1 through 10-10
Working facilities, 0-8

Notes